Fundamentals of the Stock Market

B. O'Neill Wyss

McGraw-Hill
New York San Francisco Washington, D.C.
Auckland Bogotá Caracas Lisbon London
Madrid Mexico City Milan Montreal New Delhi
San Juan Singapore Sydney Tokyo Toronto

Library of Congress Cataloging-in-Publication Data

Wyss, O'Neill.
Fundamentals of the stock market / by O'Niell Wyss.
p. cm.
Includes index
ISBN 0-07-136096-4
1. Stocks—United States. 2. Investments—United States. I. Title

HG4910.W97 2000
332.63'22'0973--dc21 00-060575

McGraw-Hill
A Division of The McGraw-Hill Companies

1 2 3 4 5 6 7 8 9 0 2CUS / 2CUS 0 9 8 7 6 5 4 3 2 1 0

ISBN 0-07-136096-4

This book is printed on recycled acid-free paper containing a minimum of 50% recycled, de-inked fiber.

Dedication

This book would not have been possible without the patience of my loving wife, Mary, and her many sacrifices when I was absent from home. Because this marks my 25th year in the investment profession, I dedicate this book to all of my colleagues who have worked so hard to help their clients understand the money-management process, and how to be patient during volatile market conditions. My goal is to increase your knowledge to use the principles that will make you successful in this career field. This book can also be used as a gift for clients and prospects to expand their knowledge and to help them become even more successful in the future. They can use it as a tool to compare your professionalism against the competition; and by knowing you follow these principles, will send you even more referrals. By working together as a team, their respect for your advice will jump to heights that have no boundaries.

Contents

Preface

This book is written for the entry-level financial professional who is ready to place and manage money for clients in one of the most exciting times in our history. The American stock market has become the most zestful phenomena for making money over the last decade. With strong and stable economic growth, along with radical changes in the financial services industry, investing in the stock market will become even more popular during the next century.

As a certified financial planner, money manager, author, and teacher, I am honored to help you understand how our markets have evolved over the years, what the current state of investing is all about, and how to prepare for a dynamic future by participating in the international stock market. Consider yourself fortunate to be in a position to help investors make decisions that were once only reserved for a select few wealthy individuals in our society. We owe the deepest gratitude to those who made sacrifices during past wars in order to ensure our freedom of choice today. As we enter the 21st century, the United States has evolved into a society of tremendous wealth, and the opportunity for making money is unlimited.

Fundamentals of the Stock Market is designed to give you a growing appreciation for the events that are shaping today's markets and to give you a thorough understanding of how the system works. Chapter 1 will examine the origins of investing and how the markets and major indexes evolved. By understanding the stock market's historical background, you can appreciate where we stand today and how the major indexes can help you manage money for clients in the future. You will learn how and why stocks are traded on the various exchanges, the importance of *Initial Public Offerings* (IPOs), and how to take advantage of market liquidity. We will study major indexes and discuss why they are so popular with investors today. You will also learn how to identify and invest in a two-tiered market. The chapter concludes with a section on predicting future market activity and how to pick consistent winners.

Before investing money for clients, you must become knowledgeable about the structure of our economy, as described in Chapter 2. This knowledge includes a basic understanding of key terms and definitions and how the Federal Reserve controls the growth of the economy. By learning about equity ownership as it relates to business cycles, you will be able to choose the best type of stock for investors in various financial situations. Behind any successful financial professional is a fundamental knowledge of economic indicators and how Federal Reserve policy affects the value of stocks.

Chapter 3 takes a hard look at factors that directly affect major price movements in the markets. You will learn to distinguish between types of common and preferred stock and the tax ramifications of individual ownership. We will examine financial statements and discover how ratio analysis plays a key role in the evaluation process. This includes the importance of earnings, book value, and cash flow. To help your clients and customers become prosperous investors, you must be able to predict future stock prices in relation to their current values. You will also learn about life cycles as part of industry analysis and stock market trends for the new millennium. Finally, we will study companies that are reshaping the new decade, and give you tips on building a new career as a financial service professional.

Stock trading has become a hot issue, especially with the explosion of the Internet. Chapter 4 will take you behind the scenes of a stock-market order and show how electronic trading makes today's instant winners and losers. You will learn the functions of floor brokers and specialists, and the importance of proper account registrations. We will study various types of orders, how to place them, and what to expect when ordering large-company versus small-company shares. We will also examine the more risky strategies of buying on margin and short selling and show why electronic trading is becoming the wave of the future. Even though the markets have converted to decimalization, we must guard against the dangers of churning. This chapter concludes with a section on the future of financial markets.

Understanding and following stock prices in the news is vital for keeping clients informed and making timely decisions in our fast-paced economy. Chapter 5 examines what you need to know when watching shows such as the "Nightly Business Report" on PBS television and how to analyze critical information in major financial publications such as *The Wall Street Journal*. You will also learn how to recognize and use symbols of various stocks on the Internet and how to spot trends with advancing or declining share volume. This chapter examines the *Dow Jones Industrial Average* (DJIA), foreign equities, and government regulations. You will also learn the best way to maintain your competency skills by using investment advisory services and professional publications.

To become a brilliant money manager, you need to sharpen your decision-making skills by using modern tools and understanding new theories. Chapter 6 will examine averages and indexes and explain the differences between fundamental and technical analyses. You will discover the hard lessons learned from a zig-zagging stock market plus how to protect clients' money. We will examine various investment styles and how to use risk-reduction strategies for different types of portfolios. Some market theories that you might want to use immediately include the Dow Theory and the Modern Portfolio Theory.

Chapter 7 will focus on goal setting and how to use investment guidelines to become even more successful. By setting portfolio parameters and understanding investment risks, you and your clients can avoid major financial mistakes in building a portfolio for the future. In this regard, we will examine domestic, foreign, and emotional risks. You will also discover the risks of investing in the new economy and how to avoid major mistakes. We will cover important topics that are often overlooked, such as smart reasons for selling a stock and how to lower risk by using equity mutual funds. We will show how to tackle challenging financial problems at various stages in the life of a client, how to set goals according to time horizons, and how to achieve specific client objectives.

Chapter 8 takes us into the dynamic world of mutual-fund investing. You will learn the benefits of owning mutual funds and how to establish a high-quality portfolio to complement individual stock holdings. A key to success in this area is understanding the various types of mutual funds and how they fit into different investment styles. Flexible purchase plans make mutual-fund ownership extremely affordable, and you will learn how to weigh risk when setting up different types of portfolios. You *must* be able to address the issue of cost, and explain to clients the flexibility in exchanging and redeeming fund shares. They should also understand various investment strategies such as dollar-cost averaging and the Modern Portfolio Theory. Investment professionals should know how to pick fund companies along with top-quality money managers. We will conclude this chapter with a section focusing on portfolio objectives and how to help four types of mutual-fund investors.

When using equities to build a portfolio, one must not ignore tax considerations. Critical issues involving ordinary income and capital gains taxes will be examined in Chapter 9. You will learn about different types of capital gains taxes and how to figure taxes in the highest marginal bracket. We will examine the issues of trading versus a buy-and-hold approach and describe how to lower taxes with individual stocks. You will learn which type of *Individual Retirement Account* (IRA) is best to use for various client situations, and how to take advantage of tax laws regarding gifts and inheritances. We will also examine the advantages of owning variable annuities, and explain how they are being used to create more retirement income. In today's competitive environment, it is critical that financial professionals know how to use variable annuities as an asset-allocation tool. We will also study whether or not to use the strategy of tax swapping. As more and more older Americans want to make financial gifts to children and grandchildren, we will show how inheritances can be passed from one generation to the next with minimal tax consequences.

To conclude our book, Chapter 10 will have a critical and frank discussion of the current investment services offered by financial institutions, and will describe the ever-changing role of the stockbroker. You will learn about dynamic changes taking place in Internet investing, and how they will directly affect your recommendations to clients. We will examine the role of various investment advisors in today's competitive environment. You will learn the tools in choosing a broker-dealer, and how to build competency as a financial professional. Also, we will examine the latest trends that are reshaping the financial services industry so you can become more successful as we enter the 21st century.

Fundamentals of the Stock Market takes you beyond the basics of investing to prepare for an exciting and profitable career as a financial professional. This book will help you become more self-confident in making recommendations, while learning how to advise investors during what has become an uncertain and volatile time in the financial markets. American investors need your services more than ever in our fast-paced and ever-changing economy as they try to make their own investment decisions. As a new or veteran financial professional, you are now ready to embark on an exciting journey that will give you the knowledge and tools to become highly successful in your chosen career field.

Despite the constant criticism that we seem to receive from the press, this book is written to help new professionals coming into the business to start off on the right foot. By understanding the current trends that are reshaping the future of our industry, they can make the best recommendations for their clients and help them avoid costly mistakes which save time and money. Most importantly, knowing your client's personality and financial background will enable you to give sound advice, become highly reputable, and help build your investment clientele within a shorter period of time.

As an entry-level professional, you will benefit from advice focused on the future. I strongly feel that our goal is to help as many people as possible sort through the maze of confusion that permeates our industry today. We must side with investors as new electronic trading means faster execution of orders at lower costs. I feel we must be direct in pointing out mistakes that clients tend to make—often unintentionally. Most importantly, we must show them how to avoid costly errors that can put them behind the eight ball in achieving future financial goals.

According to the "Jobs Rated Almanac" by Les Krantz, which was published in 2000, financial planning is one of the top careers in America today. It is very rewarding from the standpoint of both job satisfaction and financial renumeration.

Whether you are a beginner or have many years of experience, this book will give you the knowledge to become a true professional who is highly regarded in your community. By doing things differently than other people in our industry, you can build a reputation among other related professionals (such as accountants and attorneys) that will gain you many referrals. By showing that you care about a client's personal as well as business affairs, you will make yourself the professional of choice each and every time. I feel confident that you will enjoy and benefit from reading *Fundamentals of the Stock Market*. Specifically, this book is designed to be a reference tool that can be used in building your practice for many years to come.

Chapter 1

Origins: The Markets and Major Indexes

Introduction

Many years ago, Wall Street was a mysterious entity that many people shied away from because they did not understand it. People equated the term *stock* with the unknown and therefore perceived stocks to be risky. Americans did not have the communications mechanisms of today and therefore did not have the opportunity to understand Wall Street's colorful history and its vital role in shaping our economy.

About the only thing that people knew then was that Wall Street existed somewhere in New York City and that only the rich gathered there to buy and sell a paper certificate called a stock. Little did they realize that stock represented actual ownership in corporate America and that those people who were fortunate enough to own stock would make bundles of money in the future.

This chapter sets the tone for this book by giving you an increased knowledge regarding the historical background of the major stock markets. To help educate your clients, you will receive an overview of the major indexes that we use in today's markets. You will also learn why stocks are priced and how they are traded so that you will have a solid foundation of knowledge in order to answer clients' questions. Finally, an understanding of trading activity will help you make even better decisions when dealing in the after market.

The Stock Market: Historical Background

The origins of Wall Street date back to the founding of our country, when merchants used currencies to buy and sell commodities such as furs, guns, and tobacco. In 1789, Congress met on Wall Street to authorize the issue of $80 million in government bonds in order to finance the cost of the war. Shortly thereafter, stocks were created to establish the Bank of the United States and to offer shares to the public. As more bank stocks and government bonds emerged, the need for an organized market to trade these instruments developed. Stocks represented an ownership in something and the opportunity to make money as businesses grew.

Wall Street businessmen met regularly to auction stocks and bonds, and agents left securities with auctioneers who received a commission for each stock and bond that they sold. With an increased interest and the need for an improved system, 24 brokers met under a buttonwood tree on May 17, 1792 and signed what they considered to be an all-inclusive document. This document enabled them to trade securities among themselves, to maintain fixed commissions on these trades, and to avoid dealing in other auctions. We consider this event to be the actual founding of the *New York Stock Exchange* (NYSE).

In March 1817, the members adopted a formal constitution of trading rules and regulations. Exchange members could trade securities and sit at the auction for a cost of only $400 (the beginning of what is now called owning a seat on the exchange). Ironically, members never sat down while trading securities; instead, they always stood when auctioning their shares of stock. This practice continues today on major exchanges.

As trading activities increased and more members purchased a seat to trade securities, this exchange moved to larger quarters several times. Finally, in 1863, the exchange settled into its present facilities at 11 Wall Street in New York City. The actual building occupied by the New York Stock Exchange at 16 Broad Street was not finished architecturally until 1903.

During the late 1800s, the discovery of gold and the development of railroads created a large interest in owning mining and railroad stocks. People considered many of the smaller company issues to be too speculative for trading, so some non-members of the exchange took up the slack and actually traded these shares on the streets of New York City. They were called curbstone brokers and used hand signals to convey price and volume information to brokers who leaned out of second- and third-story office windows. They wore brightly colored clothes so that clerks could easily spot them in the crowd and would instantly know that certain stocks were being traded at specific landmarks or lamp posts. These street brokers later united and settled in a large building on Wall Street to form what is now known as the *American Stock Exchange* (AMEX).

As the communications media advanced in the early 1900s, people all across America began to read newspaper stories about what was taking place in New York City. They were finally discovering what Wall Street was all about. They learned that it was a marketplace where merchants, agents, and customers actually gathered together each day to buy and sell stocks and bonds. As the popularity of making money by trading these instruments grew, other companies sprang up in order to participate in this type of activity. Many of them could not afford to own a seat on the exchange and therefore began to make a market in securities of smaller companies outside the original trading process.

Brokerage companies that did not own a seat on a major exchange were called non-member firms. Their orders for exchange-listed stocks were processed through another member firm or were executed in the third market. This third market is referred to as the *Over-the-Counter Market* (OTC), where brokerage firms act as market makers for various company stocks. This term was originally referred to more than 100 years ago when securities were actually sold over the counter in stores and banks.

The Exchanges of Today

Securities exchanges today are designed to facilitate and organize the buying and selling of stocks and other securities instantaneously. Two major types of exchanges include the registered exchanges and the OTC market. Registered exchanges include the NYSE and the AMEX, which are linked electronically in order to facilitate trading activity.

Securities that are not traded on one of these two exchanges are traded on the OTC market. Dealers in these stocks must communicate with each other by using a sophisticated buy-and-sell process. This system is known as NASDAQ, where thousands of brokers and dealers communicate electronically to buy and sell shares of specific companies. This system acts as the marketplace and central clearinghouse for trading many smaller company shares.

To understand the operations of these exchanges, let's briefly examine each one.

***New York Stock Exchange* (NYSE).** This exchange is the largest equities marketplace in the world. Some 3,000 people work together each day to trade billions of shares of 3,025 companies whose combined market capitalization totals $16 trillion. The NYSE represents approximately 80 percent of the value of all publicly owned companies in the United States.

More than two-thirds of NYSE companies have listed within the last 12 years. This amount represents a cross-section of leading U.S. companies, including large, mid-size, and small capitalization companies. As of July 1999, 382 non-U.S. companies were also listed here, which is more than triple the number five years ago.

As you will learn in Chapter 4, "Trading: Buying and Selling Stocks," stock orders are referred to a floor broker who brings them to a specialist —a broker who personally matches buy and sell orders at his post on the exchange floor. Each stock is assigned a specialist who handles no more than 10 stocks. Since 1976, most orders have been transmitted electronically to specialists' screens over the *Designated Order Turnaround* (DOT) system or via the upgraded SuperDot. To accommodate the overflow of specialists and staff, the NYSE is building a new facility across the street from its present location.

A *member firm* is a company or individual that owns a seat on the exchange. This concept goes back to the days when members actually sat in assigned chairs, waiting for the name of a stock that they wanted to buy or sell to be called. To this day, only member firms can buy and sell securities on the trading floor. In order to become a member firm, a company must meet rigorous professional standards set by the exchange. The number of seats has remained constant (at 1,366) since 1953. Today, an exchange seat commands a hefty asking price—recently quoted at $1.7 million.

Institutional investors are corporations that invest on behalf of individuals and companies. They are also eligible for membership and include pension funds, mutual funds, insurance companies, and banks. Because they account for a tremendous volume of daily trading, we cannot overemphasize their importance and function as members. As the 21st century unfolds, these firms will manage more money for individuals, pension funds, and foundations.

In more recent developments, the NYSE overturned a rule that prevented its members from trading some of the most popular stocks on alternative trading systems. From now on, the biggest firms on Wall Street can trade stocks of blue-chip companies such as General Electric, IBM, and AT&T on the *Electronic Communications Networks* (ECNs), which offer cheaper and faster trading systems. This feature will help investors receive more efficient executions at the best possible prices. The move will go a long way toward improving competition and public participation in various U.S. markets.

***American Stock Exchange* (AMEX).** The AMEX is considered a secondary exchange but is also national in scope. No stocks are listed on either the NYSE or AMEX at the same time. The AMEX is also located in New York City and is distinct from the NYSE in terms of member requirements, specific companies listed, and instruments traded (in other words, a large options exchange). Because of these differences and the need to give full service, most large brokerage firms are members of both exchanges.

In an attempt to become more competitive with the NYSE, the AMEX recently developed a Web site for investors to study and analyze companies that are listed there. The Web site is www.americanstocks.com and is designed to provide earnings histories, analysts' reports, and virtually everything for discovering new investment opportunities.

The AMEX is proud to be one of the two largest options exchanges in the world. This exchange offers a diverse family of options that helps investors control risk and increase the potential to maximize profits. Having been in this specialized business for 25 years, the AMEX trades options on more than 1,000 common stocks. Its Web site at www.amex.com teaches investors about the basics of options trading, and offers a helpful educational publication.

The AMEX created and pioneered the concept of index shares. These shares work very similar to an index fund yet trade like a stock. Rather than buying a single company, an investor buys an entire stock index and gets the diversification of owning stock in many companies. Index shares offer an approach to investing that provides lower fees and expenses along with important tax efficiencies. They range in diversity and size from large to mid-cap companies and from U.S. industry sectors to indexes in 17 foreign countries.

Over-the-Counter (NASDAQ). Since its inception in February 1971, NASDAQ has been known as an industry innovator. For example, it was the first in history to use computers to gather and match buy-and-sell orders. During its first year of operation, people used NASDAQ only as a pricing system in order to facilitate trading. After a modest start in 1972, when 2.2 billion shares of 3,500 stocks changed hands, NASDAQ took off in popularity. By 1999, its trading volume had exceeded 270 billion shares, outstripping that of the NYSE by 70 billion shares.

Today, NASDAQ has become a model symbol of automation—in stark contrast to the NYSE's chaotic manual auction system. Foreign exchanges in Frankfurt, Paris, and London have emulated NASDAQ in trading electronically. As of this writing, the NYSE is practically the last exchange where people actually come together on a floor to conduct trades. However, as electronic trading accelerates, fueled by the Internet, it will be interesting to see whether the NYSE changes its system to embrace automation and became more cost efficient.

As it stands today, NASDAQ is poised to become the world's first truly global market, and ranks second among the world's securities markets in dollar volume. It is quickly becoming the market of choice for business and industry leaders worldwide. NASDAQ has helped thousands of small companies achieve tremendous growth by allowing their stock to trade publicly.

NASDAQ's future goal is to operate and regulate the most liquid, efficient, and fair securities market in the world. Through strict regulation, NASDAQ is designed for the ultimate benefit and protection of the investor. Since trading began, it has become the fastest growing market in the United States, and ranks second in the world's securities markets in terms of dollar volume.

We should note some statistical highlights here. Currently, the market value of over 5,000 companies listed on NASDAQ stands at $5 trillion, considerably more than the 3,000 plus companies listed on the NYSE. An average of 1.8 billion shares per day are traded on NASDAQ. In the 3rd quarter of 2000, the value of shares traded was $6 trillion.

Regional Stock Exchanges. There are five regional exchanges in the United States that on a typical trading day account for at least 10 percent of the 1 billion shares of stock traded on the NYSE:

Name of Exchange	Year Started	Average Daily Share Volume	Number of Stocks Traded	Cost of a Seat
Boston Stock Exchange	1834	20 million	2,000	$ 40,000
Chicago Stock Exchange	1882	55 million	4,000	$117,000
Cincinnati Stock Exchange	1885	12 million	500	$ 10,000
Pacific Exchange (San Francisco)	1882	20 million	2,600	$225,000
Philadelphia Stock Exchange	1790	8.7 million	2,600	$ 90,000

These exchanges occupy a small but busy lane on the financial superhighway. Approximately 100 million shares might pass through one or more regional exchanges during a typical trading day. For example, a St. Louis investor who buys shares in a Big Board-listed company might have that trade executed through a computer in Cincinnati or Chicago, and not on the bustling NYSE floor that is familiar to millions of television viewers.

With the way our trading systems are evolving today, centuries-old open-outcry trading (where investors bark orders on crowded floors) is giving way to more efficient electronic systems that match buyers and sellers instantaneously. Furthermore, our U.S. stock markets are now being pushed to expand trading hours, report trades in decimals rather than in fractions, and cut their transaction costs. Keeping up with these innovations will be a major challenge for the regional exchanges.

Practical .com Sites

Hundreds of Web sites exist today that all seem to be similar. Some sites provide better tools than others, however, in offering investors unique sources of information. That is what gives the sites of the NYSE, NASDAQ, the AMEX, and several smaller regional exchanges their competitive edge. These sites are storehouses of information revealing which stocks trade, for how much, and how often. They even track how sectors are faring and indicate which stocks within those groups are soaring or sagging. In fact, these exchanges are eager to share that wealth of information with investors in order to attract more trading activity.

- www.nasdaq.com and www.amex.com are virtual twins. To find out what is available on either site, you can click Site May & Site Tour. There are links for reading news stories and quotes from various markets. There are also preset and customized screens to help you search for NASDAQ stocks that meet various investment criteria. Also, you can use savings and retirement calculators, retrieve IPO information, earnings report calendars, and more. You can even set up a ticker for specific stocks that is updated every three minutes that will stay on the screen even when you are visiting other Web sites. www.nasdaq.com also offers data about stocks that are listed on NASDAQ or on the Amex. The Sector Overview pages (found by clicking the Market Activity header) enable you to view charts and comments on various sectors, including transportation and finance, with the consensus growth rates for each. Clicking any sector brings similar charts and comments on subsectors. For example, health-care subsectors include biotechnology and drugs. You can choose one of those topics for a list of all its NASDAQ or AMEX stocks, with links to a research section on each company. NASDAQ's site offers another bonus: price and volume data for pre-market (8:30 A.M. to 9:30 A.M.) *Eastern Standard Time* (EST) and after-hours (4 P.M. to 6:30 P.M. EST) trading. The Earnings page also provides useful research shortcuts. Analyst Activity calls up summaries of NASDAQ and AMEX stocks whose earnings forecasts have been revised by a great number of analysts. Analyst Forecast Change lists the new consensus estimates, highlighting the greatest percentage changes for the current week.
- www.nyse.com is the NYSE Web site. This site does not have an abundance of tools but is easier to use. Quotes for tradable stocks and funds include bar charts, trading volume, data on shares outstanding, market capitalization, dividend yield, earnings per share, and even beta (a stock's risk factor). The Data Library lists record trading volume and a trading-statistics archive. One of the site's most useful features is a geographical list of all foreign companies traded on the Big Board as American Depositary Receipts (ADRs). For example, by going to Listed Companies and clicking Geography, you will find country links that identify familiar ADRs such as Germany's Celanese and British Airways.

- Regional exchange sites also have a wealth of information. For example, www.pacificex.com is the Pacific Exchange Web site that lists 2,500 issues, including common and preferred stocks, corporate bonds, and ADRs. This site also offers quotes for all publicly traded stocks. The Philadelphia Stock Exchange, www.phlx.com, lists more than 2,300 stocks, 900 equity options, and options on 10 sector indexes. This site includes an Oil Service Sector Index Option that is the most actively traded index option on any exchange. The Boston Stock Exchange, www.bostonstock.com, trades mostly NYSE issues that are identified under Companies on its home page, while the Chicago Stock Exchange, www.chicagostockex.com, lists NYSE and AMEX shares as well as 450 large NASDAQ issues. Finally, the Arizona Stock Exchange, www.azx.com, is interesting mostly for its educational value. Its single-price auctions of NYSE, NASDAQ, and AMEX securities are available only to institutional traders.

Pricing and Trading

Stocks are priced and subsequently quoted in dollars and cents. The *asked price* is the price at which you can buy a stock. The *bid price* is the price at which you can sell a stock. The difference between the bid price and the ask price is called the *spread.* People often refer to a spread as the profit that a broker or dealer makes on a trade over and above any commission charged to the customer.

When it comes to trading, a company whose stock is traded on a national exchange usually has a smaller spread between its bid price and asked price. Conversely, a company that trades OTC will have a larger spread. For example, the spread on a recent price quoted for AT&T common stock listed on the NYSE was $44.50–$44.75, versus a recent price spread quoted for Microsoft that traded OTC for $87.25–$88.50.

The size of the spread relates directly to the level of liquidity for that particular stock in the marketplace. The amount of stock outstanding and available for trading is also a major factor. For example, a new company might issue two million shares of common stock to be traded on NASDAQ. Traders would consider this amount to be a thinly traded issue, because not that many shares are issued and outstanding (which makes for limited liquidity). In contrast, a major company such as Monsanto that is traded on the NYSE might already have one billion shares outstanding that are available for trading. Due to the popularity of a major company held by institutional investors, its shares are traded more frequently—making it highly liquid. In summary, the more shares that are available for investors to buy and sell, the more price efficient the stock will be to own.

Likewise, every company that issues stock is assigned a *symbol,* or set of letters to be used to identify its stock. These symbols make trading easier for buyers, sellers, and market makers. For example, the symbol for AT&T is T; the symbol for Microsoft is MSFT; and the symbol for Monsanto is MTC. People who watch the ticker, an electronic scoreboard that records trading activity, can look for and identify their stock with its associated symbol. We will discuss the importance of stock symbols as related to trading in Chapter 5, "Studying: How to Interpret Prices and Understand Financial News."

How and Why Stocks Are Traded

It's important to recognize the current trend of market activity from various terms used on Wall Street. A *bear market* is a market in which prices are on the decline for a period of time. Generally speaking, when prices decline by 20 percent from their previous high, we are considered to be in the type of market where there are more sellers than buyers of stock. Conversely, a *bull market* occurs when prices are rising for a prolonged period of time. Most recently, we have been in a long-term bull market since August 12, 1982, when the Federal Reserve began to lower interest rates and economic expansion accelerated. Investors are more optimistic in a bull-market environment and are more willing to buy stocks, which drives prices to even higher levels.

The perception that we are in either a bull or a bear market is based on the decisions of each individual investor. Those who have cash and are willing to buy stocks feel confident about the future and are certain they can make more money by holding this type of security. Conversely, those who need to use cash for other purposes or feel pessimistic about the money-making capability of stocks will not want to hold a security that they feel will decline in value. Depending on whether or not investors are in or out of the market at a particular point in time, they will either make or lose money, during a bullish or bear market environment.

Sometimes, as witnessed during the year 2000, the market has an indentiy crisis—it can't decide whether to act like a bull or a bear but will move sideways instead. This can be very puzzling to investors, especially when inflation is under control and no recession is in sight. But the perception of slower economic growth, higher oil prices, and weak corporate earnings will lower investor confidence and give little prospect for a boost to stock prices.

***Initial Public Offerings* (IPOs).** Depending on the type of market at any given point in time, companies might be willing to offer shares to the public—especially if there is a receptive environment. When a new business enterprise wants to raise capital for expansion and long-term growth, it will contact an *investment banker.* This person's function is to help guide the company when dealing with investors on Wall Street for the first time, and to explore alternate sources of financing when a company wants to raise money.

For example, before a company issues stock for the first time, the investment banker will examine several factors such as general economic conditions, the market environment on Wall Street, and the company's financial condition. Most importantly, potential investors want to know the company's history of profitability and the outlook for future success of its products before purchasing any new stock. These and other factors help establish an offering price for the new shares. This price is determined in advance and is considered reasonable for attracting new buyers.

If conditions look favorable for the marketing of new stock, the investment banker will negotiate an agreement to underwrite the issue by buying all of the shares and then reselling them at a predetermined price. For larger issues of stock, inviting other dealers to join in the underwriting process spreads the risk. This concept is known as a *syndicate group,* where all firms together will contract to sell the new shares to investors at a set price.

Before a new issue of stock can be sold, however, each potential buyer must receive a prospectus. This legal document is required by the *Securities and Exchange Commission* (SEC) and contains essential facts regarding the financial condition and recent operations of the company. By reading the prospectus, a potential investor can make a more informed decision before committing any money to purchase the stock.

During the most recent 10-year bull market, there were billions of dollars raised in IPOs, with the highest of over $70 billion raised during 2000. The ten best performing IPOs that went public between October 1990 and October 2000 are listed in Figure 1-1. Investors who bought and held these securities from their beginning would have made a tremendous amount of money.

After-Market Trading Activity

After a company issues its stock in the primary market, on the IPO, its shares automatically become tradable according to the supply and demand in the secondary market. Investors deal with brokers or registered representatives who act on their behalf as agents. These people must know the rules and regulations of securities trading and must be professionally licensed. They are also known as stock brokers or account

Figure 1-1 *Ten best performing IPOs during the recent bull run (October 11, 1990—October 9, 2000).*

Company	Gain
American Online	61,506%
Veritas Software	24,662
Network Appliance	14,159
CMGI	13,850
SDL	10,810
Siebel Systems	9,030
Vitesse Semiconductor	8,893
Applied Micro Circuits	8,822
Yahoo	7,653
Sanmina	7,505

executives when working for major financial institutions, as explained in Chapter 10, "Brokers: Investment Companies and Services."

These professionals are compensated by commission, charged each time a stock is bought or sold. Depending on how the order is handled and where the stock is traded, there might also be a markup or markdown on the trade. This situation will generally occur on transactions traded on the OTC market. The markup is an amount added to the purchase price of a stock, while a markdown is subtracted from the sales price of a stock. The amount is limited and regulated by the *National Association of Securities Dealers* (NASD).

Ever since trading began in 1792, commissions were fixed according to a predetermined schedule based on price and the number of shares traded on the exchange. On May 1, 1975, however, commissions became fully negotiable on all orders. An investor in today's market who would have had to pay a fixed commission previously can now bargain with a broker for the lowest rate available. As we will see in Chapter 4, trading costs have become even less expensive with the increased usage of the Internet.

More affluent individual investors or large institutions such as banks, insurance companies, and pension funds can execute what are known as *block trades.* These transactions are designed for large trades of 10,000 shares or more, and the transaction costs are even lower. With millions of shares trading hands each day, these types of orders account for the vast majority of activity which creates a more efficient market.

Major Indexes

In today's sophisticated markets, major indexes are used to gauge the performance of various industries. They are now being followed more closely by investors to help make decisions on whether to buy or sell securities. When talking about movements in the market, we need to compare them with economic indicators such as industrial production, consumer spending, changes in the money supply, and the level of corporate profits. Rates of return in various sectors of the market can be a valuable benchmark for judging the performance of actual stock portfolios.

In order to diversify money rationally among stocks, indexes are used to study the price relationship of individual stocks compared to movements in the market as a whole. This process is known as *asset allocation* and helps investors lower the overall risk in their portfolios. The best summary measure of market behavior is indexes. We will discuss the principles underlying them and the uses for which each is best suited.

There are two important issues to keep in mind when using an index:

1. Knowing the stocks that are included in each one.
2. Determining the relative importance or weight of each reported stock in its index.

These two points include the problems of sampling and weighting.

Sampling. An index can be based on a sampling of stocks or on all of the stocks. For example, the *Dow Jones Industrial Average* (DJIA) represents only 30 stocks, which constitutes a sampling of those stocks in the entire NYSE composite index. Although it is widely recognized as reflecting the general market environment, the DJIA does not represent a wide variety of stocks that might be moving in opposite directions.

The adequacy of indexes based on samples is caused by two elements: (1) the fact that stocks of relatively few companies constitute a large proportion of the value of the stocks of all companies, and (2) the tendency of all stocks to move together. Therefore, the substantial concentration of value in relatively few companies contributes to the power of small samples such as the DJIA.

In other words, if we try to measure the performance of a particular portfolio against such an index, the degree of conformity will obviously be distorted. This statement is also true regarding some mutual funds that are focused on specializing in only one industry. For example, the Fidelity Biotechnology Fund should not be expected to represent stocks in general, nor should we expect it to reflect the performance of the broader-based DJIA. Investors can also fall into the trap of thinking their portfolios are under-performing or over-performing the market by comparing their holdings of individual stocks to the wrong index.

Unfortunately, the market receives much media attention when it is going through periods of extreme volatility. Busy American investors who do not have time to sit and watch their stocks each day will receive a synopsis on the evening news. A negative report on the performance of the DJIA or NASDAQ will imply that their stocks may be following these indexes in the same direction. However, this situation might not necessarily be true, and this example shows the importance of tracking the performance of each individual holding.

Weighting. The price of each stock represented in an index must be combined in order to determine the value of the entire index. For that purpose, the index must be computed each time in order to determine the relative importance of each reported stock. Thus, higher-priced stocks of larger companies will carry a much greater weighting than lower-priced stocks of smaller companies.

The two most common ways of weighting stocks are in accordance with market value or by assigning equal weights to equal relative price changes. The former method is appropriate for indicating changes in the aggregate market value of stocks represented by an index, while the latter is more appropriate for indicating movements in the prices of typical or average stocks. For example, changes in general market value are more important for studies of relationships between stock prices and other factors in the national economy.

You must realize that value-weighted indexes attach relatively great importance to large companies and that the stocks of those companies might behave differently from the stocks of smaller companies. The main difference is shown through greater volatility in the fortunes and stock prices of small companies, and the greater tendency for the price of stocks of large companies to be moved by the general tides in the economy as a whole.

Major Indexes. Indexes that are most widely followed and used today include the following:

- ***DJIA***—Comprised of 30 large company stocks that represent all major areas of the economy. The average is price-weighted and is managed by editors of the *Wall Street Journal*, who occasionally drop or add stocks to keep the index current. The average is calculated after the close of the market each trading day and is adjusted for stock splits, substitutions, and spin-offs. This index is still the most popular benchmark and has proven reliable in reflecting general market conditions as a whole.
- ***NASDAQ Composite Index*** **(NASDAQ)**—Measures the performance of stocks traded on the OTC market and is weighted for market value. Newer or smaller companies, or those larger companies that do not want to be listed on a larger exchange, are represented in this index. In recent years, this index has been weighted more heavily toward technology companies.
- ***Standard & Poor's 500*** **(S&P 500)** ***Index***—Comprised of 500 of the largest corporations traded on the NYSE. These stocks are tracked together, and a summary measure is reported on a daily basis. This index is a popular benchmark for gauging the performance of individual stocks.
- ***Russell Indexes***—Measures the performances of stocks based on market capitalization (for example, Russell 3000 includes stocks that represent 98 percent of the total equity in market capitalization). Russell 1000 includes stocks of companies that have larger capitalization, and Russell 2000 comprises companies that have smaller capitalization.
- ***Wilshire 5000 Index***—Includes any stock traded in the United States for which information is readily available. There is a separate index for the 750 largest stocks, one for the next 1,750 companies, and one for the remaining smaller companies. This index has been gaining more attention from federal policy makers and market strategists who try to determine the next direction that the market will take. The Wilshire combines stocks as represented by the old and new economies so that people can see market activity in its entirety.
- ***Industry Indexes***—Designed to measure the performance of stocks related to a specific industry (for example, automobile, airline, financial, health care, technology, and so on)
- ***Europe, Australia, and Far East*** **(EAFE) Index**—Measures the total return of a sample of common stocks of companies in 20 European and Pacific Basin countries. This index helps gauge the performance of foreign markets as a whole.

A Special Application: Investing in a Two-Tiered Market

Sometimes it is necessary to look beyond the numbers in order to see what actually occurs in a volatile market environment. For example, the DJIA rose from 7,500 to more than 11,000 between August 1997 and June

1999. While this rise of 47 percent was considered phenomenal, it was not widespread. Despite what the general public perceived, many stocks outside the DJIA did not regain their former 1997 highs during that period. In fact, just a handful of stocks actually drove the market indexes to higher ground.

How can this situation occur? Partly, it is the result of the way that returns for the S&P 500 and NASDAQ indexes are calculated. They are based on the relative size of each company, so large companies (rather than small companies) make up a greater percentage of the total return of the S&P 500. Understanding the way in which these indexes are calculated is critical when you have two groups of stocks operating in a completely different manner. When this situation occurs, we have a *two-tiered market*.

This situation is exactly what occurred during the 12-month period ending February 22, 1999, when the S&P 500 turned in a total return of 24.4 percent. While that figure sounds outstanding, you must realize that only 20 stocks out of all 500 in this index produced 14.3 percent of the 24.4 percent total return. In other words, 20 stocks made up almost 59 percent of the entire gain of the S&P 500 during that one-year period. Unfortunately, these stocks represented only 4 percent of the entire index. This means that the other 96 percent of those companies could only manage a 10 percent return.

In examining the technology-heavily weighted NASDAQ, the two-tiered market was even more dramatic. Again, looking at the one-year returns as of February 22, 1999, the NASDAQ produced a total return of 35.3 percent. If you look at the top 20 stocks that comprise the NASDAQ, they produced 33.2 percent or 94 percent of the entire gain in this index. Amazingly, these 20 stocks represent only 0.5 percent of the total index. All the other stocks were only capable of producing a 2.1 percent gain.

This situation shows us that only a small group of stocks actually drove these indexes to new highs. Unfortunately, when the average investor hears that these indexes are moving up, he or she believes that all stocks in the index are advancing the markets. The problem occurs when these indexes are used as a comparison to a broadly diversified portfolio, which could obviously have produced a much lower return. This can result in extreme disappointment and unnecessary changes in a portfolio. In a later chapter, we will show how Modern Portfolio Theory produces a more accurate return using four asset classes.

In conclusion, do not let a two-tiered market fool you into changing an investment strategy and moving out of a diversified position. History shows that markets go back to their norms and either rise or fall on a much broader basis. We all know that diversification reduces risk over the long run and that "not putting all of your eggs in one basket" is an Investment 101 fundamental principle. As a financial professional, you should frequently review your client's portfolio to make sure that it is structured to achieve the client's future goals.

Predicting Future Market Activity

Both professional and novice investors attempt to predict future market activity every day. History shows that past performance does not predict future results, especially in the short term. However, we have a much better chance of making money over the long term, because history does tend to repeat itself. In other words, the longer we go out to measure price fluctuations, the more pronounced the risk-reward tradeoff becomes. We will discuss this subject in detail in Chapter 6, "Analysis: Tools and Theories" (under the Modern Portfolio techniques).

Unlike bonds or Treasury bills (T-bills), stocks have been a tremendous defense against rising consumer prices. History shows that they have produced returns that have outpaced inflation to help us maintain our standard of living. Since 1982, we have seen excellent returns in the U.S. stock market. However, we should not be spoiled by these large numbers; but rather, prepare for slower growth and lower returns in the years ahead. It is better to be conservative when making market projections to clients than to promise phenomenal returns which may not materialize.

This information leads us to conclude that portfolio diversification, which has worked so well in the past, will also be a prudent strategy to follow in the future. For example, an investor who owns a mix of large and small growth and value U.S. and foreign shares will reduce overall risk because these classes of stock do not move in sync. While we tend to hear arguments that concentrating on one asset class would be better based on recent results (U.S. blue chip growth stocks from 1995 to 1999), we do not know which asset class will be the biggest winner in the future. Because we have no crystal ball to make a prediction, it always makes sense to split investible assets among the previously mentioned classes of investments.

Picking Consistent Winners. In the kind of turbulent and fast-paced market we saw in the last quarter of 1999 and the early part of the year 2000, many investors just wanted to jump on the bandwagon and go along for the roller coaster ride. They did not want to study market history first to gain knowledge about investment principles. A market with this kind of momentum produced pure madness, and when it corrected, foolish investors lost huge sums of money.

In conducting market research and making recommendations for clients, you should always err on the side of caution. Whether selecting individual stocks or mutual funds, you will find that a diversified program will usually include some excellent winners. Most importantly, investors want to build faith and trust in your recommendations as a professional.

In the past, we have seen that some strategies work for a while and then fade away from popularity. For example, "Dogs of the Dow" involves buying the 10 highest-yielding stocks in the DJIA at the beginning of each year. This process usually means picking those companies whose stocks lagged in performance the previous year, and therefore ended up with the highest dividend payouts. This strategy generated decent results during the '80s and '90s, and showed that some stocks were recognized as being out of favor and subsequently had value. Investors therefore snapped them up, causing a rebound in their prices.

Although this strategy received a lot of press in the mid-1990s, the approach has not worked well recently. Generally, quality stocks that are undervalued will tend to rebound anyway, especially if we are in a bull-market environment and their earnings are rising. Over the past five years, however, we have seen fewer demand for value stocks than for growth stocks. The dogs strategy could be suffering as a result, or it could be that the approach is no longer being followed by most astute investors.

What we have witnessed recently is more of a momentum strategy being taken by investors during an optimistic bull market environment. This situation shows that the best-performing stocks from one year are tending to generate better-than-average returns the following year. Investors will want to own those stocks, especially if they are participating in the growth of the new information age economy.

Meanwhile, the worst-performing stocks keep on suffering and show a lack of performance. But history might very well repeat itself here as investors come to realize that overvaluation can only go so far and that they are better off buying undervalued stocks with a track record of solid earnings. These stocks are known as sleepers that will someday wake up and become recognized by the investment community as bargains. Therefore, it is critical to include some of these stocks as part of a client's portfolio.

Summary

As we saw in this chapter, the stock market has deep roots in American history and has come a long way since its origin. Anyone who is financially able to participate in company ownership through the purchase of common stock can reap tremendous rewards. The stock market, as measured by the S&P 500 Index, has given investors an average rate of return of 11.3 percent between 1926 and 1998. This return has enabled them to keep pace with the rate of inflation and to achieve numerous financial goals, such as saving for a college education or for a comfortable retirement.

In order to participate in this dynamic process and make intelligent recommendations for clients, you must be familiar with the function of the Federal Reserve system in our economy. Its actions will continue to play a major role in determining the direction of our financial markets in the future. Chapter 2, "Economics Basics: Terms, Definitions, Trends, and Policies," will also examine recent economic trends and describe how to interpret important economic data. By understanding the benefits of owning stock in relation to economic activity, you will find it easier to determine which types are best to own in order to achieve specific goals and objectives.

Chapter 2

Economics Basics: Terms, Definitions, Trends, and Policies

Introduction

Learning about the stock market is an inordinate task. As a professional in the field of finance, you will find that your understanding of various terms and the implications of markets moving in one direction or the other will be the key to giving sound financial advice. This chapter explains what clients need to know regarding our economy as they try to make important investment decisions. This material will also give clear insight regarding the actions of the Federal Reserve system as it goes about its main function of controlling inflation and the money supply.

A brief background on economics is in order here. We can define *economics* as the study of how wealth is created and distributed in a free society, such as the United States. Citizens are free to buy and sell the goods and services that they need, and prices are set according to the supply and demand for each type of product or service. There is interplay between major institutions, namely the government, labor, and business. They must work together in order to satisfy the needs and wants of consumers.

A number of factors affect the pricing of goods and services. *Economics 101* teaches that a high demand for consumer products will force prices up. Similarly, factors such as cost of labor and industry competition will ultimately influence the overall level of prices. For example, because consumers can borrow money at reasonable rates from various lending institutions, they will have more money to spend during an economic expansion. Conversely, when consumers experience a tightening of credit during economic recessions, they will shy away from borrowing money when interest rates are higher.

Having said that, we must explore the supply and demand for money. Financial institutions such as banks, credit unions, and consumer loan companies provide money to consumers to help stimulate economic activity. The availability of money to these institutions for lending purposes is directly affected by the monetary policy of the Federal Reserve system. We can consider "the Fed" as our nation's central bank, and its chief function is to maintain an adequate supply of money while attempting to control the rate of inflation. As our economy grows, the Fed makes funds available for business expansion and consumer spending by providing money for each of these areas. The Fed also plays a delicate balancing act by keeping interest rates and consumer prices at reasonable levels so that the economy can continue to grow at a reasonable rate.

Global Economic Expansion

Due to the recent tremendous boom in global economic expansion, we cannot ignore these important influences. As more international trade develops between all countries of the world during the next century, there will be an increase in the activities of foreign investors and more global competition. This means American businesses must compete directly with foreign companies for the dollars spent by American consumers to buy various products.

For example, the automobile industry has witnessed this intense competition. Due to their sleek styling, high quality, and reasonable prices, foreign automobiles have become very popular with American car buyers. While Detroit was asleep during the late 1900s, automobile makers such as BMW, Lexus, and Mercedes were making tremendous strides into the American market and taking away business from U.S. automobile manufacturers such as GM, Ford, and Chrysler.

To counter this type of intense competition, American companies are expanding their overseas locations in order to sell more goods and services to foreigners. In effect, when sales of U.S. goods (exports) are greater than the sale of goods made in foreign countries, we have a trade surplus that benefits our entire economy. In effect, this surplus increases the funds available for domestic spending and investment. Likewise, if foreign companies invest their dollars directly into the United States, our money supply increases—which helps reduce interest rates and stimulates greater expansion.

But in recent years we have experienced a large trade deficit, as shown in Figure 2-1. In other words, Americans are buying more goods that are made abroad, and more money is leaving this country faster than it is coming in. As of October 1999, the U.S. trade deficit stood at $25.9 billion. This figure was the seventh monthly record set in 1999, and through the first 10 months, the deficit was running at an annual rate of $262 billion. This figure far surpassed 1998's record deficit of $164.3 billion. Through the first eight months of the year 2000, the trade deficit stood at $29.4 billion.

You should note that American exports in October 1999 stood at $81.9 billion as sales of farm products, computers, and telecommunications equipment fell. Meanwhile, imports surged to a record $107.9 billion. Particularly worrisome is that the deficit at an annual rate had widened by $60 billion in that last three-month period. While this tends to be a drag on the U.S. economy, it is not expected to show any internal growth.

The administration blamed 40 percent of the widening deficit on rising oil prices. The average price of a barrel of crude oil hit $20.74 in October 1999—more than double the low in January ($9.19) as production cutbacks by oil producers and the improving global economy boosted the world's demand for oil. As the summer of 2000 approached, the price of a gallon of gas had reached $2 in some parts of the country. While the price of oil has reached $32 per barrel in November 2000, more production overseas was expected to gradually decrease this amount during 2001, reducing inflationary pressure in the U.S. economy.

Our ultimate goal is to have a trade surplus, where foreigners perceive our goods to be superior to theirs in quality and price so they will make more purchases here. In other words, an increase of money coming into the country would overtake the amount that is exiting. The more money we have to earn and keep, the more money we can spend at home to improve our quality of life in the United States.

Figure 2-1 *Trade deficit.*

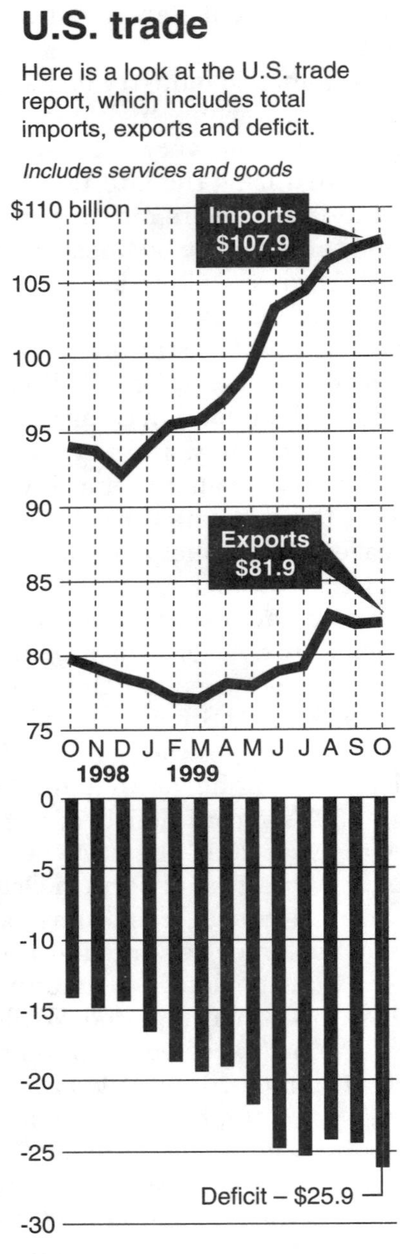

Source: Federal Reserve Bank of St. Louis

Economic Terms and Definitions

To better understand activity in the U.S. economy, let's examine some key terms and definitions and their influences on consumer spending.

- **Interest rates**—Interest rates represent the cost of money. These rates take into effect the supply and demand for money. There is a cost for the privilege of borrowing on credit, just as there is a return for saving and investing. When interest rates rise, buying on credit is more expensive, but saving and investing in *certificates of deposit* (CDs) becomes more attractive. The Fed will use this tactic to contract the money supply and to slow economic expansion. On the other hand, when the Fed wants to encourage economic growth, it will reduce interest rates—which lowers the cost of borrowing and makes savings less attractive. Figure 2-2 illustrates both short- and long-term interest rates. Short-term interest rates are represented by three-month T-bills and 90-day commercial paper. Notice how they move together and follow the prime lending rate. Long-term interest rates are represented by conventional mortgage, corporate Aaa, and 30-year Treasury bond (T-bond) rates. They also have a pattern of moving together. More recently, interest rates on short-term securities have increased to the point where they are equal to or

Figure 2-2 *Short- and long-term interest rates.*

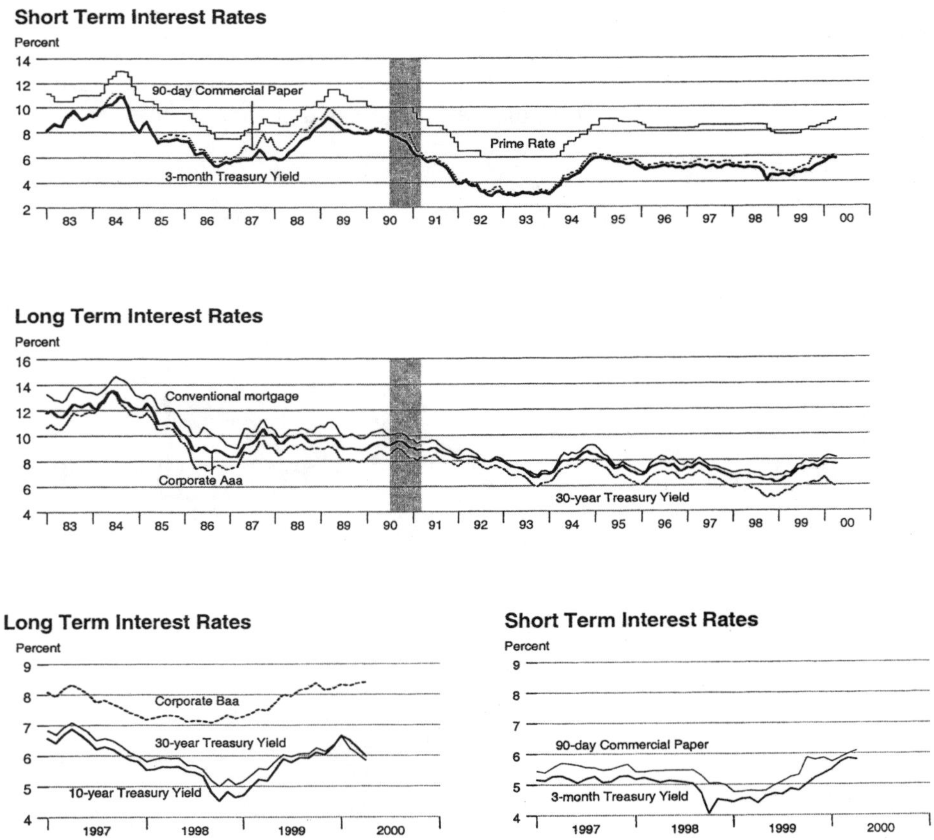

Federal Reserve Bank of St. Louis

greater than interest rates on long-term securities. This situation is sometimes referred to as an *inverted yield curve*.

- ***Consumer Price Index* (CPI)**—The CPI measures the level of inflation as reflected by changes in the price levels of consumer goods and services. As consumer prices rise due to higher demand for goods and services, the general level of inflation in the economy also rises. The cost of living will vary depending on the area of the country in which you live. For example, housing costs are much higher on the east and west coasts than they are in the Midwest. In recent years, the CPI has averaged between 1.5 percent to 3.0 percent. Figure 2-3 illustrates the activity of the CPI going back to 1975. Notice that inflation got completely out of control in the late 1970s and finally peaked at around 14.75 percent in mid-1980. Since 1981, inflation has decreased steadily, which has resulted in more economic growth and reasonable prices. More recently, the average CPI has been around 3 percent. With the Fed's actual target being closer to 2 percent, it explains the series of increases in short-term rates during the second half of 1999 and the first half of 2000.
- **Consumer spending**—Measures the demand for goods and services in a free economy. When consumers have more jobs and earn higher wages, they feel confident about the state of the economy and tend to spend more money. However, increased levels of consumer spending and borrowing can also lead to higher inflation—causing the Fed to raise interest rates to contract the money supply. This situation can lead to a subsequent reduction in the number of jobs,

Figure 2-3 *CPI activity dating back to 1975.*

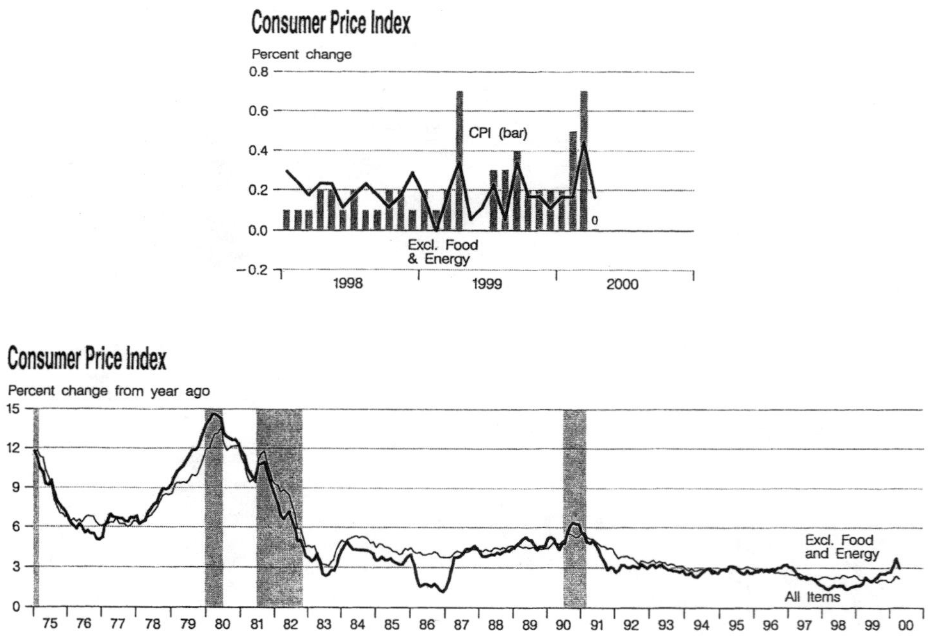

Source: Federal Reserve Bank of St. Louis

Figure 2-4 *Consumer spending.*

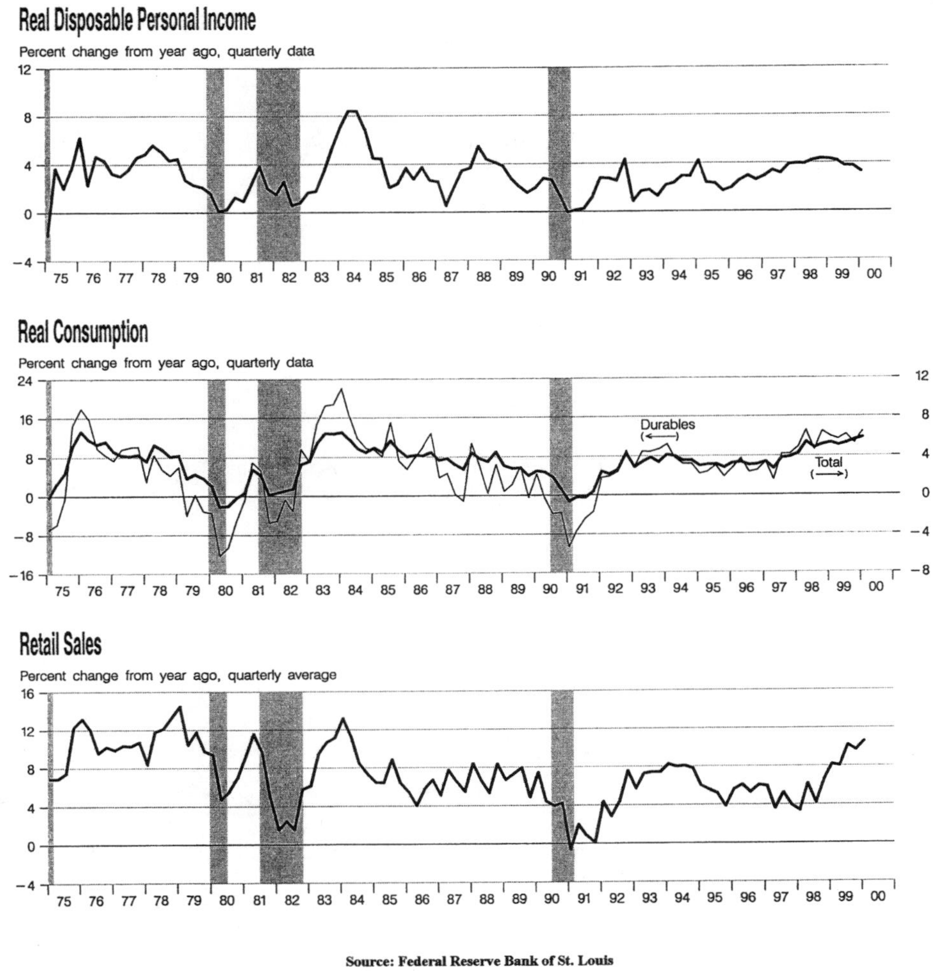

lower wages, and a negative feeling about the economy (which in turn would lower consumer spending). We can examine several graphs in Figure 2-4 as they relate to consumer spending. These figures show that as real disposable personal income goes up, real consumption or consumer spending will also rise. Positive consumer confidence is also reflected in the pattern of retail sales in a good economic environment. However, the shaded areas indicate a decline in personal income resulting in flat or negative consumption. Note a direct correlation to retail sales during these periods.

- **Money supply (M1, M2, and M3)**—Money supply measures the dollars that are available for spending in the U.S. economy. M1 represents the sum of demand deposits, coins, and currency in circulation. M2 includes all of these components plus bank savings accounts, smaller CDs (less than $100,000), and all money-market accounts. M3 includes all of these elements plus large CDs (greater than $100,000), Euro dollar deposits, and institutional money-market funds. Figure

Figure 2-5 *Changes in money supply.*

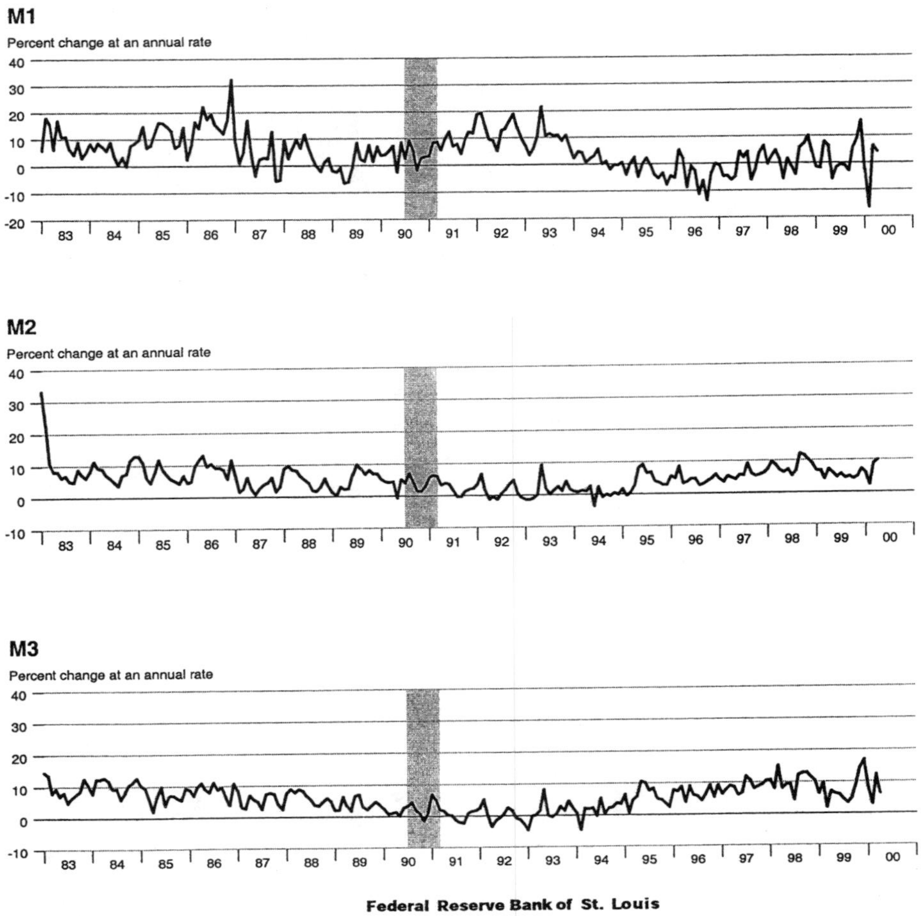

2-5 shows changes in the money supply going back to 1983. All three measures tend to be consistent with each other, based on the Federal Reserve policy of contracting or expanding money that is available for consumer spending. These statistics are reported by the Fed on a weekly basis and can be interpreted differently. When increases are reported in M1, M2, or M3, money is taken out of circulation and economic expansion levels off or tends to decline. The Fed can set targets for the levels of M1, M2, and M3. Most importantly, a balance in the money supply will help maintain economic growth without an increase in the level of inflation.

- ***Gross Domestic Product*** **(GDP)**—The GDP represents the total market value of goods and services produced in the United States for a particular period. This information is released quarterly by the Department of Commerce and is reported on television and in the business press. The percentage change is an easy way to determine the productivity in the economy. For example, Figure 2-6 shows real GDP increased to 5 percent by the end of 1999, which means that the U.S. economy produced more goods and services than it did in 1995.

Figure 2-6 *Real GDP increased to 5 percent at the end of 1999.*

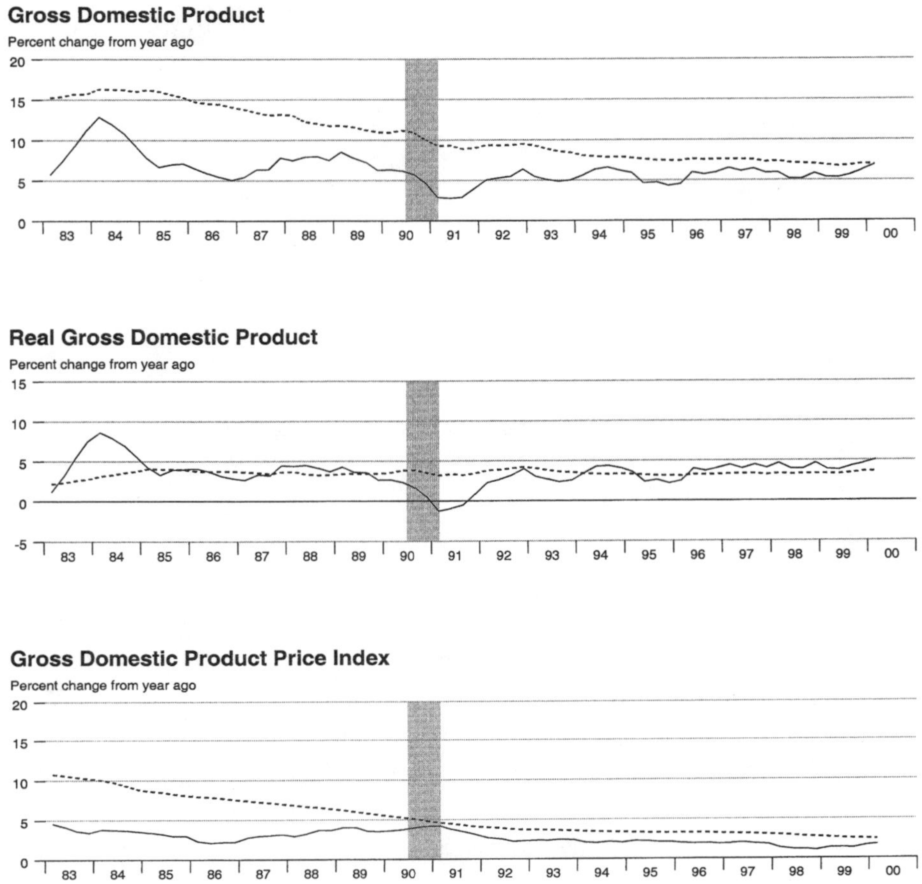

Source: Federal Reserve Bank of St. Louis

Notice how real GDP has increased steadily since our minor recession in the early 1990s. This continued expansionary phase, along with a decreasing Gross Domestic Product Price Index, makes the United States look favorable for future economic growth and will attract more foreign companies and governments that want to invest here.

- **Unemployment**—Unemployment refers to the number of people without work who are willing and able to be employed. Each month, the U.S. Bureau of Labor Statistics comes out with an employment survey. The results are measured in *frictional* and *structural unemployment*. The former is unemployment that occurs when employees lose jobs due to the poor management of a company. The latter occurs when many companies in the same sector or industry encounter financial problems and begin laying off workers. This situation often results from changes in technology, consumer preference, or political influences. Because we will always have some unemployment in the economy, a 5 percent figure is considered full employment. The higher

Figure 2-7 *Unemployment as an economic indicator.*

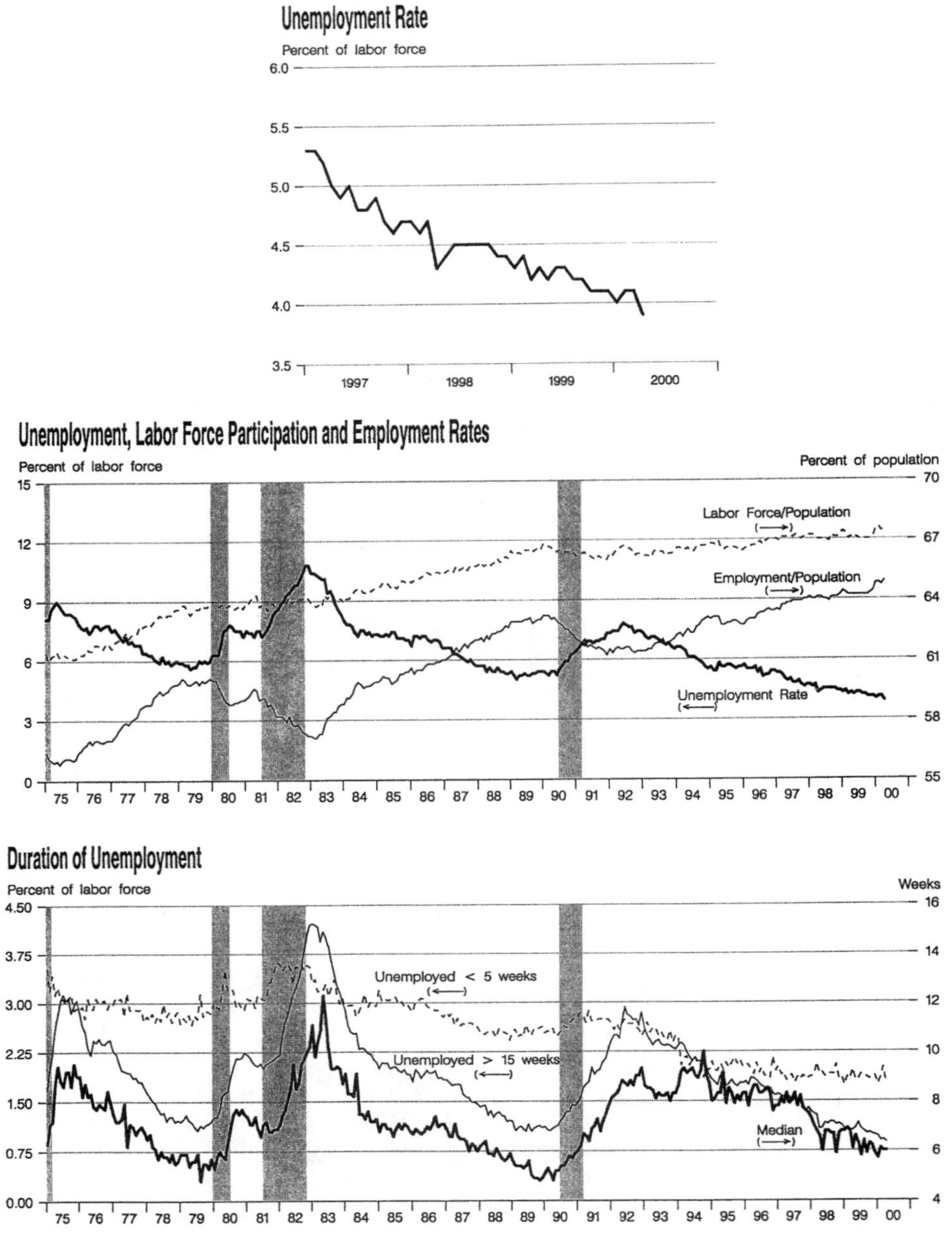

Federal Reserve Bank of St. Louis

the rate above this level, the more negative effect that unemployment will have on sales in food, housing, retail, automotive, and leisure activities. We show this economic indicator in Figure 2-7. The figure shows how a growing economic environment will create more jobs and reduce unemployment, as indicated, from 1997 to early 2000. During this time, the population of the labor force will also increase, causing the number of skilled jobs available to decrease. As workers are retrained for jobs in the new economy, the rate of unemployment will also tend to remain low. However, notice how unemployment spiked upward during recessionary periods in the U.S. economy (shaded areas).

- **Housing starts**—This term refers to the number of new homes being built at a particular point in time. An increase in housing starts reflects lower interest rates and an expanding economy. In other words, more people can afford mortgages to purchase new homes in desirable locations. Conversely, when interest rates on home loans rise, the number of housing starts will decline—which, in turn, could warn of a pending slow down of economic activity. We see this concept illustrated in Figure 2-8. As interest rates tended to remain stable and the economy expanded over the last several years, consumers will feel confident and able to afford new homes. However, when mortgage rates rose (as in late 1998 and 1999), the demand for new homes declined.
- **Prime rate**—This term refers to the rate that banks charge their best customers to borrow money. The prime rate is indirectly controlled by the Fed and is generally set by banks to acceptable levels for businesses to borrow money in an expansionary environment. As the Fed raises the discount rate, as it did in late 1999 and into mid-2000, the prime rate goes up—resulting in less borrowing and an economy that will tend to contract (refer to Figure 2-2).

The Business Cycle

Our economy functions according to a business cycle. We will typically go through four phases: expansion, peak, contraction, and trough (statistics

Figure 2-8 *Housing starts.*

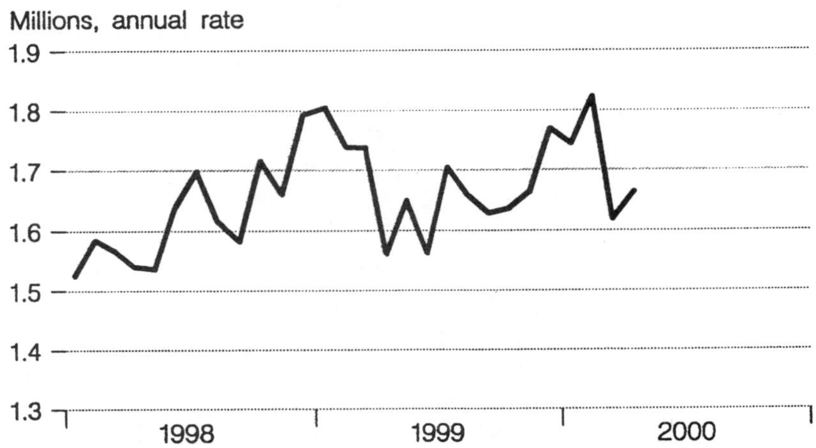

Federal Reserve Bank of St. Louis

are shown in Figure 2-9). We are currently going through an expansionary period where unemployment is low, prices are stable, inflation is steady, and corporate profits are rising. As spending during this period of prosperity matures, we will eventually come to a peak. At that time, the output of goods and services along with corresponding employment is high. Companies have expanded their factories so that they will be capable of producing more goods. But as labor demands higher wages, companies will raise prices to cover the increased costs, and consumer demand will begin to slow down. Eventually, the supply of goods will begin to exceed the demand, and more will remain unsold. Inventories of unsold goods will begin to pile up, and gradually the economy will begin to contract. In other words, prices will level off as new orders for unsold goods will decrease—as will the demand for the raw materials used to make them. The economy usually contracts as companies begin to produce less, lay off workers, and try to offset falling sales and profits. Prices for goods and services will decrease, as will the use of credit. A prolonged economic contraction of this kind is called a *recession.* The low point in the business cycle is called a trough and is marked by depressed stock prices and low consumer confidence. If this period becomes prolonged and severe, it is known as a *depression.* As the Fed lowers interest rates to encourage borrowing once again, consumers will eventually begin buying as prices for goods drop faster than income. Accumulated business inventories will begin to fall as consumers and businesses increase their purchases. As the use of credit becomes popular once again, we begin the expansionary phase once more.

Federal Reserve Policies, Rules, and Regulations. You must realize that throughout any business cycle, the Fed's job is to keep the economy moving forward. The Fed strives for continued economic growth and plays a delicate balancing act in order to achieve this goal. The Fed closely monitors the economic indicators described previously and expands and contracts the money supply by using monetary policy. As we stated earlier, if the supply of money increases, the economy is likely to expand. If the supply of money decreases, the economy is likely to contract. By raising or lowering interest rates, the Fed directly controls the demand for money.

As we enter the 21st century, dynamic changes are already taking place in our economy. Larger companies have been buying smaller ones in an attempt to reduce costs and increase profits. As we witness these consolidations in most major industries, the number of laid-off workers tends to increase. However, many are being retrained to perform more efficient functions with their new employers. This situation helps keep unemployment figures down and simultaneously raises our GDP.

As the U.S. economy becomes more technologically oriented, the cost of producing goods and services will decrease—resulting in higher corporate profits. This situation should be bullish for equity markets and should result in higher stock prices on all major exchanges. Likewise, as the rest of the free world attempts to follow the United States in this transformation, other countries will experience the same progression. There will be an increase in demand for their goods and services, and stock prices of companies will also rise. Barring any major wars or unfore-

Figure 2-9 *Expansion, peak, contraction, and trough.*

US Business Cycle Expansions and Contractions [1]

Contractions (recessions)start at the peak of a business cycle and end at the trough.

click here for more information about how the NBER's Business Cycle Dating Committee uses dates and where the current expansion ranks in terms of length

BUSINESS CYCLE REFERENCE DATES		DURATION IN MONTHS			
		Contraction	Expansion	Cycle	
Trough	Peak	(Trough From Previous Peak)	(Trough to Peak)	Trough from Previous Trough	Peak from Previous Peak
December 1854	June 1857	--	30	--	--
December 1858	October 1860	18	22	48	40
June 1861	April 1865	8	***46***	30	***54***
December 1867	June 1869	***32***	18	***78***	50
December 1870	October 1873	18	34	36	52
March 1879	March 1882	65	36	99	101
May 1885	March 1887	38	22	74	60
April 1888	July 1890	13	27	35	40
May 1891	January 1893	10	20	37	30
June 1894	December 1895	17	18	37	35
June 1897	June 1899	18	24	36	42
December 1900	September 1902	18	21	42	39
August 1904	May 1907	23	33	44	56
June 1908	January 1910	13	19	46	32
January 1912	January 1913	24	12	43	36
December 1914	August 1918	23	***44***	35	***67***
March 1919	January 1920	***7***	10	***51***	17
July 1921	May 1923	18	22	28	40
July 1924	October 1926	14	27	36	41
November 1927	August 1929	13	21	40	34
March 1933	May 1937	43	50	64	93
June 1938	February 1945	13	***80***	63	***93***
October 1945	November 1948	***8***	37	***88***	45
October 1949	July 1953	11	***45***	48	***56***
May 1954	August 1957	***10***	39	***55***	49
April 1958	April 1960	8	24	47	32
February 1961	December 1969	10	***106***	34	***116***
November 1970	November 1973	***11***	36	***117***	47
March 1975	January 1980	16	58	52	74
July 1980	July 1981	6	12	64	18
November 1982	July 1990	16	92	28	108
March 1991		8	--	100	--
Average, all cycles:					
1854-1991 (31 cycles)		18	35	53	53*
1854-1919 (16 cycles)		22	27	48	49**
1919-1945 (6 cycles)		18	35	53	53
1945-1991 (9 cycles)		11	50	61	61
Average, peacetime cycles:					
1854-1991 (26 cycles)		19	29	48	48***
1854-1919 (14 cycles)		22	24	46	47****
1919-1945 (5 cycles)		20	26	46	45
1945-1991 (7 cycles)		11	43	53	53

* 30 cycles.
** 15 cycles.
*** 25 cycles.
**** 13 cycles.

Figure 2-9B *Continued.*

Figures printed in ***bold italic*** are the wartime expansions (Civil War, World Wars I and II, Korean War, and Vietnam War); the postwar contractions, and the full cycles that include the wartime expansions.

From the U.S. Department of Commerce, Survey of Current Business, October 1994, Table C-51.

[1] **The determination that the last recession ended in March 1991 is the most recent decision of the Business Cycle Dating Committee of the National Bureau of Economic Research.**

Announcement dates:

The March 1991 trough was announced December 22, 1992.
The July 1990 peak was announced April 25, 1991.
The November 1982 trough was announced July 8, 1983.
The July 1981 peak was announced January 6, 1982.
The July 1980 trough was announced July 8, 1981.
The January 1980 peak was announced June 3, 1980.

The NBER does not define a recession in terms of two consecutive quarters of decline in real GNP. Rather, a recession is a recurring period of decline in total output, income, employment, and trade, usually lasting from six months to a year, and marked by widespread contractions in many sectors of the economy.

A growth recession is a recurring period of slow growth in total output, income, employment, and trade, usually lasting a year or more. A growth recession may encompass a recession, in which case the slowdown usually begins before the recession starts, but ends at about the same time. Slowdowns also may occur without recession, in which case the economy continues to grow, but at a pace significantly below its long-run growth

A depression is a recession that is major in both scale and duration. Further discussion of these concepts can be found in the NBER book, Business Cycles, Inflation and Forecasting, 2nd edition, by Geoffrey H. Moore, 1983, Ballinger Publishing Co., Cambridge, MA.

Source:

Public Information Office
National Bureau of Economic Research, Inc.
1050 Massachusetts Avenue
Cambridge MA 02138
USA

seen circumstances, we will have more countries joining in free world trade. As a result, this situation should result in a more prosperous global economy.

Controlling the Economy with Monetary Policy. As a government agency, the Federal Reserve controls economic activity by changing reserve requirements, using open market operations, and changing the discount rate. Let's examine each one briefly to better understand how they are used by the Fed.

One way in which the Fed can alter the money supply is by changing the level of reserves that its member banks must maintain. For example, when you make a deposit into your checking or savings account, the bank in turn lends a portion of this money and charges interest to make a profit on the loan. However, the bank is required to keep a certain percentage of your deposit on reserve at its regional Federal Reserve bank.

This percentage is known as the *reserve requirement* and is considered money that the bank cannot use for lending or investment purposes. The higher the reserve requirement, the less money that the bank has to lend out. Thus, when the Fed raises the reserve requirement, it will reduce the money supply in circulation and will generally cause interest rates to increase. Because the Fed has used other strategies to accomplish the same goal, this approach has not been a popular form of control in recent years.

This topic brings us to the more popular approach of *open-market operations,* involving the sale and purchase of government securities to investors. The Fed's *Open-Market Committee* (OMC) of 12 member banks meets eight times a year in order to evaluate U.S. economic conditions. If the OMC wants to stabilize the economy, it can alter the money supply by authorizing the purchase or sale of government securities. When buying government securities from the public, the government pays investors and increases the amount of money in circulation. This increases the amount of borrowing resulting in higher production and employment.

Conversely, when the OMC authorizes the sale of government securities, the government sells them to investors who pay to acquire them. This money goes directly to the Fed and is subsequently removed from circulation. When the money supply decreases, there is less borrowing in the economy. This situation is likely to lead to decreases in consumer demand, slower economic growth, and lower prices. Thus, the OMC has powerful control over the 12 districts of the Federal Reserve banking system.

The third and currently most popular way in which the Fed controls the money supply is by changing the *discount rate.* This rate is charged to member banks to borrow money overnight. By decreasing the discount rate, the Fed has more money available for economic growth and borrowing increases. Conversely, by increasing the discount rate, borrowing will decrease and fewer funds will be available for economic growth. These higher interest rates are passed directly to consumers as banks raise the prime lending rate to their best customers. In effect, this increase will discourage consumers and businesses from borrowing money and will tend to slow down the economy. Updated rates are available each day in the Money Rates table of the *Wall Street Journal*.

Figure 2-10 illustrates the Federal OMC's expected federal funds and discount rate dating back to 1983. These rates work together to control the amount of money in circulation. To fine-tune the economy and control inflation, the Fed will not hesitate to raise these rates. Figure 2-10 shows this to be the case in 1994 and in late 1999 into the first half of 2000.

The Federal Reserve and Economic Trends: Past, Present, and Future. As we stated earlier, the Federal Reserve acts as our central bank and controls the money supply. History has shown, however, that controlling the economy can be a difficult task. For example, during the late 1970s, poor monetary policy and political differences in Washington caused inflation to get out of control. To catch inflation, the Fed was forced

Figure 2-10 *FOMC expected federal funds rate and discount plan.*

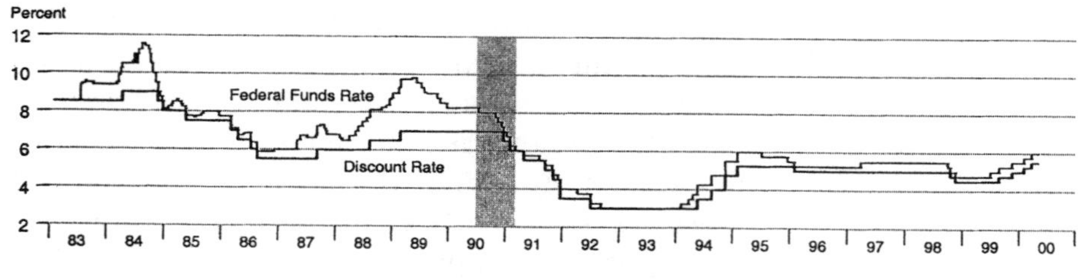

to raise interest rates, which put many people out of work and brought the economy to a standstill. As the Fed regained control of the economy during the early 1980s, however, prices fell, unemployment decreased, and economic conditions gradually improved. Since that time (and as a result of better monetary control), we have experienced tremendous economic expansion that has brought us into the boom of the 21st century.

Currently, economic growth is expected to moderate in late 2000 and into early 2001. However, investing in the high-tech sector will continue to be hot, and this area should outperform other areas of the economy. As increased demand for specialists in the new economy tends to push wages even higher, these costs will be passed on to consumers in the form of higher prices. This situation could easily lead to a modest increase in price inflation, which means that the Fed would likely raise interest rates further into 2001.

As we increase the use of computer software to run our daily lives and businesses, this industry will become an increasing part of our GDP. In the early 1980s, business software investment began to steadily increase. Currently, it adds one-fourth of a percent each year to national economic growth. As we become more of a technologically oriented society in the 21st century, this area is expected to contribute even more to GDP growth and at a much faster pace. Therefore, the outlook for jobs in this industry looks very bright.

As an important economic indicator, housing starts and the sale of new homes have been strong in recent years. This situation is due to the robust economy and a somewhat lagging effect of an immigration surge during the 1980s. There has also been an increased demand for second homes by more affluent Baby Boomers, and this expansion has fostered a rise in home ownership. As people become more established and want to stay in their well-developed neighborhoods, we will see more houses being torn down and rebuilt. An unusual period of warmer weather and shorter winters has contributed to more activity in the housing market as well.

Because our population growth will eventually peak, we will begin to limit the upside for housing starts. Other factors contributing to this trend will be a slowdown in economic growth, an increase in mortgage interest rates, and the higher cost of housing construction. As the younger generation moves into the 24 to 34 age bracket, they represent a smaller percentage of the population and will eventually undermine the demand for housing.

Foreign trade is not to be ignored. Americans have been purchasing more goods outside the United States than selling to companies overseas. As stated earlier, this situation results in a trade deficit, which can have negative implications for U.S. economic growth. The outflow of U.S. dollars to overseas markets has been a backstop for other economies in crisis and has served as an inflationary safety valve for the United States. As our economy slows in 2001, however, we will spend more dollars in the United States—and the foreign demand for U.S. goods should also increase. The trade deficit will also become more of a political issue in the years ahead.

The Outlook for Monetary Policy, Interest Rates, and Equity Markets. Milton Research, Inc. is a highly respected company that conducts research for high-profile clients in forecasting economic activity. Let's examine some of their graphs, along with the company's outlook regarding the effects that monetary policy will have on interest rates and on the equity markets in the coming years.

During 1998, there was a risk that the U.S. economy would become an island of prosperity among the weakness of other global economies. In an attempt to help the free world, the Federal Reserve bought insurance by cutting the Fed funds rate three times (75 basis points). This action triggered a massive rally in U.S. financial markets, as illustrated in Figure 2-11. During 1999, although concerns regarding global recession receded, the Fed still raised the funds rate three times (75 basis points) in order to keep U.S. inflation under control. This figure shows how this policy hurt bond performance, as reflected in long-term T-bonds, but did little to impair the demand for U.S. equities (as reflected in the rise of the S&P 500 stock index).

As long as we have increasing inflationary pressures, the Fed is likely to keep raising interest rates. Its unofficial inflation target is around 2 percent. As in the past, Federal Reserve Chairman Alan Greenspan will keep

Figure 2-11 *Cutting the Federal Reserve funds rate.*

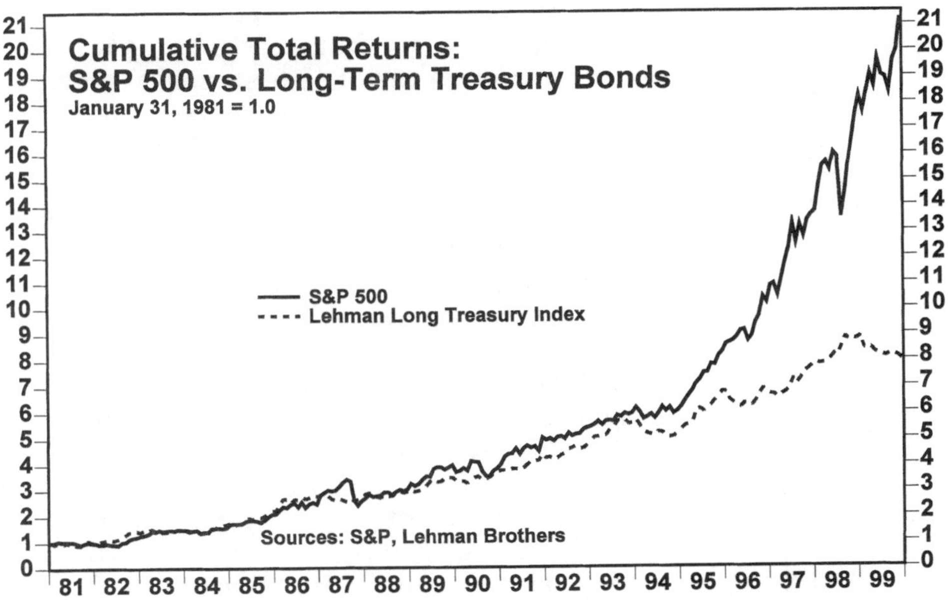

Figure 2-12 *Corporate debt and Treasury debt.*

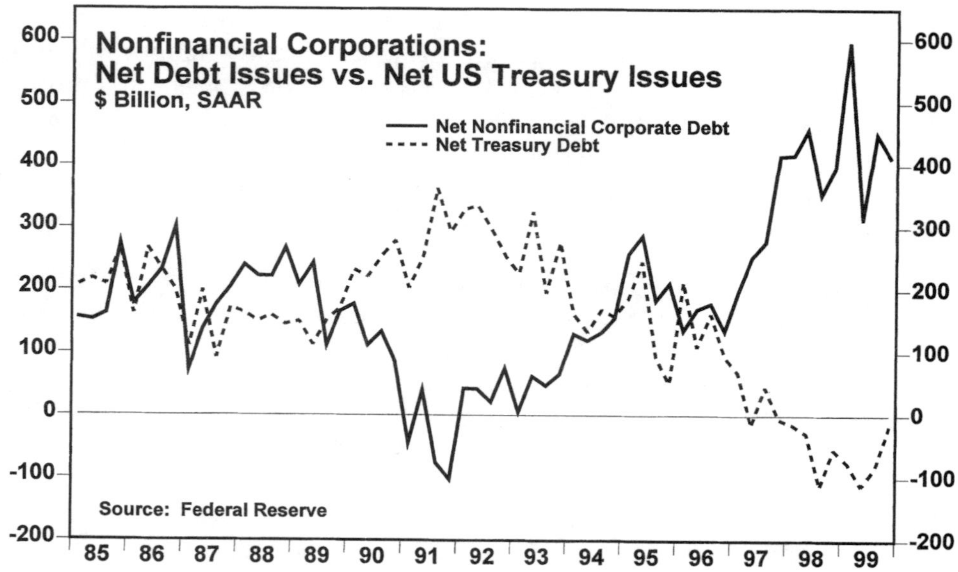

a tight rein on inflation. He has been reappointed for another term and will continue to focus on slow, yet stable growth for the U.S. economy.

Figure 2-12 shows that in recent years, corporate debt has expanded more rapidly than Treasury debt. This situation is in part due to the Fed's policy of keeping more money in circulation in an expanding economy. What we see is corporate debt inversely correlated with the volume of Treasury debt issues. Should the Fed decide to contract the money supply in order to control inflation, it would issue more Treasury securities in the near future.

Ironically, the expansion of corporate debt has been mirrored by a major reduction of corporate equity supply, as shown in Figure 2-13. With the recent trend of stock repurchase plans and consolidations, corporations have become the largest buyers of equities in recent years. While more corporate cash has been paid from share repurchases and major acquisitions, the increased demand for a dwindling stock supply has resulted in higher equity prices. This trend is expected to continue in the foreseeable future.

In regards to a leading market index, large cap stocks (as represented by the S&P 500) are significantly overvalued. In Figure 2-14, we see a phenomenal growth pattern, especially from 1995 through the end of 1999. This growth represented a 12 percent overvaluation, which seems rather large. This value is small, however, in comparison to a 23 percent overvaluation prior to the October 1987 stock market crash. Figure 2-14 would also indicate a continuing trend of higher valuations in this index, assuming favorable economic growth, low inflation, and low unemployment numbers.

Several times during 1998 and 1999, small-cap stocks were touted as offering vastly better values than large-cap stocks. While this statement has been validated, in each case, expectations of superior performance have been disappointing. Figure 2-15 shows the underperformance of

Figure 2-13 *Expansion of corporate debt.*

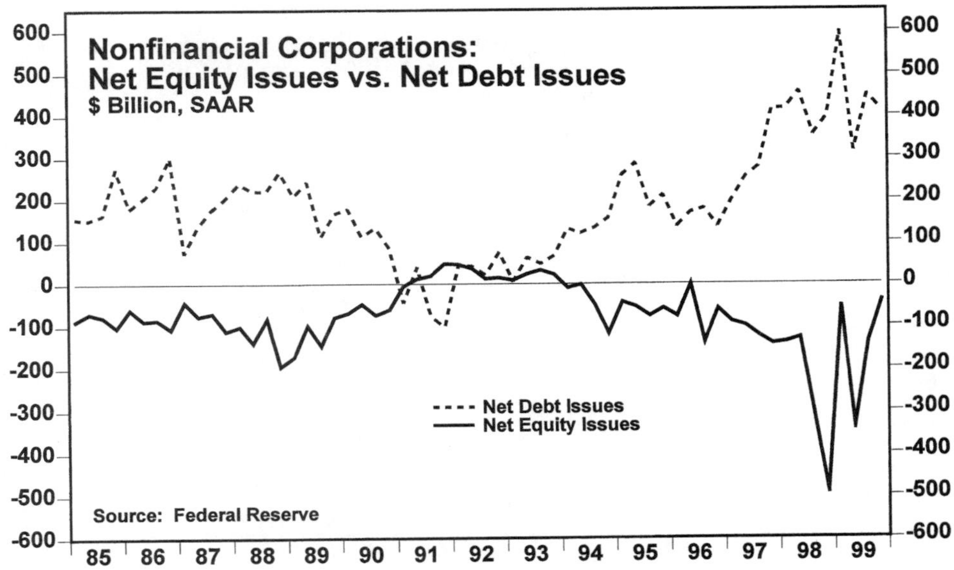

Figure 2-14 *Higher valuations.*

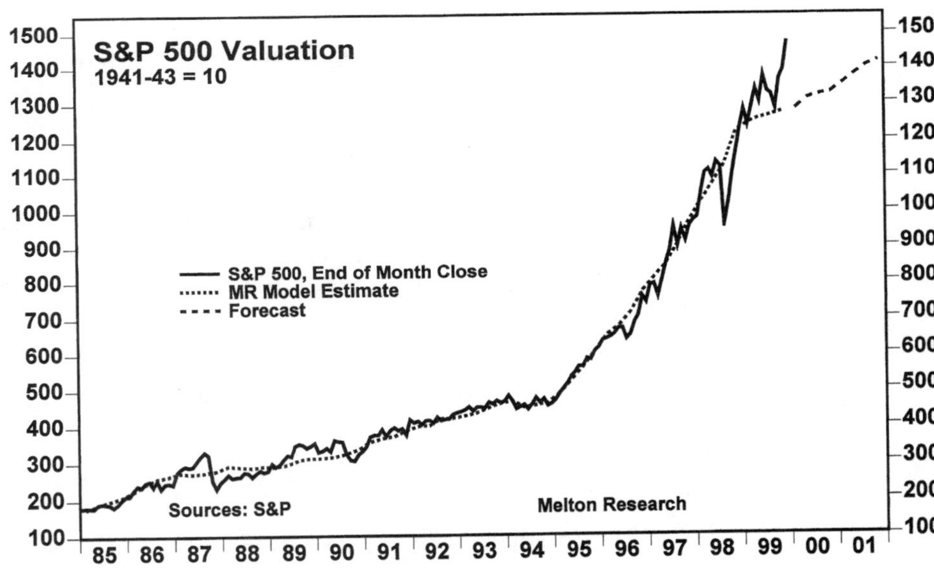

small-cap stocks, as represented by the Russell 2000 Index since mid-1994. While relative value remains in this market sector, we must remember that a sharp reversal in the large-cap market (defined as a 5 percent decline in the S&P 500 index in one month) would cause a significantly larger negative impact on the small-cap market.

Should consumer confidence remain high, resulting in increased spending in a growing U.S. economy, there is no reason to believe that small-cap stocks would not participate in a bullish market environment. During the first half of 2000, mid-cap stocks were the market leaders.

Figure 2-15 *The relative underperformance of small-cap stocks.*

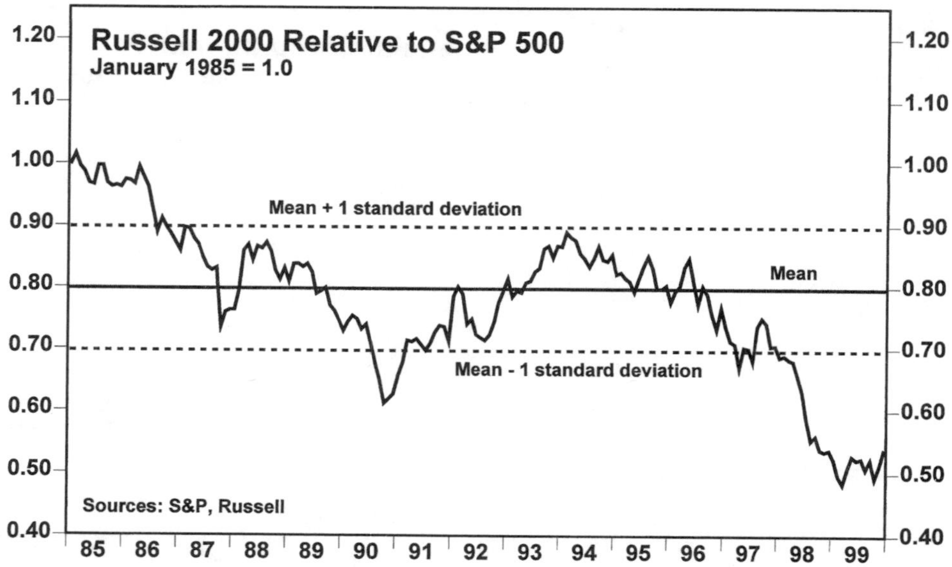

Therefore, now would be an excellent time to purchase small-cap stocks and to hold them for the foreseeable future. A portfolio balanced with a combination of large, medium, and small-cap stocks will work well to accomplish the goals of diversification with reduced risk for many clients as we enter the 21st century. The weight assigned to each class will depend on client comfort level and risk tolerance.

Finally, we have seen tremendous volatility in stock prices during 2000. Major threats to future valuation of U.S. equities would include the following: 1) Fed tightening, 2) profit disappointments, 3) dollar weakness, and 4) inflated prices. The risk of continued Fed tightening is much greater now than is generally anticipated by the investing public. In recent years, corporate profits have not been growing as fast as stock prices, and a sudden realization of this effect might slow the trend of stock-price increases in the future.

Dangerous Waters for Long-Term Investors

At the 1999 conference of the Financial Planning Association, Dr. Robert Goodman, managing director and senior economic advisor for Putnam Investors, discussed the dangers for investors in the current economic environment. "Virtually all of the economic and market commentary that investors receive from the press is geared toward the concerns of traders," he said. "The risk to long-term investors is that they give in to the temptation and try to time their long-term investment decisions on the basis of this barrage of information of largely short-term significance."

As financial professionals, we must keep an eye on what matters most to our clients—the developing long-term trends in the U.S. economy and market fundamentals. What we are seeing today are economic and market trends that are solidly positive. With technological changes and the

Fed's monitoring of monetary and fiscal policy, the U.S. equity market should reach levels that are consistent with the economy's long-term potential to grow.

In commenting on monetary policy, Dr. Goodman noted, "If, as Shakespeare wrote, all the world's a stage and all of us are merely players, it almost seems as if the members of the Federal Reserve Board are the featured actors. A few weeks before each meeting, we will see the Fed's governors speaking in various venues. One governor will seem to be hawkish on inflation and ready to raise interest rates in a preemptory attack. Another will urge patience. The chairman himself, the star of the show, will make cryptic statements that are pored over by analysts in an attempt to discern their meaning."

Now, it has become a habit that every time the Federal Reserve board decides to raise the federal funds rate, traders hope that they can make short-term profits on either bullish or bearish positions. The good news for investors, however, is that it does not matter what the Fed decides in its policy meetings. Rather, what matters most is that the Fed continues to pursue a policy that enables our economy to continue to expand at a potential growth rate that is non-inflationary.

Concerning fiscal policy, Dr. Goodman commented, "The spending and tax policies of Congress and the Administration once again will emerge as the focus of attention. This debate will be worth watching because the government's fiscal policy does indeed matter in terms of the economy's course. If monetary policy as directed by the Federal Reserve Board is the fuel that propels the country's economic machine efficiently, than fiscal policy is the steering mechanism that keeps it moving in the right direction."

What Dr. Goodman said was that politics come into play in what ultimately happens to the economy. During the 1990s, we had a competitive environment that improved the standard of living for most Americans. Capitalism rewards individuals not according to their needs, but rather according to their contribution to the system. As investors, we must keep in mind that social inequities can bring about government policy changes that could reverse the positive economic and market trends that have created so much wealth.

Regarding market volatility, Dr. Goodman is a firm believer that investors who have long-time horizons should take advantage of significant market volatility in order to position assets for the stock market's continued uptrend. We know that there has been a disparity between growth and value stocks, with the former being in favor with investors while the latter have virtually been ignored. As financial professionals advising clients, we must be aware of fundamental values staring us in the face. There will continue to be some excellent opportunities to invest as the markets pull back to more reasonable levels, most recently during the year 2000.

Our clients need to build solid equity portfolios as a basis for achieving their long-term goals. We can only be optimistic about the prospects for continued economic growth during the 21st century, and our recommendations should reflect this attitude until we have firm data to believe otherwise. In short, serious money should be invested in order to achieve both short and long-term goals in an economy that offers prosperity and growth with controlled inflation.

Summary

Is market risk being underestimated at this point? With all of these variables interacting at the same time, there is no easy way to answer this question. One thing is for certain, however: If investors anticipate a continuation of the wide market swings as witnessed during the year 2000, they will be more cautious when committing new funds in the future.

During uncertain times, investors will be eager to get your opinion on how to structure their portfolios. Your knowledge in the area of economics can be communicated to them instantly by making solid recommendations. This will make you stand out from your competition. As we will see in future chapters, a variety of equity investments should be used to lower risk and to help produce acceptable returns.

While it is easy to forget past volatility in an overly optimistic market environment, investors should also be aware of the factors that will influence economic activity in the future. Remember that a reduction in corporate profits can subsequently result in a bear-equity market environment. By understanding the economic variables discussed in this chapter, you now have a better background for what affects markets and prices, as discussed in Chapter 3, "Beginnings: What Affects Markets and Prices."

Chapter 3

Beginnings: What Affects Markets and Prices

Introduction

Now that you have an understanding of the market's historical background and why the Federal Reserve implements monetary policy, let's discuss why markets act the way they do, and what other influences affect their behavior. Ultimately people, whether professional or novice investors, make the decisions to buy or sell securities, which in turn, cause the markets to rise and fall each trading day. The information they disseminate in making their final decisions come from a variety of sources. This chapter will discuss the benefits of owning various types of stocks and how fundamental analysis influences the decision-making process. You will learn about stock market trends and which companies are revolutionizing their industries for the new millennium. Finally, we will discuss what you should do to build a successful practice as you begin a career as a financial service professional.

As we know, stock ownership is becoming more popular in American today, and is something citizens in a free and democratic society take pride in doing. History tells us that by owning a piece of corporate America, we can increase our net worth and improve our standard of living. That's why more and more people own stock in their corporate retirement plans, IRAs, and personal accounts. In particular, the performance of the markets over the last twenty years has shown the investing public that to not own stock was one of the greatest mistakes an American citizen could have made.

An American doesn't have to invest $100,000 or for that matter $10,000 to participate in the growth of a U.S. business. All he or she needs is an understanding of what asset type is being purchased, the risks involved, and how stock ownership can be personally beneficial. Beginners can start out by purchasing a small number of higher priced shares of a large corporation or more shares of an inexpensive smaller company. With a commitment as little as $500, for example, individual stocks or mutual fund shares are readily available.

Classifications of Stock

Stocks are generally divided into two main classes—common and preferred. **Common stock** actually represents the most popular form of ownership in corporate America. It gives the owner a private interest in the assets and a share in the earnings of the business. It is the most widely held type of stock, and owners participate directly in the fortunes or misfortunes of the company. Should earnings decline, an owner can expect the value of his or her shares to also go down. Conversely, should Wall Street expect higher profits in the future, the value of common stock can jump to astronomical levels.

The underlying company that issues common stock may pay a *dividend* to stockholders, which actually represents a share in the profits. People who like to receive income, or want to feel they are receiving something back for their investment enjoy owning stocks which pay dividends. The actual payments can vary each year, and are based on how much the corporate board of directors decides to pay out. Some larger companies are known for their consistent dividend payments, and are sought after by more conservative investors.

Ownership of common stock also conveys the *right to vote* on matters of interest, which includes electing members to the corporate board of directors. This is done each year at the annual meeting, where shareholders are invited to attend and can vote on other matters that affect the overall operations of the company. Those who cannot attend are sent a proxy card in the mail along with a detailed explanation of major issues to be voted upon. By signing and voting on each issue, owners can send their proxies back to be included in the final votes tabulated for the annual meeting.

When we study various indexes and hear about daily market activity, we are, in effect, being told about the movement of common stock. People want to learn more about why common stock is so popular to own, and how it can be beneficial to them. This is where you as a financial professional come into play. As you gain more knowledge about this exciting profession, you will be called upon to share your expertise and develop a client base to serve in the future.

Preferred stock also represents ownership in corporate America. Investors who like to receive a higher dividend payment and take precedence in being paid before common stockholders enjoy owning preferred stock. The term "preferred" means that owners have a claim on company profits and have a right to receive a specified dividend before common stockholders receive their payments. Likewise, should the company be sold, preferred stockholders will be paid out of the liquidating proceeds before common stockholders.

Because preferred stock is not as actively traded as common stock, owners generally cannot count on large price gains in rising markets. Likewise, they will also have less volatility in falling markets. Since dividends are fixed, their prices tend to act like bonds and will rise and fall more with changes in interest rates. Thus, preferred stock is usually owned by individuals or institutions that are seeking steady income with lower price volatility. They are not as concerned with large capital appreciation of their assets.

However, there is a special class of shares called **convertible preferred stock**. These shares may be converted into the common stock of the issuing corporation. The value of this security type is directly related to the price of the common stock into which it may be converted. There has to be a fixed ratio or number of shares of common stock that can be exchanged for the convertible preferred stock. Because dividend payments are usually higher on these securities, investors will receive more money and have less volatility than with direct ownership in the underlying common stock.

Another major difference that distinguishes these two classes of stock is *liquidity.* Common stock is considered to be highly liquid because there are more shares outstanding in actively traded markets where investors are constantly buying and selling them. Even though preferred stock issues are traded on the major exchanges, there is not as much demand for them by investors, so it is considered to be "thinly" traded. As you can see, these basic differences create the pros and cons of each class according to the investor's goals and risk tolerance.

Generally speaking, investors who seek higher appreciation potential like to own more actively traded common stock. Their goals may be college education for children, accumulating money for a down payment on a home, or planning for future retirement. On the other hand, investors who seek more income with modest appreciation potential may like to own preferred stock. Their goals may include generating more income during retirement, or owning them to complement a more conservative portfolio of corporate or government bonds. No matter the reason, each type represents actual ownership of a company, and history shows that more benefits come to owners in a free enterprise system.

Types of Common and Preferred Stock

Shares of common and preferred stock are authorized for sale to the public and subsequently issued when sold. The maximum number of shares allowed to be issued are authorized under a corporate charter. To authorize additional shares for sale requires a formal charter amendment. Likewise, the shares considered to be outstanding are the number of authorized shares that have been issued that are not yet in the hands of owners. The term "when-issued" refers to a security that is authorized but not yet issued.

Treasury stock is issued stock that has been repurchased by the company from stockholders. These shares may be held by the company for an indefinite period of time, reissued to the public at a later date, or retired permanently. Unlike issued stock, treasury stock receives no dividends and is not eligible for voting purposes.

Keep in mind that dividends on common and preferred stock can be omitted at anytime. For this reason, those investors who rely on income from equities may seek "cumulative preferred stock." The benefit of owning this type of stock comes into play if dividends are omitted by the board of directors for a certain period of time. In effect, the dividends are allowed to accumulate and eventually must be paid when funds become available. On the contrary, dividends that are omitted on common stock never have to be made up to those shareholders in the future.

"Participating preferred stock" enables the owner to share in any extra dividend payments if declared by the company. However, most issued preferred stock is "non-participating," which limits the annual return to a fixed dividend payment. For this reason, most growth oriented investors like the opportunity to receive higher dividends as reflected from increased profits and declared by the board of directors on common stock.

Many well-established companies have a history of dividend increases paid on their common stock. This is considered a benefit by many investors as a hedge against the rising cost of living. When comparing this benefit to the fixed interest rates on bonds and CDs, it is understandable why more and more investors like to purchase and hold dividend-paying stocks. They also have the added potential of price appreciation, which is not available with most bonds or CDs.

Perhaps the most popular reason why today's baby boomers and young investors like to own stock is the opportunity to make money as their shares appreciate in value. Stocks can be classified as representing either "growth" or "value." It is critical to identify the type of investors you will be working with as we enter the new millennium. They will be looking to make money in stocks, but want to own companies that are growing quickly in their industries or represent unrealized value or a combination of both.

A **growth stock** represents shares of a company whose earnings and profits are expected to grow at an above average rate in the future. For this reason, very little emphasis is given to current income. They often represent shares of very well known companies as well as those of smaller firms that may offer superior growth potential. Growth investors like to own companies that have been around for a long time, and have a history of rising profits during both good and bad times.

Growth stocks have particularly been in favor from 1995 through 1999. Figure 3-1 shows the history of the Standard & Poor's 500 Stock Index going back to 1983. This index is composed of 500 leading growth companies in the United States, and indicates excellent performance for shareholders. The average return from 1995 through 1999 was over 20% per year, indicating investor preference for growth stocks during that time.

A **value stock** is one that represents a company whose price potential has not yet been recognized by the investing public for one reason or another. Value investors like to purchase the stock of companies that have been out of favor with the market due to weak profits, changing management, or product inacceptance. The higher risk taken by value investors

Figure 3-1 *History of major U.S. growth stock.*

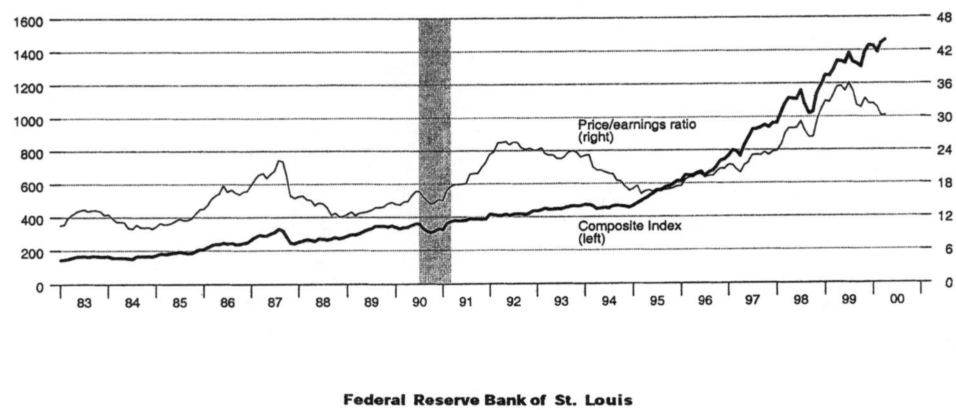

may be well rewarded if the company experiences a turnaround and suddenly becomes favorable with other market investors in the future.

These types of stocks have not performed as well during the late '90s as had growth stocks. People that owned value stocks were generally disappointed with their returns. There have been other times, however, when value stocks did outperform growth stocks. Prudent investing would stress that diversification between these classes would generally produce excellent results over longer time periods.

Table 3-1 illustrates the measure of performance from 1980–1999 between the growth and value styles of investing in large cap U.S. stocks, as represented by the S&P/Barra 500 Growth and S&P/Barra 500 Value indices.

A study of these numbers show that large cap growth stocks outperformed large cap value stocks in 13 out of the last 20 years. This would lead us to believe that American investors and institutions prefer to own large cap growth stocks as the basis for building their portfolios. During the first part of the 21st century, we may very well see a reversal in leadership as more value companies are recognized for their profitability and emerging leadership in the new economy. A financial professional should keep up with these trends and be in a position to shift client funds from

Table 3-1 *Recent history of growth versus value stocks.*

Year	S&P/Barra 500 Growth	S&P/Barra 500 Value
1999	+ 28.25%	+ 12.72%
1998	+ 42.16%	+ 14.69%
1997	+ 36.52%	+ 22.00%
1996	+ 23.97%	+ 22.00%
1995	+ 38.13%	+ 36.99%
1994	+ 3.14%	− 0.64%
1993	+ 1.68%	+ 18.61%
1992	+ 5.06%	+ 10.52%
1991	+ 38.37%	+ 22.56%
1990	+ 0.20%	− 6.85%
1989	+ 36.40%	+ 26.13%
1988	+ 11.95%	+ 21.67%
1987	+ 6.50%	+ 3.68%
1986	+ 14.50%	+ 21.67%
1985	+ 33.31%	+ 29.68%
1984	+ 2.33%	+ 10.52%
1983	+ 16.24%	+ 28.89%
1982	+ 22.03%	+ 21.04%
1981	− 9.81%	+ 0.02%
1980	+ 39.40%	+ 23.59%

one class to another. By giving high quality service in this area, you can make more money for clients and subsequently gain more referrals.

Tax Ramifications of Ownership

Short-term investors are those who sell stock and take profits in less than one year. The government wants a higher percentage of their profits, and taxes the entire gain as ordinary income in their highest tax bracket. These are known as **short-term capital gains**. For this reason, it does not make sense to buy stocks for the short-term unless the investor feels that huge profits will more than make up for the higher taxes.

On the contrary, under current tax law, stockholders are well rewarded if they can hold their stock investment for one year or longer. Any gains realized after this time are taxed at a maximum rate of 20%, rewarding the investor for taking a longer period of risk to make a profit. People in the 15% tax bracket pay a maximum tax of only 10%. These are classified as **long-term capital gains**.

Under the Taxpayer Relief Act of 1997, investors will benefit from even lower rates if stocks are held for more than five years. For example, assets purchased after December 31, 2000, and owned more than five years will be taxed at a maximum rate of 18%. People in the 15% tax bracket will pay a maximum rate of 8% starting January 1, 2001, on the sale of an asset held longer than five years, regardless of when it was acquired.

However, the ramifications of profit taking can cause havoc in the markets. For example, Figure 3-2 illustrates one of the biggest two day declines in the Dow Jones Industrial Average. As reported by the Wall Street Journal on January 5, 2000, the Dow dropped 4.34% while the NASDAQ Composite Index dropped 5.55%. Much of this decline was due to profit taking from sharp gains made by investors during late 1999. In effect, they waited to sell and lock in profits that wouldn't be taxed until the year 2000.

For those investors who buy stocks that depreciate in value, they can sell shares and take either a **short or long-term capital loss** depending on the time period previously stated. Currently, we are allowed to offset short and long-term gains and losses against each other for tax purposes. Any excess losses over and above this amount can be taken up to $3,000 per year against ordinary income. The balance of losses can than be carried over to offset profits in succeeding years.

While no one enjoys selling stock at a loss, it can sometimes be beneficial if the investor is trying to lower his or her income tax bracket. If a company falls upon hard times and the outlook for future profitability looks grim, it may make more sense to go ahead and sell to realize the tax loss for the current year. Also, taking a loss and repositioning the funds into a better investment will oftentimes be more advantageous for the future.

Figure 3-2 *Selling afte a new year begins.*

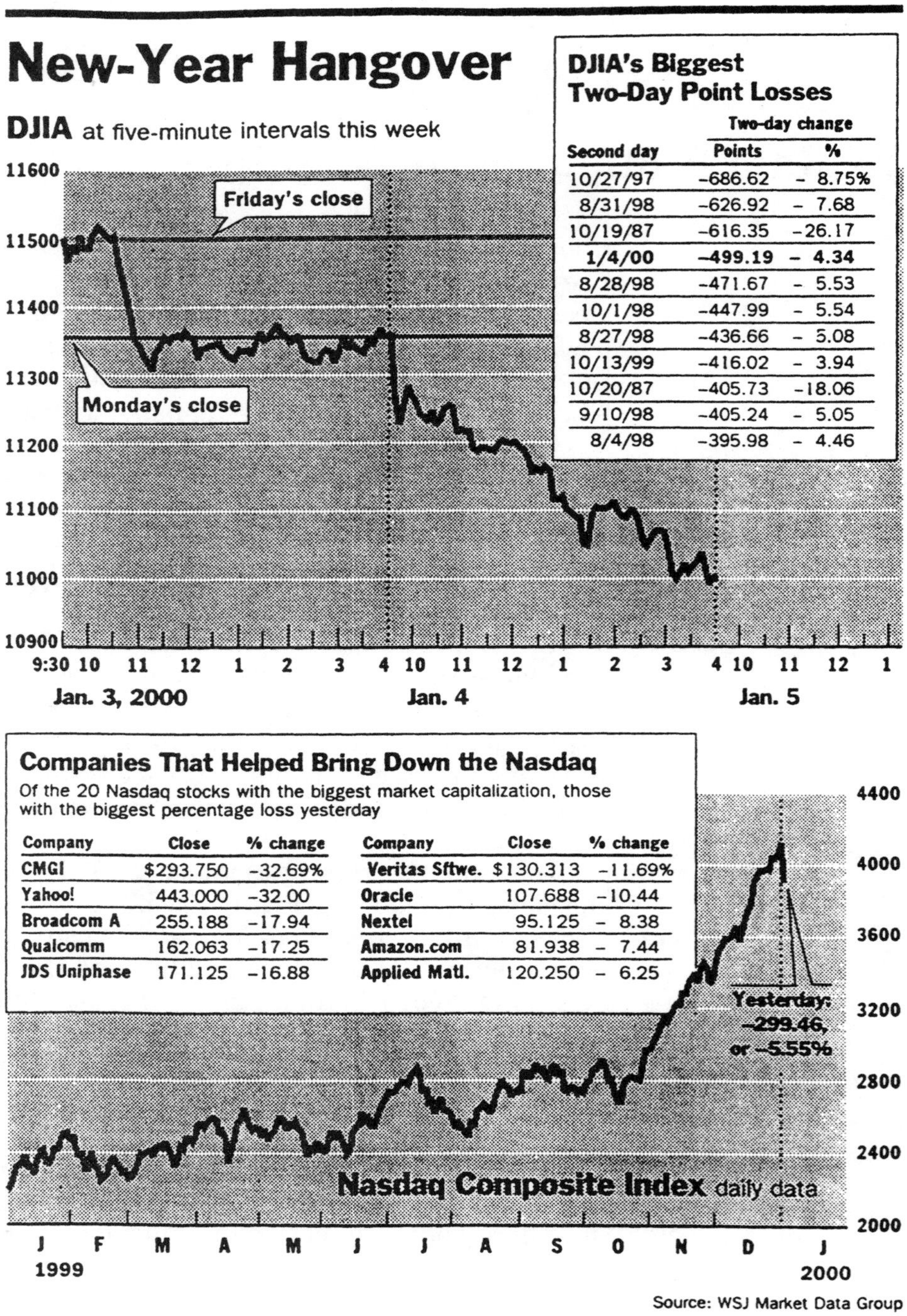

DJIA's Biggest Two-Day Point Losses

Second day	Two-day change Points	%
10/27/97	-686.62	- 8.75%
8/31/98	-626.92	- 7.68
10/19/87	-616.35	-26.17
1/4/00	**-499.19**	**- 4.34**
8/28/98	-471.67	- 5.53
10/1/98	-447.99	- 5.54
8/27/98	-436.66	- 5.08
10/13/99	-416.02	- 3.94
10/20/87	-405.73	-18.06
9/10/98	-405.24	- 5.05
8/4/98	-395.98	- 4.46

Companies That Helped Bring Down the Nasdaq

Of the 20 Nasdaq stocks with the biggest market capitalization, those with the biggest percentage loss yesterday

Company	Close	% change	Company	Close	% change
CMGI	$293.750	-32.69%	Veritas Sftwe.	$130.313	-11.69%
Yahoo!	443.000	-32.00	Oracle	107.688	-10.44
Broadcom A	255.188	-17.94	Nextel	95.125	- 8.38
Qualcomm	162.063	-17.25	Amazon.com	81.938	- 7.44
JDS Uniphase	171.125	-16.88	Applied Matl.	120.250	- 6.25

Financial Statements and Ratio Analysis

Before purchasing any stock, the potential investor must analyze the underlying company to make sure invested capital has a chance of appreciating in value. **Fundamental analysis** examines a number of mathematical equations to determine the true value of an underlying security. This exercise involves closely examining a company's income statement and balance sheet. Before recommending a stock to any investor, a financial professional should understand its intrinsic value and the potential for future appreciation.

The **Income Statement** shows a company's business activity for a given year, and whether it made money for its shareholders. For example, Figure 3-3 illustrates the 1999 Consolidated Income Statement for Anheuser-Busch Companies as stated in their 1999 Annual Report. This includes the sales, expenses, net income and earnings that were made for the past twelve months as compared to the two previous years. Potential investors will want to examine the Income Statement for a number of years to make sure there is a growing trend of profitability, and the likeliness of it lasting into the future.

More specifically, sales will show the demand for the company's products during this period. The cost of products and services will show how money was spent to manufacture these products, including materials, wages, energy and other production costs. If sales exceeded the cost of production, there will be a "gross profit."

A non-cash item that does not directly affect profits is called "depreciation." Companies may take as an expense a reasonable allowance for the exhaustion, wear and tear of property used in their businesses. Over time,

Figure 3-3 *Anheiser-Busch Companies Income statements.*

Consolidated Statement of Income
Anheuser-Busch Companies and Subsidiaries

YEAR ENDED DECEMBER 31 *(in millions)*	1999	1998	1997
Sales	$13,723.3	$ 13,207.9	$12,832.4
Excise taxes	(2,019.6)	(1,962.1)	(1,766.2)
Net sales	11,703.7	11,245.8	11,066.2
Cost of products and services	(7,254.4)	(7,162.5)	(7,096.9)
Gross profit	4,449.3	4,083.3	3,969.3
Marketing, distribution and administrative expenses	(2,147.0)	(1,958.0)	(1,916.3)
Operating income	2,302.3	2,125.3	2,053.0
Interest expense	(307.8)	(291.5)	(261.2)
Interest capitalized	18.2	26.0	42.1
Interest income	4.3	5.8	7.9
Other expense, net	(9.4)	(13.0)	(9.3)
Income before income taxes	2,007.6	1,852.6	1,832.5
Provision for income taxes	(762.9)	(704.3)	(703.6)
Equity income, net of tax	157.5	85.0	50.3
Income before cumulative effect of accounting change	1,402.2	1,233.3	1,179.2
Cumulative effect of accounting change, net of tax benefit of $6.2	—	—	(10.0)
Net income	$ 1,402.2	$ 1,233.3	$ 1,169.2
Basic earnings per share:			
Income before cumulative effect of accounting change	$ 2.99	$ 2.56	$ 2.39
Cumulative effect of accounting change	—	—	(.02)
Net income	$ 2.99	$ 2.56	$ 2.37
Diluted earnings per share:			
Income before cumulative effect of accounting change	$ 2.94	$ 2.53	$ 2.36
Cumulative effect of accounting change	—	—	(.02)
Net income	$ 2.94	$ 2.53	$ 2.34

these assets wear out and therefore represent a major cost in operating the business. A company's operating profit is calculated by deducting the cost of sales, marketing, distribution and administrative expenses, and depreciation from its total sales.

Finally, after all costs and expenses are deducted from total revenues, we can see the difference as represented in "Income Before Taxes." This will either rise or fall depending on the fortunes or misfortunes of the company within its own industry. The ensuing profit a company earns after deducting federal taxes is called "Net Income."

Earnings per share is derived by dividing net income by the current number of common shares outstanding at the end of the current year. For Anheuser-Busch, an accounting change in 1999 reduced it from $2.99 to $2.94. This is the figure that has most interest to potential investors. As earnings rise on a year-by-year comparison, it shows that shareholders are getting more value for their invested dollars.

There are several important ratios that can be derived from an analysis of the Income Statement. The **Net Profit Margin** is computed by dividing net earnings by total revenues, and measures the profitability after all expenses and taxes have been paid. For Anheuser-Busch, this calculation is $1402.2/$13,723.3 or 10.22%. Generally speaking, the higher the number, the more profits are being made for shareholders.

The **Operating Profit Margin** is calculated by dividing operating income by total sales. The resulting number tells investors how profitable the products are to manufacture and sell. For Anheuser-Busch, this calculation is $2302.3/$13,723.3 or 16.78%. Again, a rising percentage on a year-by-year comparison is what we are looking for.

Finally, the **Tax Rate** is calculated by dividing taxes paid by profits before taxes. It shows the percent of profits paid to federal, state, local, and foreign governments. For Anheuser-Busch, this calculation is $762.9/$2007.6 or 38%. Generally, the more a company makes, the higher will be its tax rate. As taxes rise over the years, we want to make sure the higher trend in earnings per share is not affected.

In summary, we want to see a positive trend in these numbers. A company with good management will show rising sales and gross profits. Figures to the contrary may indicate a struggle to gain market share in the industry. We also want to see rising figures in operating income and equity income after tax. These figures will reflect underlying strength in the value of its common stock. Finally, rising net income will be reflected in earnings per share. The longer we can go back and establish a good trend here, especially during both good and bad economic periods, the better we can lay the foundation for a solid, high quality stock portfolio for our clients.

The **Balance Sheet** presents a snap shot of the company's financial condition at the end of a given year. This includes the assets (what the company owns), liabilities (what the company owes), and the stockholders' equity (difference between assets and liabilities). Figure 3-4 illustrates the 1999 Consolidated Balance Sheet for Anheuser-Busch Companies as stated in their 1999 Annual Report. Most importantly, this represents the financial strength of a company, and tells a potential investor whether too much debt is being incurred in an attempt to increase profitability.

Figure 3-4 *Anheiser-Busch Companies balance sheets.*

Consolidated Balance Sheet
Anheuser-Busch Companies and Subsidiaries

YEAR ENDED DECEMBER 31 *(in millions)*	1999	1998
Assets		
Current Assets:		
Cash and marketable securities	$ 152.1	$ 224.8
Accounts and notes receivable, less allowance for doubtful accounts of $6.4 in 1999 and $5.5 in 1998	629.0	610.1
Inventories:		
Raw materials and supplies	378.2	362.9
Work in process	84.7	90.7
Finished goods	160.9	169.8
Total inventories	623.8	623.4
Other current assets	195.7	182.1
Total current assets	1,600.6	1,640.4
Investments in affiliated companies	2,012.5	1,880.6
Other assets	1,062.7	1,114.3
Plant and equipment, net	7,964.6	7,849.0
Total Assets	$12,640.4	$12,484.3
Liabilities and Shareholders Equity		
Current Liabilities:		
Accounts payable	$ 932.6	$ 905.7
Short-term debt	242.3	—
Accrued salaries, wages and benefits	263.0	256.3
Accrued taxes	164.2	193.6
Other current liabilities	385.1	374.7
Total current liabilities	1,987.2	1,730.3
Postretirement benefits	506.4	515.8
Long-term debt	4,880.6	4,718.6
Deferred income taxes	1,344.7	1,303.6
Common Stock and Other Shareholders Equity:		
Common stock, $1.00 par value, authorized 1.6 billion shares	716,1	712.7
Capital in excess of par value	1,241.0	1,117.5
Retained earnings	9,181.2	8,320.7
Accumulated other comprehensive income:		
Foreign currency translation adjustment	(175.0)	(205.6)
	10,963.3	9,945.3
Treasury stock, at cost	(6,831.3)	(5,482.1)
ESOP debt guarantee	(210.5)	(247.2)
	3,921.5	4,216.0
Commitments and contingencies	—	—
Total Liabilities and Equity	$12,640.4	$12,484.3

You will notice this balance sheet is divided into two main parts. Assets and liabilities are further sub-divided into "current" and "long-term." Generally, current assets are those expected to be converted into cash within twelve months, while current liabilities are obligations that will be paid within the next twelve months. Long-term assets are those that will be held by the company for longer than twelve months, while long-term liabilities will have to be repaid sometime beyond twelve months of the statement date.

Shareholders' Equity (net worth) represents the value of stockholders' ownership in the company. For Anheuser-Busch, it is total assets minus total liabilities which is $12,640.4 − $8,718.9 = $3,921.5. An increasing amount of net worth will show strength in the company's financial position, and is a positive indicator for shareholders.

There are several ratios that should be considered when analyzing the Balance Sheet. The **Current Ratio** is calculated by dividing current assets by current liabilities, and is one important measure of financial strength. We generally look for a ratio of 2 or higher to measure how quickly assets can be converted into cash. For Anheuser-Busch, this calculation is $1600.6/$1987.2 or .8055. Newer businesses often have a lower current ratio, but over time it should improve as cash flow increases and short-term liabilities are paid off. Generally speaking, over 1.0 is an acceptable ratio—the higher it goes, the better.

The **Acid Test Ratio** shows the relationship of cash and marketable securities to current liabilities. The higher the total of cash plus marketable securities is to total current liabilities, the better the ability to pay off current debts within a shorter period of time. For Anheuser-Busch, this calculation is $781.1 ($152.1 + $629.0)/$1987.2 or 39.31%.

The **Capitalization** of a company is represented by long-term debt plus equity. The higher total stockholders' equity is to long-term debt, the less danger to stockholders. A low amount of debt is more desirable since it allows management greater flexibility during periods of slower sales in a down business cycle. For Anheuser-Busch, this calculation is $4880.6/$3921.5 or 1.24.

Book Value is calculated by dividing the amount of stockholders' equity by the result of net income by earnings per share, and determines the amount of equity behind each share. We look for a trend of increasing book value as a company grows and increases in profitability. This figure will also tend to support a rising stock price. The book value for Anheuser-Busch is $3921.5/$4192.6 (net income of $1402.2 × earning per share of $2.99) or .9353.

Another important ratio is **Return on Equity,** and is calculated by dividing net earnings from the Income Statement by stockholders' equity from the Balance Sheet. This figure is expressed as a percent, and if multiplied by book value per share will also equal earnings per share. An acceptable level of return on equity for most major U.S. industries has been 14%. For Anheuser-Busch, this calculation is $1402.2/$3921.5 or 35.76%.

Finally, it is important to compare ratios of specific companies to their own industry averages. If financial progress can be expected from a growing company, its underlying stock price will rise over time. The stockholders should expect to enjoy steady improvement in revenues, as well as healthy and expanding profit margins. This should also lead to a sharing in the profits as reflected in higher dividend payments in the future.

Industry Analysis

Not only is it important to understand how to evaluate individual companies, but to study critical factors that affect the industries they exist in. What type of competition do they face both now and into the future? Do their products and services enable them to gain an increased market share? Is the industry cyclical or is there a constant demand for its products and services during both good and bad times?

These are some important questions that must be answered before advising clients. While research can identify some tremendous opportunities for individual stock purchases, prices will also be directly affected by what happens in the underlying industry during economic expansion or contraction. Let's look at some specific examples, and why it's important to identify life cycles.

All industries go through a **life cycle** that is similar to that experienced by individuals. Industries are born as a result of technological innovations. For example, the invention of computer chips lead to the revolution of the personal computer industry. In other cases, changes in one area often create a rebirth in another. For example, old movies have been put out on video tapes that can now be rented at Blockbuster stores all across America.

In examining Figure 3-5, we see how the life cycle of an industry takes place. Initially, many companies enter an industry which causes rapid growth (t_0 to t_1). But as the number of participants increases, the markets become saturated and the rate of growth begins to level off or even decline (t_1 to t_2). This produces a phase of consolidation, where some firms fail and cease operations while others merge with stronger companies that absorb the weaker ones. Surviving firms enjoy the benefits of a larger market share and the increased capacity to survive. Finally, we see a period of maturity (t_2 to t_3) with a few large remaining participants that share in a stable market, but the overall growth rate will be modest from this point forward.

The time period necessary for a life cycle can be long or short. It depends on a number of factors, including the amount of funds needed to start operations, legal barriers to entry such as patents, competition, and the rate of technological change. The easier it is to enter a market, the quicker it becomes saturated with participants. For example, while once

Figure 3-5 *U.S. industry growth cycle. Courtesy of Harcourt, The Dryden Press.*

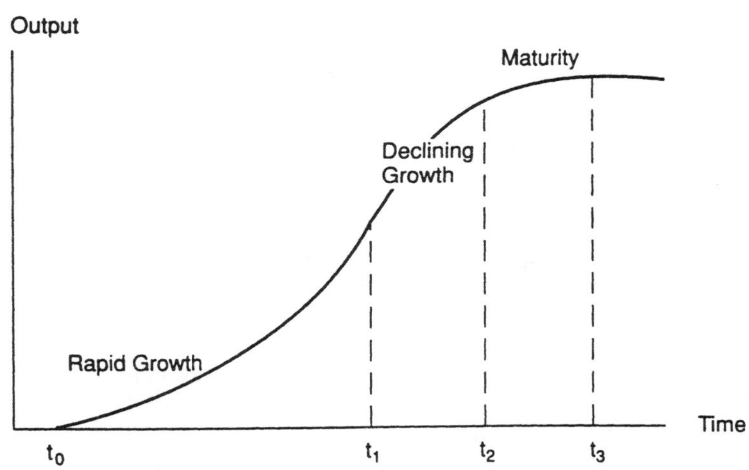

Source: Mayo, H. B. *Investments: An Introduction*, Third Edition. The Dryden Press, Hartcourt.

McDonald's and Burger King were the only name companies in the fast-food industry, today's market is saturated by many more companies giving increased competition to the leaders.

In some cases, saturated domestic markets have encouraged firms to expand abroad. For example, due to a national anti-smoking campaign, Phillip Morris and American Brands have experienced declining U.S. cigarette sales. This, in turn, has forced them to expand sales efforts into foreign countries to maintain profitability. Ironically, many other industries had already made this transition many years ago. In the soft drink industry, for example, Coca-Cola's foreign sales now generate over half its yearly revenues.

When picking individual stocks, it is critical to know what type of industry the underlying company is participating in. Where does it fall in the life cycle of its industry? Is it a smaller company about to experience rapid growth or is it a larger company that has already matured? Keep in mind that a portfolio of rapidly growing companies will have the potential for higher returns but also higher volatility levels. On the other hand, a portfolio with mature companies will have less volatility risk. Clients should always be fitted with a portfolio designed for their risk tolerance and comfort levels.

Some industries are very sensitive to changes in the level of economic activity. These are called **cyclical industries**, and include such common examples as the automotive and building industries. Since consumers can defer spending on such high-priced items from year to year, sales in these industries will fluctuate directly with the economy. On the other hand, other industries are quite resistant to recessions and are classified as **non-cyclical**. Some examples include food processing and retailing. Since people have to eat, such purchases cannot be deferred, even during a recession.

Just because a company may be classified in either of these two industries does not mean its stock should be avoided. Securities markets will smooth out the fluctuations in earnings so the firm's value is related to its performance over a certain time period. Most importantly, the flow of dividend income and the growth in earnings over many years will ultimately determine the value of the shares. In summary, we can say that an investment in a cyclical industry firm will be riskier than a firm in a more stable industry.

Other Critical Factors

In addition to studying the type of industry a company operates in, the investor must also consider such factors as government regulations, labor conditions, and the financing requirements of the industry. Some industries are more heavily regulated than others. For example, utilities such as electric and gas, along with telecommunications companies are subject to a large amount of regulation as to the prices they can charge customers. A company which operates in a state with a strict regulatory environment will likely keep more cash in reserves and pay lower dividends to its shareholders. Also, stock prices could be adversely affected should regulations become stricter, which in effect would cause a lower demand for its shares.

Labor conditions also affect the analysis of an industry. The heavy presence of unions, or the industry's need for skilled labor, can have a negative impact on earnings. History shows that union demands for higher wages (i.e. the Airline Pilots' Association or the United Mine Workers) can negatively affect company earnings through strikes and expensive long-term contracts. Recently, we have experienced an economy with low unemployment. The need for specialized labor in this type of environment will often result in more generous salaries, resulting in an effort to bid away skilled workers from other firms. A keen assessment of these factors can give considerable insight into the risk associated with investing in a particular industry.

The need for various types of financing can also have a tremendous impact on a company's earnings. Industries that are growing or use a large amount of plant space and equipment need more funds than more stable and less capital intensive industries. For example, firms in the oil drilling industry require large investments in rigs, pipe, and transportation systems. This type of equipment is usually financed by the issuance of bonds, which must be repaid to lenders as principal and interest. If the company decides to finance its expansion through equities, the increase in market shares will tend to dilute earnings. Thus, the need for funds by a company can have a direct impact on the valuation of its stock because such financing will have a positive or negative implication on the firm's earnings.

Stock Market Trends for the New Millennium

We know the history of the stock market does not always repeat itself. Stocks that experienced whopping gains during the 1990s won't necessarily repeat in the new millennium. Markets don't always go up, and sometimes the declines can be very painful. But history shows that investors with strong enough nerves to keep much of their wealth in stocks over long time spans have consistently outperformed investors using more cautious strategies. With the innovations of new technologies that promise to make our lives easier and longer, the chance to invest in tomorrow's growth industries has seldom looked more enticing.

Traditionally, people have set aside money for their children's college education, for a home down payment, and even for retirement at age 65. How you advise clients to invest money will partially be affected by the generation you live in. The older you are, the more you will be inclined to follow these traditional values. However, those in a younger generation will likely experience a dynamic transformation of goals and values.

In our fast growing economy, younger workers change jobs an average of seven times during their careers. So getting a good education to keep up with changing technology may be a goal that never stops until retirement. With more money being passed down and inherited by younger Americans, the line between owning and renting real estate may become a blur. Affluence may cause people of all ages to enter and exit the workforce at various times. For example, people may use part of an inheritance to travel around the world, or to retire early and work part-time in a small business.

Let's take a perceptive approach to project what the market could look like by the year 2025. Figure 3-6 shows how the leading market indexes closed on December 31, 1999. Even compared to 1998, this one year of change was dynamic. It marked the fifth consecutive year of unprecedented growth for the broader market averages. The overall average return between these nine indexes for 1999 was up 22.14%. Historically, the market, as measured by the S&P 500 Index, has been up an average of 11.6% since 1926. Depending on your point of view, and whether you are from an older or younger generation, projections can be made using any range of these averages.

If we consider the old norm as now becoming conservative, an investment of $100,000 with an average return of 11.6% would grow to $1,432,650 by 2025. A more aggressive return, using our computed average of 22.14%, would mean an investment of $100,000 would grow to $2,734,390 by 2025. Those who are confirmed bulls might even be tempted to use a

Figure 3-6 *Returns of leading market indexes.*

	12/31/99 CLOSE	% CHG. FROM 9/30/99	% CHG. FROM 12/31/98
DJIA	11497.12	**+11.22%**	+25.22%
DJ U.S. Market	1390.32	**+15.15**	+18.90
DJ World	193.39	**−10.24**	− 4.64
S&P 500	1469.25	**+14.54**	+19.53
NYSE Comp.	650.30	**+ 9.70**	+ 9.15
Nasdaq Comp.	4069.31	**+48.18**	+85.59
Amex	876.97	**+11.26**	+27.28
Value Line	431.03	**+ 3.20**	− 1.40
Russell 2000	504.75	**+18.13**	+19.62

Source: WSJ Market Data Group.

higher average. However, it would be wise to employ a more moderate approach and use an average somewhere in between these two. These figures were computed using interpretation and based on the Standard Table of Compound Interest.

Just as the industrial revolution reshaped our economy during the 1920s, so will the technological revolution bring about major changes during the 21st century. Each industry, whether in financial services, biotechnology, electronics, health care or technology, will have its leading companies. They will spend millions on advertising and have brand names that are so strong that they could almost be thought of as a monopoly. Examples of three current leaders include Microsoft, Coca-Cola, and Wal-Mart. When considering the purchase of individual stocks, brand leadership should be an important part of the investment decision.

As companies become larger and tend to monopolize an industry, they will be subjected to intense government regulation. For example, in May 2000, the U.S. government proposed splitting Microsoft into two pieces. The Justice Department and seventeen states involved in an antitrust case said the company used illegal methods to protect its monopoly in computer operating systems. Under the proposal, one company would possess the dominant Windows operating system while the other would control everything else Microsoft produces, including its lucrative Office Suite and Internet services.

Meanwhile, Microsoft offered to restrict its business practices for four years. It also promised to guarantee that its partners and other software developers get the same access to Windows technology as its own internal developers enjoy. However, the Justice Department dismissed the company's counterproposal as inadequate. The settlement of this case will ultimately affect the value of Microsoft stock.

Many investment strategists would also agree that investing in foreign securities is a way to diversify and take advantage of global capitalization. Figure 3-7 shows the performance of the world's stock markets during 1999. The Internet and other new technologies are making it easier for investors to analyze and buy securities across international borders. Valuations are particularly attractive outside the United States, as many companies in other countries will benefit from higher earnings growth and the recovering global economy.

As can be seen from Figure 3-7, emerging markets of smaller countries represent an astounding 85% of the world's population. They are growing in their importance to the global economy, and account for 19% of the world's GDP. As the industrialization process continues in these emerging countries, their share of world imports is expected to increase from 19% to 38% over the next two decades. As a way to reduce volatility, international diversification may offer a particularly effective way to cushion the short-term swings that affect individual stocks in the U.S. markets.

Companies Shaping the New Decade

What companies should clients focus on at the start of the new millennium? The answer may lie in those that have already revolutionized their

Figure 3-7 *World's stock markets performance.*

● How the world's stock markets, both large and small, did in 1999. Survey by Birinyi Associates, Inc. Changes were computed based on the years performance of the local stock index, or, as noted, by change in market capitalization. Figures are preliminary.

Argentina	+28.00	Macedonia*	−6.90
Armenia	+23.34	Malawi	+39.27
Australia	+12.05	Malaysia	+38.59
Austria	+6.87	Malta	+154.62
Bahrain	+1.06	Mauritius	−6.07
Bangladesh	−11.87	Mexico	+80.06
Barbados	−9.03	Moldova*	+781.00
Belgium	−4.95	Mongolia	+5.96
Bermuda	−1.07	Morocco	−4.57
Bolivia*	+14.70	Nairobi	−22.38
Botswana	+47.86	Namibia	+48.11
Brazil	+151.93	Nepal	+48.50
Bulgaria*	+434.20	Netherlands	+24.71
Canada	+36.65	New Zealand	+6.85
Chile	+43.76	Nigeria	−8.42
China (Shen)	+58.01	Norway	+42.27
China (Shan)	+32.04	Oman	+9.10
Colombia	−10.05	Pakistan	+49.05
Costa Rica	+60.68	Palestine	+52.77
Croatia	−0.93	Panama	−15.24
Cyprus	+688.13	Peru	+37.41
Czech Rep.	+24.23	Philippines	+8.85
Denmark	+16.57	Poland	+43.80
Ecuador	+45.94	Portugal	+10.15
Egypt	+42.50	Qatar	−0.44
El Salvador*	+49.34	Romania	+28.88
Estonia	+38.32	Russia	+260.68
Fiji*	+22.25	Saudi Arabia	+39.10
Finland	+161.98	Singapore	+78.04
France	+51.12	Slovakia	−18.01
Germany	+39.10	Slovenia	+4.92
Ghana	+14.21	South Africa	+69.42
Greece	+102.19	South Korea	+82.78
Hong Kong	+68.80	Spain	+18.35
Hungary	+39.82	Sri Lanka	+3.08
Iceland	+47.45	Swaziland	+5.91
India	+63.83	Sweden	+70.96
Indonesia	+70.06	Switzerland	+5.72
Iran	+29.96	Taiwan	+31.63
Ireland	+0.43	Thailand	+35.44
Israel	+62.47	Trinidad&Tobago	−4.31
Italy	+22.30	Tunisia	+74.21
Ivory Coast	−10.45	Turkey	+385.03
Jamaica	+6.31	U.A.E.	−12.72
Japan	+36.79	Ukraine	+81.22
Jordan	−5.10	U.K.	+17.81
Kenya	−22.24	U.S.	+25.22
Kuwait	−9.26	Uzbekistan	−43.80
Latvia	−10.57	Venezuela	+13.14
Lebanon	−20.88	Zambia	+21.65
Lithuania	+0.01	Zimbabwe	+125.12

* Based on market value change.
NOTE: Bulgaria, Macedonia, Moldova and Uzbekistan as of 9/30; Nepal as of 11/11; Bolivia as of 11/30; Saudi Arabia as of 12/22

Source: WSJ Market Data Group.

industries at the end of the last century. These include such giants as Microsoft, Wal-Mart, Dell Computer, IBM, and General Motors. Figure 3-8 shows these among the 20 companies certified as "mavericks" for having revolutionized or rewritten the rules in their industries. This survey was conducted for the *Wall Street Journal* by the Reputation Institute of New York as published in January 2000.

Figure 3-8 *Leading companies of the new decade.*

The Mavericks

MAVERICK RANK	COMPANY	REPUTATION RANK
1	Microsoft	7
2	Apple	18
3	Wal-Mart/Sam's Club	2
4	AOL/Netscape	14
5	Amazon	8
6	eBay	13
7	Dell	5
8	Saturn	17
9	IBM	9
10	Yahoo!	8
11	Home Depot	3
12	DaimlerChrysler/ Dodge	15
13	AT&T	12
14	Intel	1 (tie)
15	Gateway	4
16	Cisco	10
17	Lucent	6
18	Ford	16
19	Ben & Jerry's	1 (tie)
20	MCI WorldCom	19

Source: Reputation Institute

You will notice that 12 of these "mavericks" are Internet or computer related companies. With the explosion in popularity of this industry, it's not surprising to see such names as Apple, AOL/Netscape, Amazon, eBay, Yahoo, and Intel. The rest come from older and more established industries such as retailing and auto manufacturing.

It's important to keep in mind that companies we hear about today that tend to dominate the Web are not guaranteed of retaining their leadership in the future. For example, just as AT&T was forced to break up into the Baby Bells during the last century, the government's attack on Microsoft shows it would like to stimulate more competition from other firms within the industry. These companies will challenge the dominance of its Windows software, and eventually gain more market share and revenue growth. The same thing happened to IBM in the computer hardware industry during the latter part of the 20th century.

A related study by Dr. Charles Fombrun, a New York University professor, and Harris Interactive asked respondents to rate the reputations of these 20 companies. The study used criteria such as emotional appeal and the quality of a firm's products or services. When we compare the maverick rankings with the companies' reputation ratings, things become more interesting.

For example, Microsoft—the Redmond, Washington software giant—ranked Number 1 on the public's list of maverick companies. Microsoft fell to seventh in terms of reputation, however, because respondents blasted the company for making unreliable, difficult-to-use products that are only marginally better than earlier software versions. Similarly, Apple Computer ranked second among revolutionary companies but fell near the bottom for its corporate reputation. On the other hand, ice-cream maker Ben & Jerry's ranked only 19th in being thought of as an industry innovator but tied for first place in terms of its progressive reputation with consumers.

From this study, we can draw the conclusion that nothing lasts indefinitely. An investor who buys stocks in these companies will tend to be well rewarded as long as the reputation of high-quality products offered at reasonable prices persists. The old philosophy of buying stocks and putting them away forever, however, is now outdated. With the ever-increasing volatility of market prices and Internet trading, each stock in one's portfolio must be monitored more frequently. The use of fundamental analysis learned in this chapter along with underlying quality and reputation will be critical to the success of a portfolio's performance in the future.

Beginning a New Career as a Financial Professional

As you begin a new career, keep in mind that building competence is a key element in what clients look for in an investment professional. In today's competitive market environment, you need to combine services that clients desire—along with a streamlined business model. Here are five steps to follow in order to accomplish this goal:

1. **Define your ideal client**—What types of clients would you like to work with in the foreseeable future? You will find it tempting to be all things to all people because of your desire to help everyone. However, focusing on a market niche will help you better serve your chosen clients with less effort. For example, you might want to serve widows, retirees, or even affluent Baby Boomers. If you ask an experienced financial professional, most will tell you that 20 percent of their clients generate around 80 percent of their business revenue. You can quickly increase profits by designing your business to ser-

vice a particular group of people. By becoming an expert in solving their unique problems, your business will grow faster and become even more lucrative as new clients refer their friends to you. Next, determine the minimum account size with which you want to work. Although your decision is not binding in the beginning, you will eventually want to work with clients who have a larger asset base that makes it more profitable for your business to grow. While fee-based advisers need a higher amount of assets in order to be profitable, commission brokers can usually accept and work with smaller amounts.

2. **Match personalities with your comfort level**—What are the personality traits of people you enjoy the most? With which type of people are you most compatible? Knowing the psychological makeup of the people with whom you come in contact will help identify your ideal clients. Aggressive or driver personalities are inclined to seek speculative, high-performance investments. While they are not opposed to taking on more risks, they will usually blame you if something goes wrong. Because they want to make their own decisions, they will tend to shy away from your services and generally will not make good clients. Some people will like to get your investment advice but might be inclined to second-guess or devalue your opinion. These uncertain personalities are focused on beating the market but somehow think that they can do a better job than you can. Obviously, while they might do some business with you in the beginning, they are not likely to value your recommendations long enough to continue building a solid relationship. Patient investors will likely be your best customers. They tend to find money and investing overwhelming and are looking for someone who can help them preserve their asset base. Generally speaking, they have worked long and hard in order to accumulate their assets and want a professional to guide them in the complete decision-making process. They tend to be older and more conservative and are motivated more by fear than by greed. If you meet their emotional and financial needs, these people are the best clients for building an efficient and profitable business.
3. **Identify what they value**—Determine what is most important to your clients so that you can fulfill their expectations and needs. In David Bach's workshop on "Smart Women Finish Rich," this knowledge is a key ingredient to building a successful relationship. How can you match your products or services to what your clients hold in high esteem? Men are usually quite different than women in what they value. Men will look more at tangible things and avoid emotional issues. They are more goal oriented and want quicker results. Women, however, will usually be more patient and focus on a long-term approach to investing. Volatile markets will not cause them to shift course in mid-stream, as men tend to do.
4. **Give clients what they are looking for**—They want your guidance in making a complicated financial world easier to understand. They need to place the burden of responsibility on your shoulders. Keep them informed through newsletters, and invite them to workshops and seminars that you sponsor. Encourage them to bring friends and relatives to these educational meetings. Design your

business around your client base. Give them a combination of institutional money-management choices and personal financial planning. They want to rely on a higher level of competency that they cannot find in others. If you have a business that is designed to meet the needs of your ideal clients and are able to give them outstanding service, your professional practice can grow with unlimited opportunities.

5. **Build a team-centered practice**—You *must* build your practice by delegating authority to others while you focus on meeting with clients face-to-face. As your practice grows, hire individuals who can take responsibilities away from you—and focus on serving the needs of clients. Start with an administrative assistant who can take over clerical responsibilities. Then, hire a marketing person to organize special events, public relations, and referral-generating programs. Remember, you cannot do everything without hurting your real value to existing clients. Develop a business model that will mark specific objectives and yearly growth. By targeting specific markets and identifying ideal clients, you will build an organization that is highly profitable and efficient. By doing things that create emotional bonds between you and your clients, you can design a profitable and efficient business that meets not only your goals but also the needs of your clients. As our industry continues to change during the 21st century, your ability to use these strategies will help ensure your survival and property.

Chapter 4

Trading: Buying and Selling Stocks

Introduction

In order to take advantage of trends that will affect various markets in the new millennium, you must understand the process of buying and selling stocks. This includes the various types of orders that you can execute on the exchanges, how electronic trading works, how to lock in profits or limit losses, and who becomes involved in executing a successful transaction. This chapter will conclude with a discussion of how the history of buying and selling in the financial markets can teach us about where other markets might be heading in the future.

As mentioned in the previous chapter, an investor who is preparing for the new millennium will want an investment professional to be proactive. In other words, you must constantly monitor the development of a new portfolio and provide proper supervision in order to ensure that trades will be executed correctly. Whether using a traditional broker from a large wirehouse or trading online, the astute investor will only be successful if he or she is directly involved in the entire process.

Our ultimate goal is to select stocks that will create a high-quality portfolio. Depending on their goals and risk tolerance, we know that investors have different personal objectives. For example, a younger investor might be accumulating money to purchase a house or start an educational fund for a child. An older and more seasoned investor, however, might be building capital in order to prepare for eventual retirement or to pass on money to family members as an inheritance. Whatever the reason, the importance of understanding how individual stocks are traded is critical to prosperous money management.

As we enter the 21st century, more individual investors will want to take responsibility for the performance of their portfolios. They will be tempted to become their own money managers and as such take the entire matter more seriously. They might tell you that they cannot decide whether to become a stock trader or a portfolio manager. Let's look at the difference between the two and see how you can advise this type of client.

Stock traders are willing to buy and sell shares on any given day during regular market hours. They constantly monitor market activity and are ready to make a move on a minute's notice. Thus, their goal is to make money as quickly as possible, and they are willing to assume a higher degree of risk with their trading activity. Once more, the temptation to be a stock trader is more prevalent today with the ease of setting up an online trading account.

Portfolio managers buy and sell stocks with the intention of holding their securities for longer periods of time (usually quarterly, semi-annually, or yearly). Their goals are to make profits by using a strong, fundamental analysis approach as described in Chapter Three. Once they make a decision to purchase a stock, they monitor the basics of the underlying company to decide when to sell their position at a later date. They might also buy and hold securities for more than a year in order to reap the rewards of lower taxes resulting from long-term capital gains.

Whether clients want to trade stocks by searching for quick profits or want to build a portfolio over a longer term, you must go through the trading mechanics. As stated earlier, the trading of common stock occurs in a number of major market systems, including national stock exchanges, regional stock exchanges, and on the *over-the-counter* (OTC) market. In addition, independently owned and operated electronic trading systems are available for trading common stock. Let's examine the mechanics for trading stocks in our free economic society.

Brokers and Dealers

The ultimate success of market trading relies on brokers and dealers. A *broker,* usually referred to as a *registered representative* or *account executive*, is a person who is licensed in securities (possesses a Series 7 license) and is authorized to act as an agent for an investor who wishes to execute an order. This person is responsible for acting on behalf of a client based on the highest ethical standards. In other words, the broker cannot take a position in a stock that would result in a conflict of interest or improper recommendation. The broker should also guard against churning or trading stock in a client's account unnecessarily in order to generate excess commissions. When an investor uses a broker to execute trades, he or she expects the highest standards of professionalism along with a high degree of trust that bonds the relationship.

On the contrary, a *dealer* is an entity or company that is willing to buy or sell a stock for its own account. Many large brokerage firms have representatives located on the floor of the stock exchange who are known as "specialists." They stand ready to buy stock for their inventory or to sell stock that reduces their inventory. At any given time, dealers declare their willingness to buy a stock at a specific price (bid price) that is less than the price for which they are willing to sell the same stock (its asked or offer price).

This process is critically important, because an imbalance of orders can hit the market at any given time. For example, negative news about a company might cause traders to place a large number of sell orders. This temporary disparity would tend to push the stock price much lower without a balance of buyers willing to purchase the stock on the other side.

Dealers help to stabilize the markets by acting as a buffer between the buy and sell side of market traders. They work with one another on the exchange floor in order to provide liquidity and price stability. Dealers who have a supply of stock in their inventory are willing to sell it to those dealers who want to purchase the stock for their traders. We can view the bid-ask spread as the price charged by dealers for supplying liquidity and stability resulting from short-term order imbalances.

When a stock is more tradable, the balance between its bid and ask price will be better. Not only are investors concerned with this liquidity feature, but they also want to trade at reasonable prices because market conditions can change quickly. Some dealers have a privileged position to know the pricing of a particular stock when they keep the books on special orders. This privilege enables them to be in a much better position to influence the price information that they signal to market participants with their bids and offers.

Traders must realize that a bid-ask spread is also affected by the dealer's direct cost of doing business. Some examples are the costs of equipment, administrative and operations staff, and order processing costs. With the ever-increasing technological advances in machinery, dealers must keep up to date by purchasing or leasing newer types of equipment. They also want to hire only the most competent people to run their organizations. Finally, dealers must pay their brokers competitive commissions and offer qualified retirement plans in order to retain their services and to generate future revenues.

Dealers must also be compensated for bearing two major risks. This compensation might involve carrying a stock inventory (a long position) or selling a stock that is not in inventory (a short position). First, there is always uncertainty concerning the future price of a stock. A dealer who has a long position is concerned that the price will fall in the future, creating an excess inventory of unsold stock. On the other hand, a dealer who has a short position is concerned that a sudden price rise would cause a buyback at a much higher price.

The second type of risk is associated with the amount of time that it will take to unwind a position and the uncertainty in doing so. This situation primarily depends on the frequency of transactions that take place for a particular security. The greater the number of buy and sell orders for a stock, the less time that a dealer has to maintain a position. A stock that is infrequently traded, however, poses a much greater risk, because its price could decline during a longer holding period.

Floor Brokers and Specialists

Several types of members work on the trading floor of the major exchanges, and each plays a distinct role in the auction process.

A *floor broker* acts as an agent, representing customer orders to buy or sell stock. There are two main types of floor brokers: commissioned and independent. Brokerage houses that are members of the *New York Stock Exchange* (NYSE) employ commission brokers. A commission broker executes the orders of the firm's customers. Independent brokers work for themselves. Although not affiliated with any brokerage house, they handle orders for brokerage houses that do not have full-time brokers, whose brokers are off the floor, or whose brokers are too busy to handle a specific order. Their fee is fully negotiable depending on the size and difficulty of the order that they are trading.

A *specialist* performs five essential functions:

- **Manages the auction process**—To maintain a fair and orderly market in a particular security, the specialist establishes the opening price for that security every day. Then, during the day, he or she continually quotes the current bid and offer prices to brokers.
- **Executes orders for floor brokers**—The specialist can execute an order immediately or hold the order and execute it when the stock

reaches the specific price requested by the customer. As a dealer, the specialist will buy or sell stock from his or her own inventory in order to keep the market liquid or to prevent rapid price changes.

- **Serves as a catalyst**—Specialists are the point of contact between brokers who have buy and sell orders. The specialist acts as a catalyst, bringing buyers and sellers together and enabling a transaction to take place that otherwise would not have occurred.
- **Provides capital**—If buy orders temporarily outpace sell orders (or conversely, if sell orders outpace buy orders), the specialist is required to use his firm's own capital to minimize the imbalance. He or she performs this task by buying or selling against the trend of the market until a price is reached at which public supply and demand are once again in balance.
- **Stabilizes prices**—To ensure that stock trading moves smoothly with minimal price fluctuations, the specialist will step in against the market trend. Specialists buy and sell stock in order to cushion temporary imbalances and to avoid unreasonable price variations.

Suppose your client works in the health-care industry and wants to purchase shares in the drug company Pfizer (PFE). He or she gives you an order to buy 200 shares at a specified price. You in turn relay the order to a floor broker who is physically located on the floor of the NYSE where Pfizer trades. If the floor broker cannot immediately fill your order to purchase 200 shares at the price that your client wants, the order goes to the Pfizer specialist. This person keeps a record of all unfilled orders on Pfizer. As the market price of Pfizer moves up and down during the trading day, the specialist looks for opportunities to fill each order.

Account Registrations. Before you can place an order for a client, you must know how to open and register the account. There are many different situations of which you should be aware, and proper registration in the beginning can save you headaches later. You *must* know how each account should be set up and what type of ownership is best for each client. The most common types of account registrations are as follows:

- **Individual account**—For single people who want sole ownership and control of assets.
- **Joint ownership**—Includes joint tenancy ($^{50}/_{50}$ ownership), joint tenants with right of survivorship (should one tenant die, the surviving tenant receives full ownership of all assets in the account), tenants in common (if one tenant dies, the account is divided according to the percentage on the joint agreement), tenants by entirety (each tenant has full interest in the securities, and upon the death of one tenant, the entire asset is transferred to the survivor), and community property (for husband and wife only; upon the death of either spouse, the survivor takes half and the remaining half is probated and taxable).
- **Custodian accounts**—Set up under the *Uniform Gift to Minors Act* (UGMA) in each state, according to specific laws. UGMA enables the

legal transfer of property to a minor without the expense of creating a trust and the cost of a bond. Property that can be given is generally limited to cash, securities, mutual funds, and life/annuity contracts. Investment earnings in the account (dividends and interest) are the property of the minor (using his or her Social Security number) and must be reinvested by the custodian according to the Prudent Man Rule (in the minor's best interest).

- **Guardian-conservatorship accounts**—This account is established for a minor who does not have a parental guardian. A court will appoint a guardian or conservatorship until the minor reaches the age of maturity. In addition, there can only be one child whose Social Security number is used per account.
- **Estate accounts**—Where a decedent leaves his or her properties to specifically named heirs upon his or her death. If no will exists, the court will appoint an executor or administrator to oversee the assets.
- **Corporate account**—For an entity that operates under a legal name. The federal tax ID number must be used at all times, and all corporations are exempt from federal withholding.
- **Investment club accounts**—All names of the club members must be written on the investment club agreement, and it must have a tax ID number.
- **Trust accounts**—A legal entity with assets managed by a trustee for the benefit of the beneficiaries. A trust is made up of three persons: the settlor or trustor (owner), the trustee (manager), and the beneficiary (ultimate recipient). A trust tax ID number must be assigned to this type of account. The most common types of trusts are living (made during the lifetime of the trustor), testamentary (directed by the last will and testament of the trustor), revocable (can be revoked by the trustor at any time), irrevocable (cannot be changed or revoked by the trustor), pension (made up by the employer for the employee's retirement benefits), corporate (an employer who offers his or her employees profit-sharing benefits), and private (set up when there are several trustees, enabling the trustees to act as a unit).
- **Power of attorney**—A legal instrument authorizing someone to act as the attorney or agent of the grantor. These accounts are used when the person who has the stock registered to them is incompetent and needs a coherent individual to serve as power of attorney over their possessions.
- **Transfer on death (individual or joint)**—Permits a security owner to designate a beneficiary upon registration of securities and to pass the assets directly to the beneficiary(ies) without probate.

Types of Orders. Now, let's examine the types of orders that you can place in order to buy and sell on the floor of an exchange, such as the NYSE. You should know which type of order to place in relation to the client's desire to buy and sell securities. There are orders for every type of investor, from those who want quick executions to those who want to wait for a specific price.

Keep in mind that stock prices are now quoted in decimals, where each cent counts. Prior to this, price quotes were in sixteenths of a point.

In other words, prices for stocks were in 6.25-cent increments. For example, if PFE is quoted at 34 $^{1}/_{16}$ on the NYSE, this value converted into real dollars equals $34.0625 per share. A stock price of 48 $^{13}/_{16}$ is converted to $48 plus 13 times $0.0625, or $48.8125.

Generally, most investors place orders in round lots versus odd lots. Each *round lot* represents 100 shares of stock. Whether the order is for 500 shares of *General Motors* (GM) stock on the NYSE or 800 shares of Microsoft (MSFT) on the OTC market, the order is considered a round-lot order. If an investor does not have enough money to buy in round lots, then he or she can trade in odd lots.

An *odd-lot* order is a trade of fewer than 100 shares and can actually be in any amount. Higher-price stocks, such as those of Internet companies, will often create many odd-lot orders. Investors usually pay a one-sixteenth-point markup per odd-lot trade. This added fee is charged for the extra handling incurred in smaller trades. For example, if the price of a stock is $150 per share, an odd-lot trade of 50 shares would cost $150.0625 per share.

Market Orders. This is the simplest because it is executed at the best price available at the time the order is placed. A *market order* simply means buying or selling at the current market price. The investor is willing to accept the trade price when it occurs. Market orders have priority on the trading floor, because they can be executed quickly as buy and sell orders reach the market at the same time. In effect, the order that has the best price receives the highest priority. For example, when a buyer is willing to pay a higher price for a stock, his or her order is filled more quickly. Conversely, when a seller is willing to take less for his or her stock, the order is filled more quickly.

Figure 4-1 shows two sample trading tickets from Pershing, a division of *Donaldson, Lufkin, & Jenrette Securities Corporation* (DLJSC). These tickets are marked as stock buy and sell orders. The client's name and account number are placed on each ticket along with the agreed-upon commission. To avoid three-day settlement problems, buy orders must usually have funds (cash) already in the account, and sell orders must have the securities long (already fully paid for) in the account. There is currently a move to shorten settlements to one day, which would save millions of dollars each year.

Specialists will always execute a market order first, so the turnaround time is much shorter. More importantly, stocks that are actively traded will have a closer spread between the bid and asked price. The price that an investor receives when buying or selling this type of stock will be close to the last quotation that he or she received. For example, Ford Motor Company had much bad publicity during 2000 as a result of installing defective Firestone tires on many of its SUVs. As a result of accidents which resulted in a number of deaths, its stock became very volatile (see Figure 4-2). If Ford Motor Company (F) stock is trading between 24.50 to 25.00, a broker could execute a market order for 24.75.

Because of the massive influx of orders received on the floor of an organized exchange, there must be a priority as to the handling of orders that arrive at the same time. Generally, we might think of the first order in as the first one that should be executed. But higher priority can be

Figure 4-1 *Two sample trading tickets from Pershing.*

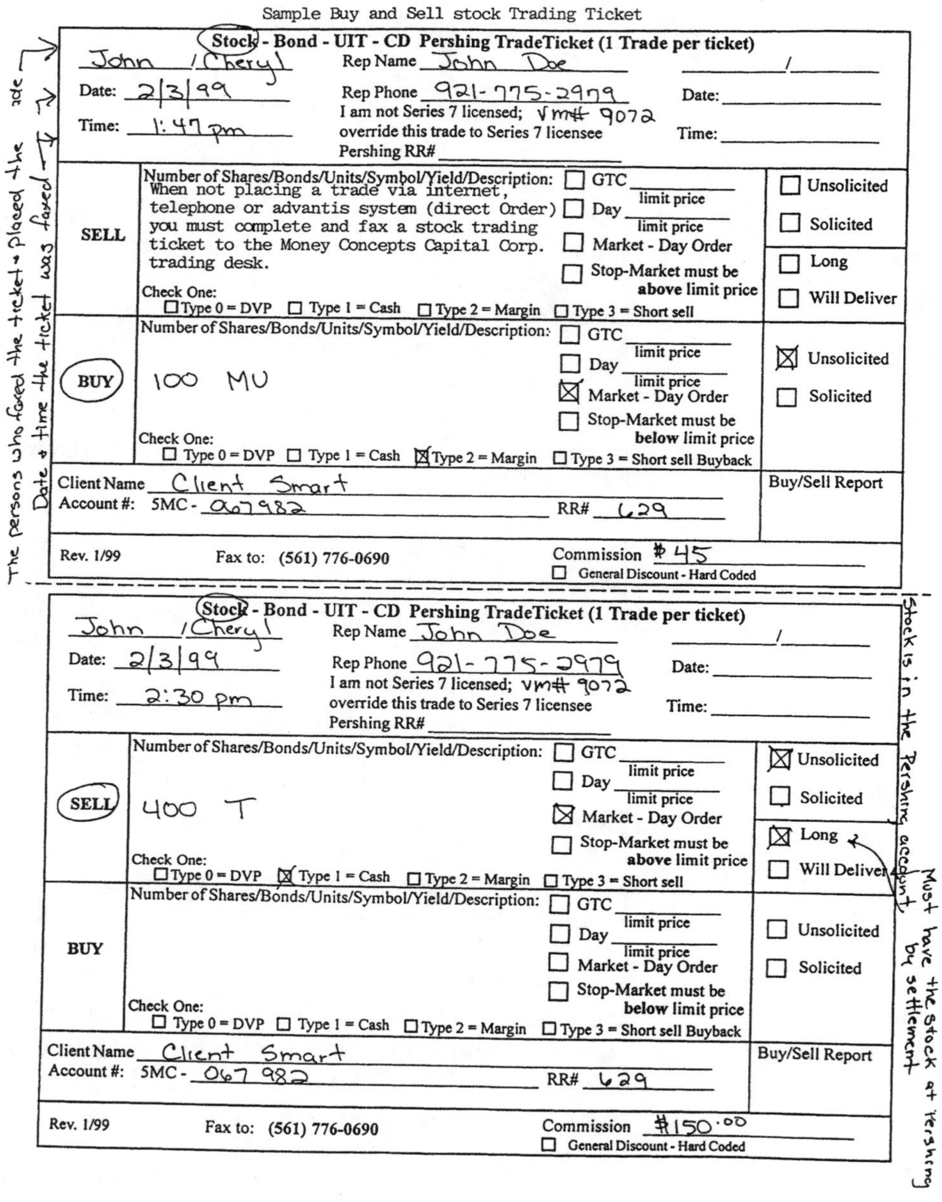

Sample Buy and Sell stock Trading Ticket

Stock - Bond - UIT - CD Pershing TradeTicket (1 Trade per ticket)

John / Cheryl Rep Name John Doe /

Date: 2/3/99 Rep Phone 921-775-2979 Date:

Time: 1:47 pm I am not Series 7 licensed; VM# 9072 override this trade to Series 7 licensee Time:

Pershing RR#

SELL — Number of Shares/Bonds/Units/Symbol/Yield/Description: When not placing a trade via internet, telephone or advantis system (direct Order) you must complete and fax a stock trading ticket to the Money Concepts Capital Corp. trading desk.

☐ GTC limit price ☐ Day limit price ☐ Market - Day Order ☐ Stop-Market must be above limit price

☐ Unsolicited ☐ Solicited ☐ Long ☐ Will Deliver

Check One: ☐ Type 0 = DVP ☐ Type 1 = Cash ☐ Type 2 = Margin ☐ Type 3 = Short sell

BUY — Number of Shares/Bonds/Units/Symbol/Yield/Description: 100 MU

☐ GTC limit price ☐ Day limit price ☒ Market - Day Order ☐ Stop-Market must be below limit price

☒ Unsolicited ☐ Solicited

Check One: ☐ Type 0 = DVP ☐ Type 1 = Cash ☒ Type 2 = Margin ☐ Type 3 = Short sell Buyback

Client Name Client Smart Buy/Sell Report

Account #: 5MC- 067982 RR# 629

Rev. 1/99 Fax to: (561) 776-0690 Commission $45

☐ General Discount - Hard Coded

The persons who faxed the ticket + placed the trade

Date + time the ticket was faxed

Stock - Bond - UIT - CD Pershing TradeTicket (1 Trade per ticket)

John / Cheryl Rep Name John Doe /

Date: 2/3/99 Rep Phone 921-775-2979 Date:

Time: 2:30 pm I am not Series 7 licensed; VM# 9072 override this trade to Series 7 licensee Time:

Pershing RR#

SELL — Number of Shares/Bonds/Units/Symbol/Yield/Description: 400 T

☐ GTC limit price ☐ Day limit price ☒ Market - Day Order ☐ Stop-Market must be above limit price

☒ Unsolicited ☐ Solicited ☒ Long ☐ Will Deliver

Check One: ☐ Type 0 = DVP ☒ Type 1 = Cash ☐ Type 2 = Margin ☐ Type 3 = Short sell

BUY — Number of Shares/Bonds/Units/Symbol/Yield/Description:

☐ GTC limit price ☐ Day limit price ☐ Market - Day Order ☐ Stop-Market must be below limit price

☐ Unsolicited ☐ Solicited

Check One: ☐ Type 0 = DVP ☐ Type 1 = Cash ☐ Type 2 = Margin ☐ Type 3 = Short sell Buyback

Client Name Client Smart Buy/Sell Report

Account #: 5MC- 067 982 RR# 629

Rev. 1/99 Fax to: (561) 776-0690 Commission $150.00

☐ General Discount - Hard Coded

Stock is in the Pershing account

Must have the stock at Pershing by settlement

given to certain types of market participants. For example, exchange rules require that orders received from the public be given priority over those received from member firms that are trading for their own accounts.

Limit Orders. For investors who want to pay a specific price for their stock, a limit order is the most desirable type of order to place. Specifically, *limit orders* indicate the price that you want to pay or receive for buying or selling shares. The trade will not take place until the limit price is reached. With this type of order, there is no latitude for negotiating for either a lower or higher price.

Figure 4-2 *Two sample limit order tickets from Pershing.*

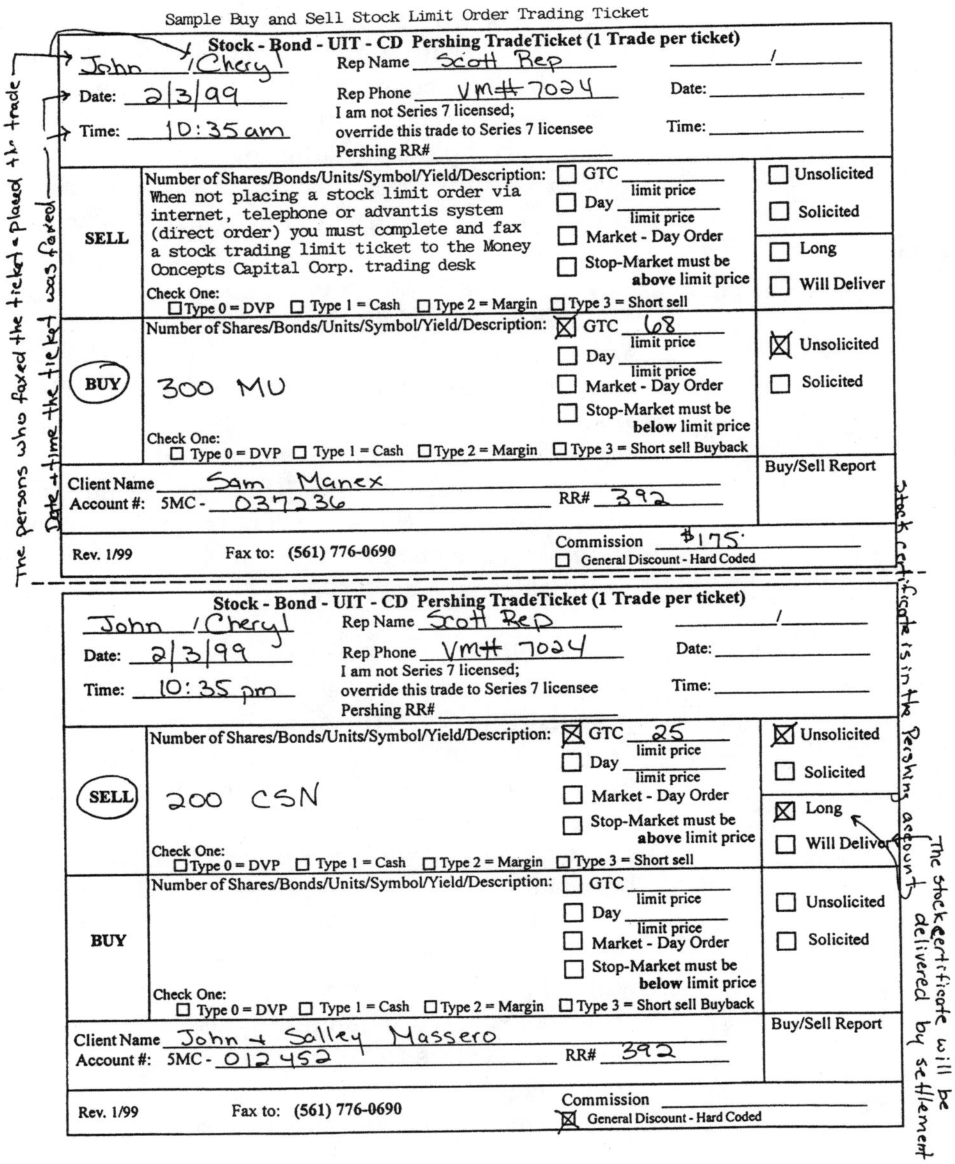
Sample Buy and Sell Stock Limit Order Trading Ticket

Stock - Bond - UIT - CD Pershing TradeTicket (1 Trade per ticket)

John /Cheryl Rep Name Scott Rep /
Date: 2/3/99 Rep Phone VM# 7024 Date:
Time: 10:35 am I am not Series 7 licensed; override this trade to Series 7 licensee Time:
Pershing RR#

SELL — Number of Shares/Bonds/Units/Symbol/Yield/Description: When not placing a stock limit order via internet, telephone or advantis system (direct order) you must complete and fax a stock trading limit ticket to the Money Concepts Capital Corp. trading desk
☐ GTC limit price ☐ Day limit price ☐ Market - Day Order ☐ Stop-Market must be above limit price
☐ Unsolicited ☐ Solicited ☐ Long ☐ Will Deliver
Check One: ☐ Type 0 = DVP ☐ Type 1 = Cash ☐ Type 2 = Margin ☐ Type 3 = Short sell

BUY — Number of Shares/Bonds/Units/Symbol/Yield/Description: 300 MU
☒ GTC 68 limit price ☐ Day limit price ☐ Market - Day Order ☐ Stop-Market must be below limit price
☒ Unsolicited ☐ Solicited
Check One: ☐ Type 0 = DVP ☐ Type 1 = Cash ☐ Type 2 = Margin ☐ Type 3 = Short sell Buyback

Client Name Sam Manex
Account #: 5MC- 037236 RR# 392 Buy/Sell Report
Rev. 1/99 Fax to: (561) 776-0690 Commission $175. ☐ General Discount - Hard Coded

Stock - Bond - UIT - CD Pershing TradeTicket (1 Trade per ticket)

John /Cheryl Rep Name Scott Rep /
Date: 2/3/99 Rep Phone VM# 7024 Date:
Time: 10:35 pm I am not Series 7 licensed; override this trade to Series 7 licensee Time:
Pershing RR#

SELL — Number of Shares/Bonds/Units/Symbol/Yield/Description: 200 CSN
☒ GTC 25 limit price ☐ Day limit price ☐ Market - Day Order ☐ Stop-Market must be above limit price
☒ Unsolicited ☐ Solicited ☒ Long ☐ Will Deliver
Check One: ☐ Type 0 = DVP ☐ Type 1 = Cash ☐ Type 2 = Margin ☐ Type 3 = Short sell

BUY — Number of Shares/Bonds/Units/Symbol/Yield/Description:
☐ GTC limit price ☐ Day limit price ☐ Market - Day Order ☐ Stop-Market must be below limit price
☐ Unsolicited ☐ Solicited
Check One: ☐ Type 0 = DVP ☐ Type 1 = Cash ☐ Type 2 = Margin ☐ Type 3 = Short sell Buyback

Client Name John + Salley Massero
Account #: 5MC- 012452 RR# 392 Buy/Sell Report
Rev. 1/99 Fax to: (561) 776-0690 Commission ☒ General Discount - Hard Coded

For example, Mr. Jones might want to buy shares of Boeing (BA) at $45. Although the stock is currently trading at $48, Mr. Jones is willing to pay no more than $45 per share. If the stock moves down in price, the order can be executed at $45, and Mr. Jones will have bought the stock at a more reasonable price. However, if the stock continues to move up and never comes back down to $45, Mr. Jones will not be able to purchase unless he cancels the limit order and places a market order in its place.

The limit order is also considered conditional because it is executed only if the limit price or a better price can be obtained. A *buy limit order* designates that a stock can be purchased only at a specific price or lower.

A *sell limit order* authorizes the stock to be sold at a specific price or higher. For example, assume Mr. Jones' wife is also an investor for her own account. She owns shares of Lands End (LE) that are currently trading at $34.75, and she needs to sell some shares in order to fund a vacation on a cruise liner. She places a limit order to sell 100 shares at $38. If the price goes up to this level or higher, the order is executed. If the price drops from its current range, she will have to wait or change her order if she wants to sell her stock.

An example of a Pershing limit order ticket appears in Figure 4-2. Note the limit price that is set for both the buy and sell orders. These orders are also marked *Good Until Canceled* (GTC), meaning they will stay active until executed or canceled by the client. A day limit order is only good for a specified date.

The danger of a limit order is that there is no guarantee that the order will ever be executed. If it is not executable at the time it reaches the exchange floor, the order is recorded in the specialist's book. Once the market price hits the designated or limit price, the specialist will then attempt to match up all sellers and buyers. But because market orders are always executed first, there might not be enough shares at the limit price to execute the order. Therefore, make sure that investors specify a time limit for either a GTC or day order, and that they understand the ramifications of each type.

Stop Orders. A *stop order* is considered conditional because it specifies a trade that is not to be executed until the market moves to a designated price. At that time, the order becomes a market order. For example, a stop order to buy stipulates that an order is not to be executed until the market price of a stock rises to a specific price. Conversely, a stop order to sell indicates that an order is not to be completed until the market price of a stock drops to a specified price. Once that designated price is reached, it becomes a market order and is executed immediately.

For example, suppose that Mr. Jones wants to buy BA stock, but not at the current price of $48. He wants to be sure that if the price goes up, he will not pay more than $51. When he places a stop order to buy at $51, the order is executed when and if the price reaches $51. In the case of Mrs. Jones, she wants to be sure not to sell her LE stock at less than $30 per share. Therefore, she can place her stop order to sell at $30.

An investor can also place a *stop-limit order*. In effect, this order type is a stop order that designates a limit price on the stock. In comparison to a stop order, which is automatically executed when the stop is reached, a stop-limit order becomes a limit order when the stop is reached. In other words, the investor can limit the execution price after the stop is activated. However, the limit price can never be reached after the order is activated.

Special Orders. An order that automatically becomes a market order when a designated price is reached is called a *market-if-touched order*. This type of order is the opposite of a stop order, because the market must fall back to a given price in order for the order to be executed as a buy order. Likewise, a sell order becomes a market order when the market falls to a given price. To distinguish between a stop order and a market-if-touched order, the former is designed to get out of an existing position at an acceptable price, while the latter is designed to get into a position at an agreeable price.

Another type of order can be classified as time specific. For example, an order to buy or sell at the opening of the market is called an *opening order.* A *closing order* indicates that a trade is to be executed only within a closing period of the business day. A *fill-or-kill order* is an order that must be executed upon reaching the trading floor or it is immediately canceled. Other orders might designate a specific time period in which they are effective—a day, a week, a month, or even a given time during a regular trading day.

Buying on Margin. When an investor does not have enough money to pay cash for the entire purchase of an order, credit must be arranged in order to *buy on margin.* Before a margin transaction takes place, a special account needs to be opened at the brokerage house or dealer's office. In effect, this account enables the investor to apply for a line of credit—except the money is used exclusively to buy stock.

The Fed and the NASD have established special rules regarding the requirements for margin trading. Currently, a 50-percent margin is required on an account in order for this type of trade to be executed. In other words, when stock is purchased on margin, cash in the amount of 50 percent of the total purchase price must already be credited in the brokerage account.

For example, suppose that you wanted to buy 100 shares of Xerox, which is currently being offered at $45 per share. The regular full price for this trade would be $4,500 (excluding commissions). If you purchase these shares on margin, you will owe $2,250 or one-half the total cost. This amount already has to be in the account or deposited with your broker as collateral. The broker pays for the rest of the trade ($2,250) and will charge interest that is payable monthly on the outstanding balance. Keep in mind that the interest can be higher than the bank rate, because the brokerage firm must borrow the money from the bank to loan you.

People buy stock on margin to put up a smaller amount of money for the purpose of *leverage.* In effect, a small amount of money is used to control a larger amount of underlying security value. When an investor purchases stock on margin, the potential return is much greater if the stock price goes up, because the broker was paid only half of the original purchase price.

For example, let's assume you paid $45 per share to acquire that 100 shares of Xerox. If the price goes up to $60, the gain is $15 per share. But because you only paid half of the $45 per share to buy the stock, your actual rate of return is about 67 percent ($15 gain divided by $22.50 original per-share payment). Although this rate does not include the interest paid on the margin account or the brokerage commission, you still have a much higher gain than if you had paid the entire $4,500 in cash initially.

While this concept sounds like a wonderful idea, remember that stocks can also fall in price, which causes the opposite effect. If that happens, the broker might ask you to come up with some additional cash in order to maintain a minimum margin requirement. This situation is classified as a *margin call.* The broker's loan amount in your account does not fall with the stock price; instead, only your invested amount loses value. In other words, the broker does not share in the market risk with you.

Let's return to our original example. Suppose that the market value of your Xerox falls to \$3,200 from the initial \$4,500 purchase price. The equity in your account drops to \$950 (\$3,200 market value minus \$2,250 initial equity). If the margin requirement is 35 percent of the current market value, or \$1,120 (\$3,200 × .35), you must add \$170 to your equity at the brokerage house (\$1,120 − \$950). By law, you must bring your margin account back up to its minimum value.

The margin call gives the investor two choices: either depositing cash or equivalent valued securities, or selling out the entire position and settling the account with the broker in full. To illustrate our example, if you sell the original 100 shares of Xerox at \$3,200 after its decline, you owe the broker \$2,250 (the original amount borrowed) plus interest on the margin account and a sales commission. In effect, you are left with less than \$950, meaning that your real loss is \$1,300 (\$2,250 − \$950).

Keep in mind that investors take full responsibility for making the decision to purchase stock on margin. In a bullish market environment, doing so can be extremely tempting—especially if cash for investing is not readily available. Traders take an especially high risk because they are in and out of stocks frequently. Unless the client is a wealthy individual, most brokerage firms will generally require traders to keep plenty of cash in reserve in order to cover any margin calls. Longer-term investors are more suitable for margin buying, because they generally only receive occasional margin calls and can cover their positions by depositing other marketable securities.

Short Selling. When we think of trading in an ordinary sense, we would buy a stock first and then sell it later—hopefully for a profit. With a *short sale,* we do just the opposite. We sell the stock first and then buy it back later in order to cover the stock that we initially sold. Does this process sound confusing? Let's go through an example to see why anyone would want to employ such a strategy.

First of all, short sellers tend to be pessimistic and expect the stock price to decline. This situation could result from falling company profits or earnings per share, a cut in the dividend rate, or a change in management that is anticipated to negatively affect the company as a whole. No matter the reason, these investors will be bearish on that particular stock.

Reacting just the opposite of margin buyers, who are bullish and expect a stock to rise in value, the short seller wants to profit from a fall in the stock's price. First, a margin account must be established with the broker. Then, instead of borrowing cash on margin, the short seller borrows stock from the broker. The stock can then be sold at a higher price, in anticipation that it will fall in value and can be bought back at a much lower price.

Let's assume that the brokerage house can borrow stock shares that the investor wants to short. The shares are placed in the account and are delivered to the buyer when sold. The investor is now short the stock and will need to buy the stock back later to deliver to the broker. The goal is to eventually repurchase the shares at a lower price, return them to the broker, and keep the difference as a profit. If the stock's price rises, however, the investor might have to buy back the shares at a higher price and incur a loss.

Here is a hypothetical example of how short selling works. Suppose you learn that Boeing lost a big government contract to build military planes at its old McDonnell-Douglas facility in St. Louis. You anticipate that its profits for the year will drop substantially and will negatively effect the price of its stock. To try to take advantage of the situation, you borrow 100 shares from your broker and sell Boeing stock for $48 per share. This sale nets you $4,800 (excluding commissions), but you still owe the broker 100 shares of BA stock. Two months later, your intuition is correct, and BA stock has dropped to $40 per share. You now decide to repurchase 100 shares of BA at $4,000 in order to cover the shares that you borrowed from the broker initially. In effect, the broker receives these shares back, and you walk away with an $800 profit (excluding commissions).

Just as in margin trading, a short seller also incurs risk. Let's suppose that after two months, the Saudi Arabian government awards Boeing a large contract to build fighter planes for its country. In anticipation of higher profits for the year, market forces push the price of BA stock higher instead of lower. The stock now trades at $62 per share, so you decide to recover the stock and close out your position with the broker. In effect, you will lose $1,400 plus commissions—because buying back the stock cost you $6,200.

To protect yourself from this embarrassing position, you could have placed a *stop-loss buy order* on the BA stock. Therefore, if the stock you sold at $48 increases to $54, an automatic stock repurchase is initiated for 100 shares of BA. While you are guaranteed to lose, this situation is not as bad as letting your shares get out of hand and escalating to an even higher price (and subsequently higher loss).

OTC Transactions. Securities of stock issued to the general public that are not traded on an exchange are traded OTC. This market is also referred to as *National Association of Security Dealers Automated Quotation* (NASDAQ) system. As described in Chapter 1, "Origins: The Markets and Major Indices," the OTC market does not have a trading floor. Rather, trades take place by means of a computerized quotation system at brokerage counters and desks.

This broader market has what is known as second-tier stocks, which include solid, reputable companies. However, they generally have lower capitalization, (shares outstanding), and trade for lower prices than those on the major exchanges. For example, one classification is known as *emerging growth stocks.* These stocks represent younger companies that have tremendous growth potential but have fewer assurances of long-term success.

As trading takes place, broker-dealers act as market makers for various stocks. The computerized trading system enables them to interact immediately when executing orders, providing instant liquidity for the market to function. For example, a stock might have a bid price of $15.00 and an ask price of $15.75. An investor who wants to buy shares would pay $15.75 per share, and an investor who wants to sell shares would get

$15.00 per share. The difference is called the *spread* and is split between the two firms that are involved in the transaction.

The reporting of NASDAQ national market issues is similar to the reporting of listed securities. In Figure 4-3, we see how the *Wall Street Journal* reports security activity for the NASDAQ on a typical trading day. The information includes the 52-week high and low prices, the company's symbol, dividend, the volume of transactions, the high, low, and closing prices of that particular trading day, and the net change from the previous day. Some papers also include the yield and profits/earnings (P/E) ratio.

For example, let's look at Compuware (symbol CPWR). We can tell that this is a volatile stock from examining its 52-week high and low price (40 – 12.66). This company does not pay a dividend and had a P/E of 11 at the time. Shares trading hands were 53,287 on August 2, 2000. The high was 8.06; the low was 7.78; and the closing price was 7.84. This stock was off .16 from the previous day's close. Thus, we can obtain a lot of information just be studying this one report.

In addition to listed securities and stocks traded OTC, large block transactions are executed by brokers who are referred to as the third market. The activity in this market takes place when institutional investors (such as pension plans, mutual funds, or insurance companies) buy and sell large amounts of shares for their accounts. These transactions usually involve 10,000 shares or more and are called blocks of stocks. The brokers who organize and execute these types of trades are called block positioners.

Figure 4-3 The Wall Street Journal *security activity reports for NASDAQ.*

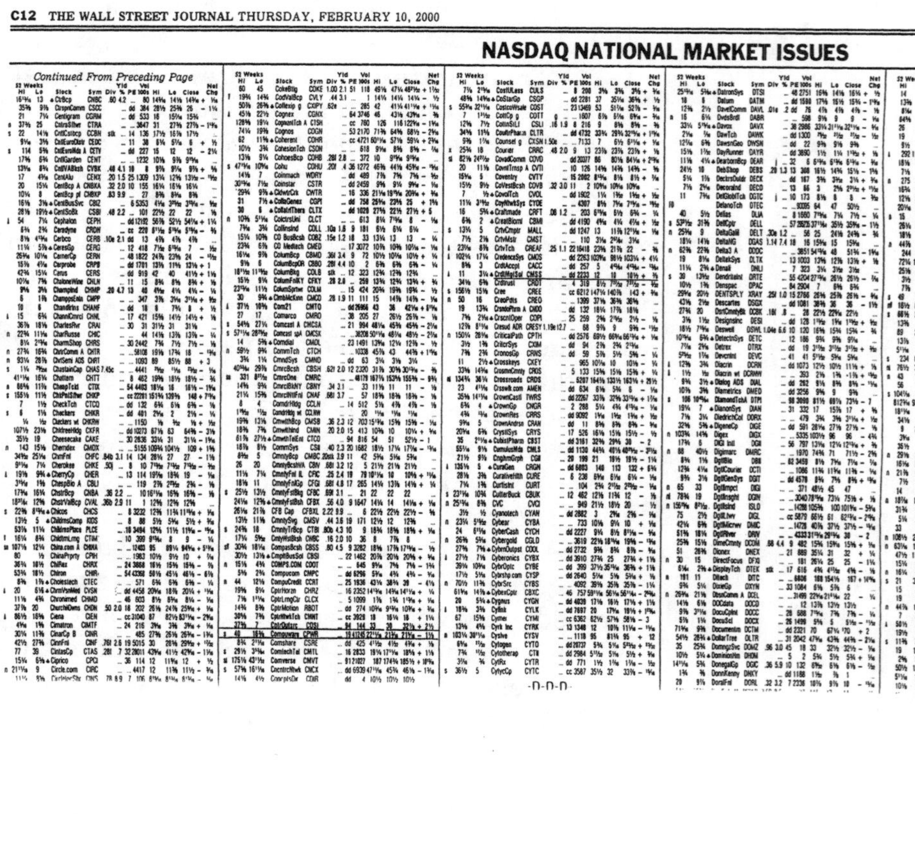
C12 THE WALL STREET JOURNAL THURSDAY, FEBRUARY 10, 2000

NASDAQ NATIONAL MARKET ISSUES

Continued From Preceding Page

Usually, institutional investors work through a large brokerage firm in order to complete the transaction. They can also work independently, however, in a *fourth market* over a computerized trading system called Instinet. The system is limited to subscribers only and provides bid and ask price quotations plus executing orders. This activity is reported in the financial press as composite transactions, just as trades on the various exchanges are reported.

Block trades, the third market, and the fourth market offer institutional investors two advantages over individual traders: lower transaction costs and quicker executions. Due to increased competition among brokerage firms for this type of business, the commissions charged to institutional investors have greatly decreased. The effort to refine trading and changes in the regulatory environment has greatly improved efficiency in the market system for the execution of security orders.

Decimals Come to the Markets

After years of delay, the *Securities and Exchange Commission* (SEC) has given major stock markets permission to convert the pricing of stocks and options to decimals from fractions. The new quotes will replace the 200-year-old tradition of using fractions of a dollar, such as $^1/_8$ for 12.5 cents. Advocates believe that decimals will shrink bid-ask spreads and save investors up to $3 million a day in commissions.

It didn't take long for investors to adjust to decimal pricing. Hundreds of newspapers that publish stock prices have switched to the decimal format. Web sites and monthly brokerage statements regularly display decimal prices, as well. U.S. securities markets are also adopting the international practice of decimal pricing in order to remain competitive, and this is a crucial step in the right direction.

Supporters say that using the decimal system will help ordinary investors by narrowing the difference between a stock's best bid and asking prices, known as the spread. Spreads typically vary from .125 cents to 50 cents—an amount that adds up to a sizable profit for brokers who take a percentage based on the size of the spread. This situation will definitely be a win-win for investors and will make our markets much more attractive to foreign investors in the future.

Disappearance of the Spread

Supply and demand determine stock prices, and the difference between what the seller asks and what the buyer bids (the spread) is where specialists make part of their profits. Most revenue comes from the companies that the specialist represents and is somewhat tied to trading volume, so it is in the specialist's best interest to facilitate trading. However, the spread is gradually disappearing from most NYSE trades. With most orders being matched directly and electronically, there is almost zero spread.

In contrast, all 500 NASDAQ market makers—rather than having specific stocks assigned to them—can compete for every stock transaction. *Electronic Communications Networks* (ECNs) have gained popularity thanks to the Internet. By using ECN, brokers can automatically and instantly match buy and sell orders and eliminate the spread when executing trades. If no match is found, the order is posted in an electronic trading book that lists the would-be buyer and seller, the number of shares to be transacted, and the price. NASDAQ market makers look at the book and try to fill the orders. If an ECN fails to find a match, however, and NASDAQ market makers cannot make the deal, then the trade might never be executed.

That is one advantage of the specialist system: every order that comes in goes through to completion. NYSE rules require specialists to help maintain an orderly market. For example, if no buyer comes forward for shares that someone wants to sell, the specialist will buy them to sell later. As mentioned earlier, this process is called making a market in the stock.

Another argument for ECNs is that they save investors money, because trades executed by machines are fair and honest and make no errors. Also, the speed of ECNs reduces the chance of a price changing between the times when a trade is requested and executed. Here, we see that the shift to electronic trading benefits the active trader the most. Per-transaction trading costs drop, and market orders most often get filled at the trader's price.

Electronic Trading: The Wave of the Future

The Internet is forcing a revolution in personal investing as we dive into the 21st century. Nothing is sacred anymore, and even traditional full-service brokers are joining the online trading boom in order to retain clients and keep up with the competition. As Americans become more independent and want to make their own investment decisions, more will naturally go to the Internet to buy and sell securities in an attempt to lower trading costs.

Although online trading has made these times exciting for individual clients, they can also be the most confusing of times. The recent bull market has generated a surge in the popularity of online trading and has put investing within the reach of nearly everyone. Not only can investors buy and sell stocks for a minimal cost, but the availability of stock research on the Internet can tempt anyone to become an instant Warren Buffett.

A June 1999 survey by Gomez Advisors, Inc. (a Lincoln, Massachusetts Internet research firm) and Harris Interactive, Inc. (a Rochester, New York market-research firm) found that 16.3 million people were poised to begin trading online. Scrambling to sign up these investors, traditional brokerage firms have increased their Internet offerings. For example, a recent Internet search on the Yahoo! Web site detected more than 80 firms that offer some type of online trading service.

Basic online investing involves a cheaper or easier way of running a brokerage account. These methods are for people who like to pick investments themselves. Instead of calling a broker with a traditional order to buy or sell, you send the broker the order online. These accounts typically go through discount stock brokers who give no investment advice.

Some of the leading online brokerage company websites include the following:

- **Merrill Lynch & Co.**—www.mldirect.ml.com
- **Charles Schwab Corp.**—www.schwab.com
- **E*Trade Group, Inc.**—www.etrade.com
- **Ameritrade Holding Corp.**—www.ameritrade.com
- **Powerstreet**—www.fidelity.com
- **DLJdirect, Inc.**—www.dljdirect.com
- **TD Waterhouse Group, Inc.**—www.waterhouse.com
- **Datek Online Brokerage Services**—www.datek.com
- **Morgan Stanley Dean Witter Online**—www.online.msdw.com
- **National Discount Brokers Group, Inc.**—www.ndb.com

The Danger of Churning

For years, experts, planners, and regulators have argued over the appropriate minimum time that a stock should be held before it is sold. How much time should pass after an investor buys stock before his planner can suggest selling in order to buy another equity? There is an obvious potential for abuse here, because commission-based planners or brokers can make more money just by recommending trades.

There have been numerous cases in which licensed securities professionals have been accused of *churning* their client's accounts. In effect, they recommend a buy and sell of the same security within a relatively short period of time in order to make more income from commissions. With the lower commission structure of most broker-dealers today, however, this argument is harder to prove.

The SEC is the watchdog of the industry and tries to clamp down on abuses in this area. More violations are likely to occur in the mutual-fund industry, where higher commissions and charges are common for investors. Occasionally, you might find an investor who has suffered from this type of abuse. Most importantly, you must have a valid reason for recommending a repositioning of funds in a portfolio.

As a new financial professional, you must structure your practice to install confidence in clients that this type of situation will not occur. Frequent reviews do not mean that drastic changes will be made to portfolios. Rather, some minor repositioning could take place only if the situation warrants. For example, a stock that no longer fits the criteria of achieving a particular goal might be considered for repositioning into a better investment that has a much better chance of accomplishing the objective. Once clients are aware that you have their best interest in mind, they will not worry about abuse and frequent trading of their investments.

The Future of Financial Markets

As we have seen so far in this book, the stock market is rich in tradition, and technology is becoming more of a factor in changing the way in which business will be conducted in the future. Just over the past decade, for example, technology and financial theory have come together to set off a gush of new products. Everything in the future will be aimed at reducing costs and redistributing risk so that the investor can make better decisions.

What trends should you be aware of as a financial professional, in order to bring maximum value to your clients?

- First, more and more goods and services will be sold through auctions. The pricing of Internet transactions makes it more cost efficient to buy both tangible and intangible goods and services. The pricing effectively eliminates the middle man, so pricing can become more competitive. As more mergers and acquisitions take place in financial services, auctions will become the wave of the future.
- The pool of potential buyers and sellers will greatly enlarge. This situation will favor the cheapest supplier and keenest buyer and will thus lower the cost of labor and boost productivity. Not only will this situation have a tremendous impact on the consumer durable goods markets, but it will also affect the demand for intangible products. For example, as the number of Baby Boomers using the Internet for online trading increases, it will encourage a more efficient market with faster executions and more reliable pricing of securities.
- Prices will lose their anchors and float more freely. Just as the *Dow Jones Industrial Average* (DJIA) fluctuates from hour to hour, the same situation has occurred for airline-ticket pricing. Initially, there was only one class of airline travel. But with technology and deregulation, airlines learned to use sophisticated software to change ticket prices depending on the time of day, day of the week, the flexibility of the ticket, and so on. Priceline.com, Inc. went the last step to create an online market that enables travelers to pay an infinite variety of fares.
- Falling transaction costs and more efficient pricing will encourage people to swap what they have more frequently. For example, just as $10 stock commissions have turned many long-term investors into day traders, people will more readily trade up to a new pair of skis if they can sell their old ones at a fair price without paying a chunk of the proceeds to a broker.

- Products will become more standard so that buyers will not need to see what they buy every time. In fact, Internet shopping will compete heavily with catalog shopping for quantity purchases. Because we deal with intangibles in this industry, people will want quicker buy and sell executions of securities and will expect to pay a minimal commissions or transaction cost in order to do so.

The Opportunity to Specialize

All this change and technological innovation in the securities markets may sound discouraging, but it actually gives you the opportunity to specialize in helping clients. You will encounter many people who already have these types of accounts. Rather than turn them away, you can show them the benefits of your expertise in other areas.

For example, an investment plan using Modern Portfolio Theory (described in a later chapter) will complement an individual trading account using four investment classes and a strategy called rebalancing to achieve long-term objectives. You will learn how this concept works to increase returns and lower risk associated with individual stocks.

You could focus on retirement planning using employee benefits. In this career field, you can study to become a *Retirement Benefits Specialist* (RBS). You would learn all about different retirement plans, the benefits associated with each type, and how clients can use them to maximize tax savings. Long-term retirement planning is directly related to individual securities.

Finally, you can help younger Americans to receive an inheritance from their parents. If they haven't earned the money through their own efforts, there is a sense of insecurity and the goal of not to blow it. Two websites to explore in this area include www.inheritance-project.com and www.thewealthconservancy.com. Giving financial advice to wealthy people is one of the best services that professionals in our industry can offer to high net worth clients.

Chapter 5

Studying: How to Interpret Prices and Understand Financial News

Introduction

Once we know the fundamentals of pricing, do our homework on stock selection, and actually make a purchase for a client, the next step is to track the activity of this new asset. We want to follow its progress and be able to understand why it trades higher or lower on any given day. Financial information is vitally important in our fast-paced world, and we need to know how to follow daily market activity in order to give outstanding service.

In essence, this chapter will show why so many people open their daily newspapers to the business section before reading any other section. Whether contemplating the purchase of a new stock or just keeping track of interest rates, many Americans devote a special time and place to following the financial markets. While access to the Internet enables us to track the value of holdings instantly, this method does not give the proper time to contemplate making long-term investment decisions. We will discover here why investors believe that reading financial news is a meaningful part of their everyday lives.

When you read the financial section of a newspaper, you can compare the experience to watching a football game. This includes knowing the rules, what to look for, and how to identify a few key players. Just as a quarterback's goal is to lead his team to a successful score, the financial reader wants to find and interpret news that will enable him or her to make a profitable decision. Now let's proceed with identifying a strategic approach to finding the most important financial news sources so that our client's chances of winning are enhanced.

Ticker-Tape Language

Before analyzing current and future financial news sources, let's step back in time 133 years and walk onto the floor of the *New York Stock Exchange* (NYSE). In 1867, the first stock ticker machine was installed in order to connect the exchange to other brokerage offices in New York City and around the country. A thin piece of paper reported the transactions of buyers and sellers and showed the results of each stock trade. You might remember pictures of miles of ticker tape spread all over the floor of the exchanges and also cluttering the offices of major broker-dealers.

The reports on this tape enabled buyers and sellers to react instantly to the same information. As advances in electronics took over, transaction times dropped to a minimum—and trades were executed instantly. While today's fast-paced world has outdated the old ticker tape, some electronic ticker machines are still mounted high above reception rooms in major brokerage offices in order to give investors time to sit back and contemplate their next moves. Also, despite incremental advances in technology, that method is still basically how many people buy and sell securities today.

In order to make the ticker tape more time efficient, symbols were assigned to each stock and were reported on the tape as trades were executed. For example, a transaction involving 100 shares of Ford Motor Company at a price of $45 would appear as F 45. After reading this report, a buyer could place an order at a price of 44 $^7/_8$ in an attempt to get a lower price, while a seller could place an order for 45 $^1/_8$ (hoping to get a higher price). For someone who is wishing to buy or sell the stock instantly, a market order would be placed within this narrow spread—knowing that the executed price would be somewhere close to $45.

Share Volume and Trading

As a financial professional, you should be aware that the best place to find the most comprehensive information about daily market activity is in *The Wall Street Journal*. This newspaper keeps investors up to date on details of what happened during the previous trading session. One area of importance is tracking the number of shares that were traded on various exchanges the previous day.

Figure 5-1 illustrates the *Wall Street Journal* trading report for February 25, 2000. The breakdown of trading on the NYSE during normal business hours shows that more than 1.1 billion shares traded hands on Thursday, February 24, and more than 975 million shares were traded on Wednesday, February 23. This report also shows the trading volume in NYSE stocks taking place on other exchanges such as Chicago, Philadelphia, Boston, and Cincinnati. For those interested investors, trading volume is also broken down every half hour. The bar chart on the bottom shows NYSE volume in millions of shares going back six months. As more interest in owning stocks becomes apparent, we can logically see a corresponding increase in the overall trading activity.

After the close of business, each exchange totals the number of shares traded during the day. The total volume of the NYSE, however, is the figure used most often by news commentators to describe the day's market activity. Since the 1950s, volume has steadily increased due to a larger number of outstanding shares issued by more American companies. Also, trading activity has increased due to greater involvement from institutional investors (such as mutual funds, pension funds, insurance companies, and banks).

Figure 5-2 illustrates the most actively traded stock issues on February 24, 2000 on three major exchanges. Names will typically be of the largest companies whose shares were traded in the millions. This synopsis also gives the closing price of each issue and point change from the previous day. Investors who like to own stocks with plenty of liquidity will have a special interest in this report. On this particular day, America Online was the most actively traded issue on NYSE with more than 42

Figure 5-1 *The* Wall Street Journal *trading report for February 25, 2000.*

BREAKDOWN OF TRADING IN NYSE STOCKS (9:30 a.m. to 4 p.m. Eastern time)

BY MARKET	THU	WED	WK AGO
New York	1,167,855,750	975,476,590	1,029,598,930
Chicago	37,791,700	59,958,200	57,625,100
CBOE		100	300
Pacific	21,272,800	18,456,500	17,840,900
NASD	127,630,570	106,779,930	96,907,050
Phila	8,974,100	7,405,300	8,171,500
Boston	24,893,900	19,439,100	21,224,800
Cincinnati	18,307,000	14,768,800	14,843,300
Composite	1,406,725,820	1,202,284,520	1,246,211,880

NYSE first crossing 4,980,600 shares, value n.a.
Second (basket) 42,153,485 shares, value $1,952,644,070
[1]The net difference of the number of stocks closing higher than their previous trade from those closing lower; NYSE trading only.
[2]A comparison of the number of advancing and declining issues with the volume of shares rising and falling. Generally, an Arms of less than 1.00 indicates buying demand; above 1.00 indicates selling pressure.
z-NYSE or Amex only.

½-HOURLY	THU	WED	WK AGO
9:30-10	147,600,000	125,220,000	135,840,000
10-10:30	113,160,000	94,424,000	112,061,000
10:30-11	100,130,000	71,506,000	76,959,000
11-11:30	91,230,000	69,790,000	73,960,000
11:30-12	73,320,000	57,030,000	61,820,000
12-12:30	59,340,000	53,440,000	60,670,000
12:30-1	60,080,000	46,950,000	58,130,000
1-1:30	54,420,000	47,810,000	58,410,000
1:30-2	54,290,000	59,520,000	66,280,000
2-2:30	83,910,000	67,740,000	60,310,000
2:30-3	68,790,000	62,300,000	64,190,000
3-3:30	107,620,000	76,310,000	79,990,000
3:30-4	153,965,750	143,436,590	120,978,930

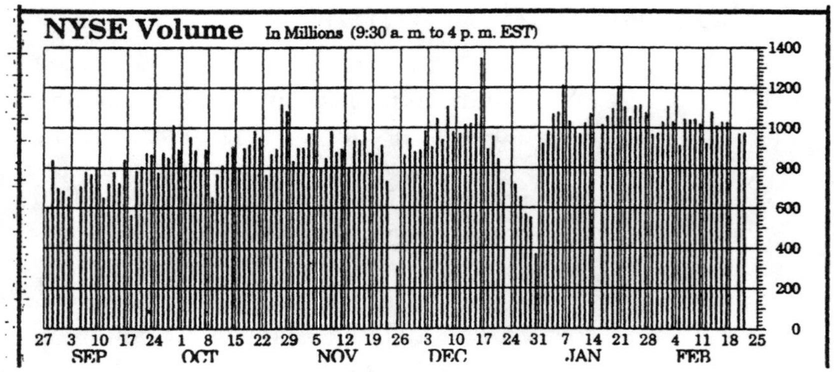

Source: *Republished with permission of Dow Jones from WSJ Market Data Group Year 2000; Permission conveyed through Copyright Clearance Center.*

million shares, while Dell Computer was the most actively traded issue on NASDAQ with more than 60 million shares.

If a particular stock is not on this list, an investor or professional advisor should not be overly concerned. Although they tend to get less attention, many other types of stocks also trade with a high volume each day. The activity of a particular issue can be checked for volume of shares traded by using the Internet and by searching any number of Web sites that track the activities of individual companies.

For example, Corporate Information (www.corporateinformation.com) is an excellent site that contains thousands of research reports, company profiles, and many categorized links. This site also has a complete company extensions guide (such as Corp. or Inc.) for every possible corporate extension around the world. An investor can conduct company searches by country, industry, or specific company. Each link offers impressive capabilities that can be an invaluable research tool for advising clients.

As market trading becomes more popular, more attention will also be given to the Late Trading Snapshot (illustrated in Figure 5-3). In the figure, this snapshot shows activity that took place from 4 P.M. to 6:35 P.M. Eastern time on February 24, 2000. The snapshot also includes the most active issues, along with late price-percentage gainers and losers.

.Figure 5-2 *Most actively traded stocks on February 24, 2000 on three major exchanges (from* The Wall Street Journal*).*

MOST ACTIVE ISSUES

NYSE	VOLUME	CLOSE	CHANGE
AmOnline	42,178,700	60 1/8	+ 3 3/8
LucentTch	26,913,000	55 7/8	+ 3 3/16
Citigroup	23,603,300	49 3/8	− 1 1/4
Compaq	22,874,300	25 15/16	+ 3/4
WalMart	19,399,800	44 5/8	− 2 1/2
SBC Comm	12,850,500	35 3/8	+ 1/8
NewbrNtwk	12,664,300	33 1/2	+ 11/16
PhilipMor	11,925,700	20 1/16	− 3/8
AT&T	10,844,300	45 3/4	− 1 1/8
ArrowElec	10,314,700	32	+ 9
Pfizer	9,286,600	33 1/16	+ 1/16
JohnsJohns	9,244,000	73 3/4	− 2 9/16
GenElec	9,204,800	131	+ 1/16
Merck	9,066,800	61 3/8	− 1 15/16
IBM	9,054,700	110 7/8	+ 2
NASDAQ			
DellCptr	60,602,700	42 3/8	+ 1
Intel	41,273,600	114 1/4	+ 5 3/16
CiscoSys	36,229,100	137 1/4	− 1 3/8
OracleCp	34,382,700	61 15/16	− 1 1/8
Microsft	33,348,800	94 3/4	+ 1/2
Qualcomm	25,561,600	139 11/16	− 7 3/16
Tellabs	21,794,700	51 11/16	− 2 1/8
3ComCp	18,973,700	83	+ 5 3/8
SunMicrsys	18,486,400	96 7/8	+ 2 1/4
MCI Wrldcm	16,366,900	46 15/16	+ 1/2
JDS Uniphs	15,619,800	258	+ 22 1/2
ImagingTch	14,844,500	1 19/32	+ 1/32
Compuware	13,801,100	22 3/16	+ 13/16
AMEX			
NASDAQ100	24,419,300	213	+ 4 39/64
SPDR	16,587,500	135 9/16	− 15/16
DJIA Diam	4,515,400	100 15/16	− 1 9/32
DaytonMng	2,929,000	7/64	....
HooprHolm	1,851,300	27 7/8	+ 2 3/8

Source: *Republished with permission of Dow Jones from WSJ Market Data Group Year 2000; Permission conveyed through Copyright Clearance Center.*

Often, special news announcements regarding individual companies will come out after the close of regular market hours and can have a profound effect on after-hours trading. Investors who study this report before the market opens the following morning will know whether a stock of particular interest has been positively or negatively affected. Late trading activity can often give a clue as to the type of action that will take place during the next trading day.

Bids and Offers: Understanding Stock Market Tables

You will also notice in Figure 5-3 the various ways in which trading activity is reported as it pertains to each individual stock under the heading "New York Stock Exchange Composite Transactions." The following list is a summary of each column and describe how to interpret this critical data.

Figure 5-3 *Late trading snapshot.*

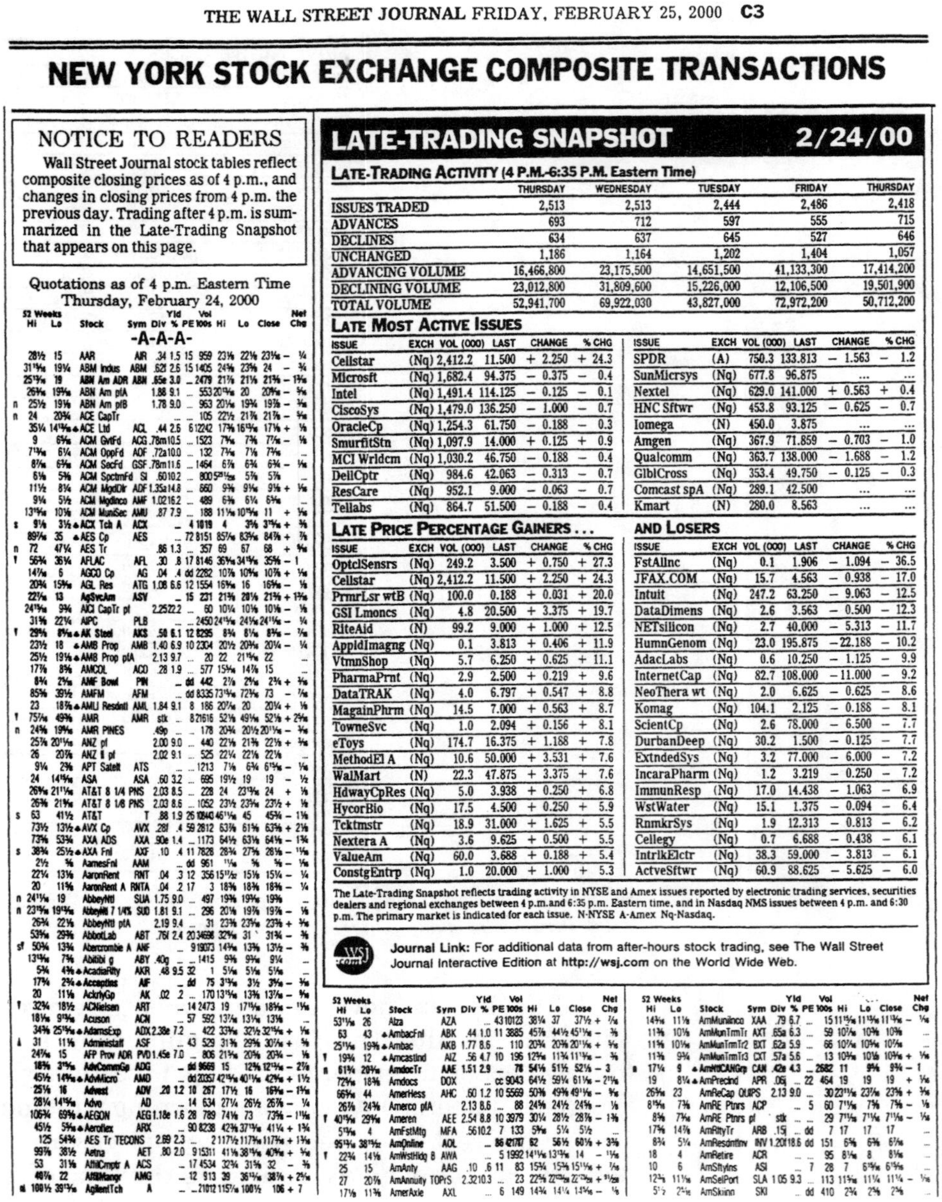

THE WALL STREET JOURNAL FRIDAY, FEBRUARY 25, 2000 C3

NEW YORK STOCK EXCHANGE COMPOSITE TRANSACTIONS

NOTICE TO READERS

Wall Street Journal stock tables reflect composite closing prices as of 4 p.m., and changes in closing prices from 4 p.m. the previous day. Trading after 4 p.m. is summarized in the Late-Trading Snapshot that appears on this page.

Quotations as of 4 p.m. Eastern Time Thursday, February 24, 2000

-A-A-A-

LATE-TRADING SNAPSHOT 2/24/00

LATE-TRADING ACTIVITY (4 P.M.-6:35 P.M. Eastern Time)

	THURSDAY	WEDNESDAY	TUESDAY	FRIDAY	THURSDAY
ISSUES TRADED	2,513	2,513	2,444	2,486	2,418
ADVANCES	693	712	597	555	715
DECLINES	634	637	645	527	646
UNCHANGED	1,186	1,164	1,202	1,404	1,057
ADVANCING VOLUME	16,466,800	23,175,500	14,651,500	41,133,300	17,414,200
DECLINING VOLUME	23,012,800	31,809,600	15,226,000	12,106,500	19,501,900
TOTAL VOLUME	52,941,700	69,922,030	43,827,000	72,972,200	50,712,200

LATE MOST ACTIVE ISSUES

ISSUE	EXCH	VOL (000)	LAST	CHANGE	% CHG	ISSUE	EXCH	VOL (000)	LAST	CHANGE	% CHG
Cellstar	(Nq)	2,412.2	11.500	+ 2.250	+ 24.3	SPDR	(A)	750.3	133.813	– 1.563	– 1.2
Microsft	(Nq)	1,682.4	94.375	– 0.375	– 0.4	SunMicrsys	(Nq)	677.8	96.875	...	...
Intel	(Nq)	1,491.4	114.125	– 0.125	– 0.1	Nextel	(Nq)	629.0	141.000	+ 0.563	+ 0.4
CiscoSys	(Nq)	1,479.0	136.250	– 1.000	– 0.7	HNC Sftwr	(Nq)	453.8	93.125	– 0.625	– 0.7
OracleCp	(Nq)	1,254.3	61.750	– 0.188	– 0.3	Iomega	(N)	450.0	3.875	...	...
SmurfitStn	(Nq)	1,097.9	14.000	+ 0.125	+ 0.9	Amgen	(Nq)	367.9	71.859	– 0.703	– 1.0
MCI Wrldcm	(Nq)	1,030.2	46.750	– 0.188	– 0.4	Qualcomm	(Nq)	363.7	138.000	– 1.688	– 1.2
DellCptr	(Nq)	984.6	42.063	– 0.313	– 0.7	GlblCross	(Nq)	353.4	49.750	– 0.125	– 0.3
ResCare	(Nq)	952.1	9.000	– 0.063	– 0.7	Comcast spA	(Nq)	289.1	42.500	...	...
Tellabs	(Nq)	864.7	51.500	– 0.188	– 0.4	Kmart	(N)	280.0	8.563	...	...

LATE PRICE PERCENTAGE GAINERS . . . AND LOSERS

ISSUE	EXCH	VOL (000)	LAST	CHANGE	% CHG	ISSUE	EXCH	VOL (000)	LAST	CHANGE	% CHG
OptclSensrs	(Nq)	249.2	3.500	+ 0.750	+ 27.3	FstAllnc	(Nq)	0.1	1.906	– 1.094	– 36.5
Cellstar	(Nq)	2,412.2	11.500	+ 2.250	+ 24.3	JFAX.COM	(Nq)	15.7	4.563	– 0.938	– 17.0
PrmrLsr wtB	(Nq)	100.0	0.188	+ 0.031	+ 20.0	Intuit	(Nq)	247.2	63.250	– 9.063	– 12.5
GSI Lmoncs	(Nq)	4.8	20.500	+ 3.375	+ 19.7	DataDimens	(Nq)	2.6	3.563	– 0.500	– 12.3
RiteAid	(N)	99.2	9.000	+ 1.000	+ 12.5	NETsilicon	(Nq)	2.7	40.000	– 5.313	– 11.7
Appldlmagng	(Nq)	0.1	3.813	+ 0.406	+ 11.9	HumnGenom	(Nq)	23.0	195.875	– 22.188	– 10.2
VtmnShop	(Nq)	5.7	6.250	+ 0.625	+ 11.1	AdacLabs	(Nq)	0.6	10.250	– 1.125	– 9.9
PharmaPrnt	(Nq)	2.9	2.500	+ 0.219	+ 9.6	InternetCap	(Nq)	82.7	108.000	– 11.000	– 9.2
DataTRAK	(Nq)	4.0	6.797	+ 0.547	+ 8.8	NeoThera wt	(Nq)	2.0	6.625	– 0.625	– 8.6
MagainPhrm	(Nq)	14.5	7.000	+ 0.563	+ 8.7	Komag	(Nq)	104.1	2.125	– 0.188	– 8.1
TowneSvc	(Nq)	1.0	2.094	+ 0.156	+ 8.1	ScientCp	(Nq)	2.6	78.000	– 6.500	– 7.7
eToys	(Nq)	174.7	16.375	+ 1.188	+ 7.8	DurbanDeep	(Nq)	30.2	1.500	– 0.125	– 7.7
MethodEl A	(Nq)	10.6	50.000	+ 3.531	+ 7.6	ExtndedSys	(Nq)	3.2	77.000	– 6.000	– 7.2
WalMart	(N)	22.3	47.875	+ 3.375	+ 7.6	IncaraPharm	(Nq)	1.2	3.219	– 0.250	– 7.2
HdwayCpRes	(Nq)	5.0	3.938	+ 0.250	+ 6.8	ImmunResp	(Nq)	17.0	14.438	– 1.063	– 6.9
HycorBio	(Nq)	17.5	4.500	+ 0.250	+ 5.9	WstWater	(Nq)	15.1	1.375	– 0.094	– 6.4
Tcktmstr	(Nq)	18.9	31.000	+ 1.625	+ 5.5	RnmkrSys	(Nq)	1.9	12.313	– 0.813	– 6.2
Nextera A	(Nq)	3.6	9.625	+ 0.500	+ 5.5	Cellegy	(Nq)	0.7	6.688	– 0.438	– 6.1
ValueAm	(Nq)	60.0	3.688	+ 0.188	+ 5.4	IntrlkElctr	(Nq)	38.3	59.000	– 3.813	– 6.1
ConstgEntrp	(Nq)	1.0	20.000	+ 1.000	+ 5.3	ActveSftwr	(Nq)	60.9	88.625	– 5.625	– 6.0

The Late-Trading Snapshot reflects trading activity in NYSE and Amex issues reported by electronic trading services, securities dealers and regional exchanges between 4 p.m.and 6:35 p.m. Eastern time, and in Nasdaq NMS issues between 4 p.m. and 6:30 p.m. The primary market is indicated for each issue. N-NYSE A-Amex Nq-Nasdaq.

Journal Link: For additional data from after-hours stock trading, see The Wall Street Journal Interactive Edition at http://wsj.com on the World Wide Web.

Source: *Republished with permission of Dow Jones from WSJ Market Data Group Year 2000; Permission conveyed through Copyright Clearance Center.*

- **52-Week Hi and Lo**—States the highest and lowest prices paid for each stock over the past 52 weeks, excluding the latest-day's trading activity. The investor will know exactly where the current price falls within this range, and whether or not the stock is overpriced or underpriced in relation to its closing prices over the last year. Many decisions are made each day based on just this one set of numbers.
- **Stock Name & Symbol**—Shows all stocks listed alphabetically by name and the accompanying symbol for each stock. Each stock is assigned a letter symbol to make trading easier on the exchange

floor, and many investors like to learn and follow their favorites—especially if they are watching the electronic ticker board or CNBC television.

- **Dividend**—States the per-share dividend in dollars and cents. The stock's annual cash payout, if any, is based on the rate of the last quarterly payout to shareholders. Those investors who are interested in income will study this column carefully to determine the appropriateness of individual stocks for their particular situation.
- **Yield (percentage)**—Obtained by dividing the cash dividend by the closing price of the stock. This number enables dividend yields to be compared with other stocks of a similar nature and with the interest rates paid on various types of bonds and cash instruments. You will note how yields on common stocks are generally always lower than yields on preferred stocks.
- **Price/earnings ratio**—Used as an indicator of relative stock performance. The P/E ratio is calculated by dividing the latest closing price by the available earnings per share over the last four quarters. A high P/E ratio indicates a stock price that is a high multiple of the company's earnings, and might suggest optimism about the future of the company. A low P/E ratio represents lower investor favor and might suggest pessimism about the future of a company. Reasons for high and low P/Es include the company's growth outlook, the industry in which it is competing, its perceived risk, and the stability of its earnings.
- **Vol 100s (volume)**—Indicates the number of shares that were traded in each stock on the previous trading day. This number is expressed in hundreds (for example, AAR = 959, or 95,900 shares were traded). Stocks that have unusually high trading volumes compared with that stock's average trading volume are underlined. An *n* will also indicate a new issue of stock. High volume also indicates favorable or unfavorable momentum for a stock, depending on its upward or downward movement in price.
- **Hi-Lo-Close-Net Chg**—These columns represent the latest-day's price data—high, low, close, and change from the previous day's closing. Stocks that close up or down more than 5 percent from the previous day's closing price are represented in bold. Investors can get a good sense for trading activity by examining the difference between these numbers. A separate table also lists new highs and lows of both NYSE and NASDAQ stocks. When many issues reach new highs, there tends to be more buying pressure or bullish sentiment in the market. Conversely, when many issues reach new lows, there tends to be more selling pressure or bearish sentiment in various markets.

The Dow Jones Averages

Up until now, the Dow Jones has been the most popular indicator of overall, day-to-day stock market activity. Charles H. Dow, one of the founders of the Dow Jones Company and first editor of *The Wall Street Journal*, is credited with the original 1884 calculation. His intention was to express the general level and trend of the stock market by using the average prices of a few representative stocks.

His first stock average appeared on July 3, 1884, in the *Customer's Afternoon Letter*, a two-page financial news bulletin that had been distributed daily by Dow Jones since November of the previous year. Only 11 stocks were included in the first index, and nine of them were railroad issues (which reflected the importance of this mode of transportation back in those early days).

In 1896, there were two Dow Jones averages. Most important was the Dow Jones Railroad Average, comprised of 20 rail stocks. As more forms of transportation became popular in later years, the *Dow Jones Transportation Average* (DJTA) evolved with a mixture of railroads, airlines, and trucking companies. The second contained 12 stocks that represented other types of businesses and was called the *Dow Jones Industrial Average* (DJIA). This roster was increased to 20 stocks in 1916 and then to 30 stocks on October 1, 1928.

A third average, called the *Dow Jones Utility Average* (DJUA), was established with 20 stocks in 1929 and was later reduced to 15 stocks (as it is today). These three averages—the 30 industrials, the 20 transportation, and the 15 utilities—together comprise the fourth average known as the *65 Dow Jones Composite*. The 65 current stocks used to make up this index appear in Figure 5-4.

You will find it interesting to compare these three indices. Companies used from the DJIA will give a broad mix from American industries, while those of the DJTA and DJUA will focus more on two specific industries. You will also note that most of these companies are considered solid and have been in business for a long time. They have withstood economic recessions and continue to be leaders in their respective industries. Should you be called upon to make recommendations for building a high quality portfolio for the future, a number of these companies would make excellent choices as a foundation for your client's future success.

Trading activity in these indices, as reported in *The Wall Street Journal*, is graphed in Figure 5-5. The figure also reports component volume in each average along with the net change for each stock from the previous-day's trading. Investors studying these graphs will also get a feel for how some leading stocks in major U.S. industries have performed over the past six months.

Note how the DJIA had an excellent fourth quarter in 1999 while the DJTA was virtually flat and the DJUA suffered a decline. This situation means they do not always move together at any particular point in time. This information also proves how important diversification is in structuring a portfolio in order to reduce risk. While it is important to understand why each of these averages performed the way they did during that period, you must stress that investors not make future decisions based solely on past results.

As you can see, a typical daily graph of the Dow Jones averages is fairly self-explanatory. For example, a vertical line or bar is drawn for each day. The top of the line indicates the high of the day, and the bottom indicates the low. The tiny horizontal crossbar represents the closing level

Figure 5-4 *65 Dow Jones Composite prices and weighting as of Nov. 7, 2000 (part 1 of 3).*

Dow Jones Industrial Average

Company Name	Symbol	Price	Weighting(%)
Alcoa Inc.	AA	29.0000	1.567
American Express Co.	AXP	60.9375	3.293
AT&T Corp.	T	22.4375	1.212
Boeing Co.	BA	65.1875	3.523
Catepillar Inc.	CAT	36.1250	1.952
Citigroup, Inc.	C	54.7500	2.959
Coca-Cola Co.	KO	60.0625	3.246
DuPont Co.	DD	43.3125	2.340
Eastman Kodak Co.	EK	47.8750	2.587
Exxon Mobil Corp.	XOM	89.0000	4.810
General Electric Co.	GE	54.9375	2.969
General Motors Co.	GM	57.0000	3.080
Home Depot Inc.	HD	41.3750	2.236
Honeywell International	HON	54.2500	2.932
Hewlett-Packard Co.	HWP	47.4375	2.563
Intl Business Machines	IBM	102.3125	5.529
Intel Corpl	INTC	46.1875	2.496
International Paper Co.	IP	36.8750	1.992
J.P. Morgan & Co.	JPM	163.0625	8.812
Johnson & Johnson	JNJ	92.1250	4.979
McDonald's Corp.	MCD	31.7500	1.715
Merck & Co.	MRK	86.8750	4.695
Microsoft Corp.	MSFT	70.5000	3.810
Minnesota Minning & Manufacturing Co.	MMM	96.9375	5.239
Philip Morris Cos.	MO	35.2500	1.905

Figure 5-4 *Continued.*

Procter & Gamble Co.	**PG**	**68.4375**	**3.698**
SBC Communications	**SBC**	**57.0625**	**3.084**
United Technologies Co.	**UTX**	**68.0625**	**3.678**
Wal-Mart Stores, Inc.	**WMT**	**48.9375**	**2.644**
Walt Disney Co.	**DIS**	**37.1250**	**2.006**

Dow Jones Transportation Average

Airborne Freight Corp.	**ABF**	**10.0000**	**1.727**
Alexander & Baldwin, Inc.	**ALEX**	**25.8125**	**4.459**
AMR Corp.	**AMR**	**32.8750**	**5.680**
Burlington Northern Santa Fe Corp.	**BNI**	**26.4375**	**4.567**
CNF Transportation Inc.	**CNF**	**28.0000**	**4.837**
CSX Corp.	**CSX**	**26.1875**	**4.524**
Delta Air Lines, Inc.	**DAL**	**46.5000**	**8.034**
Federal Express Corp.	**FDX**	**46.0299**	**7.952**
GATX Corp.	**GMT**	**44.8750**	**7.753**
J.B. Hunt Transportation Services	**JBHT**	**12.7500**	**2.202**
Norfolk Southern Corp.	**NSC**	**14.9375**	**2.580**
Northwest Airlines Corp.	**NWAC**	**28.5000**	**4.924**
Roadway Express, Inc.	**ROAD**	**21.4375**	**3.703**
Ryder System, Inc.	**R**	**18.7500**	**3.239**
Southwest Airlines Co.	**LUV**	**29.1875**	**5.042**
UAL Corp.	**UAL**	**37.5625**	**6.489**
Union Pacific Corp.	**UNP**	**48.1250**	**8.314**
US Airways Group, Inc.	**U**	**37.3125**	**6.446**

Figure 5-4 *Continued.*

US Freightways	**USFC**	**25.6250**	**4.427**
Yellow Corp.	**YELL**	**17.8750**	**3.088**
	Dow Jones Utility Average		
AES Corp.	**AES**	**64.1875**	**9.413**
American Electric Power	**AEP**	**40.9375**	**6.003**
Consolidated Edison Inc.	**ED**	**34.5625**	**5.068**
Dominion Resources Inc.	**D**	**58.0625**	**8.515**
Duke Energy Corp.	**DUK**	**85.2500**	**12.500**
Edison International	**EIX**	**22.6875**	**3.327**
Enron Corp.	**ENE**	**81.8125**	**11.990**
Exelon Corp.	**EXC**	**56.4375**	**8.276**
NiSource Inc.	**NI**	**24.6250**	**3.611**
PG&E Corp.	**PCG**	**26.5625**	**3.895**
Public Service Enterprise	**PEG**	**39.4375**	**5.783**
Reliant Energy	**REI**	**39.1875**	**5.747**
Southern Co.	**SO**	**28.6875**	**4.207**
Texas Utilities Co.	**TXU**	**36.5000**	**5.352**
Williams Co.	**WMB**	**42.9375**	**6.296**

of that trading day. The greater the distance between the top and bottom of each line, the more volatile that average experienced for that particular trading day.

Over the years, the widely followed DJIA has changed considerably with many substitutions. Fewer than 20 of the original 30 stocks in 1928 remain, and only General Electric (of the present industrial average) was included in Dow's initial computation. Expanding its reporting services over the years, Dow Jones now calculates thousands of indices around the world.

Computation of the Dow Jones Averages

In the beginning, computing the average was relatively simple. If there were 12 stocks, the prices were added together and divided by 12. Over

Figure 5-5 *65 Dow Jones Composit Trading activity.*

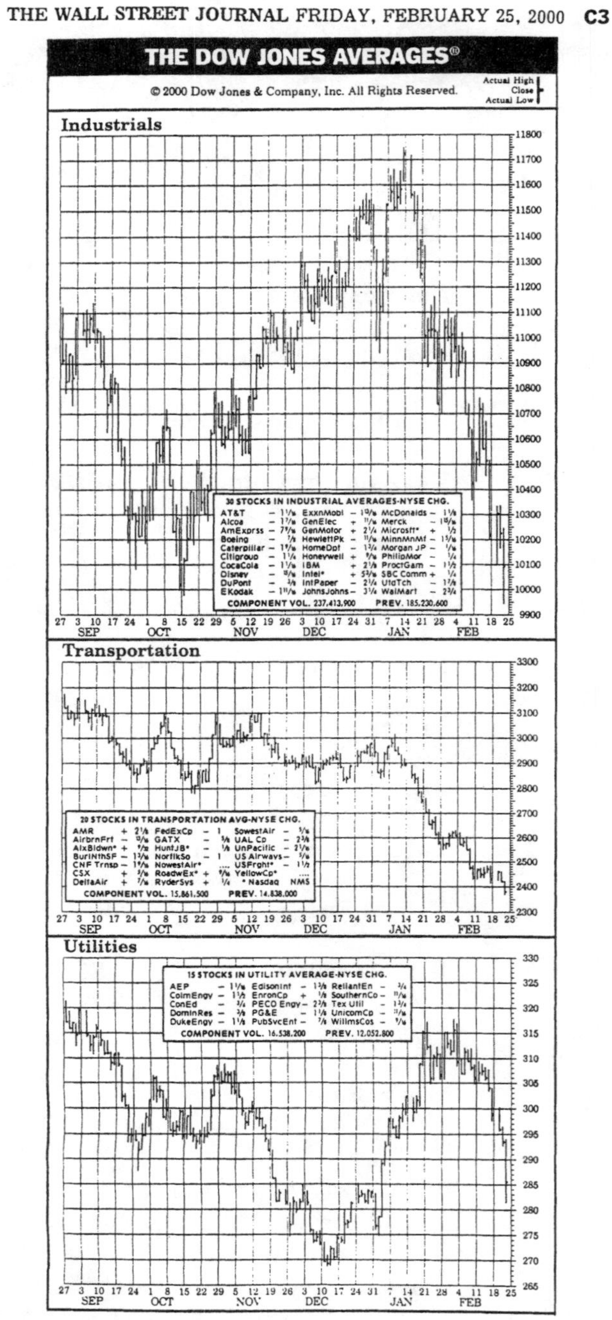

Source: *Republished with permission of Dow Jones from WSJ Market Data Group Year 2000; Permission conveyed through Copyright Clearance Center.*

time, the divisor had to be changed in order to reflect adjustments for *stock splits.* This situation takes place when the market price of a stock advances to where it is perceived that the stock is losing appeal for investors. The company's board of directors will often vote to split the stock and formally declare a stock split. For example, a two-for-one split results in issuing one new share for each share that is currently outstanding. In other words, on the effective date, each share of stock is now worth only half of the original market price.

If the new stock price was simply substituted for the old one, these stock splits would produce many distortions. Let's assume that three stocks are selling at $40, $60, and $80, respectively. This makes the average price of these three stocks $60. Now, let's assume that the $80 stock splits two for one, which will make the new shares sell for $40. The new average price of these three stocks is now $46.67, which is a distortion in comparison to the previous average.

Therefore, an adjustment must be made in order to compensate (so that the average will remain at $60). To perform this task, we must change the divisor or the number divided into the total of the stock prices. In this case, the new divisor is 2.33, rather than 3. Thus, this new figure would be used in any subsequent computations of the average.

Since its invention, the divisor has been changed numerous times (mostly downward). This information explains why the DJIA can be reported as 10,000 while no single stock in the average is even close to that price. This method also explains the wide movements of the average in comparison to the general level of stock prices. From this perspective, we should think of the DJIA as more of an index or indicator.

In recent years, public interest in the stock market has exploded. As a result, a variety of price-trend indicators are now available from other sources. These indicators include Standard & Poor's, Inc. and the NYSE itself. Because each index is useful to investors in a variety of ways, no single index tells the market's entire story on a particular trading day. Because of its history and familiarity, however, the Dow still ranks as the most widely used indicator of stock market action (at least, with older investors). The NASDAQ has also become more popular with younger investors, because it represents many technology stocks and newer companies that have tremendous growth potential in the new economy.

Selection of the Dow Stocks

The structure of the Dow is aimed at tracking underlying market trends over a period of time from a number of major industries. It is easy to misunderstand why only 30 stocks are used when trying to gauge a market that is composed of thousands of common stock issues. Other market indices contain more issues than the Dow, but they react more to fluctuations in lower-priced stocks. For example, changes in investor sentiment or unusually heavy trading volume in certain industries can cause these indicators to change sharply.

The reason why the Dow is so respected today is because its 30 component companies represent broad market activity throughout American industry. These stocks are widely held by individuals, institutional investors, and many pension funds. In fact, by the end of the third quarter of 1997, these 30 stocks represented about 19 percent of the 9.5 trillion plus market of all stocks in the United States.

Changes in the components are made entirely by the editors of *The Wall Street Journal*, independently of each listed company. Most substitutions are made as a result of mergers, such as the Exxon Mobil Corporation (formally listed as Exxon). From time to time, however, changes are also made in order to achieve better representation. For example, the recent additions of the Intel Corporation, the Microsoft Corporation, and SBC Communications, Inc. were warranted due to the rapidly growing trends of a more technologically oriented U.S. economy.

The dynamic changes in the high-technology and telecommunications industries have also increased the demand for stocks traded on the NASDAQ. As a result, this index is now quoted daily by the news media (along with the DJIA) in order to cover much broader activity in U.S. markets. The emergence and development of Internet companies and information technology will continue to change our economy from an industrialized nation into a nation of rapid communications growth, where greater efficiency should help us lead the rest of the world into the 21st century.

Foreign Equities

In recent years, individual investors have been attracted by generous returns and the excitement of owning shares in foreign securities. These equities consist of companies that are incorporated and listed on overseas stock exchanges that generally are not subsidiaries of U.S. corporations. For example, there are stock exchanges in London, Paris, Tokyo, and other foreign financial centers. These securities can be purchased through U.S. brokers who have access to trading on these exchanges.

However, the easiest way to buy foreign stocks is to purchase the shares of firms that are already traded on U.S. exchanges or through U.S. OTC markets. To be eligible for trading, foreign securities must be registered and comply with various regulations of the SEC.

Figure 5-6 shows some foreign firms whose shares are traded in the United States. This figure gives the company, its symbol, the country of origin, its primary industry, and where the shares are actually traded. For example, stocks of large foreign corporations such as Telefonos de Mex L, Sony, Nortel Networks, and KLM Royal Dutch Airlines are traded on the NYSE. Others such as Japan Airlines, Volkswagenwerk, and Wal-Mart de Mexico trade on the NASDAQ.

Our domestic markets do not actually trade in foreign shares; instead, they trade receipts for each stock issue (called an *American depository receipt* [ADR]). There are two types of ADRs. Sponsored ADRs are created when a foreign company wants its shares to trade in the United States. The company employs a bank to create the ADRs and to act as a transfer agent. Unsponsored ADRs come into existence when a brokerage firm

Figure 5-6 *Examples of foreign firms whose shares are traded in the United States.*

Selected Foreign Securities Traded on Various Exchanges

Firm	Symbol	Country	Industry	Traded
Hatachi, Ltd.	HIT	Japan	Electronics	NYSE
Imperial Group	ITY	Britain	Tobacco	NYSE
Japan Airlines	JAPNY	Japan	Airline	NASDAQ
KLM Royal Dutch Air	KLM	Netherlands	Airline	NYSE
Nortel Networks	NT	Canada	Telephone	NYSE
SONY	SNE	Japan	Electronics	NYSE
Telefonus do Mex L	TMX	Mexico	Telecom	NYSE
Volkswagenwerk	VLKAY	Germany	Automobiles	NASDAQ
Wal-Mart de Mexico	WMMVY	Mexico	Retailer	NASDAQ

believes that there will be sufficient interest to make a market in a foreign stock. The firm will buy a block of securities and hire a commercial bank to create the ADRs and then act as a transfer agent.

The creation of ADRs simplifies the trading in foreign securities for U.S. investors and offers some benefits. First, ADRs reduce the risk of fraud. For example, if an investor bought a foreign stock issued by a German company, the stock certificate would be drafted in German. Because the U.S. investor probably cannot read German, he or she could become a victim to a phony certificate. The issuance of ADRs solves this problem, because the certificates are always printed in English. Thus, the issuing agent certifies the authenticity of the certificate. Remember that the ADR represents only the underlying securities held by the agent, and the ADR is not an obligation of the firm that issued the stock.

Second, ADRs are convenient. In other words, securities do not have to be delivered by international mail; rather, their prices are quoted in dollars. Any dividend payments are also delivered in dollars. Furthermore, the ADR can represent any number of foreign shares. For example, a Japanese stock that trades for a low price of $2 per share would be considered a penny stock in the United States. To make the price comparable to U.S. securities, an ADR can represent 10 Japanese shares that would translate to a price of $20.

Sometimes there are no ADRs issued for the stock that an American investor wishes to purchase. In that case, the actual foreign securities will have to be ordered. The stock would be purchased in the appropriate foreign market, and the shares would be acquired through exchanges or OTC from dealers who make a market in that security. After settlement of the completed purchase, an investor can either leave the securities registered with the broker or take full delivery of the certificate.

The prices of a number of foreign stocks are given daily in *The Wall Street Journal*. Figure 5-7 illustrates closing prices and the net change for a particular trading day. Also note that there is no reporting the volume of transactions, P/E ratios, or dividends. Because this is only a small sampling, investors who wish to track more of these stocks will require access to foreign publications such as the *Financial Times*, a British newspaper that is similar in structure to *The Wall Street Journal*.

Figure 5-7 also shows the activity in the major foreign stock-market indices. This figure shows the net and percentage change from the previous trading day and the *year-to-date* (YTD) net and percentage changes. A study of these markets shows that a number of them were up at the time of printing while the major U.S. markets were down. For a U.S. investor who had not previously thought about single country risk, this action might warrant serious consideration for buying foreign securities in order to diversify a portfolio made up entirely of U.S. stocks.

The Dow Jones Global Indexes from *The Wall Street Journal* are illustrated in Figure 5-8. First, nearly 3,000 companies from 16 countries and 120 industry groups go into an extensive foreign listing. The groupings divide these stocks into nine sectors that reflect large segments of the world economy. Countries are constantly being added to the index as the global economy grows and changes. Over time, the listing will include every country whose stocks are available to foreign investors.

As U.S. investor interest continues to grow in these global markets, this index will give them a feel for stock-performance activity in foreign countries. This index also provides investors with a more geographical perspective. When studying individual securities, they can also measure performance against their peers on a global, regional, or national basis.

Finally, the Dow Jones Global Industry Groups are illustrated in Figure 5-9. This table shows the relative performance of broad economic sectors from the United States, the Americas, Europe, Asia and the Pacific, and the entire world. The activity reflects the previous trading day and any percentage changes for the YTD. Consider the wealth of information from this table alone. An investor who wishes to place money into an industry within a specific region of the world will know immediately whether or not this action would be warranted.

While investors hear about political events that take place in foreign countries from our daily news services, it is much harder to obtain information concerning economic and financial forces that affect global markets. For this reason, many investors find it more convenient to purchase shares of mutual funds that specialize in foreign investing. Professional money managers who watch over this area will select the stocks or bonds to make up the portfolios. In Chapter 8, "Diversifying with Mutual Funds," we will focus on the advantages of this strategy for investors who wish to diversify their portfolios internationally.

Figure 5-7 *Prices of foreign stock, closing prices, and the net change for a particular trading day.*

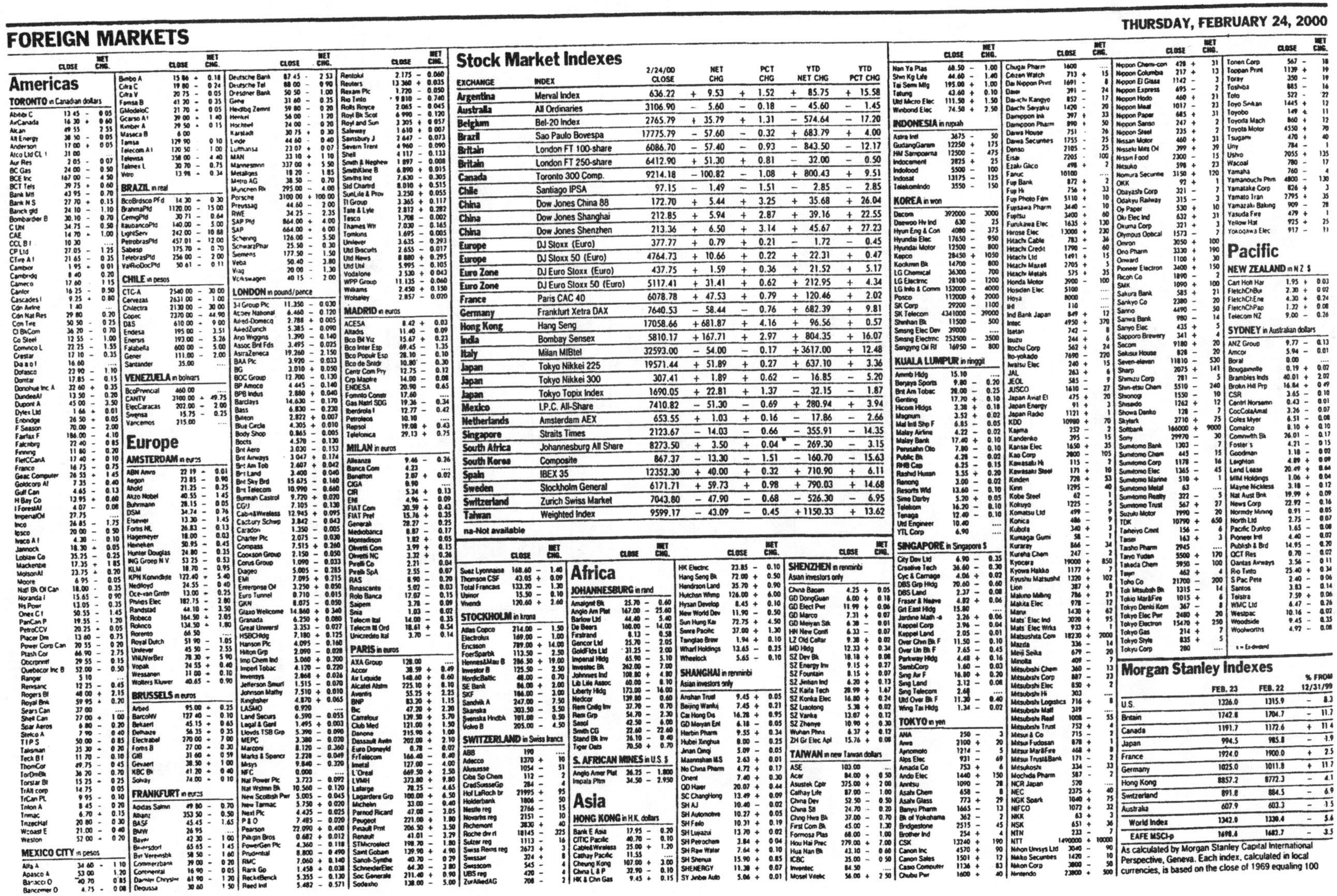

FOREIGN MARKETS

THURSDAY, FEBRUARY 24, 2000

Stock Market Indexes

EXCHANGE	INDEX	2/24/00 CLOSE	NET CHG	PCT CHG	YTD NET CHG	YTD PCT CHG
Argentina	Merval Index	636.22	+ 9.53	+ 1.52	+ 85.75	+ 15.58
Australia	All Ordinaries	3106.90	– 5.60	– 0.18	– 45.60	– 1.45
Belgium	Bel-20 Index	2765.79	+ 35.79	+ 1.31	– 574.64	– 17.20
Brazil	Sao Paulo Bovespa	17775.79	– 57.60	– 0.32	+ 683.79	+ 4.00
Britain	London FT 100-share	6086.70	– 57.40	– 0.93	– 843.50	– 12.17
Britain	London FT 250-share	6412.90	+ 51.30	+ 0.81	– 32.00	– 0.50
Canada	Toronto 300 Comp.	9214.18	– 100.82	– 1.08	+ 800.43	+ 9.51
Chile	Santiago IPSA	97.15	– 1.49	– 1.51	– 2.85	– 2.85
China	Dow Jones China 88	172.70	+ 5.44	+ 3.25	+ 35.68	+ 26.04
China	Dow Jones Shanghai	212.85	+ 5.94	+ 2.87	+ 39.16	+ 22.55
China	Dow Jones Shenzhen	213.36	+ 6.50	+ 3.14	+ 45.67	+ 27.23
Europe	DJ Stoxx (Euro)	377.77	+ 0.79	+ 0.21	– 1.72	– 0.45
Europe	DJ Stoxx 50 (Euro)	4764.73	+ 10.66	+ 0.22	+ 22.31	+ 0.47
Euro Zone	DJ Euro Stoxx (Euro)	437.75	+ 1.59	+ 0.36	+ 21.52	+ 5.17
Euro Zone	DJ Euro Stoxx 50 (Euro)	5117.41	+ 31.41	+ 0.62	+ 212.95	+ 4.34
France	Paris CAC 40	6078.78	+ 47.53	+ 0.79	+ 120.46	+ 2.02
Germany	Frankfurt Xetra DAX	7640.53	– 58.44	– 0.76	+ 682.39	+ 9.81
Hong Kong	Hang Seng	17058.66	+ 681.87	+ 4.16	+ 96.56	+ 0.57
India	Bombay Sensex	5810.17	+ 167.71	+ 2.97	+ 804.35	+ 16.07
Italy	Milan MIBtel	32593.00	– 54.00	– 0.17	+ 3617.00	+ 12.48
Japan	Tokyo Nikkei 225	19571.44	+ 51.89	+ 0.27	+ 637.10	+ 3.36
Japan	Tokyo Nikkei 300	307.41	+ 1.89	+ 0.62	– 16.85	– 5.20
Japan	Tokyo Topix Index	1690.05	+ 22.81	+ 1.37	– 32.15	– 1.87
Mexico	I.P.C. All-Share	7410.82	– 51.30	– 0.69	+ 280.94	+ 3.94
Netherlands	Amsterdam AEX	653.55	+ 1.03	+ 0.16	– 17.86	– 2.66
Singapore	Straits Times	2123.67	– 14.03	– 0.66	– 355.91	– 14.35
South Africa	Johannesburg All Share	8273.50	+ 3.50	+ 0.04	– 269.30	– 3.15
South Korea	Composite	867.37	– 13.30	– 1.51	– 160.70	– 15.63
Spain	IBEX 35	12352.30	+ 40.00	+ 0.32	+ 710.90	+ 6.11
Sweden	Stockholm General	6171.71	+ 59.73	+ 0.98	+ 790.03	+ 14.68
Switzerland	Zurich Swiss Market	7043.80	– 47.90	– 0.68	– 526.30	– 6.95
Taiwan	Weighted Index	9599.17	– 43.09	– 0.45	+ 1150.33	+ 13.62

na-Not available

Morgan Stanley Indexes

	FEB. 23	FEB. 22	% FROM 12/31/99
U.S.	1326.0	1315.9	– 8.3
Britain	1742.8	1704.7	– 11.7
Canada	1191.7	1172.6	+ 11.4
Japan	994.5	985.8	– 1.9
France	1924.0	1900.0	+ 2.5
Germany	1025.0	1011.8	+ 11.7
Hong Kong	8857.2	8772.3	– 4.1
Switzerland	891.8	884.5	– 6.9
Australia	607.9	603.3	– 1.5
World Index	1342.0	1330.4	– 5.6
EAFE MSCI-p	1698.6	1682.7	– 3.5

As calculated by Morgan Stanley Capital International Perspective, Geneva. Each index, calculated in local currencies, is based on the close of 1969 equaling 100

x = Ex-dividend

Source: *Republished with permission of Dow Jones from WSJ Market Data Group Year 2000; Permission conveyed through Copyright Clearance Center.*

Figure 5-8 *The Dow Jones Global Indexes from* The Wall Street Journal.

5:30 p.m., Thursday, February 24, 2000

REGION/ COUNTRY	DJ GLOBAL INDEXES, LOCAL CURRENCY	PCT. CHG.	IN U.S. DOLLARS: 5:30 P.M. INDEX	CHG.	PCT. CHG.	12-MO HIGH	12-MO LOW	12-MO CHG.	PCT. CHG.	FROM 12/31	PCT. CHG.
Americas			**319.85**	**− 1.21**	**− 0.38**	**341.34**	**281.95**	**+ 33.72**	**+ 11.79**	**−21.49**	**− 6.30**
Brazil†	1633	− 0.39	353.76	0.00	0.00	380.32	162.04	+188.97	+114.68	− 6.50	− 1.80
Canada	279.07	− 1.79	221.67	− 3.29	− 1.46	231.50	142.36	+ 74.62	+ 50.74	+14.49	+ 6.99
Chile	237.31	− 1.13	175.36	− 1.94	− 1.09	196.18	130.95	+ 40.17	+ 29.71	+ 2.00	+ 1.15
Mexico	551.11	− 0.83	180.32	− 1.61	− 0.88	188.87	94.23	+ 82.56	+ 84.45	+10.03	+ 5.89
U.S.	329.88	− 0.32	329.88	− 1.06	− 0.32	354.84	297.09	+ 28.49	+ 9.45	−24.97	− 7.04
Venezuela	386.14	+ 0.24	36.05	+ 0.04	+ 0.11	47.83	29.12	+ 5.71	+ 18.82	+ 1.39	+ 4.00
Latin America			**208.15**	**− 1.19**	**− 0.57**	**220.92**	**112.57**	**+ 92.79**	**+ 80.43**	**+ 4.03**	**+ 1.98**
Europe/Africa			**269.25**	**− 2.06**	**− 0.76**	**278.76**	**223.65**	**+ 38.15**	**+ 16.51**	**− 6.14**	**− 2.23**
Austria	110.62	− 1.06	85.29	− 1.82	− 2.09	113.74	82.40	− 18.89	− 18.13	−12.69	−12.95
Belgium	249.34	+ 1.32	192.40	+ 0.50	+ 0.26	271.50	189.31	− 79.10	− 29.14	−44.92	−18.93
Denmark	258.16	− 0.60	203.74	− 3.42	− 1.65	207.16	156.84	+ 32.52	+ 18.99	+ 3.38	+ 1.69
Finland	2391.28	+ 3.03	1654.39	+31.74	+ 1.96	1695.71	621.01	+1010.6	+156.99	+124.12	+ 8.11
France	366.29	+ 0.87	287.23	− 0.53	− 0.18	296.11	209.30	+ 68.01	+ 31.03	+ 1.23	+ 0.43
Germany	424.04	− 0.66	326.15	− 5.65	− 1.70	331.80	223.12	+ 89.15	+ 37.61	+26.37	+ 8.80
Greece	812.41	+ 3.86	423.83	+11.17	+ 2.71	513.15	302.06	+ 77.39	+ 22.34	− 9.65	− 2.23
Ireland	364.44	+ 0.62	270.62	− 1.18	− 0.43	347.59	256.12	− 70.88	− 20.76	−15.21	− 5.32
Italy	439.72	+ 0.13	278.16	− 2.58	− 0.92	280.74	193.78	+ 56.89	+ 25.71	+28.61	+11.46
Netherlands	460.45	+ 0.01	354.19	− 3.70	− 1.03	378.35	304.78	+ 35.48	+ 11.13	−16.21	− 4.38
Norway	204.11	− 0.03	148.84	− 0.91	− 0.61	160.33	115.78	+ 32.02	+ 27.41	− 5.95	− 3.84
Portugal	455.56	+ 0.35	304.92	− 2.16	− 0.70	307.08	229.73	+ 18.68	+ 6.53	+28.40	+10.27
South Africa	259.53	− 0.01	112.34	− 0.18	− 0.16	129.31	74.49	+ 37.37	+ 49.83	− 3.63	− 3.13
Spain	496.50	+ 0.26	287.68	− 2.27	− 0.78	289.95	231.54	+ 27.65	+ 10.63	+ 4.82	+ 1.70
Sweden	788.60	+ 1.41	509.10	+ 4.59	+ 0.91	509.10	252.37	+243.58	+ 91.74	+76.39	+17.65
Switzerland	403.01	− 0.65	337.57	− 5.20	− 1.52	385.50	324.56	− 39.92	− 10.58	−31.82	− 8.61
United Kingdom	229.18	− 0.94	196.24	− 2.33	− 1.17	228.42	192.82	− 5.57	− 2.76	−29.74	−13.16
Europe/Africa (ex. South Africa)			**278.36**	**− 2.16**	**− 0.77**	**288.20**	**232.06**	**+ 38.34**	**+ 15.98**	**− 6.32**	**− 2.22**
Europe/Africa (ex. U.K. & S. Africa)			**330.01**	**− 2.01**	**− 0.61**	**332.02**	**253.28**	**+ 66.04**	**+ 25.02**	**+ 8.42**	**+ 2.62**
Asia/Pacific			**118.91**	**+ 1.07**	**+ 0.91**	**132.88**	**77.12**	**+ 39.31**	**+ 49.38**	**−12.63**	**− 9.60**
Australia	194.42	− 0.14	157.12	− 2.01	− 1.26	174.04	145.50	+ 7.05	+ 4.70	−12.84	− 7.56
Hong Kong	378.25	+ 4.35	378.01	+15.74	+ 4.34	392.24	192.05	+185.96	+ 96.83	+24.58	+ 6.95
Indonesia	203.22	− 1.90	53.76	− 2.00	− 3.59	82.35	32.70	+ 17.21	+ 47.08	−17.96	−25.04
Japan	96.79	+ 1.34	108.58	+ 1.22	+ 1.14	125.05	69.36	+ 35.71	+ 49.01	−15.53	−12.51
Malaysia	194.69	+ 0.21	139.42	+ 0.29	+ 0.21	140.29	65.65	+ 65.85	+ 89.51	+27.65	+24.74
New Zealand	135.99	− 0.81	122.36	− 1.58	− 1.27	158.16	119.44	− 17.38	− 12.44	−19.03	−13.46
Philippines	171.59	− 1.48	109.24	− 2.19	− 1.97	175.79	108.86	− 12.18	− 10.03	−21.35	−16.35
Singapore	146.06	− 0.92	137.97	− 1.57	− 1.13	177.91	100.93	+ 36.50	+ 35.96	−32.58	−19.10
South Korea	156.97	− 2.11	104.12	− 2.99	− 2.79	134.76	52.62	+ 51.50	+ 97.86	−24.85	−19.27
Taiwan	238.08	− 0.24	199.88	− 0.80	− 0.40	212.80	118.51	+ 80.34	+ 67.22	+24.43	+13.92
Thailand	73.66	+ 2.09	45.56	+ 0.86	+ 1.92	59.51	36.03	+ 9.53	+ 26.46	−10.02	−18.03
Asia/Pacific (ex. Japan)			**187.73**	**+ 0.65**	**+ 0.35**	**199.46**	**125.01**	**+ 62.73**	**+ 50.18**	**− 4.14**	**− 2.16**
World (ex. U.S.)			**185.12**	**− 0.37**	**− 0.20**	**195.54**	**140.09**	**+ 40.68**	**+ 28.16**	**− 8.53**	**− 4.40**
DJ WORLD STOCK INDEX			**239.35**	**− 0.62**	**− 0.26**	**254.04**	**197.91**	**+ 37.19**	**+ 18.40**	**−14.43**	**− 5.68**

Indexes based on 12/31/91=100.
†Local currency index shown in 000s.

Source: *Republished with permission of Dow Jones from WSJ Market Data Group Year 2000; Permission conveyed through Copyright Clearance Center.*

Markets Diary

For investors who do not have the time to thoroughly read all of the information in *The Wall Street Journal*, they can quickly obtain results from the previous-day's market activity by glancing at the Markets Diary section in the top left-hand corner of Section C of *The Wall Street Journal*.

Figure 5-9A *The Dow Jones Global Industry Groups (part 1 of 2).*

Industry Group Performance

U.S.			WORLD		AMERICAS		EUROPE		ASIA/PACIFIC	
6:30 P.M. 02/24/2000	% CHG. YTD		5:30 P.M. 02/24/2000	% CHG. YTD	5:30 P.M. 02/24/2000	% CHG. YTD	5:30 P.M. 02/24/2000	% CHG. YTD	5:30 P.M. 02/24/2000	% CHG. YTD
149.17	– 20.30	**Basic Materials**	129.75	– 15.58	155.62	– 18.54	188.88	– 17.96	76.38	– 8.05
160.98	– 18.68	**Chemicals**	174.36	– 12.38	188.94	– 19.01	205.68	– 12.53	107.82	+ 0.42
196.35	– 20.28	Chem-commodity	209.76	– 12.15	222.41	– 20.10	261.60	– 12.23	127.23	+ 1.93
125.69	– 15.60	Chem-specialty	123.04	– 12.81	139.98	– 16.58	136.73	– 12.90	71.80	– 3.93
141.60	– 25.87	**Forest products & paper**	115.14	– 21.20	143.80	– 22.03	126.22	– 26.70	60.79	– 7.33
162.46	– 28.24	Forest products	127.79	– 23.73	151.92	– 25.33	0.00	0.00	61.42	– 13.67
152.41	– 24.10	Paper products	111.46	– 20.25	138.12	– 19.81	124.79	– 26.70	61.43	– 5.04
129.17	– 18.29	**Mining & Metals**	96.70	– 17.11	119.94	– 15.18	180.73	– 23.36	61.10	– 16.22
288.99	– 16.32	Aluminum	218.93	– 16.08	281.18	– 16.18	331.27	– 14.30	47.86	– 18.11
205.55	+ 8.42	Mining, diversified	135.35	– 25.15	112.77	– 6.68	208.72	– 30.10	112.85	– 28.33
115.38	– 26.72	Non-Ferrous (ex Alum)	82.22	– 14.48	87.71	– 19.80	84.90	– 16.55	70.88	– 2.16
48.64	– 7.52	Precious metals	87.97	– 8.79	77.16	– 10.00	257.71	+ 7.64	39.90	– 14.68
89.36	– 24.42	Steel	71.96	– 16.96	103.14	– 19.33	148.44	– 20.61	55.65	– 14.01
285.91	– 16.37	**Consumer, Cyclical**	225.97	– 9.66	296.11	– 15.24	222.10	– 1.33	161.10	– 6.07
495.79	– 12.20	**Advertising & Media**	475.74	+ 9.78	461.56	– 9.14	505.10	+ 38.60	473.10	+ 30.03
652.83	– 20.33	Advertising	792.98	– 13.60	649.82	– 21.05	1371.69	+ 14.69	0.00	0.00
800.66	– 7.18	Broadcasting	663.34	+ 11.53	683.65	– 5.00	668.18	+ 48.17	733.83	+ 28.98
231.65	– 20.71	Publishing	321.72	+ 13.71	240.89	– 13.44	350.24	+ 31.35	444.14	+ 33.93
318.39	– 11.08	**Auto mfg & parts**	208.81	– 11.97	296.79	– 10.39	165.87	– 16.49	193.31	– 10.27
423.28	– 10.66	Auto manufacturers	248.11	– 12.89	429.16	– 10.66	162.93	– 16.40	235.02	– 11.72
189.45	– 11.31	Auto parts	118.11	– 10.32	139.67	– 8.33	197.30	– 24.36	98.96	– 9.70
68.38	– 16.46	Tires & Rubber	149.13	– 4.29	71.39	– 19.91	173.93	– 12.37	176.79	+ 3.77
279.37	– 5.10	**Entertainment**	243.78	– 2.18	324.04	– 3.16	131.93	+ 1.22	228.15	– 1.83
150.18	– 16.82	Casinos	136.57	– 2.06	196.45	– 17.98	131.45	+ 4.26	84.52	+ 13.80
132.32	+ 8.46	Consumer electronics	291.91	– 9.79	0.00	0.00	96.90	+ 0.41	297.16	– 9.81
532.97	+ 8.98	Entertainment	588.96	+ 16.52	565.41	+ 12.69	301.73	+ 47.61	582.24	+ 32.29
245.78	– 7.62	Recreation products	175.64	– 3.69	260.55	– 7.28	48.41	– 19.22	134.63	+ 18.55
205.99	– 21.03	Restaurants	203.29	– 16.87	218.05	– 22.02	126.86	– 8.19	95.15	– 1.76
147.61	– 12.07	Toys	142.23	+ 13.21	142.97	– 11.95	0.00	0.00	161.65	+ 26.10
139.18	– 23.43	**Home const & furn**	94.02	– 20.57	137.88	– 23.51	135.91	– 20.82	80.49	– 16.25
145.80	– 26.11	Furnishings	112.61	– 21.48	140.41	– 25.88	176.71	– 17.64	76.40	– 13.11
116.89	– 14.25	Home construction	80.89	– 19.23	132.06	– 16.37	80.12	– 27.48	75.05	– 17.80
262.37	– 23.90	**Retailers**	198.98	– 22.81	262.84	– 23.63	205.16	– 20.66	85.52	– 27.24
227.12	– 16.44	Retailers,apparel	259.57	– 12.62	265.90	– 14.17	845.84	– 6.83	66.06	– 25.01
250.92	– 32.58	Retailers,broadline	177.18	– 29.32	240.15	– 31.23	172.09	– 24.95	84.79	– 27.91
253.19	– 11.22	Retailers,drug-based	244.85	– 12.67	380.73	– 10.85	86.65	– 23.45	0.00	0.00
312.68	– 18.17	Retailers,specialty	249.29	– 17.73	328.85	– 18.46	146.41	– 18.99	53.26	– 11.48
75.90	– 25.55	**Textile & Apparel**	106.34	– 14.62	77.61	– 29.87	232.22	– 12.26	54.67	– 6.93
71.01	– 13.77	Clothing/Fabrics	108.47	– 10.72	65.91	– 15.28	257.36	– 11.32	55.28	– 7.21
81.76	– 38.44	Footwear	82.08	– 39.79	91.12	– 44.11	45.00	– 34.92	37.32	– 0.54
163.71	– 14.65	**Travel**	128.65	– 14.69	209.42	– 14.57	126.00	– 15.10	64.03	– 14.63
161.29	– 13.95	Airlines	125.24	– 13.20	170.40	– 12.72	141.18	– 13.42	69.45	– 13.52
194.56	– 16.66	Lodging	123.47	– 18.94	239.03	– 16.74	144.42	– 20.59	51.23	– 19.01
206.16	– 15.73	**Consumer, Non-Cycl**	172.62	– 15.81	202.10	– 16.39	159.91	– 11.82	126.20	– 20.60
919.90	– 15.94	**Consumer services**	434.04	– 18.91	477.36	– 18.72	92.88	– 14.83	167.11	– 8.76
197.86	– 12.16	**Cosmetics**	264.32	– 14.01	208.71	– 12.32	484.09	– 15.73	188.57	– 14.39
158.02	– 14.28	**Food retailers**	229.36	– 23.25	175.43	– 12.95	203.17	– 18.32	334.39	– 32.21
167.46	– 14.41	**Food & Beverage**	134.75	– 11.36	164.65	– 14.46	140.25	– 8.84	71.23	– 5.03
0.00	0.00	Agriculture	177.93	+ 2.83	0.00	0.00	0.00	0.00	177.93	+ 2.83
190.02	– 16.92	Distillers & Brewers	114.24	– 8.66	167.84	– 17.08	112.20	– 6.37	89.92	– 2.32
112.37	– 18.88	Food	117.33	– 13.16	113.07	– 19.74	154.22	– 9.89	63.06	– 4.98
242.59	– 10.25	Soft drinks	228.19	– 10.35	242.45	– 9.98	382.03	– 11.18	58.53	– 22.34
256.27	– 20.37	**Household products**	259.91	– 19.79	294.70	– 20.35	74.21	– 5.26	39.81	– 16.91
73.63	– 21.74	Durable	75.24	– 20.86	92.89	– 21.13	0.00	0.00	29.89	– 18.75
294.55	– 20.24	Non-durable	306.99	– 19.73	336.34	– 20.30	74.21	– 5.26	63.48	– 15.15
67.24	– 13.91	**Tobacco**	100.00	– 11.79	87.51	– 9.91	140.92	– 13.81	119.34	– 13.22
202.71	– 7.74	**Energy**	188.58	– 13.53	204.06	– 8.66	210.02	– 18.27	42.79	– 20.50
33.13	– 23.72	**Coal**	49.69	– 3.49	61.34	+ 9.36	0.00	0.00	22.57	– 19.10
203.08	– 7.73	**Oil & Gas**	189.99	– 13.54	204.91	– 8.68	210.02	– 18.27	43.62	– 20.53
211.88	– 13.11	Oil cos, major	216.34	– 16.06	208.70	– 13.19	223.10	– 18.17	0.00	0.00
97.46	– 13.61	Oil cos, secondary	108.02	– 13.40	130.60	– 10.65	129.14	– 13.75	43.91	– 20.55
322.91	+ 5.58	Oil drilling	332.23	+ 5.59	457.75	+ 5.62	68.42	+ 5.03	0.00	0.00
222.21	+ 11.12	Oilfield equip/svcs	209.06	+ 9.50	216.60	+ 10.51	174.08	– 1.46	78.70	– 19.53
371.74	+ 16.64	Pipelines	286.85	– 5.66	300.06	+ 7.78	113.47	– 25.58	0.00	0.00
300.09	– 15.36	**Financial**	173.35	– 13.22	305.30	– 15.27	241.25	– 12.24	75.51	– 11.36

Source: *Republished with permission of Dow Jones from WSJ Market Data Group Year 2000; Permission conveyed through Copyright Clearance Center.*

Just as the daily business section of any local newspaper would give market results from the previous day, this section shows activity from five indices and major international exchanges.

Figure 5-10 shows this information from February 24, 2000. Listed major indexes include the DJIA, DJUS Total Markets, S&P 500, NASDAQ, and Russell 2000. Included are the closing averages, net changes for the

Figure 5-9B *Continued.*

242.59 − 10.25	Soft drinks	228.19 − 10.35	242.45 − 9.98	352.03 − 11.18	58.53 − 22.34
256.27 − 20.37	**Household products**	259.91 − 19.79	294.70 − 20.35	74.21 − 5.26	39.81 − 16.91
73.63 − 21.74	Durable	75.24 − 20.86	92.89 − 21.13	0.00 0.00	29.89 − 18.75
294.55 − 20.24	Non-durable	306.99 − 19.73	336.34 − 20.30	74.21 − 5.26	63.48 − 15.15
67.24 − 13.91	**Tobacco**	100.00 − 11.79	87.51 − 9.91	140.92 − 13.81	119.34 − 13.22
202.71 − 7.74	**Energy**	188.58 − 13.53	204.06 − 8.66	210.02 − 18.27	42.79 − 20.50
33.13 − 23.72	**Coal**	49.69 − 3.49	61.34 + 9.36	0.00 0.00	22.57 − 19.10
203.08 − 7.73	**Oil & Gas**	189.99 − 13.54	204.91 − 8.68	210.02 − 18.27	43.62 − 20.53
211.88 − 13.11	Oil cos, major	216.34 − 16.06	208.70 − 13.19	223.10 − 18.17	0.00 0.00
97.46 − 13.61	Oil cos, secondary	108.02 − 13.40	130.60 − 10.65	129.14 − 13.75	43.91 − 20.55
322.91 + 5.58	Oil drilling	332.23 + 5.59	457.75 + 5.62	68.42 + 5.03	0.00 0.00
222.21 + 11.12	Oilfield equip/svcs	209.06 + 9.50	216.60 + 10.51	174.08 − 1.46	78.70 − 19.53
371.74 + 16.64	Pipelines	286.85 − 5.66	300.06 + 7.78	113.47 − 25.58	0.00 0.00
300.09 − 15.36	**Financial**	173.35 − 13.22	305.30 − 15.27	241.25 − 12.24	75.51 − 11.36
287.57 − 15.92	**Banks**	141.07 − 14.38	276.39 − 15.03	242.28 − 12.38	62.54 − 17.50
231.94 − 22.75	**Insurance**	227.32 − 16.09	248.21 − 23.59	263.04 − 11.23	64.88 − 15.71
351.04 − 23.70	Full line	267.98 − 16.47	278.29 − 23.84	258.95 − 12.34	116.74 − 14.06
230.02 − 26.97	Life	228.72 − 19.44	216.40 − 27.14	268.58 − 17.08	175.68 + 1.76
144.35 − 16.20	Property/Casualty	177.95 − 9.85	189.61 − 18.60	310.22 + 11.52	55.54 − 21.74
122.14 − 2.89	**Real estate**	103.21 − 8.86	53.42 − 3.72	82.68 − 12.16	124.10 − 10.31
447.46 − 12.54	**Specialty Finance**	288.95 − 9.25	440.86 − 12.37	271.12 − 14.12	129.37 + 10.78
414.77 − 16.52	**Diversified financial**	313.70 − 14.36	436.65 − 16.17	263.64 − 14.80	117.28 − 2.90
219.43 − 15.97	**Savings & loan (US only)**	162.56 − 17.62	162.56 − 17.62	0.00 0.00	0.00 0.00
739.08 − 1.54	**Securities brokers**	293.38 + 6.88	681.97 − 0.81	341.15 + 1.20	156.73 + 22.95
271.56 + 3.02	**Healthcare**	260.85 − 3.34	277.69 − 1.04	257.78 − 11.09	189.35 + 8.14
123.14 − 16.24	**Healthcare poviders**	122.69 − 17.23	131.18 − 19.27	2605.03 − 5.60	63.14 + 14.96
221.83 + 6.57	**Medical Products**	239.87 + 3.44	250.67 + 5.01	153.46 − 8.76	247.75 − 3.53
337.62 + 29.48	Advcd Med Devices	367.68 + 23.09	409.93 + 25.78	128.87 + 0.83	204.27 + 0.05
160.87 − 10.31	Medical supplies	178.05 − 9.94	176.24 − 10.45	144.61 − 15.21	240.20 − 4.51
326.80 + 3.62	**Pharma & Biotech**	276.90 − 3.59	310.91 − 0.98	260.55 − 11.21	185.51 + 10.05
684.93 + 42.66	Biotechnology	363.73 + 21.25	393.64 + 21.56	18.11 + 14.67	71.38 − 13.61
288.23 − 4.68	Pharmaceuticals	262.66 − 6.80	286.93 − 6.09	261.93 − 11.40	188.04 + 10.30
286.55 − 7.02	**Industrial**	184.79 − 7.80	286.30 − 9.65	235.59 + 1.84	101.96 − 12.18
157.01 − 14.04	**Aerospace/Defense**	199.62 − 14.29	220.40 − 14.10	211.25 − 12.50	174.46 − 15.98
148.38 − 17.36	**Construction & Materials**	79.37 − 9.17	118.44 − 18.23	150.64 − 9.31	38.37 − 4.34
166.66 − 19.04	Building materials	101.13 − 15.36	137.80 − 18.76	132.98 − 19.05	63.98 − 5.80
110.12 − 8.63	Heavy construction	56.14 + 2.01	65.93 − 14.62	184.91 + 10.15	24.85 − 2.94
102.28 − 26.67	**Containers & pkging**	75.66 − 23.04	94.77 − 27.98	107.31 − 20.30	60.56 − 12.42
353.54 + 9.80	**Industrial Equipment**	254.95 − 6.83	382.54 + 7.14	310.54 − 0.86	178.51 − 17.13
401.19 + 22.08	Adv industrial equip	652.34 + 3.96	821.25 + 44.92	650.58 + 13.82	391.87 − 26.89
303.80 − 5.25	Elec comps & equip	228.00 − 14.11	262.00 − 16.02	277.16 − 9.64	195.04 − 14.28
226.75 + 14.34	Factory equipment	103.18 − 6.52	82.29 − 17.77	118.96 − 3.99	110.75 − 6.50
255.33 − 21.69	Heavy machinery	101.31 − 17.42	242.22 − 19.85	58.40 − 8.42	49.54 − 13.85
205.06 − 1.09	**Industrial services**	166.75 − 0.88	150.91 − 4.92	309.26 + 11.37	138.05 − 2.78
271.10 − 0.45	Industrial svcs	184.15 − 0.64	209.47 − 4.41	308.60 + 11.61	139.91 − 3.08
43.18 − 14.23	Pollution control	55.08 − 8.44	38.95 − 13.66	255.02 − 3.85	81.60 + 15.71
137.73 − 16.53	**Industrial transportation**	95.05 − 15.12	129.36 − 18.11	137.13 − 17.81	70.92 − 11.97
291.52 − 17.24	Air freight	266.05 − 16.81	296.60 − 16.81	0.00 0.00	0.00 0.00
111.24 − 13.03	Marine transport	104.90 − 12.55	88.04 − 13.82	201.05 − 14.12	50.15 − 8.91
125.51 − 17.27	Railroads	83.22 − 15.15	117.15 − 19.79	15.13 − 29.92	68.42 − 9.61
115.10 − 11.88	Trucking	108.80 − 18.64	96.81 − 12.21	0.00 0.00	118.65 − 20.35
466.66 − 15.54	**Industrial, diversified**	337.82 − 8.82	470.86 − 14.57	281.89 + 11.19	49.93 − 11.79
161.40 − 15.72	**Transportation equip**	60.86 − 20.29	167.56 − 18.55	0.00 0.00	18.06 − 23.60
159.89 − 17.08	Land transportation	113.38 − 19.29	167.56 − 18.55	0.00 0.00	26.45 − 23.76
92.98 + 1.36	Shipbuilding	16.12 − 23.98	0.00 0.00	0.00 0.00	16.27 − 23.98
1344.10 + 13.08	**Technology**	985.31 + 9.00	1186.20 + 9.67	863.24 + 20.49	387.34 − 12.03
1343.08 + 18.70	**Hardware & Equipment**	964.48 + 12.04	1160.52 + 15.22	880.27 + 19.65	419.83 − 12.46
2542.69 + 9.98	Communications tech	1043.96 + 9.32	1427.28 + 7.33	919.18 + 19.20	452.38 − 26.44
818.72 + 7.83	Computers	728.93 + 2.18	829.72 + 5.99	14.43 + 2.74	341.04 − 16.61
317.52 + 2.72	Office equipment	246.03 + 1.74	245.81 + 3.46	70.16 − 23.53	275.28 + 1.06
3130.35 + 46.61	Semiconductors	1746.80 + 31.32	3202.45 + 44.33	521.05 + 25.86	462.57 − 2.37
1348.58 + 1.10	**Software**	1180.18 − 0.46	1266.81 − 3.43	609.20 + 24.90	555.71 − 12.52
312.20 − 12.54	**Telecommunications**	438.54 + 0.31	314.75 − 11.38	683.30 + 13.89	308.40 − 4.91
289.93 − 14.41	**Fixed Line Comm**	381.87 − 1.52	286.17 − 12.35	633.72 + 12.90	232.85 − 13.42
1075.36 + 6.14	**Wireless Comm**	1024.90 + 5.11	1295.91 + 4.50	1127.81 + 16.97	469.62 − 0.68
118.63 + 0.44	**Utilities**	121.54 − 0.28	114.55 − 0.68	223.03 + 5.85	68.34 − 12.21
114.46 + 1.28	**Electric**	110.20 − 2.14	110.74 − 0.10	218.23 + 0.64	71.07 − 11.05
162.79 − 6.62	**Gas**	118.02 − 8.41	158.59 − 5.58	232.62 − 1.67	57.75 − 17.60
192.02 − 9.12	**Water**	270.84 + 14.76	188.49 − 6.40	274.77 + 16.69	0.00 0.00

Indexes based on 12/31/91=100

Source: *Republished with permission of Dow Jones from WSJ Market Data Group Year 2000; Permission conveyed through Copyright Clearance Center.*

day, changes in percentage, 12 month high and low, and 12 month change in average and percentage. These are also reflected in year-to-date changes. This will be of particular importance to an investor who already has money committed to these markets, and to those contemplating a decision based on the previous day's market results.

Figure 5-10 *Activity from five indices and major international exchanges for February 24, 2000.*

MARKETS DIARY **2/24/00**

STOCKS Dow Jones Industrial Average **10092.63 -133.10**

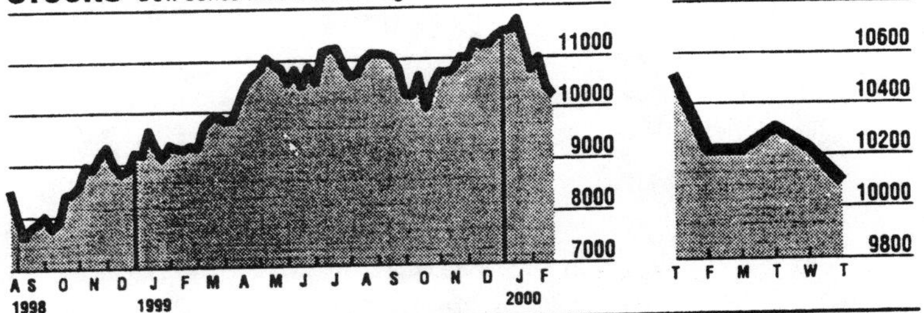

INDEX	CLOSE	NET CHNG	PCT CHNG	12-MO HIGH	12-MO LOW	12-MO CHNG	PCT	FROM 12/31	PCT
DJIA	10092.63	-133.10	-1.30	11722.98	9275.88	+726.29	+7.75	-1404.49	-12.22
DJ US Total Market	326.20	-0.28	-0.09	341.57	279.27	+43.59	+15.42	-15.37	-4.50
S&P 500	1353.43	-7.26	-0.53	1469.25	1225.50	+108.41	+8.71	-115.82	-7.88
NasdaqComp.	4617.65	+67.32	+1.48	4617.65	2259.03	+2290.83	+98.45	+548.34	+13.48
Russell 2000	554.04	+4.13	+0.75	558.42	383.37	+161.32	+41.08	+49.29	+9.77

INT'L STOCKS DJ World Stock Index (excl. U.S.) **185.12 -0.24**

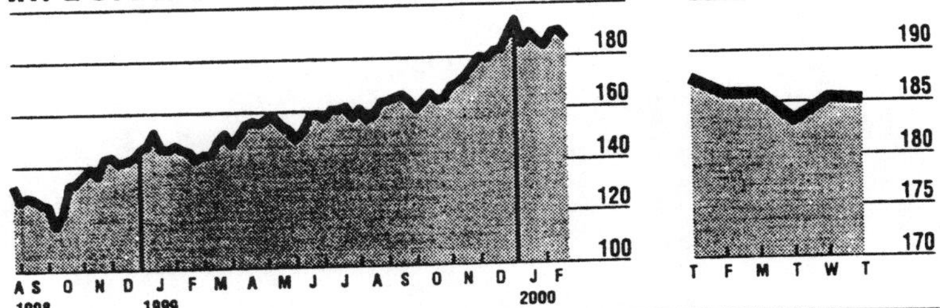

INDEX	CLOSE	NET CHNG	PCT CHNG	12-MO HIGH	12-MO LOW	12-MO CHNG	PCT	FROM 12/31	PCT
DJ World (ex. U.S.)	p185.12	-0.24	-0.13	195.28	140.03	+40.74	+28.22	-8.27	-4.28
MSCI EAFE (Prelim.)	1696.70	-1.88	-0.11	1774.13	1331.10	+325.30	+23.72	-63.34	-3.60
London (FT 100)	6086.7	-57.4	-0.93	6930.2	5869.2	-119.80	-1.93	-843.5	-12.17
Tokyo (Nikkei 225)	19571.44	+51.89	+0.27	20007.77	13921.06	+5100.99	+35.25	+637.10	+3.36
Frankfurt (Xetra DAX)	7640.53	-58.44	-0.76	7709.27	4668.52	+2721.98	+55.34	+682.39	+9.81
Paris (CAC-40)	6078.78	+47.53	+0.79	6297.66	4004.16	+1926.22	+46.39	+120.46	+2.02

Source: *Republished with permission of Dow Jones from WSJ Market Data Group Year 2000; Permission conveyed through Copyright Clearance Center.*

International stocks represented by the DJ World Stock Index are also graphed and shown in Figure 5-10. This information includes indices from DJ World, *Europe, Asia, & Far East* (EAFE), London, Tokyo, Frankfurt, and Paris. This index also shows the closing averages along with net changes for the day in dollars and percentages. As with U.S. stocks, the 12-month high and low and percentage change is also shown. An investor who is monitoring overseas market activity will find this section of particular interest.

Investor Protection: Government Regulations

While there are many publications and magazines available to investors on newsstands and in subscription form, the government has an obligation to protect investors by promoting honest and fair practices when it comes to company information. In order to make rational decisions, investors must be provided with what is called *full disclosure.* In other words, publicly held companies must publish financial and other critical information that would affect the value of their securities in the open market.

While regulations are designed to prevent fraud and the manipulation of stock prices in the securities markets, they cannot protect investors from making mistakes based on the human emotions of greed or fear. In other words, federal legislation governing the securities industry cannot ensure that investors will profit from their investment decisions, but this legislation is solely intended to ensure fair market practices.

There are also state laws that help reduce fraudulent securities practices. They generally require the following: 1) the filing of financial information regarding new securities with state regulatory bodies, 2) new securities meeting specific standards before they can be sold to the public, and 3) securities firms and individual brokers being licensed in their specific state. Each state securities commissioner must enforce these rules.

Specific Legislation

The first modern legislation governing the securities industry was the creation of the *Security Act of 1933.* This act focused on the issuance of new securities and required them to be registered with the SEC. Today, this process consists of supplying the SEC with information concerning the company, the nature of its business, competition, and its overall financial position. Upon approval, this information is then summarized and printed in a prospectus. The chief purpose of this legal document is to make the formal offer to sell the new securities to the public.

When all material facts that might affect the value of the company's shares have been fully disclosed in the prospectus, the new stock is then released for sale. As the new securities begin trading, each buyer *must* be given a copy of the prospectus. The firms that are involved with issuing the new securities must exercise extreme caution when preparing this legal document. An investor who incurs a loss can file suit to recover these losses if the prospectus contains false or misleading information. Liability for this loss might rest with the company, with its officers or directors, with the brokerage firm that markets the new issue, or with any professionals who assisted with preparing the documents.

Not only are investors who purchase new securities protected, but the government also issued the *Securities Act of 1934* to extend these regulations to existing securities. In other words, publicly held companies must keep current the information that is already on file with the SEC. This task is performed annually through the filing of a *10-K report.* While containing a substantial amount of factual information concerning the company, this report is sent to shareholders in more friendly and readable format in the company's annual report (see Figure 5-11).

With the ever-changing environment of corporate America, companies have an obligation to release any information that might materially affect the value of their securities on the open market. News programs that specialize in this area include the Nightly Business Report on PBS and daily news announcements on CNBC. Sometimes a company will ask the SEC to halt trading in its stock pending a special news release that can be prepared and disseminated in a timely manner.

Despite efforts to protect investors and give them time to make rational decisions, disclosure laws do not require a company to tell everything about its operations. In order to be competitive in their industries, all

Figure 5-11 *The company's annual report.*

firms have patents and secured information that they need to keep secret. Remember, the purpose of full disclosure is not to restrict the company's business operations but to fairly inform investors so that they can make intelligent decisions.

The SEC also prohibits company employees from using privileged information for personal gain. Top-level officers and directors, as well as lower-ranking employees, often have access to critical news before it reaches the general public. This situation is referred to as *inside information* and can enhance the employees' abilities to make huge profits or avoid large losses. For example, if an employee knows about a pending lawsuit that could negatively affect the stock price once the litigation is announced, he or she cannot sell the stock before the announcement is made to the public. Such actions would be considered illegal and would directly result in criminal prosecution.

All officers and directors must report their individual stock holdings and any changes in these positions to the SEC. This action helps determine whether any illegal transactions have taken place prior to a public announcement that affected the value of the company's securities. If insiders do profit illegally from the use of such information, they can be prosecuted as criminals and must return any gains directly to the company.

Other Published Information Sources

Most major brokerage firms have research staffs that publish special reports. These can include a general analysis of current economic conditions or specific recommendations for industries and individual stocks. In order to compete effectively and to take credit for timely information to customers, the firms' research staffs will attempt to identify undervalued securities that have the potential for price appreciation. There is usually no additional charge to send these reports to current or potential customers, because the cost is already built into the company's commissions and fee structure.

Most reports will give a thorough analysis and conclude with a buy, sell, or hold recommendation. There will tend to be a natural bias to encourage the purchase of securities, so most reports that are published will be slanted toward the buying of specific stocks. An outright sell will encourage the investor to liquidate all existing shares for a number of specific reasons, which might include a reduction in profits, dividends, or business-related activity. A hold will encourage the investor to neither buy any new shares of a specific security nor to sell any shares that might already be held in an existing account.

In a country that emphasizes freedom of speech and freedom of the press, investors are often overloaded with information. A decision to buy, sell, or hold should generally be made with financial goals in mind. While a pure speculator in the market will tend to make quicker judgments, a long-term investor who likes to buy and hold securities will not be as hasty when making a monetary commitment.

Keep in mind that each client or project will have his or her own risk tolerance and comfort level when it comes to investing money. For that reason, it is critical that financial planners, stock brokers, and investment advisors recognize these personality traits at the beginning of a relationship. They should also work closely with their clients in order to help disseminate information that will lead to a logical and sensible decision.

Besides the wealth of information contained in *The Wall Street Journal*, there are other newspapers that benefit the investment community. These publications include *Barron's*, the *Investors Business Daily*, the *Over-the-Counter Weekly Review*, and *The Wall Street Transcript*. *Barron's* is of particular interest, because it is published every Monday and contains a comprehensive summary of activity from the previous week. This information includes a weekly securities activity report, various feature articles, and investment advisory reports. The *Barron's* Confidence Index is designed to identify the level of investors' confidence as related to the price movements between high- and low-quality bonds.

Financial Magazines

There is no end to the ever-increasing variety of magazines that report financial news. Among the most popular are *Forbes*, *Money Magazine*, *Business Week*, *Fortune*, and *Financial World*. Each one has its own style and flavor for reporting the latest news. Full-time staff writers will have weekly or monthly columns that are followed by avid readers. These publications will contain articles that report on the general financial community and also on specific companies.

Sometimes a magazine will devote an issue to specific topics. For example, *Forbes* has its "Annual Report on American Industry" that ranks more than 1,000 companies related to sales, growth in earnings, return on equity, and stock price performance. This issue makes it easy to find information because the publication classifies companies within their respective industries. Other useful information in the publication includes the use of debt and profit margins for American industry.

In conjunction with specialized information, these publications will have articles about individual companies and will report on performance of the best stocks or mutual funds within a specified period. The danger here is that investors tend to only use this information to make critical decisions. We know, however, that past performance cannot guarantee future results. Therefore, you should focus on the outlook for specific industries or individual companies when advising clients whether or not to invest.

Investment Advisory Services

Most libraries subscribe to a number of services that investors can review in order to obtain additional information. One of the oldest and most reliable sources is from *Standard & Poor's*, which publishes reports about individual companies. Figure 5-12 shows an example of a stock report on the Microsoft Corporation. This report includes a summary of company operations, an opinion based on technical indicators (such as stock price,

Figure 5-12 *A Microsoft Corporation stock report.*

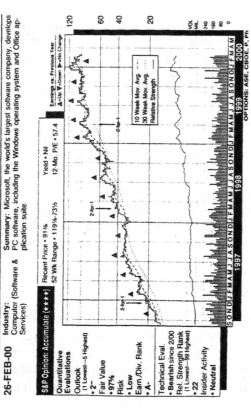

STANDARD
&POOR'S
STOCK REPORTS

Microsoft Corp.

Nasdaq Symbol **MSFT**

In S&P 500

26-FEB-00

Industry: Computer (Software & Services)

Summary: Microsoft, the world's largest software company, develops PC software, including the Windows operating system and Office application suite.

S&P Opinion: Accumulate (★★★★)

Recent Price • 91⅛ — Yield • Nil
52 Wk Range • 119⅞-73½ — 12-Mo. P/E • 57.4

Quantitative Evaluations
Outlook
(1 Lowest—5 Highest)
• 2⁻
Fair Value
• 97⅝
Risk
• Low
Earn./Div. Rank
• A-

Technical Eval.
• **Bearish** since 2/00
Rel. Strength Rank
(1 Lowest—99 Highest)
• 22
Insider Activity
• **Neutral**

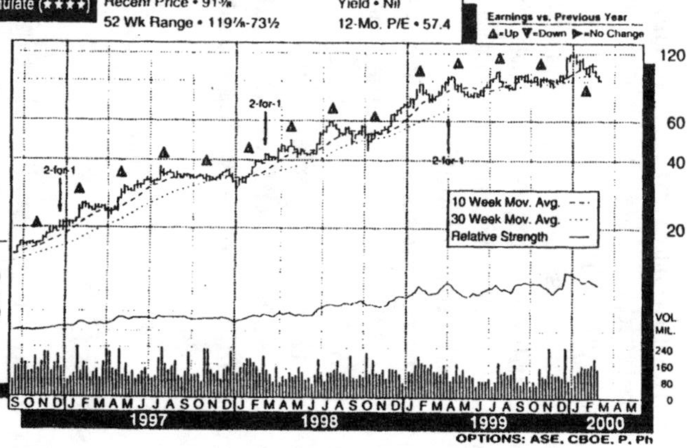

OPTIONS: ASE, CBOE, P, Ph

Overview - 19-JAN-00

We expect revenues to increase about 21% in FY 00 (Jun.), following a 29% gain in FY 99. Sales have been buoyed recently by the launch of Office 2000 in June 1999. However, sales of Windows were weak in the December quarter due to lower corporate PC demand, as well as customer anticipation of the February 17 launch of Windows 2000. We expect PC demand to remain healthy, and Windows 2000 should spur strong revenue growth. We also expect continued contributions from SQL Server sales and on-line advertising. Operating margins may narrow slightly, due to higher R&D expenses and sales and marketing costs. However, higher investment income should boost net margins.

Valuation - 19-JAN-00

Microsoft reported much better than expected earnings in the December quarter. However, most of the upside came from higher than expected investment gains. Otherwise, revenues and earnings were about as expected. We expect Windows 2000, as well as Office 2000, to fuel the company's revenue growth over the next couple of years. In addition, SQL Server, the company's database software, is showing strong growth. In search of longer term growth, the company has been investing in numerous other ventures, such as cable and telecom companies. MSFT's many Internet properties are experiencing rapid revenue growth, both from advertising and from e-commerce. The company's cash and equity investments combined total nearly $38 billion, leading to high levels of interest income and investment gains. The shares continue to merit their premium valuation in light of MSFT's strong competitive position and its future growth prospects.

Key Stock Statistics

S&P EPS Est. 2000	1.70	Tang. Bk. Value/Share	5.37
P/E on S&P Est. 2000	53.7	Beta	1.45
S&P EPS Est. 2001	1.92	Shareholders	53,400
Dividend Rate/Share	Nil	Market cap. (B)	$475.3
Shs. outstg. (M)	5204.9	Inst. holdings	41%
Avg. daily vol. (M)	33.275		

Value of $10,000 invested 5 years ago: $ 119,509

Fiscal Year Ending Jun. 30

	2000	1999	1998	1997	1996	1995
Revenues (Million $)						
1Q	5,384	4,193	3,130	2,295	2,016	1,247
2Q	6,110	5,795	3,585	2,680	2,195	1,482
3Q	—	4,595	3,774	3,208	2,205	1,587
4Q	—	5,764	3,995	3,175	2,255	1,621
Yr.	—	19,747	14,484	11,358	8,671	5,937
Earnings Per Share ($)						
1Q	**0.40**	**0.31**	0.13	0.12	0.10	0.06
2Q	**0.44**	**0.36**	**0.21**	0.14	0.11	0.08
3Q	—	**0.35**	**0.25**	0.20	0.11	0.08
4Q	—	**0.40**	**0.25**	0.20	0.11	0.07
Yr.	—	**1.42**	**0.83**	**0.66**	0.43	0.29

Next earnings report expected: late April

Dividend Data

Amount ($)	Date Decl.	Ex-Div. Date	Stock of Record	Payment Date
2-for-1	Jan. 25	Mar. 29	Mar. 12	Mar. 26 '99

STANDARD
&POOR'S
STOCK REPORTS

Microsoft Corporation

26-FEB-00

Business Summary - 19-JAN-00

Microsoft, the dominant player in the PC software market, rose to prominence on the popularity of its operating systems software. The company now rules the business applications software market, and has set its sights on becoming the leading provider of software and services for the Internet.

The company is best known for its operating systems software programs, which run approximately 90% of the PCs currently in use. Its original DOS operating system gave way to Windows, a graphical user interface program run in conjunction with DOS, which made using a PC easier. Windows 98, MSFT's latest version of its flagship PC operating system, was introduced in June 1998. Windows NT is an operating system for servers, to help build and deploy distributed applications for networked PCs. The next version, to be named Windows 2000, will be released in February 2000. MSFT also provides an operating system, Windows CE, for communications, entertainment and mobile computing devices.

MSFT entered the business applications market in the early 1990s via a line-up of strong offerings, combined with aggressive and innovative marketing and sales techniques. Its Office suite, which includes the popular Word (word processing), Excel (spreadsheet), PowerPoint (graphics), Access (database management) and Outlook (messaging and collaboration) software programs, dominates the application software market just as Windows dominates operating systems. Office 2000, the latest version, was introduced in June 1999. Other applications include SQL Server, a database management system, and software development tools.

The Consumer and Other division provides services to consumers over the Internet, as well as software solutions and services for businesses to conduct commerce on the Internet. Services include The Microsoft Network (MSN Internet Access), which provides dial-up Internet access, free Web-based e-mail through MSN Hotmail, and Microsoft MSN Messenger Service; WebTV, an on-line service that enables consumers to experience the Internet through their televisions via set-top terminals; MSN Portal, which provides services on the Internet via the home page as well as several Web sites. Sites include CarPoint, Expedia, HomeAdvisor, MoneyCentral and MSNBC. Microsoft also sells platforms that power the MSN vertical services, such as Passport and LinkExchange. This segment also offers software product categories including learning, productivity, personal finance, and entertainment, as well as hardware peripherals.

Microsoft is currently on trial in an antitrust suit brought against the company by the U.S. Department of Justice. The government alleges that MSFT is using its monopoly in one industry to gain unfair advantage in others.

Per Share Data ($) (Year Ended Jun. 30)	1999	1998	1997	1996	1995	1994	1993	1992	1991	1990
Tangible Bk. Val.	5.37	3.17	2.04	1.45	1.13	0.96	0.72	0.49	0.32	0.22
Cash Flow	1.60	1.02	0.76	0.52	0.34	0.28	0.23	0.17	0.12	0.08
Earnings	1.42	0.83	0.66	0.43	0.29	0.23	0.20	0.15	0.10	0.07
Dividends	Nil	Nil	Nil	Nil	Nil	Nil	Nil	Nil	Nil	Nil
Payout Ratio	Nil	Nil	Nil	Nil	Nil	Nil	Nil	Nil	Nil	Nil
Prices - High	119⅞	72	37¾	21½	13⅝	8⅛	6⅛	6	4⅝	2¼
- Low	68	31⅛	20¼	10	7¼	4⅞	4⅜	4⅛	2¹¹⁄₁₆	1³⁄₁₆
P/E Ratio - High	84	86	57	50	47	35	31	39	45	35
- Low	48	37	31	23	25	21	22	27	20	18
Income Statement Analysis (Million $)										
Revs.	19,747	14,484	11,358	8,671	5,937	4,649	3,753	2,759	1,843	1,183
Oper. Inc.	10,938	7,964	5,687	3,558	2,307	1,963	1,464	1,097	714	434
Depr.	1,010	1,024	557	480	269	237	138	101	67.0	46.0
Int. Exp.	Nil	Nil	Nil	Nil	Nil	2.0	1.0	2.0	4.5	3.6
Pretax Inc.	11,891	7,117	5,314	3,379	2,167	1,722	1,401	1,041	671	411
Eff. Tax Rate	35%	37%	35%	35%	33%	33%	32%	32%	31%	32%
Net Inc.	7,785	4,490	3,439	2,195	1,453	1,146	953	708	463	279
Balance Sheet & Other Fin. Data (Million $)										
Cash	17,236	13,927	8,966	6,940	4,750	3,614	2,290	1,345	686	449
Curr. Assets	20,233	15,889	10,373	7,839	5,620	4,312	2,850	1,770	1,029	720
Total Assets	37,156	22,357	14,387	10,093	7,210	5,363	3,805	2,640	1,644	1,105
Curr. Liab.	8,718	5,730	3,610	2,425	1,347	913	563	447	293	187
LT Debt	Nil	Nil	Nil	Nil	Nil	Nil	Nil	Nil	Nil	Nil
Common Eqty.	27,458	15,647	9,797	6,908	5,333	4,450	3,242	2,193	1,351	919
Total Cap.	28,438	16,627	10,777	7,033	5,458	4,450	3,242	2,193	1,351	919
Cap. Exp.	583	656	499	494	495	278	239	318	275	159
Cash Flow	8,767	5,486	3,996	2,675	1,722	1,383	1,091	809	530	326
Curr. Ratio	2.3	2.8	2.9	3.2	4.2	4.7	5.1	4.0	3.5	3.9
% LT Debt of Cap.	Nil	Nil	Nil	Nil	Nil	Nil	Nil	Nil	Nil	Nil
% Net Inc.of Revs.	39.4	31.0	30.3	25.3	24.5	24.7	25.4	25.7	25.1	23.6
% Ret. on Assets	26.2	24.4	28.2	25.4	23.1	25.0	29.1	32.5	33.4	30.1
% Ret. on Equity	36.0	35.1	41.2	35.9	29.7	29.8	34.6	39.3	40.4	37.1

Data as orig reptd.; bef. results of disc opers/spec. items. Per share data adj. for stk. divs. Bold denotes diluted EPS (FASB 128)-prior periods restated. E-Estimated. NA-Not Available. NM-Not Meaningful. NR-Not Ranked.

Office—One Microsoft Way, Redmond, WA 98052-6399. **Tel**—(206) 882-8080. **Website**—http://www.microsoft.com **Chrmn & CEO**—W. H. Gates III. **Pres**—S. Ballmer. **EVP & COO**—R. J. Herbold. **SVP-Fin & CFO**—G. B. Maffei. **SVP & Secy**—W. H. Neukom. **Investor Contact**—Carla Lewis (425-936-3703). **Dirs**—P. G. Allen, W. H. Gates III, R. Hackborn, D. F. Marquardt, W. G. Reed Jr., J. A. Shirley. **Transfer Agent**—ChaseMellon Shareholder Services, Ridgefield Park, NJ. **Incorporated**—in Washington in 1981; reincorporated in Delaware in 1986. **Empl**— 31,400. **S&P Analyst:** Brian Goodstadt, CFA volume, and moving averages), an overview, a valuation, and key stock statistics. The Business Summary is of particular interest to those who want to learn more about current and future operations of the company. In addition, critical financial data is listed from the latest income statement and balance sheet.

Another popular service is from the Value Line Investment Survey, which contains information about selected industries and individual companies. For example, Figure 5-13 shows a report for the Intel Corporation that contains a large amount of user friendly information. While the data is based on facts, it also projects information about items such as earnings per share, sales, and dividends. This type of report is ideal for an analytical investor who loves to make decisions by studying numbers. This survey also has an easy-to-understand report regarding current and future company activity, and how the company expects the stock to perform over the next three to five years.

Another condensed source of information is contained in the *Standard & Poor's Stock Guide*, which is published monthly. It is generally distributed to both full-service and discount brokerage firms. Figure 5-14 reproduces a page from the January 2000 edition. For example, Index number 42 on pages 206 and 207 of the January 2000 edition highlights the activity of Wal-Mart stores. There is a considerable amount of information, including price-range history and data concerning dividends, earnings per share, various balance sheet items, and market capitalization. This booklet packs a lot of data into a small space and is therefore widely used as a quick and easy-to-use monthly reference guide.

Academic and Professional Publications

The information in these publications is more specialized and written for the financial professional. The *Financial Analysts Journal* is exclusively devoted to the professional who specializes in analyzing individual companies (such as a chartered financial analyst). The *Journal of Finance* is published for those who are doing research on specialized financial topics. Articles published by academicians and industry professionals often appear in the *Journal of Portfolio Management*.

There are a number of monthly or quarterly publications designed for investment brokers or financial planners. *Stockbroker Magazine* deals with current issues and companies related to the brokerage industry. *Investment Advisor* discusses issues pertaining to professionals who give advice for a fee. The *Journal of Financial Planning* is published exclusively for members of the Financial Planning Association. It discusses issues and strategies pertaining to the investment industry. *Research* highlights profiles of successful brokers and information about individual companies.

Internet Web Sites

The Web is bringing Wall Street everywhere to everybody who wants to receive the information. Any laptop computer that has Web access can

Figure 5-13 *An Intel Corporation report.*

INTEL NDQ-INTC | RECENT PRICE **103** D | P/E RATIO **40.9** (Trailing: 40.9 Median: 13.0) | RELATIVE P/E RATIO **2.69** | DIV'D YLD **0.1%** | VALUE LINE **1064**

TIMELINESS **2** Lowered 5/14/99
SAFETY **3** New 7/27/90
TECHNICAL **2** Raised 1/21/00
BETA 1.05 (1.00 = Market)

2002-04 PROJECTIONS

	Price	Gain	Ann'l Total Return
High	120	(+15%)	4%
Low	80	(-20%)	-6%

Insider Decisions

	F	M	A	M	J	J	A	S	O
to Buy	0	0	0	0	0	1	0	0	0
Options	0	0	3	0	2	2	0	0	0
to Sell	1	0	3	0	0	2	0	0	3

Institutional Decisions

	1Q1999	2Q1999	3Q1999
to Buy	660	644	620
to Sell	484	491	529
Hld's(000)	1815536	1707348	1770987

	1988	1989	1990	1991	1992	1993	1994	1995	1996	1997	1998	1999
High:	2.3	2.3	3.3	3.7	5.7	9.3	9.2	19.6	35.4	51.0	63.1	89.5
Low:	1.2	1.4	1.8	2.4	2.9	5.3	7.0	7.9	12.5	31.4	32.8	50.1

Target Price Range 2002 | 2003 | 2004

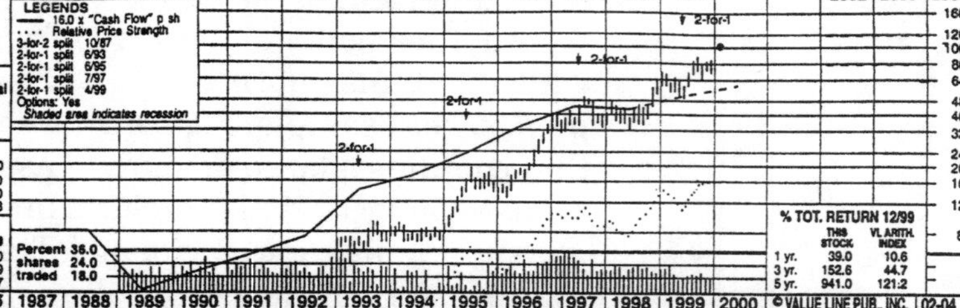

1983	1984	1985	1986	1987	1988	1989	1990	1991	1992	1993	1994	1995	1996	1997	1998	1999	2000	© VALUE LINE PUB., INC.	02-04
.42	.60	.49	.45	.71	1.00	1.06	1.23	1.46	1.75	2.63	3.49	4.93	6.35	7.70	7.93	*8.45*	*9.30*	Sales per sh	*14.50*
.08	.11	.06	.01	.13	.23	.23	.30	.37	.48	.90	1.09	1.48	2.15	2.81	2.71	*3.25*	*3.75*	"Cash Flow" per sh	*5.50*
.04	.06	--	d.07	.06	.16	.15	.20	.24	.31	.65	.73	.99	1.45	1.94	1.73	2.33	*2.80*	Earnings per sh A	*4.00*
--	--	--	--	--	--	--	--	--	.01	.03	.03	.04	.05	.06	.07	.09	*.12*	Div'ds Decl'd per sh B ■	*.17*
.05	.14	.08	.05	.11	.17	.14	.21	.29	.37	.58	.74	1.08	.92	1.38	1.07	*1.00*	*1.40*	Cap'l Spending per sh	*1.25*
.42	.50	.51	.45	.49	.72	.86	1.12	1.35	1.63	2.24	2.80	3.70	5.14	5.93	7.05	*9.35*	*10.15*	Book Value per sh	*15.00*
2680.8	2732.0	2785.9	2826.6	2693.3	2888.6	2952.3	3194.4	3262.8	3348.7	3344.0	3304.0	3284.0	3284.0	3256.0	3315.0	*3484.0*	*3550.0*	Common Shs Outst'g C	*3650.0*
32.0	21.2	NMF	--	28.7	11.4	12.6	12.3	12.2	12.3	11.3	10.7	13.9	14.2	20.6	24.3	29.5		Avg Ann'l P/E Ratio	*25.0*
2.71	1.97	NMF	--	1.92	.95	.95	.91	.78	.75	.67	.70	.93	.89	1.19	1.29	1.66		Relative P/E Ratio	*1.65*
--	--	--	--	--	--	--	--	--	.2%	.3%	.4%	.3%	.2%	.1%	.1%	.1%		Avg Ann'l Div'd Yield	*.2%*

CAPITAL STRUCTURE as of 9/25/99
Total Debt $1048 mill. Due in 5 Yrs $377 mill.
LT Debt $884 mill. LT Interest $55.0 mill.
(Total interest coverage over 60x) (3% of Cap'l)

Leases, Uncapitalized Annual rentals $35.0 mill.
Pension Liability None

Pfd Stock None

Com. Stock 3,341,000 shs. (97% of Cap'l)
MARKET CAP: $304 billion (Large Cap)

1989	1990	1991	1992	1993	1994	1995	1996	1997	1998	1999	2000		02-04
3126.8	3921.3	4778.6	5844.0	8782.0	11521	16202	20847	25070	26273	29389	*33000*	Sales ($mill)	*53000*
26.8%	29.3%	31.4%	34.4%	46.8%	42.2%	40.9%	45.3%	48.2%	43.2%	*45.0%*	*46.5%*	Operating Margin	*47.5%*
237.2	292.4	418.3	517.6	717.0	1028.0	1371.0	1888.0	2192.0	2807	*3200*	*3400*	Depreciation ($mill)	*5500*
444.0	650.3	794.6	1076.8	2277.0	2562.5	3491.0	5157.0	6945.0	6178.0	*8100*	*9940*	Net Profit ($mill)	*14600*
32.9%	34.1%	33.5%	32.0%	35.0%	36.5%	36.8%	35.0%	34.8%	33.6%	*35.0%*	*31.7%*	Income Tax Rate	*33.0%*
14.2%	16.6%	16.6%	18.4%	25.9%	22.2%	21.5%	24.7%	27.7%	23.5%	*27.6%*	*30.1%*	Net Profit Margin	*27.5%*
1241.7	1805.4	2376.2	2849.1	3369.0	3143.0	4478.0	8821.0	9847.0	7671.0	10720	*12525*	Working Cap'l ($mill)	*18000*
412.5	344.6	362.5	249.0	426.0	392.0	400.0	728.0	448.1	702.0	955	*1000*	Long-Term Debt ($mill)	*'750*
2548.8	3591.5	4417.9	5444.6	7500.0	9267.0	12140	16872	19295	23377	32535	*36000*	Shr. Equity ($mill)	*55000*
15.7%	17.0%	17.2%	19.2%	28.9%	26.7%	28.0%	29.4%	35.2%	25.7%	*23.5%*	*27.0%*	Return on Total Cap'l	*26.0%*
17.4%	18.1%	18.0%	19.8%	30.4%	27.7%	28.8%	30.6%	36.0%	26.4%	*25.0%*	*27.5%*	Return on Shr. Equity	*26.5%*
17.4%	18.1%	18.0%	19.4%	29.2%	26.7%	27.8%	29.7%	35.1%	25.5%	*23.5%*	*24.5%*	Retained to Com Eq	*25.5%*
	--	--	2%	4%	4%	3%	3%	3%	4%	*4%*	*5%*	All Div'ds to Net Prof	*4%*

CURRENT POSITION ($MILL.)	1997	1998	9/25/99
Cash Assets	9732.0	7310.0	11891.0
Receivables	3438.0	3527.0	3494.0
Inventory (FIFO)	1697.0	1582.0	1626.0
Other	1000.0	1056.0	905.0
Current Assets	15867.0	13475.0	17916.0
Accts Payable	1407.0	1244.0	4459.0
Debt Due	322.0	159.0	164.0
Other	4291.0	4401.0	1766.0
Current Liab.	6020.0	5804.0	6389.0

ANNUAL RATES of change (per sh)	Past 10 Yrs.	Past 5 Yrs.	Est'd '96-'98 to '02-'04
Sales	26.0%	30.5%	*12.0%*
"Cash Flow"	35.5%	34.5%	*13.0%*
Earnings	42.0	34.0%	*15.0%*
Dividends	--	38.0%	*22.0%*
Book Value	27.0%	28.0%	*16.5%*

Cal-endar	QUARTERLY SALES ($ mill.) Mar.31	Jun.30	Sep.30	Dec.31	Full Year
1996	4644	4621	5142	6440	20847
1997	6448	5960	6155	6507	25070
1998	6001	5927	6731	7614	26273
1999	7103	6746	7328	8212	29389
2000	*7950*	*7750*	*8300*	*9000*	*33000*

Cal-endar	EARNINGS PER SHARE A Mar.31	Jun.30	Sep.30	Dec.31	Full Year
1996	.26	.29	.37	.53	1.45
1997	.55	.46	.44	.49	1.94
1998	.36	.33	.45	.59	1.73
1999	.57	.52	.55	.69	2.33
2000	*.66*	*.62*	*.70*	*.82*	*2.80*

Cal-endar	QUARTERLY DIVIDENDS PAID B ■ Mar.31	Jun.30	Sep.30	Dec.31	Full Year
1996	.01	.01	.013	.013	.05
1997	.013	.013	.015	.015	.06
1998	.015	.015	.015	.02	.07
1999	.02	.02	.02	.03	.09
2000					

BUSINESS: Intel Corporation is a leading manufacturer of integrated circuits. Markets served: primarily makers of personal computers; also communications, industrial automation, military, and other electronic equipment. Main products: microprocessors (notably, the Pentium series), microcontrollers, and memory chips. Also sells computer modules and boards, and network products. Foreign business: about 56% of '98 sales. R&D: 9.5% of sales. '98 depreciation rate: 13.3%. Has about 64,500 employees, 203,000 shareholders. Officers/Directors own 6.4% of stock (4/99 proxy). Chairman & C.E.O.: A.S. Grove. President: C.R. Barrett. Incorporated: Delaware. Address: 2200 Mission College Blvd., Santa Clara, CA 95052-8119. Tel: 408-765-8080. Web: www.intc.com.

Intel reported a 34% year-over-year share-net gain for 1999, despite pressures on gross margins during the earlier part of the year. Intel's gross profits had been hindered due to the popularity of the sub-$1000 PC, which resulted in increased demand for lower-end chips. Furthermore, INTC's largest competitor in the semiconductor market, Advanced Micro Devices (AMD), boosted its market share, mostly in the lower-margined area. Indeed, this resulted in intense competition and, consequently, reduced average selling prices for lower-end chips. In response, however, Intel ramped up production of its lower-end *Celeron* chips, and also introduced the *Celeron* 533 processor, which is the fastest chip the company offers in the sub-$1,000 market. Too, INTC has begun to shift production of its *Pentium 3* microprocessors (including the recently-introduced 800 MHz chip) to a 0.18 micron manufacturing process from a 0.35 process, which will reduce unit costs. Consequently, margins rebounded during 1999's fourth quarter, which helped lift bottom-line results 17% on a year-over-year basis.

AMD recently announced a supply-agreement with Gateway. This was due to Gateway's preannounced revenue shortfall, which resulted from a shortage of Intel computer components during the December quarter. (Intel had been Gateway's exclusive supplier.) However, we do not believe that this will significantly alter Intel's earnings prospects.

The key avenue for growth going forward will likely be the Internet and communications markets. The overwhelming popularity of the Internet has resulted in a need for more network servers and other networking devices. In fact, Intel has made several acquisitions in these areas over the past couple of years, the two most recent large purchases being DSP Communications and Level One. Looking ahead, we believe that INTC will continue to augment its presence in the high-growth communications industry.

Intel shares are timely, although much of the issue's 3- to 5-year appreciation potential appears to be reflected in the current price. However, acquisitions, particularly in the Internet-related areas, could add meaningfully to our projections.

Alan G. House *January 21, 2000*

(A) Diluted earnings. Excludes nonrecurring gains (losses): '84, $0.02; '86, $0.01; '87, $0.05; '89, ($0.02); '91, $0.02; '92, ($0.01); '93, $0.01; '94, ($0.16); '95, $0.04; '98 Q1, ($0.05); '99, (22¢). Next earnings report due mid-April. (B) Next dividend meeting about mid-April. Next ex-date about April 29. Dividend payment dates about first of March, June, September, December. ■ Dividend reinvestment plan available. (C) In millions, adjusted for stock splits. (D) Price as of 12:30 pm on 1/14/00.

Company's Financial Strength	A++
Stock's Price Stability	40
Price Growth Persistence	100
Earnings Predictability	55

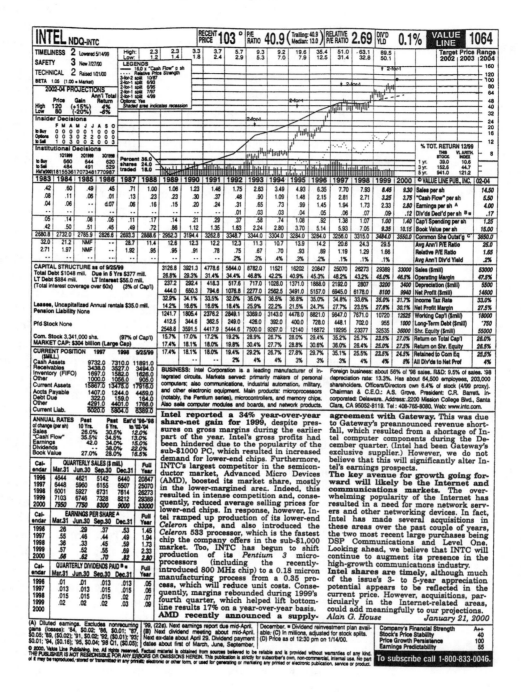

now bring the amateur browser loads of critical corporate research and investment information. Investors can retrieve the latest news and even track the results of their own portfolios on a daily basis.

While there are new sites popping up all the time, some are more useful than others. For example, The Motley Fool at www.fool.com offers a wide array of links and information for anyone who is remotely interested in money. Investors can watch a running tab on the Dow and obtain stock

Figure 5-14A *A page from the January 2000* Standard & Poor's Stock Guide *(part 1 of 2).*

206 VIS-WAR Standard & Poor's

¶ S&P 500 # MidCap 400 ✦ SmallCap 600 • Options

Index	Ticker	Name of Issue (Call Price of Pfd. Stocks)	Market	Com. Rank. & Pfd. Rating	Inst. Hold Cos	Inst. Hold Shs. (000)	Principal Business	Price Range 1971-97 High	1971-97 Low	1998 High	1998 Low	1999 High	1999 Low	Dec. Sales in 100s	Dec. 1999 Last Sale Or Bid High	Low	Last	%Div Yield	P-E Ratio	EPS 5 Yr Growth	% Annualized Total Return 12 Mo	36 Mo	60 Mo
#1•[1]	VSH	✓Vishay Intertechnology	NY,B,Ch,Ph,P	B	279	60193	Electronic resistive systems	30 11/16	1/16	18 3/4	7 3/4	32	8 3/4	107718	32	25 11/16	31 3/4	...	38	-39	173	26.6	17.5
✦2•[2]	VSIO	✓Visio Corp	NNM	NR	174	18076	Dvlp drawing/diagramm'g softwr	42 3/4	8	50 3/4	14	48 11/16	21 1/4	112791	48 11/16	35 3/4	47 1/2	...	39	...	29.9	24.3	...
3	VEI	✓Vista Energy Resources	AS	NR	2	2	Oil & gas explor,dev,prod'n	...	...	3 3/8	1 3/8	2 3/4	1 1/8	1578	2	1 1/2	2	...	d	...	-5.9	...	...
4	WS	Wrrt(Pur at com at $4)	AS	....	1			4 1/8	1/8	2 1/8	1/2	1 1/16	3/8	131	1/2	1/8	1/2	...	..	...	...	...	...
5	VGZ	✓Vista Gold	AS,To,Ph	C	6	4674	Gold/mineral explor'n,devel	14 3/4	3/16	1	1/8	1/4	1/8	51858	1/8	1/8	1/8	...	d	Neg	-39.7	-59.1	-44.3
6	VDAT	✓Visual Data	NNM	NR	15	377	Produce visual on-line info	6 1/2	2 3/8	7 3/16	1 3/16	46 1/2	6 1/4	104461	17 11/16	9 3/4	11 1/2	...	d	-30	67.3	...	...
7	VNWK	✓Visual Networks	NNM	NR	173	16545	Mfr computer systems	...	...	39 3/4	16 3/8	81 1/2	25 1/2	73354	81 1/2	57 3/4	79 3/4	...	..	...	111	...	...
#8•[3]	VISX	✓VISX Inc	NNM,Ch	B-	439	40915	Mfr vision correct'n sys	10 3/16	1 1/16	22	4 7/8	103 7/8	21 1/2	1082225	90 1/8	48 15/16	51 3/4	...	38	NM	141	112	82.1
9	VSF	✓Vita Food Products	AS	NR	1	15	Produce/mkt specialty food pds	4	1 1/4	2 3/8	1/4	3 3/4	7/8	763	2 1/4	1 11/16	1 7/8	...	d	...	114	...	...
10	WS	Wrrt(Pur 1 com at $9)	AS	....	2	5		3/8	1/8	5/16	1/32	1/4	1/16	212	1/16	1/16	1/16	...	..	...	...	...	...
11	VTCH	✓Vitech America	NNM	NR	17	4713	Mfr/distr computer eqp	20 15/16	7 3/8	21 1/4	7 1/2	15 1/2	6	14708	8 3/4	6	8	...	d	Neg	-48.1	-2.1	...
#12•[4]	VTSS	✓Vitesse Semiconductor	NNM	B-	546	123155	Dvlp,mfr integrated circuits	14 1/8	1/2	24 11/16	8 9/16	55 3/4	20 3/8	392976	53 11/16	44 1/8	52 7/16	...	...	NM	130	91.1	128
13	VTNA	Vitran Corp	NNM,To	NR	11	1398	Freight services	7	2 3/8	6 1/2	1 3/8	6 3/4	4 3/4	199	5 9/16	4 7/8	5 3/8	1.3	4	...	6.2	31.2	...
14	VITR	✓Vitria Technology	NNM	NR	28	913	Dvlp e-business software	...	...	...	...	310	16	42860	310	103	234	...	..	...	...	...	...
15•[5]	VTO	✓Vitro,Sociedad Anonima ADS[54]	NY,Ph,P	NR	42	13922	Mfr flat glass/glass products	26 7/8	4 3/4	13 3/8	3 1/4	7 1/2	3 1/2	46044	5 7/8	4 3/4	5 1/2	4.7	d	-46	26.2	2.5	-11.4
16•[2]	VVUS	✓Vivus Inc	NNM	NR	51	5795	Dvlp stge:pharmac'l R&D	41 1/4	5 3/8	15 1/2	2 1/16	6	1 15/16	556561	6	1 15/16	3 1/8	...	18	NM	21.7	-44.1	-16.1
17	VIXL	✓Vixel Corp	NNM	NR	..	...	Computer software & systems	...	...	...	...	53 1/2	17	145491	44	17	17 1/16	...	..	...	...	...	...
#18•[5]	VL	✓Vlasic Foods Intl	NY	NR	139	10791	Mfr/dvlp specialty foods	...	...	27	13 11/16	23 7/16	4 15/16	39789	8 9/16	4 15/16	5 11/16	...	d	...	-76.1	...	...
19	VOCL	✓VocalTec Commun Ltd	NNM	NR	11	343	Voice/audio communic softwr	33 1/4	3 7/8	24 3/8	5 9/16	19 3/4	8	51157	19 3/4	13	16 3/8	...	d	-41	48.9	41.8	...
•20•[6]	VOD	✓Vodafone AirTouch ADR[55]	NY,Ch,Ph,P	NR	1167	546658	Mobile telecom svcs in U.K.	15 1/16	1 15/16	33 3/8	13 11/16	53 3/8	33 1/8	616148	53 1/4	47	49 1/2	0.4	52	8	54.6	83.7	51.3
21	VTEK	✓Vodavi Technology	NNM	NR	1	3	Dgn/dvp telephone sys & prd	8 7/8	2 1/8	5 3/8	1 3/4	3 3/4	1 7/8	3303	3 1/4	2 3/8	3 1/16	...	9	14	11.3	-4.9	...
✦22	VOL	✓Volt Info Sciences	NY	B	90	5262	Tech svs: mfr typesetters	70 1/4	1/16	58 1/8	15 9/16	27 7/16	15 1/2	5016	27 7/16	19 7/8	23 7/8	...	13	16	5.8	-6.4	20.4
23•[7]	VOLVY	✓Volvo AB 'B' ADR[57]	NNM	NR	38	4659	Swedish auto,truck,bus mfg	30 3/8	4 11/16	35 1/2	19 1/4	32 1/4	23 3/4	19134	25 7/8	23 3/4	25 1/8	2.4	14	8	11.3	...	...
24	VOO	✓Vornado Operating	AS	NR	46	1094	Real estate investments	...	...	8 1/2	5 3/4	10	5 3/4	2430	6 13/16	5 3/4	6	...	..	...	-25.6	...	...
25	VNO	✓Vornado Realty Trust	NY,B,Ch,Ph	NR	221	57304	Real estate investment trust	47 3/8	3/16	49 15/16	26	40	29 11/16	57072	33 15/16	29 11/16	32 1/2	e5.9	11	13	...	...	...
26	Pr A	$3.25 Cv'A'Pfd([60]NC)	NY	BBB-	45	4628		68 3/4	48 3/4	70 1/2	39 1/4	56	43	13730	47 3/4	43	46 3/4	7.0	..	...	...	...	...
27•[5]	VOYN	✓Voyager.net	NNM	NR	29	3473	Dial-up internet svc provider	...	...	...	...	20 1/2	6 9/16	74832	11 9/16	7 3/4	9 9/16	...	..	...	...	...	...
28	VSEC	VSE Corp	NNM	B+	5	25	Engin'g,dev,test,mgmt svc	17 9/16	5/8	13	5 1/2	12 1/4	6 3/4	100	9	7 1/8	7 3/4	1.8	11	-23	-28.4	-11.7	10.8
29	VIS	✓VSI Holdings	AS	NR	4	309	Mktg svcs/Entmt/Retail	17	1/8	8 1/8	3 3/16	7 1/4	3	4902	4 3/4	3	4 7/16	...	49	NM	-15.5	55.2	51.2
30•[8]	VTEL	✓Vtel Corp	NNM	C	34	5423	Mfr multimedia conferenc'g sys	26	3 1/2	7 11/16	2 1/2	9 1/4	2	52900	3 15/16	3	3 1/4	...	d	Neg	28.1	-31.0	-17.7
31	VUL	✓Vulcan Int'l Corp	AS,Ch	B	13	141	Shoe lasts,heels:bowl pins	40	1 1/2	41 1/4	30	38 1/8	26 3/4	288	31 1/2	30 1/8	31 1/2	2.5	35	82	-4.8	3.1	15.6
¶32•[9]	VMC	✓Vulcan Materials	NY,B,Ch,Ph	A	355	63178	Constr'n materials/chemicals	34 3/4	7/8	44 11/16	31 5/16	51 1/4	34 9/16	38859	41	36 3/4	39 15/16	2.0	18	20	-7.5	27.7	21.5
33	VYSI	✓Vysis Inc	NNM	NR	7	1167	Cancer product R & D	...	...	12 3/4	3	6 13/16	2 7/16	10143	3 15/16	2 7/16	3 3/4	...	d	...	-32.6	...	...
✦34	WDFC	✓W D-40 Co	NNM	B+	138	5298	Aerosol lubricant/rust prev	32 7/8	5/8	33	20	29 1/8	17 3/4	14185	24	17 3/4	22 1/8	5.8	16	1	-18.7	-0.2	5.1
✦35•[5]	WNC	✓Wabash National	NY,Ph,P	NR	147	16537	Mfr/mkt truck trailers	43 1/2	8 11/16	31 7/8	10 1/4	22 1/2	10 7/8	18780	15 3/4	13 1/16	15	1.1	13	...	-25.5	-5.9	-16.9
¶36•[1]	WB	✓Wachovia Corp	NY,B,Ph,P	A-	628	102786	Comml bkg, N.&S.Carolina, GA	83 15/16	2 1/16	96 15/16	72 3/4	92 5/16	65 7/16	96982	80 1/16	65 7/16	68	3.2	14	8	-20.3	9.0	19.4
37	WAK	✓Wackenhut Corp Cl'A'	NY,Ch	B	69	1860	Investigative/security sv/sys	31	13/16	26	18	29 3/4	12 3/8	6832	14 15/16	12 3/8	14 15/16	...	12	21	-40.9	-3.6	17.3
38	WAK B	✓ Cl'B'	NY,Ch	B	41	6915		27 7/8	6	23	14 15/16	24	8 1/8	14667	10 15/16	8 1/8	10 9/16	...	8	21	-52.6	-11.1	11.6
39•[4]	WHC	✓Wackenhut Corrections	NY,Ch,Ph	NR	77	6199	Oper correctional facilities	45	4 1/2	30 7/8	15	28 9/16	9 3/4	21666	12 9/16	9 3/4	11 11/16	...	13	43	-59.2	-16.4	7.0
40•[2]	WDR	✓Waddell & Reed Fin'l 'A'	NY,Ph	NR	271	24487	Investment mgmt svcs	...	...	28	16 7/16	28	18 9/16	12491	27 9/16	24 3/4	27 1/8	2.0	19	...	17.2	...	...
41	WDR.B	Cl'B'	NY	NR	133	16924		...	...	24 1/8	18 3/4	27 3/4	18 1/4	8853	25 1/4	23 1/8	25 1/8	2.1	18	...	10.6	...	...
¶42•[10]	WMT	✓Wal-Mart Stores	NY,B,Ch,P	A+	1897	1580519	Operates discount stores	20 15/16	1/64	41 3/8	18 3/4	70 1/4	38 11/16	1370434	70 1/4	57	69 1/8	0.3	55	16	70.5	83.6	46.5
43	WDN	✓Walden Residential Prop	NY,Ch	NR	113	8918	Real estate investment trust	26 7/8	16 1/4	27 1/8	19 1/4	21 15/16	16	24563	21 3/8	20 7/16	21 3/8	8.9	41	-6	17.0	4.2	13.5
44	Pr B	9.16% Sr'B'Cv Pfd([61]25)	NY	NR	16	1151		30 1/2	23	30 1/2	22 3/8	25 1/8	20 1/16	231	24 1/8	23	24 3/16	9.3	..	...	...	...	...
¶45•[11]	WAG	✓Walgreen Co	NY,B,Ch,P	A+	964	509151	Major retail drug chain	16 13/16	1/16	30 9/16	14 3/4	33 15/16	22 11/16	419706	32 7/8	27 1/4	29 1/4	0.5	47	17	6.4	46.6	43.0
46	WSDI	✓Wall Street Deli	NNM	C	13	402	Operates fast food restaurants	14 1/2	1 1/8	5 1/8	3	5 1/8	1	2674	1 3/8	1	1 1/8	...	d	-28	-67.3	-40.2	-35.1
#47•[2]	WCS	✓Wallace Computer Svc	NY,Ch,Ph,P	A	218	32210	Business forms:comm'l print	40 3/4	7/8	40	15 7/16	27 1/4	14 15/16	67209	20 3/8	14 15/16	16 3/8	4.0	9	7	-34.9	-19.6	5.1
48•[12]	WLT	✓Walter Industries	NY	NR	97	31880	Homebuilding Prd & svcs	22	11 13/16	22 3/8	10 3/8	16 7/16	7 15/16	18567	11 1/2	7 15/16	10 13/16	...	14	NM	-29.2	-8.4	...
#49•[3]	WAC	✓Warnaco Group'A'	NY,Ph,P	B-	242	45348	Mfr women's intimate apparel	35 9/16	10 1/2	44 7/16	18 1/2	30 3/8	10 1/8	193937	13 7/16	10 1/8	12 9/16	2.9	6	1	-50.5	-24.4	-5.5
¶50•[11]	WLA	✓Warner-Lambert	NY,B,C,Ch,P,Ph	A-	1654	559969	Drugs:toiletries:food:gum	50 7/8	1 7/16	85 15/16	39 3/8	93 15/16	60 15/16	569181	90	79 3/8	81 15/16	1.0	43	...	10.2	50.3	47.5

Uniform Footnote Explanations-See Page 1. Other: [1]P:Cycle 1. [2]Ph:Cycle 3. [3]ASE:Cycle 3. [4]CBOE:Cycle 1. [5]CBOE:Cycle 2. [6]ASE,CBOE,P:Cycle 3. [7]CBOE,Ph:Cycle 1. [8]CBOE:Cycle 3. [9]P:Cycle 2. [10]ASE,CBOE,P,Ph:Cycle 3. [11]ASE:Cycle 1. [12]Ph:Cycle 1. [51]If com exceeds $6 for 90 con days. [52]Fiscal Dec'95 & prior in Cdn Funds. [53]If com exceeds $11.40 for 20 of 30 con trad days. [54]Ea ADS rep 3 ord. [55]Each ADR rep 10 ord shr,5p. [56]Approx. [57]Each ADR rep 1 Cl'B' shr 25 SEK. [58]11 Wk Dec'98. [59]Stk dstr of Vornado Oper Co. [60]Fr 4-1-2001 into 0.68728 com,re-spec cond. [61]Re-spec cond. [62]Spcl Redm'Ir 4-1-2001 into 1.38465 com,re-spec cond. [63]8 Mo Sep'95. [64]Fiscal Dec'95 & prior. [65]12 Mo Jul'96. [66]®$3.80,'96. [67]Fr 4-30-2006,or earlier to preserve'REIT'status. [68]To be determined.

Figure 5-14B *Continued.*

Common and Convertible Preferred Stocks

Index	Cash Divs. Ea.Yr. Since	Dividends: Latest Payment: Period $	Date	Ex. Div.	Total $: So Far 1999	Ind. Rate	Paid 1998	Financial Position Mil-$: Cash& Equiv.	Curr. Assets	Curr. Liab.	Balance Sheet Date
1♦	....	5%Stk	6-11-98	5-28	...	Nil	5%Stk	102	960	328	9-30-99
2♦	....	None Since Public			...	Nil	....	112	153	42.0	6-30-99
3	....	None Since Public			...	Nil	....	0.02	4.62	4.84	9-30-99
4	....	Terms&trad. basis should			be checked in detail			Wrrts expire 11-1-2002			
5	....	None Paid			...	Nil	....	3.92	14.5	6.05	6-30-99
6	....	None Since Public			...	Nil	....	5.70	7.71	1.86	6-30-99
7	....	None Since Public			...	Nil	....	54.9	73.3	32.1	9-30-99
8♦	....	None Since Public			...	Nil	....	225	310	50.5	9-30-99
9	....	None Since Public			...	Nil	....	0.08	7.18	3.95	9-30-99
10	....	Terms&trad. basis should			be checked in detail			Wrrts expire 1-16-2002			
11♦	....	Wrrt	3-22-99		Wrrt	Nil	....	9.59	89.8	50.2	9-30-99
12♦	....	None Since Public			...	Nil	....	198	320	27.0	6-30-99
13	1995	gS0.035	12-31-99	12-13	g0.07	0.07	g0.07	n/a	62.6	64.7	j6-30-99
14♦	....	None Since Public			...	Nil	....	65.9	75.2	17.7	6-30-99
15♦	1992	0.26¼	4-14-99	3-31	0.26¼	0.26	0.246	78.0	729	606	12-31-98
16♦	....	None Since Public			...	Nil	....	42.2	49.4	33.0	9-30-99
17	....	None Since Public			...	Nil	....	Equity per shr $1.18			7-04-99
18	....	None Since Public			...	Nil	....	0.26	298	143	10-31-99
19	....	None Since Public			...	Nil	....	36.4	50.4	7.85	12-31-98
20♦	1989	[60]0.106	2-21-00	11-23	0.211	0.21	0.19	6.10	792	1530	j3-31-99
21	....	None Since Public			...	Nil	....	2.38	21.6	5.96	9-30-99
22♦	....	0.003	11-15-67	10-10	...	Nil	....	24.9	437	284	7-30-99
23♦	1984	0.606	5-17-99	4-29	0.606	0.61	0.554	20224	105046	81375	j12-31-98
24	....	None Since Public			...	Nil	....	Total Assets $23.6M			9-30-99
25♦	1990	†Q0.48	11-16-99	11-4	†1.807	1.92	h[58]1.64	Total Assets $5.31M			9-30-99
26	1997	Q0.81¼	1-3-00	12-20	3.25	3.25	3.25	Cv into 1.38465 com			
27	....	None Since Public			...	Nil	....	17.7	22.0	15.4	9-30-99
28♦	1973	Q0.036	2-22-00	1-28	0.144	0.14	0.144	0.29	25.6	13.2	9-30-99
29	....	None Since Public			...	Nil	....	0.64	61.6	56.9	6-30-99
30	....	None Since Public			...	Nil	....	12.7	60.4	48.8	10-31-99
31	1976	Q0.20	12-15-99	12-1	0.80	0.80	0.80	47.8	50.8	18.2	9-30-99
32♦	1934	Q0.19½	12-10-99	11-22	0.78	0.78	0.693	84.6	703	494	9-30-99
33	....	None Since Public			...	Nil	....	9.98	18.7	9.10	9-30-99
34♦	1973	Q0.32	1-28-00	1-5	1.28	1.28	1.28	9.94	52.1	20.4	8-31-99
35♦	1993	Q0.04	1-27-00	1-11	0.15	0.16	0.14	32.4	443	180	9-30-99
36	1936	Q0.54	12-1-99	11-2	2.06	2.16	1.86	Total Deposits $39708.85M			9-30-99
37♦	1966	Div Discontinued 5-7-99			0.15	Nil	0.29	Total Assets $465.00M			10-03-99
38♦	1993	Div Discontinued 5-7-99			0.15	Nil	0.29	....	...	...	
39♦	....	None Since Public			...	Nil	....	22.7	107	36.7	10-03-99
40	1998	Q0.13¼	2-1-00	1-7	0.53	0.53	0.39¾	146	184	225	9-30-99
41	1999	Q0.13¼	2-1-00	1-7	0.53	0.53	....	....	...	...	
42♦	1973	Q0.05	1-10-00	12-15	0.18¾	0.20	0.15	1435	26955	28992	10-31-99
43	1994	Q0.48¾	12-1-99	11-16	1.93	1.93	1.93	Total Assets $1497.44M			9-30-99
44	1996	Q0.57¼	12-1-99	11-16	2.29	2.29	2.29	Cv into 1.1406 com			
45♦	1933	Q0.034	12-11-99	11-10	0.13¼	0.135	0.12⅝	142	3222	1924	8-31-99
46	....	None Since Public			...	Nil	....	1.22	4.68	6.88	10-02-99
47♦	1933	Q0.16½	3-20-00	2-28	0.64½	0.66	0.62½	13.3	458	214	10-31-99
48	1999	0.03	11-30-99	11-8	0.03	[60]....	....	Total Assets $3366.73M			8-31-99
49♦	1995	Q0.09	1-6-00	12-3	0.36	0.36	0.36	13.8	1045	740	10-02-99
50♦	1926	Q0.20	12-10-99	11-3	0.80	0.80	0.64	1600	5049	3378	9-30-99

Index	Capitalization: Lg Trm Debt Mil-$	Shs. 000: Pfd.	Com.	Earnings $ Per Shr.: Years End	1995	1996	1997	1998	1999	Last 12 Mos.	Interim Earnings: Period	$ per Shr.: 1998	1999	Index
1♦	724	...	±84657	Dc	v±1.18	±v0.62	±v0.63	v±0.10	E0.88†	0.11	9 Mo Sep	v0.54	v0.55	1
2♦	....	...	30166	Sp	p0.10	0.38	v0.44	v0.89	Pv1.23	1.23				2
3	52.6	...	16367	Dc	...	...	vpd0.03	vd1.95	....	d1.89	9 Mo Sep	vd0.05	v0.01	3
4	....	...	4739	Dc	...	....	...	....	....	....	Callable at 8¢[51]			4
5	14.2	...	90715	Dc	[52]0.07	vd0.21	vd0.61	vd0.02	....	d0.13	6 Mo Jun	v0.03	vd0.08	5
6	0.91	...	8234	Sp	d0.43	d1.35	vd1.42	vd1.06	Pvd1.20	d1.20				6
7	0.87	...	24761	Dc	...	...	vpd0.01	v0.02	....	0.37	9 Mo Sep	vd0.40	vd0.05	7
8♦	....	...	64313	Dc	vd0.30	v0.27	v0.23	v0.39	E1.36	1.23	9 Mo Sep	v0.13	v0.97	8
9	4.03	...	3707	Dc	p0.07	v0.28	vd0.25	vd0.16	....	d0.01	9 Mo Sep	vd0.18	vd0.03	9
10	....	...	750	Dc	...	...	....	....	....	....	Callable at 1¢[53]			10
11♦	52.2	...	15196	Dc	v0.76	v0.85	v1.06	v1.34	....	d1.06	9 Mo Sep	v0.92	vd1.48	11
12♦	....	...	153470	Sp	0.02	0.11	v0.22	v0.34	Pv0.42	0.42				12
13	62.0	...	9888	Dc	v0.32	v0.05	v0.54	v0.83	....	j0.97	9 Mo Sep	v0.63	v0.77	13
14♦	....	...	30959	Dc	...	...	...	vpd0.48	....	....	9 Mo Sep	n/a	vpd0.49	14
15♦	1298	...	314000	Dc	0.59	Δd4.53	Δv1.05	vΔd0.73	....	d0.73				15
16♦	....	...	32156	Dc	vd0.85	vd0.55	v1.03	vd2.52	....	0.18	9 Mo Sep	vd2.55	v0.15	16
17	p10.2	p...	★21629	Dc	....	....	...	pvd1.42	....	....	6 Mo Jun	n/a	pvd0.61	17
18	499	...	45502	Jl	...	....	pv1.10	vpd0.52	vd2.78	d2.79	3 Mo Oct	v0.10	v0.09	18
19	....	...	11413	Dc	d0.23	vd0.86	vd0.89	vd2.08	....	d2.40	9 Mo Sep	vd1.71	vd2.03	19
20♦	1700	...	p2921400	Mr	0.31	v0.39	v0.46	v0.68	E0.95	0.26	6 Mo Sep	v0.37	vd0.05	20
21	9.74	...	4342	Dc	v0.17	vd1.02	v0.05	v0.23	....	0.33	9 Mo Sep	v0.15	v0.25	21
22♦	56.2	...	15030	Oc	□1.13	□1.51	v2.62	v1.37	Pv1.91	1.91				22
23♦	26012	...	±442000	Dc	3.03	3.94	v2.98	v2.35	E1.80	8.86	6 Mo Jun	v1.27	v7.78	23
24	4.59	...	4068	Dc	...	...	...	v[44]d0.22	....	....	9 Mo Sep	n/a	vd1.18	24
25♦	2073	13789	85948	Dc	v1.12	v1.25	v0.79	v1.59	E3.10	1.91	9 Mo Sep	v1.19	v1.51	25
26	....	5789	...	Dc	...	...	...	....	....	....	'REIT status'redm provision anytime[142]			26
27	1.84	...	p31650	Dc	...	...	...	vpd1.05	....	....	9 Mo Sep	n/a	vpd0.45	27
28♦	6.34	...	2115	Dc	v0.76	v0.79	vd0.68	v0.75	....	0.69	9 Mo Sep	v0.49	v0.43	28
29	19.3	...	32611	Sp	r[43]d0.03	d0.80	vp0.18	v0.27	....	0.09	9 Mo Jun	v0.20	v0.02	29
30	0.25	...	24534	Jl	[44]0.30	p[44]d0.57	vd2.45	v0.12	vd0.66	d0.56	3 Mo Oct	vd0.32	vd0.22	30
31	....	...	1094	Dc	vd0.07	v1.63	v1.44	v1.23	....	0.91	6 Mo Jun	v0.69	v0.37	31
32♦	688	...	100049	Dc	v1.54	v1.79	v2.03	v2.50	E2.26	2.29	9 Mo Sep	v1.92	v1.71	32
33	0.14	...	9926	Dc	...	pd2.98	vd15.89	vd1.91	....	d1.40	9 Mo Sep	vd1.35	vd0.84	33
34♦	14.1	...	15603	Au	1.33	v1.38	v1.37	v1.40	v1.41	1.37	3 Mo Nov	v0.24	v0.20	34
35♦	162	482	22979	Dc	v1.34	v0.19	v0.74	v0.99	....	1.17	9 Mo Sep	v0.92	v1.10	35
36	8576	...	202743	Dc	v3.36	v[44]3.65	v2.94	v4.18	E4.95	4.79	9 Mo Sep	v3.01	v3.62	36
37♦	8.40	...	±14967	Dc	v±0.60	v±0.65	±v0.01	v□1.03	....	1.23	9 Mo Sep	v□±0.72	v±0.92	37
38♦	....	...	†11111	Dc	±0.60	±0.66	±v0.01	□v±1.03	....	1.23	9 Mo Sep	v±□0.72	v±0.92	38
39♦	....	...	22387	Dc	v0.25	v0.37	v0.52	v□0.74	....	0.91	9 Mo Sep	v□0.55	v0.72	39
40	....	...	±57885	Dc	...	...	pv1.10	v1.27	....	1.45	9 Mo Sep	v0.94	v1.12	40
41	....	...	31912	Dc	...	...	pv±1.10	v1.27	....	1.37	3 Mo Mar	0.25	v±0.35	41
42♦	16559	...	4453743	Ja	v0.60	v0.67	v0.78	v0.99	E1.25	1.17	9 Mo Oct	v0.64	v0.82	42
43	768	6993	25465	Dc	v□0.80	□v1.02	v□0.55	v□0.60	....	0.53	9 Mo Sep	v□0.64	v□0.57	43
44	....	1709	...	Dc	...	...	...	....	....	....				44
45♦	....	...	1004000	Au	0.33	v0.38	v0.44	v0.54	v0.62	0.62				45
46	....	...	2896	Je	vd0.27	vd0.72	v0.02	vd1.24	vd0.79	d0.87	3 Mo Sep	v0.01	vd0.07	46
47♦	406	...	41887	Jl	1.23	1.60	v1.86	v1.71	v1.80	1.84	3 Mo Oct	v0.40	v0.44	47
48	2335	...	50036	My	pd0.75	□d1.56	v0.67	v□1.08	v0.69	0.76	3 Mo Aug	v0.17	v0.24	48
49♦	847	...	55635	Dc	v□1.10	vd0.16	v0.42	v□0.22	E1.92↓	1.15	9 Mo Sep	v□0.72	v1.65	49
50♦	1281	...	858661	Dc	v0.90	v0.95	v1.04	v1.48	E1.92	....	9 Mo Sep	n/a	v1.41	50

♦Stock Splits & Divs By Line Reference Index [1]2-for-1,'95:5-for-4,'99. [2]2-for-1,'97. [8]2-for-1,'99(twice). [11]10%,'98. [12]3-for-2,'97:2-for-1,'98,'99. [14]To split 2-for-1,ex Jan 19,'00. [15]6-for-5,'95. [16]2-for-1,'97. [20]5-for-1,'99. [22]2-for-1,'95:3-for-2,'97. [23]5-for-1,'94:No adj for stk dstr of Swedish Match,'96. [25]2-for-1,'97. [28]2-for-1,'96:5-for-4,'98. [32]3-for-1,'99. [34]2-for-1,'97. [35]3-for-2,'94. [37]5-for-4 in Cl'B',95,'96. [38]5-for-4,'95,'96. [39]2-for-1,'96. [42]2-for-1,'99. [45]2-for-1,'95,'97,'99. [47]2-for-1,'96. [49]2-for-1,'94. [50]2-for-1,'96:3-for-1,'98.

quotes and valuable tips. This site also has many how-to links about finance for both the personal and professional investor.

Another site is www.money.net. It claims to be the first and only site that enables users to track a portfolio in real time for free without buying expensive hardware or downloading additional software. After a portfolio has been set up, the site will track security values and enable the user to save the information electronically. This site is simple to use and has an extremely content-rich homepage.

Finally, various search engines will enable you to gather all kinds of information. Your *Internet Service Provider* (ISP) can generally recommend sources for seeking out the best investment information on the World Wide Web. Most individual companies have their own Web sites for browsers, while brokerage and investment firms have a wide array of data to discover in this ever-changing world of financial information.

Chapter 6

Analysis: Tools and Theories

Introduction

This chapter will cover an area that is critical for making client recommendations. We must understand the volatility of various averages and indices. Advising clients in guarding against uncertain risk is important. In structuring portfolios, we need to strategize in order to reach specific objectives. The use of fundamental and technical analyses must be weighed together when making a decision to purchase both individual stocks and mutual funds. Finally, an understanding of market theories will help us structure portfolios in the most prudent manner thus reducing instability.

We have seen how volatile the markets can be when overvaluation occurs. For example, the week ending April 14, 2000 saw major U.S. markets experience a free fall. Figure 6-1 illustrates graphically how the *Dow Jones Industrial Average* (DJIA) fell by 7.3 percent and the NASDAQ dropped by 25 percent. Even in one day, the indices can lose significant value, as shown on Friday, April 14 with the Dow off 5.7 percent and the NASDAQ off 9.7 percent.

This kind of market activity is scary to most investors, whether they are new or experienced. This particular sell-off resulted from a combination of factors, including fears of rising interest rates in anticipation of higher inflation, an over-extension of investors covering margin debt, and a correction to more realistic values in technology stocks. Many new investors who had never experienced a major market correction received a taste of what it was really like to actually lose money. Likewise, experienced investors who had not taken the time to diversify their money into foreign securities received a dose of reality by of having all their eggs in one basket (in this case, the U.S. equities market).

Likewise, this kind of volatility makes all the difference in the world to short-term investors. Those who are in the market to make a quick profit will lose big when the market decides that it is time for the bears to suddenly take charge. Making a killing in the market literally means attempting to make big profits without suffering huge losses. Most short-

Figure 6-1 *DJIA and NASDAQ falls the week ending April 14, 2000.*

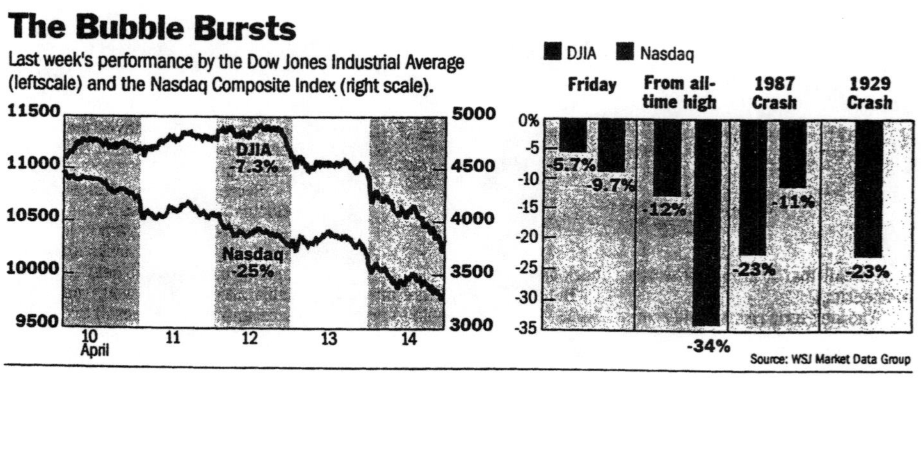

term traders look for the former to occur and never think that the latter will ever happen. They hope to be in a cash position if and when the market turns south.

For patient, long-term investors, however, this type of pullback can be viewed as a minor hiccup. For example, they know that the tumble in high-flying technology stocks is just a reminder of the importance of diversification. By spreading their investment dollars across several asset sectors, the losses do not cut so deeply nor hurt nearly as much. This situation gives us an excellent opportunity to examine various market indices and to show why diversification is such a powerful tool for successful investment-planning.

Averages and Indices

Figure 6-2 shows the activity on the DJIA during the past one and five year periods. The top graph shows that the index of 30 large company stocks had not changed much during the one-year period from April 1999 to April 2000. The index had struggled to gain higher ground as it fought the change in popularity to new economy stocks in the NASDAQ. We do see an excellent gain in these averages, however, from a low of slightly higher than 4,000 to a high of 11,908 over the past five years in the bottom graph. A short-term investor would not look as favorably upon the one-year index as a long-term investor who is patiently awaiting a rise in blue-chip stocks.

The *Standard & Poor's 500* (S&P 500) Index—Figure 6-3 shows a similar pattern to the DJIA, but with a representation of the 500 largest stocks traded on the NYSE. The top graph shows a low of 1,233.70 in October 1999 compared to a high of 1,553.11 in March 2000, or a rise of 26 percent. The five-year graph was also favorable and would have spurred buying activity from both short-term and long-term investors who had studied it.

The NASDAQ Composite Index (NASDAQ)—Figure 6-4 shows a sharp rise in this index from October 1999 through March 2000. The 52-week low of 2,329.87, compared to the high of 5,132.52, represents a gain of 120 percent. Clearly, this type of activity would make it tempting for any investor to jump on board for the perceived ride to much higher profits. However the five-year graph would clearly indicate some built-in speculation with the sudden jump during 1999. This situation would have warned the long-term investor that diversification of the indices described previously would have been a prudent strategy to help lower the overall market risk of being only in the NASDAQ.

The Russell 2000 Index (Russell 2000)—Figure 6-5 represents companies with much smaller capitalizations. The one-year graph shows similar activity to the NASDAQ Composite Index, while the five-year graph shows a more pronounced decline during 1998. In this case, the five-year graph would have given more of a precautionary warning of just how volatile this index can be. Long-term investors would have been more inclined to diversify their holdings away from this market sector into larger-cap stocks.

Figure 6-2 *DJIA activity.*

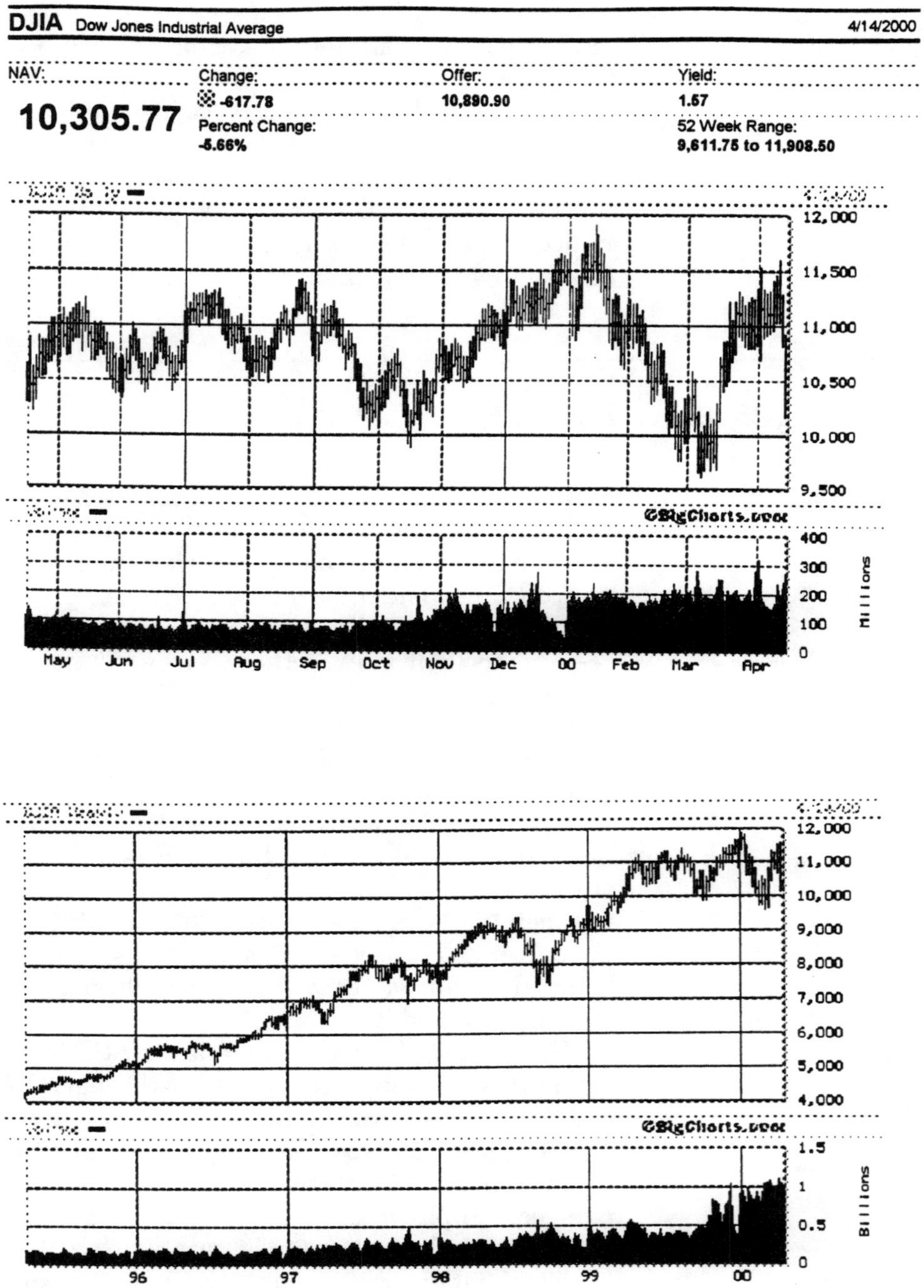

Mainstay Institutional Funds EAFE Index Fund (EAFE)—As shown in Figure 6-6, the EAFE measures the return of foreign company stocks in different countries around the world. With a low of $11.34 in June 1999 to a high of $13.88 in late-December 1999, investors would have realized a gain of 22 percent. The five-year graph, however, shows a slightly negative return. As mentioned earlier, investors would not have suffered as

Figure 6-3 *Representation of the 500 largest stocks traded on the NYSE.*

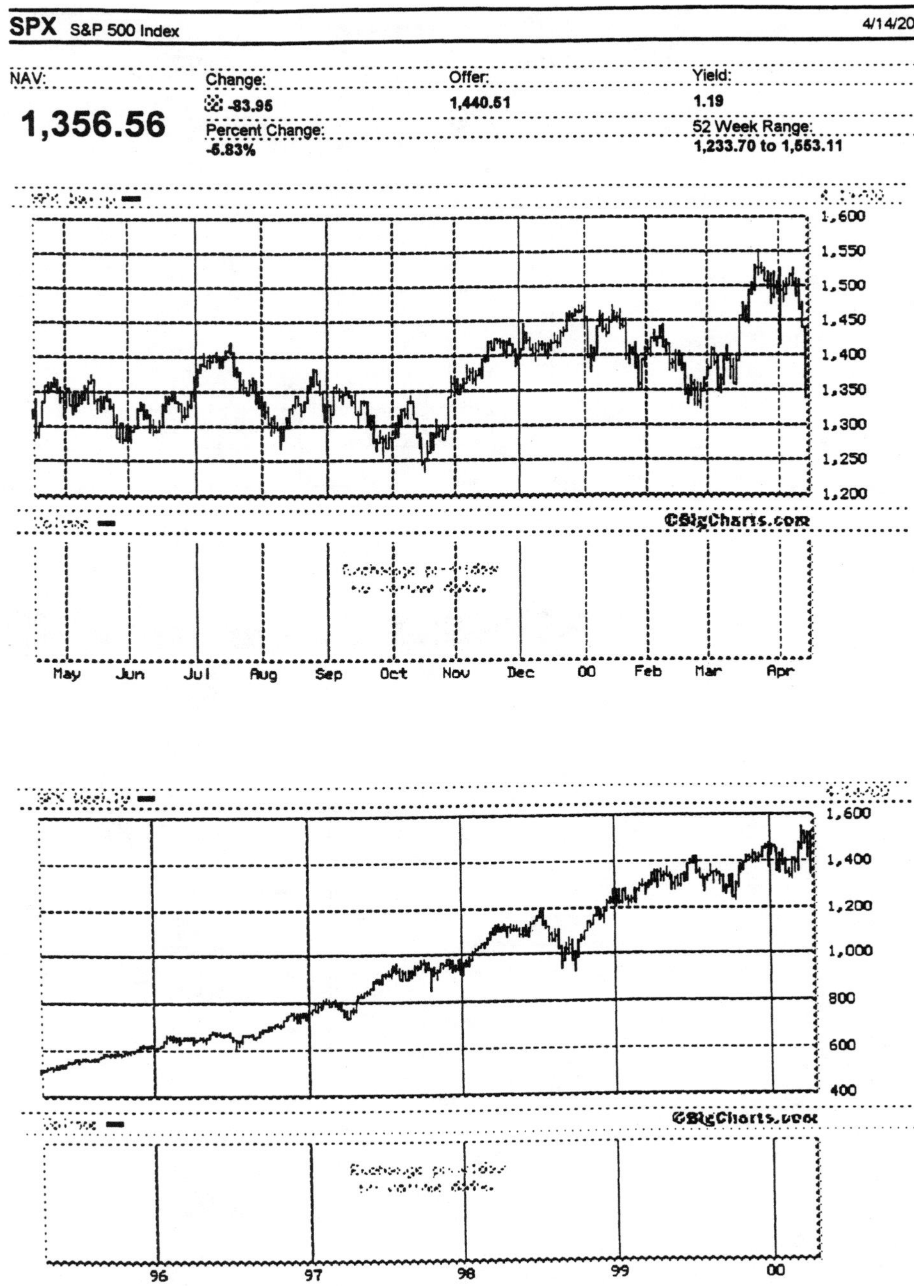

severe of a decline during the first quarter of 2000 by having a portion of their U.S. stock portfolio in this area.

In summary, the more negatively correlated that one index is to the other, the more true diversification that we have available to a given portfolio. In other words, in structuring an investment program, we want the client to diversify across several areas that do not necessarily move either up or down with each other at the same time. Rather, we would like to see

Figure 6-4 *A sharp rise in the NASDAQ Composite Index.*

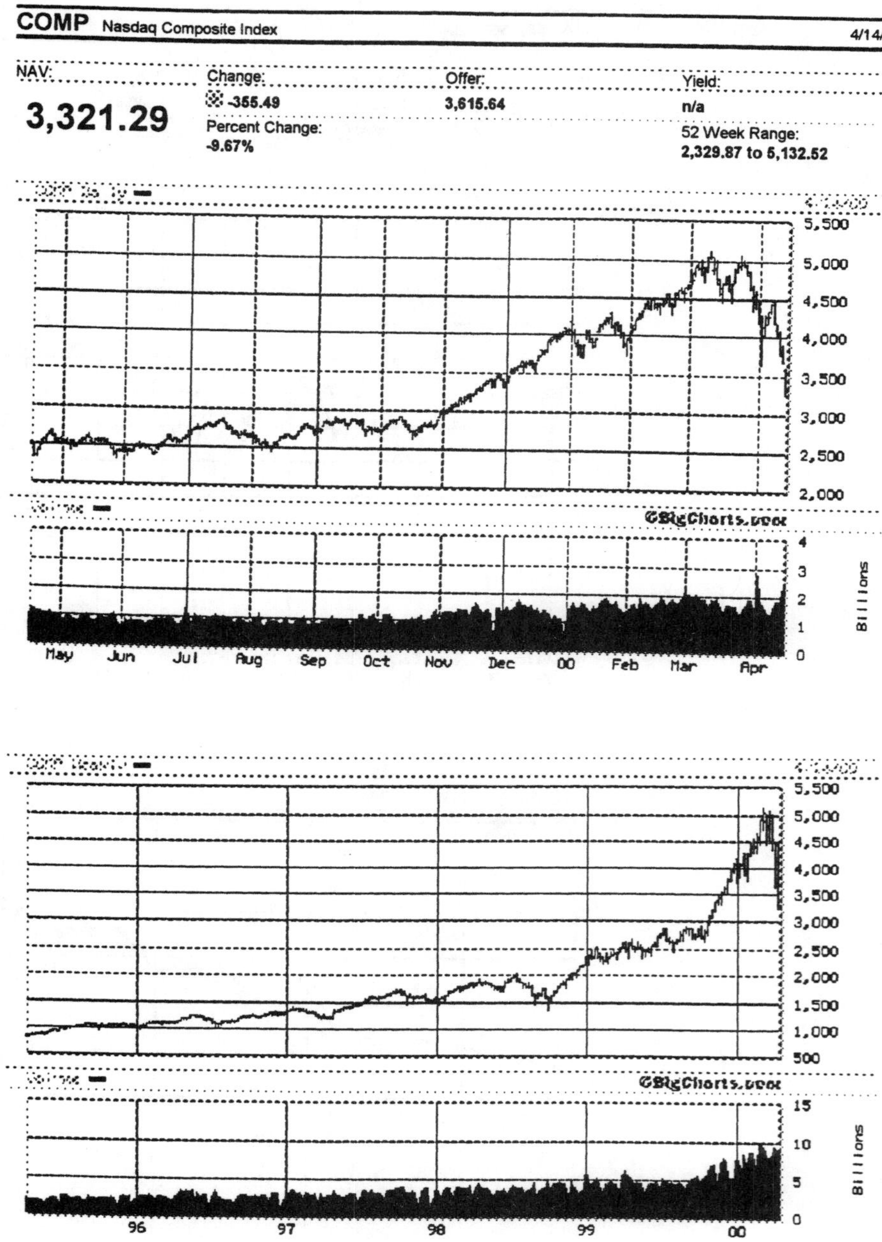

movements in the opposite direction. This situation resulted during the first quarter of 2000, with the NASDAQ moving up sharply while the DJIA was declining significantly.

Don't get me wrong—we are not against a portfolio of all U.S. stocks. Rather, we want to help guard against having a significant amount of money in any one index that falls substantially. During a bull market and favorable economic conditions, both large and small company stocks will tend to rise together. But a slowdown in consumer spending and a subsequent reduction in economic growth will more than likely cause stocks in all categories to decline.

Figure 6-5 *Companies that have much smaller capitalizations.*

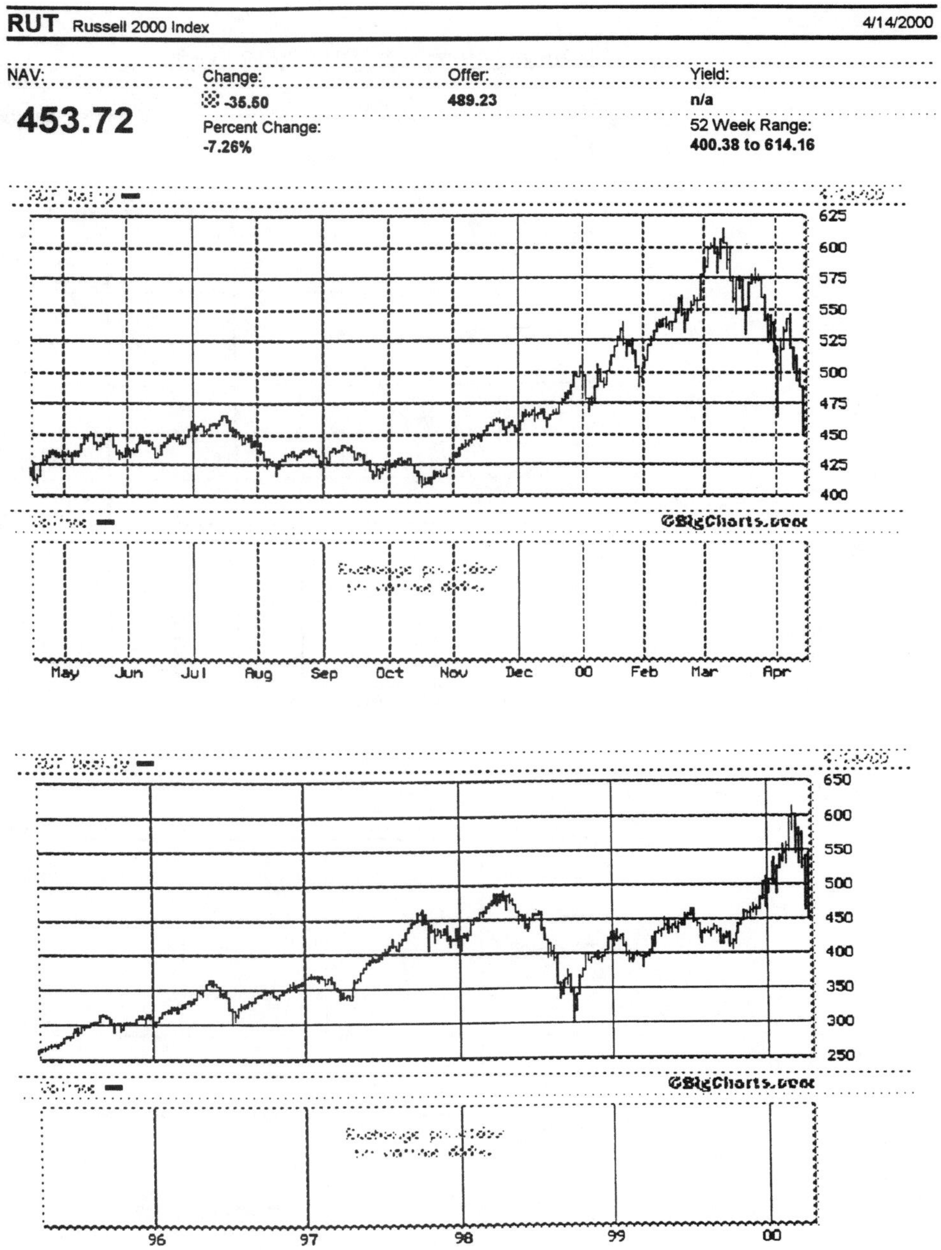

Lessons to Learn from an Erratic Stock Market

As we have observed during the year 2000, investors lose plenty of sleep during periods of high market volatility. This situation gives us some important lessons to recognize as we head into the future:

1. **Stocks should never be detached from other investment classes**—It is essential to compare them with two main alternatives:

Figure 6-6 *The EAFE measures the return of foreign-company stocks in different countries.*

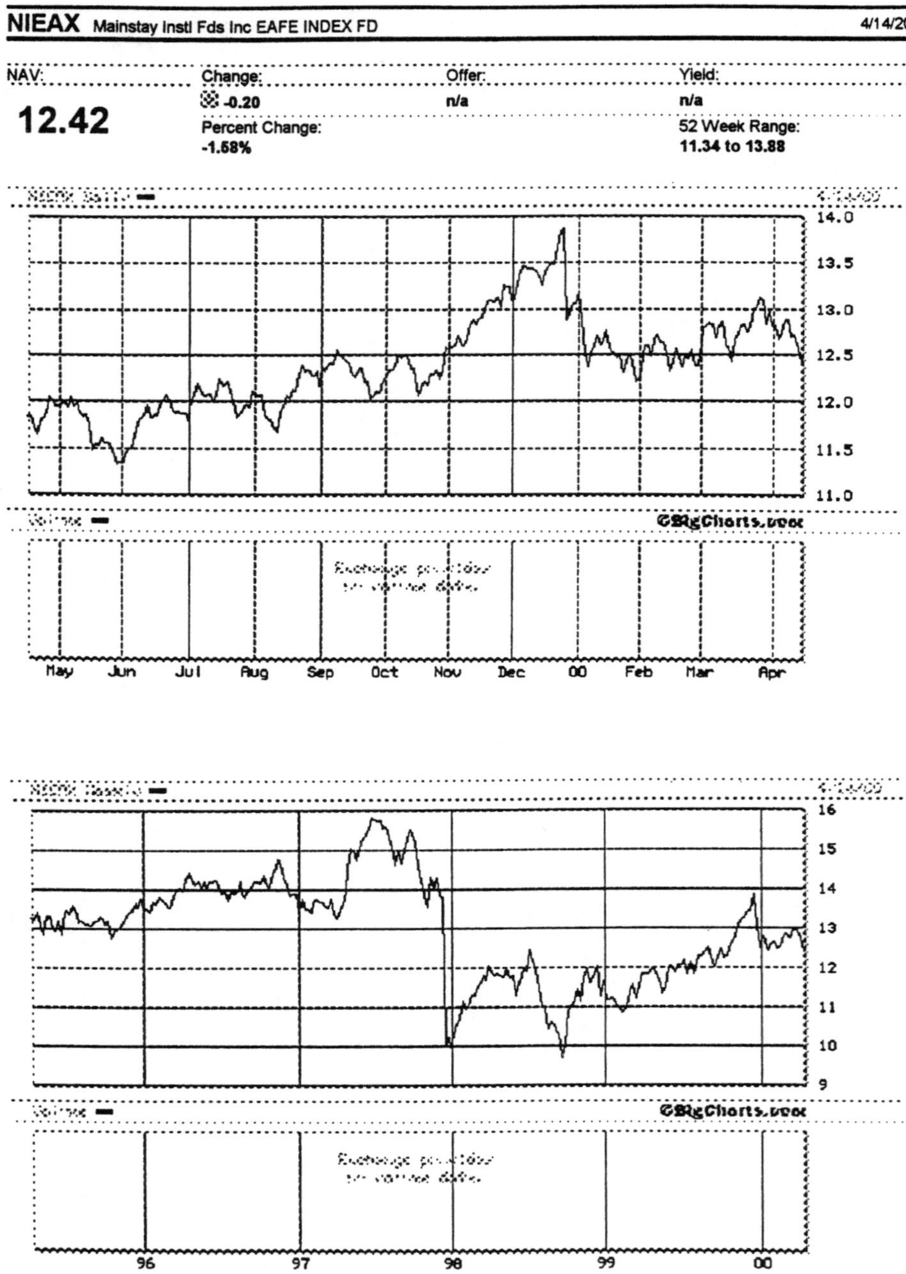

bonds and cash investments. These alternatives include government and corporate bonds, along with money-market funds and Treasury bills (T-bills). For example, in late 1999, equities seemed impervious to rising short-term interest rates. But in the first half of 2000, rising rates finally took their toll on many blue-chip as well as small company stocks. This proves that if interest rates rise long enough, stocks will eventually become vulnerable. This tends to make bonds a more attractive alternative.

2. **Conventional insight does not always hold true. Usually, when large-company stocks decline in value, small company shares get beaten to a pulp**—But just the opposite happened during the first quarter of 2000 when the DJIA was dropping and the NASDAQ was rising. Although this situation might be unusual, it underscores the reason for broad stock market diversification. Remember, no one has a crystal ball to forecast what investment class will do well at any particular point in time, you should spread your bets among al clases of stock.
3. **Don't hold too much money in one stock**—On March 7, 2000, the Procter & Gamble Company, one of the largest blue-chip stocks, announced that operating earnings would fall far short of expectations for the year. That day, its stock plunged 31 percent. This shows it is dangerous to have a lot of money invested in just one stock. Clearly, specific company risk can strike at any time, no matter how sound its current financial condition. The problem is that forecasting corporate earnings with true accuracy is a difficult task, even for professional analysts.
4. **Contrary to popular opinion, owning an index mutual fund does not always reduce risk. An investor who owns the Standard & Poor's 500 stock index is making a bet on only large-company stocks**—It is more prudent to spread bets across a combination of large, medium, and small U.S. stocks and foreign shares. For example, an investor could own 25 percent in a foreign stock index fund along with 75 percent in a Wilshire 5000 index fund, which tracks the performance of almost all U.S. stocks (both large and small). This combination would have fared much better than sole ownership in the S&P 500 during the recent market decline.
5. **It is best to be patient when investing for the long term**—Investors should have goals they are striving to attain. This gives them more time to weather the ups and downs of the stock market. For example, a ten-year investment program designed to accumulate money for a college education should be monitored closely. If properly set up in the beginning, it will not need to be changed during a weak period in the market.
6. **Never place short-term savings into stocks in an attempt to make a killing in the market**—For example, people who sell a house and plan to buy another home in six months should not be tempted to invest all the proceeds in stocks in order to come up with a higher down payment. This kind of erroneous decision would have come back to haunt investors in the spring of 2000, especially if they had invested in the technology sector. By definition, an investment in stocks needs a minimum of five years to overcome any losses along the way. Therefore, short-term money should clearly be in *certificates of deposit* (CDs), money-market funds, or at most, an intermediate-term bond fund.
7. **Don't try to time the market**—With the type of volatility we experienced during the year 2000, short-term investors took a beating they will never forget. History shows that investors usually buy high and sell low due to the emotions of greed and fear. Take a common sense appraoch and be patient using the long-term investment approach.

Guarding Against Risk: Protecting Clients' Money

Even though no one knows when the next full-fledged bear market will occur, it does not mean we can't prepare for it. Start by figuring out how risky a portfolio is through its current structure. First, add up the total value of all of the investments. Then, group them into three categories: stocks, bonds, and cash. Next, divide the amount in each category by the total value of the portfolio. For example, let's say a portfolio adds up to $100,000 ($85,000 in stocks, $10,000 in bonds, and $5,000 in cash). Very simply, the allocation is 85 percent in stocks, 10 percent in bonds, and 5 percent in cash.

During the last prolonged bear market from January 1973 through December 1974, the stock market fell by 41 percent, and this type of portfolio would have shrunk by 34 percent. If the initial $100,000 would have dropped to $66,000 in 34 months, would the client have panicked and sold stocks for a loss? This kind of test will confront investors in a bear market environment. If they have to cash out in order to get a decent night's sleep, they need to make some radical changes in their portfolios before these events occur:

1. Use a conservative strategy for money that will be needed within the next three years. For example, if the client needs funds for a vacation or for a child's education, the funds should be put into a bank, money-market fund, or short-term bond fund. Specific sums that will be needed for the short term should not be in the stock market.
2. Consider the client's risk tolerance. Decide if your client could withstand a sudden drop in value without feeling that he or she had to bail out. For example, if a client wanted the total drop in the portfolio not to exceed 30 percent, you should limit stock holdings to 60 percent. Put the remaining 40 percent in bonds or money-market funds.
3. Strive for the best return with the least volatility. A $^{60}/_{40}$ mix of stocks to bonds has historically been the proper allocation for most people. For more aggressive investors, consider a $^{70}/_{30}$ stock-to-bond mix. For more conservative investors, consider a $^{50}/_{50}$ mix of stocks to bonds.
4. Make sure that you have true diversification. It's going to depend on age and financial objectives. Many Americans today are heavily invested in big U.S. companies, which performed spectacularly well during most of the 1990s. But your client needs investments for more than one economic climate. Your best protection against an unknown future is a well-diversified portfolio, which even includes foreign securities.
5. Stock investments should include big and small companies in different industries and in different countries. You might want to keep 15 percent to 20 percent of the allocation in international funds. As for bond funds, select one with a short-term maturity (1 to 5 years) and one with an intermediate-term maturity (6 to 12 years). Although

longer-term bonds yield more, it is not enough to justify their extra risk should interest rates rise again.

6. Do not choose investments based solely on past returns. Although it is human nature to do so, this approach is a terrible way to structure a portfolio. The danger is that investments with good recent returns all fall into the current "hot" category, and will usually be recommended by most financial publications. A diversified portfolio is the best way to be sure that you will have money in this year's best-performing investments.
7. Diversification will not prevent you from ever losing money. However, you will lose less than you would with a sole collection of high fliers that all nose-dive together. As we have seen during the year 2000, diversification can be the difference between losing 15 percent and losing 75 percent.

Using Capitalization and Investment Styles for Better Balance

While Chapter 8, "Diversifying with Mutual Funds," will discuss in detail the characteristics of investing in mutual funds, we cannot treat the subject of equity investing without mentioning styles and general categories. For example, if we take a portfolio of individual stocks and put them under professional management, we have what is known as an equity mutual fund. While most American investors are familiar with this concept, many are unfamiliar with style analysis and how to diversify a portfolio according to risk and return.

An equity mutual fund is usually governed by an investment style, which is dictated by the fund's stated objective. The two chief investment styles are growth and value. A *growth investment style* seeks long-term capital appreciation. This growth will often come from large companies that have been around for a long period of time and that might already be leaders in their industries. This growth will also be found in emerging or innovative industries that will grow at an above-average rate. A *value investment style* attempts to identify quality, undervalued stocks with long-term growth potential. These companies might have been out of favor with investors due to lower earnings, a temporary decrease in dividends, or unfavorable conditions within their industries.

Because value and growth styles generally experience negative correlation, they are ideal for investment-planning purposes. Figure 6-7 shows how they have reacted to each other over time. A portfolio designed to hold one style of stocks will react just the opposite of the other style. While investors may have preference for one style over another, an ownership in both styles will lower risk in an attempt to achieve specific financial goals. Remember, overall portfolio performance has been based less on picking individual winners and more on adhering to an asset-allocation strategy.

Similar to investment style, capitalization (the worth of all of the shares of a given stock) is another area of consideration when examining mutual

Figure 6-7 *Value and growth styles.*

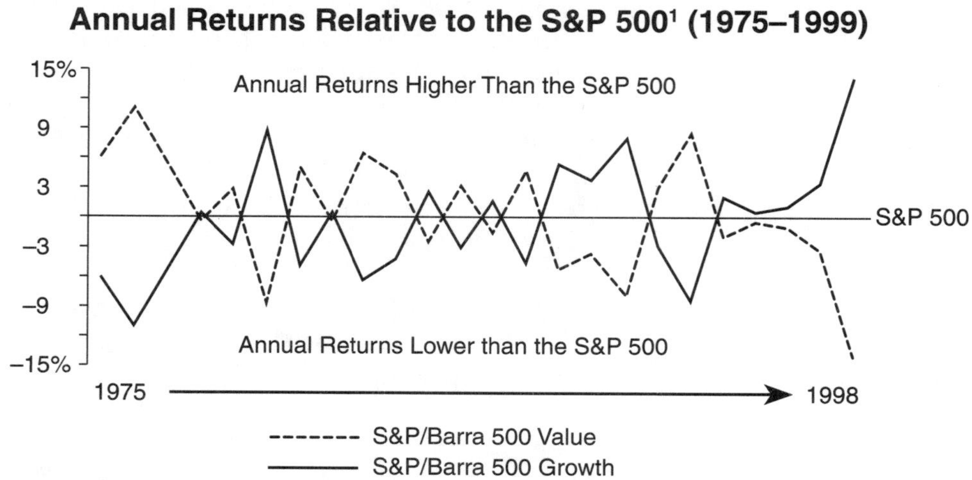

[1] Returns are shown as a percentage relative to the annual returns of the S&P 500 Index.

Figure 6-8 *Domestic equity funds.*

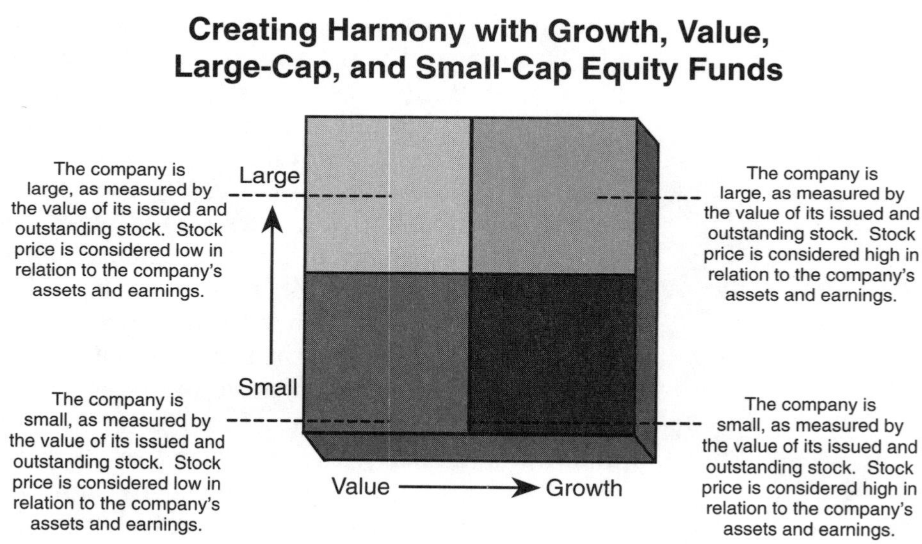

funds. Large-cap funds (with portfolios of companies whose stock is usually worth $1 billion or more) and their complement, small-cap funds, offer another level of diversification. Truly diversifying a portfolio means to invest across styles and in different levels of capitalization. All domestic equity funds fall somewhere within the four quadrants of the chart shown in Figure 6-8.

A balanced approach builds a portfolio by taking style and capitalization into account. For example, overweighing a portfolio with certain types of funds (small-cap growth, for example) will affect the overall risk and return profile. In other words, it will completely match the characteristics of that investment (for better or for worse). On the other hand, asset allocation attempts to limit exposure to the risk that is inherent in individual markets by diversifying over different investments.

When allocating client assets, you should seriously consider adding non-U.S. investments to the overall mix. There are three key benefits in doing so:

1. **Potential for better returns**—You gain access to more investment opportunities than the ones that exist in the United States alone. The United States has rarely been the Number 1 performing equity market in any given year. Furthermore, more than 50 percent of the world's stock market opportunities exist outside the United States.
2. **Opportunity to reduce overall risk**—You can actually lower volitility in the entire portfolio. Stock markets in foreign countries tend to move in different directions. Therefore, international investing enables you to put true diversification to work for your client.
3. **A small allocation can have a positive impact on total investment results**—Figure 6-9 illustrates how various combinations of U.S. and foreign investments compare with a U.S.-only portfolio on a

Figure 6-9 *Various combinations of U.S. and foreign investments compared with a U.S.-only portfolio on a risk-versus-return basis.*

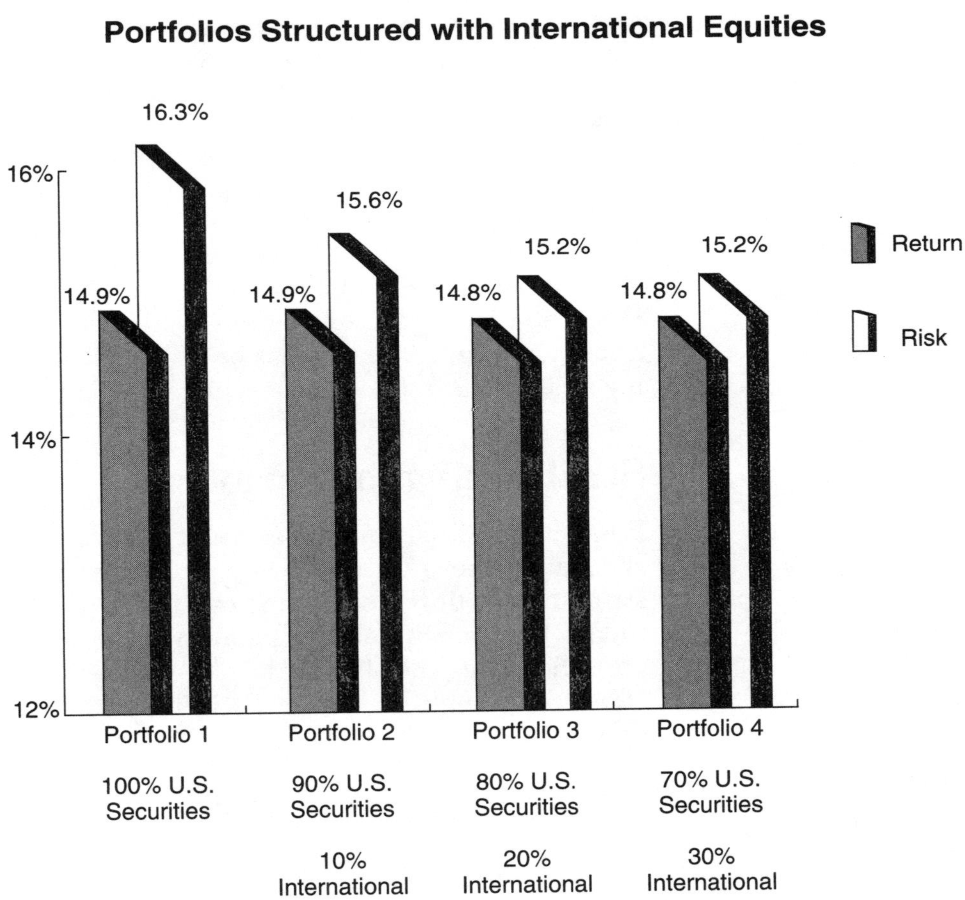

risk-versus-return basis. Surprisingly, the return was almost identical for the 20-year period ending December 31, 1998. Most importantly, however, as foreign securities were added to the mix, the level of risk decreased for the investor.

Degrees of Caution When Using Fixed-Income Securities

Fixed-income funds offered by major mutual-fund companies today generally fall into one of four categories. *Government bond funds* are known for their high quality and reliability for paying principal and interest payments by holding bonds that are backed by the U.S. government. *Municipal bond funds* give the opportunity to earn tax-free income from state and local government bonds. *Corporate bond funds* are known for their higher yields and total return potential from taking on some level of credit risk. Finally, *international bond funds* are structured for the higher yield and total return potential from foreign government and/or corporate bonds.

Regardless of which category a bond fund falls into, its risk can be quickly assessed in two terms: average credit rating and average maturity. *Average credit rating* defines the risk of bond defaults, which is generally more important in economic recessions. *Average maturity* defines the sensitivity of a fund's price to changes in interest rates. When rates rise, prices go down. Conversely, when rates fall, prices go up. *Duration* is used to predict this relationship. For example, the longer the bond's duration, the more that its price will move up and down with changes in interest rates.

Figure 6-10 shows the degree of caution that must be taken with fixed-income investments. Lower credit ratings mean a higher default risk, while higher credit ratings mean a lower default risk. Standard & Poor's and Moody's define actual credit risk. In working with an investor, a financial professional must be aware of these risks and fit the investments to a comfort level that will help balance the client's portfolio.

Strategizing for Various Portfolios

Financial professionals must use a strategy that will complement their client's tolerance for risk. They must understand how portfolios can be structured to fit the needs and comfort level of their investors. According to Van Kamper Funds, the following information helps identify optimal portfolios along the efficient frontier for various asset classes. This data is effective through December 31, 1998 and is not meant to be representative of the past or future performance of any mutual fund.

1. **Growth investor (see Figure 6-11)**—Will be comfortable with having most of the portfolio in equity positions. This factor includes 85 percent domestic equity and 15 percent in international equity.

Figure 6-10 *Degree of caution required for fixed-income investments.*

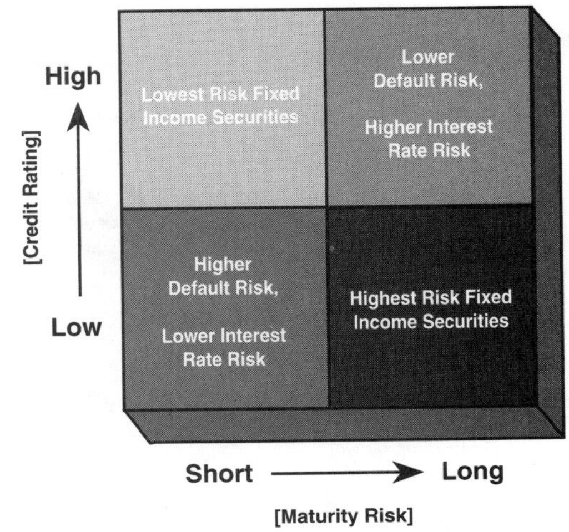

Credit Risk

S&P/Moody's	What the Ratings Mean
AAA/Aaa	The highest ratings. The issuer's ability to pay interest and principal payments is extremely strong.
AA/Aa	The issuer's ability to pay interest and principal payments is very strong, just slightly less than the issuer of an AAA rating.
A/A	The issuer's ability to meet its financial commitment is strong, however, changes in circumstances and/or economic conditions could impair the financial strength.
BBB/Baa	Lowest ratings still considered "investment grade." The issuer has adequate protection parameters. However, changes in circumstances or economic conditions are more likely to affect these issuers.
BB/Ba and lower	Speculative ratings. Issuer faces major ongoing uncertainties that could lead, or have already led, to inadequate capacity to meet financial commitments.

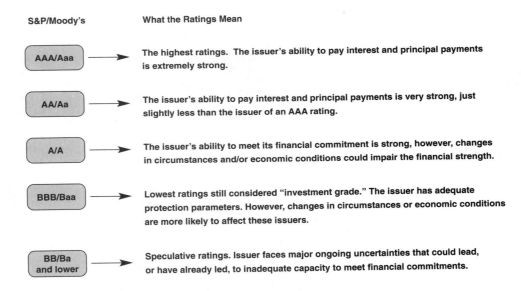

Source: Standard & Poor's and Moody's.

The domestic equity is broken down between large- and small-cap value and growth funds. The international equity is divided between foreign stock (large company) and emerging small-company stock funds. Historical performance shows the highest risk during the first year, along with the lowest returns. You will note, however, that risk declines sufficiently with just a five-year holding period while returns increase slightly.

2. **Moderate growth investor (see Figure 6-12)**—Will have 80 percent in equities, 15 percent in fixed income, and 5 percent in cash.

Figure 6-11 *Growth investor; for invenstors comfortable with risk and hoping to maximize long-term performance.*

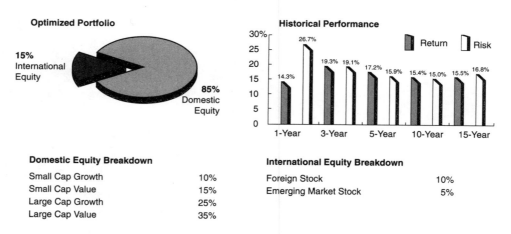

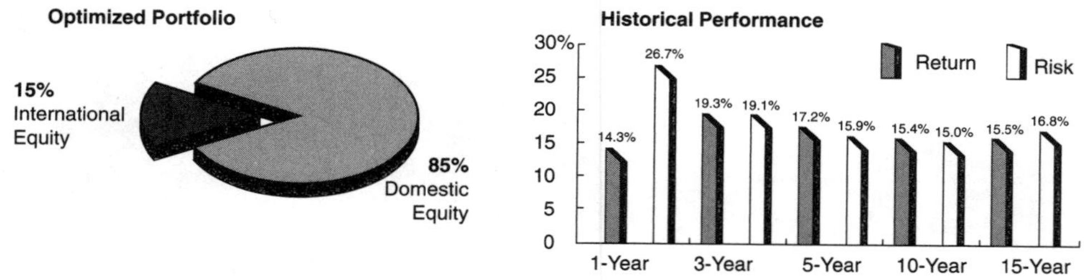

Domestic Equity Breakdown

Small Cap Growth	10%
Small Cap Value	15%
Large Cap Growth	25%
Large Cap Value	35%

International Equity Breakdown

Foreign Stock	10%
Emerging Market Stock	5%

Figure 6-12 *Moderate growth investor; for investors willing to assume more risk in an attempt to achieve better performance than cautious investments over the long term.*

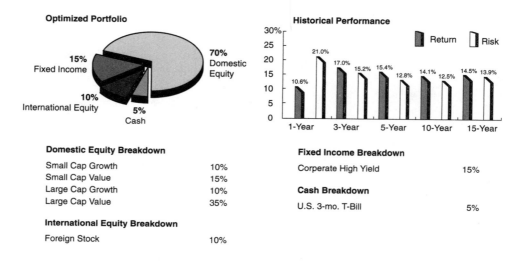

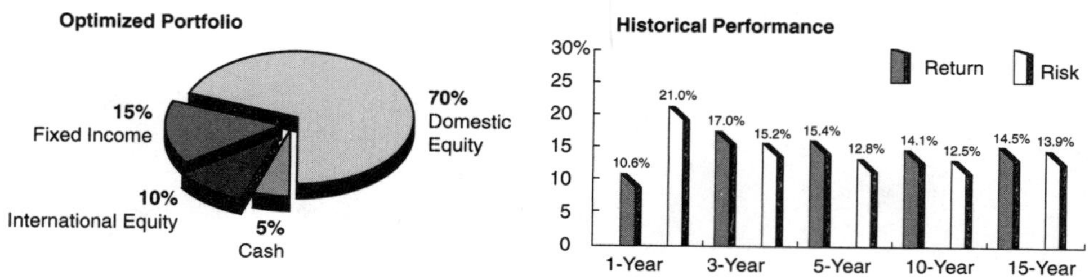

Domestic Equity Breakdown

Small Cap Growth	10%
Small Cap Value	15%
Large Cap Growth	10%
Large Cap Value	35%

International Equity Breakdown

Foreign Stock	10%

Fixed Income Breakdown

Corperate High Yield	15%

Cash Breakdown

U.S. 3-mo. T-Bill	5%

This investor will also have a mix of small- and large-cap growth and value funds, plus the foreign stock component in the international equity area. Because a moderate growth investor is willing to take more risks, he or she will usually include a high-yield corporate bond fund along with a small amount of money in a three-month T-bill. You will note quite a significant drop in both risk and return during the first year. By the 15th year, risk and return are within 16 basis points of each other.

3. **Moderate investor (see Figure 6-13)**—Will have 60 percent in equities along with a higher allocation to cash and fixed-income securities. As with Figure 6-12, an argument could be made that a higher amount (15 percent to 20 percent) should be placed in international funds. But most U.S. investors do not feel that comfortable with for-

Figure 6-13 *Moderate investor; for investors seeking growth in combination with potentially less risk over the long term.*

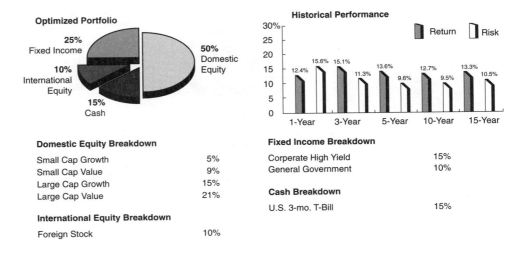

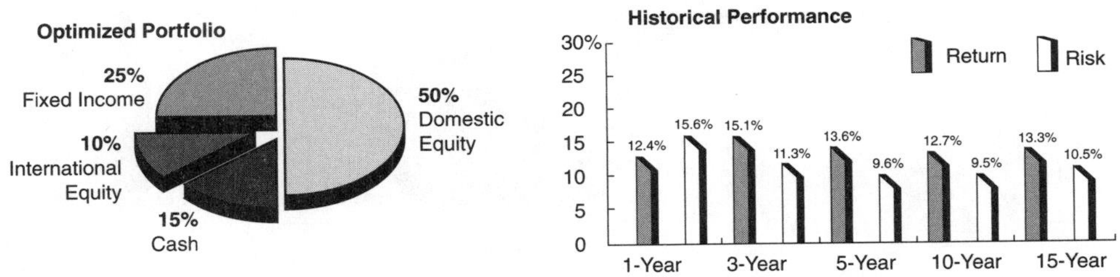

Domestic Equity Breakdown

Small Cap Growth	5%
Small Cap Value	9%
Large Cap Growth	15%
Large Cap Value	21%

International Equity Breakdown

Foreign Stock	10%

Fixed Income Breakdown

Corperate High Yield	15%
General Government	10%

Cash Breakdown

U.S. 3-mo. T-Bill	15%

Figure 6-14 *Moderate, cautious investor, for investors seeking an element of growth in combination with capital preservation.*

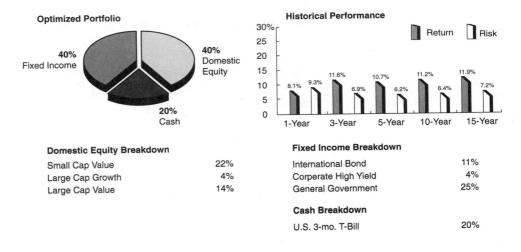

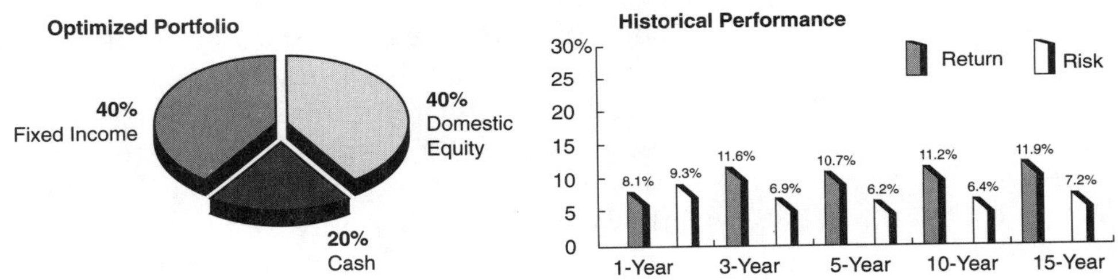

Domestic Equity Breakdown

Small Cap Value	22%
Large Cap Growth	4%
Large Cap Value	14%

Fixed Income Breakdown

International Bond	11%
Corperate High Yield	4%
General Government	25%

Cash Breakdown

U.S. 3-mo. T-Bill	20%

eign securities and will usually have a smaller allocation in them. The more moderate we become, the more we allocate to large-cap growth and value stocks. This investor will also include a general government bond fund to strengthen the fixed-income portion of the portfolio.

4. **Moderate, cautious investor (see Figure 6-14)**—Shows an optimal portfolio with 40 percent domestic equity, 40 percent fixed income, and 20 percent cash. There is no hesitation to abandon the foreign stock position, because there is more comfort in holding the international bond fund. In an effort to be more conservative, this investor will increase the government bond fund to 25 percent and the cash position to 20 percent. A typical U.S. retiree would feel very comfortable with this type of diversification. Without worrying about

Figure 6-15 *Cautious investor; for investors whose primary concern is long-term captial preservation.*

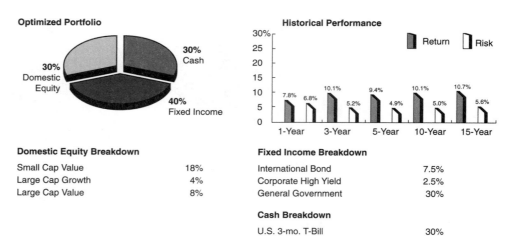

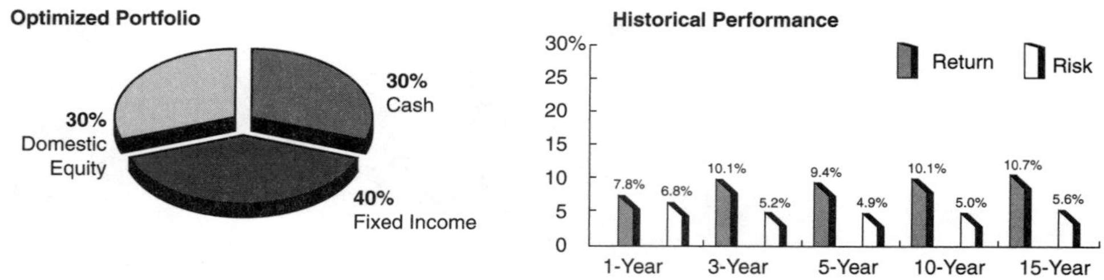

Domestic Equity Breakdown

Small Cap Value	18%
Large Cap Growth	4%
Large Cap Value	8%

Fixed Income Breakdown

International Bond	7.5%
Corporate High Yield	2.5%
General Government	30%

Cash Breakdown

U.S. 3-mo. T-Bill	30%

high returns, this investor is satisfied with an average return of around 11 percent, along with a lower level of risk.

5. **Cautious investor (see Figure 6-15)**—Would prefer less volatile investments, but knows that there must be some growth in the portfolio in order to keep up with higher inflation and a longer life expectancy. Domestic equity now accounts for only 30 percent, while fixed income remains at 40 percent (with the safety of cash increasing to 30 percent). The historical return will still be in the area of 10 percent, and the risk factor is even lower. Investors in this category will typically be in their late 70s or older and will want to pass as much of their estate on to family or heirs without unnecessary risk.

Exchange-Traded Portfolios

The public is just now becoming aware of exchange-traded index funds. Spiders (SPY), S&P's depository receipts, trace the price and dividend yield of the S&P 500 Index. Diamonds (DIA) track the DJIA and its 30 blue-chip stocks. Due to the surge in Internet-related equities, the NASDAQ 100 tracking stock (QQQ) is suddenly popular.

Mid-cap Spiders (MDY) track the S&P Mid-Cap 400 Index. Select sector Spiders (various symbols) slice the S&P 500 into nine separately traded instrument-based subsectors, including Basic Industries, Consumer Services, Consumer Staples, Cyclicals/Transportation, Energy, Financial, Industrial, Technology, and Utilities. Along with all of these components comes increased advertising, public relations, press coverage, and investor questions.

World Equity Benchmark Shares (WEBS) are designed to mirror the performance of the *Morgan Stanley Capital International* (MSCI) Index in a specific country. WEBS, traded on the *American Stock Exchange* (AMEX) under various symbols, offers 17 country-specific index-fund securities in Europe, Asia, and Mexico. WEBS enables an investor or portfolio manager to short international markets, and it provides an interesting cost-effective alternative to closed-end country funds.

Exchange-traded portfolios are similar to index-based mutual funds in that investors or advisors who manage clients' money can buy the equivalent of a stock portfolio in a single investment. But unlike a fund, one can buy and sell shares of exchange-traded securities just like other stocks during the trading day. Current prices are available throughout the day, and like other stocks, they can be sold short.

The purchase price is the investor's tax basis, and shares can be held for long-term gain. Fans of these products praise their tax efficiency, because they tend not to make taxable distributions to shareholders. Opponents think that they are a threat to the mutual fund industry, and that they come at a time when the retail mutual funds are experiencing slower growth.

Index investing has ridden the coattails of a bull market to popularity. Like other index vehicles, there is no protection on the down side. As a financial professional, you should realize that exchange-traded indices offer a set of new tools that require explanation, research, and all of the steps in the investment-management consulting process in order to be effective. A disclaimer on the AMEX Web site (www.amex.com) declares in capital letters, "ADVICE FROM A SECURITIES PROFESSIONAL IS STRONGLY RECOMMENDED."

The Benefits of Fundamental Analysis

Before deciding whether a stock is worthwhile to purchase, you want to examine all of the known facts about that particular company. This statement brings us to the concept of fundamental analysis, which examines factors such as a company's earnings per share, income statement, balance sheet, and quality of management. To evaluate the overall environment in which the company operates, you should also examine cultural and political trends, activity within the industry, and the general direction of the economy.

Even though we touched upon this area in an earlier chapter, it warrants a more thorough examination here. Companies that are in better financial condition will be more competitive within their industry and will be better capable of exploiting upcoming business opportunities. When evaluating a stock before purchase, successful advisors scrutinize a variety of financial indicators. The following information will help you when working with clients to choose appropriate stock investments:

- **Earnings per share**—Earnings per share is a popular indicator of a company's financial well-being. This information is determined by dividing a company's net income by the total number of common shares outstanding. A stock's price tends to keep pace with the growth or decline in its earnings. That is one reason why companies that have steady growth in earnings are usually favored by both novice and professional investors alike. Despite changes in investor sentiment over individual stocks, the most common fundamental information that they want to know is, "Is this company making money?" "What will my invested dollar be worth in the future?" If the trend in earnings per share has been good in the past or if the outlook is excellent for the company, it might be worth buying some of the company's stock and holding it for future appreciation.

- **P/E multiple**—The price/earnings multiple is determined by dividing the current market price of a stock by its earnings per share. For example, a stock whose earnings per share is $3 and whose stock price is $60 has a P/E multiple of $20 ($60 divided by $3). Also referred to as the P/E ratio, this indicator tells investors how much they are paying for a company's earning power. Whether the price seems reasonable or extravagant, it could be based upon severely depressed earnings (a value stock) or upon a track record of consistent profitability (a growth stock). The trick is to identify sound companies that are trading at P/E multiples that are lower than the average for companies in the same industry. Ideally, a good company that is trading at a below-average P/E multiple should rise in value at a greater rate than its industry peers once the market identifies its real value.
- **Book value**—The difference between a company's assets and its liabilities, divided by the number of shares outstanding, will give you its book value per share. We use this indicator to locate companies whose market price is attractive in relation to their book value. But we must be careful to remember that the asset values on a company's balance sheet do not represent the current market value of its assets. We must try to find companies that have asset values that are understated, rather than overstated. For example, some companies have assets that, because of the rules of accounting, are actually valued on their balance sheets at a fraction of what they are really worth. For this reason, oil companies might be attractive to value investors, because many own vast tracts of oil-rich land that are valued on their balance sheets at much less than they are thought to be worth.
- **Leverage**—Leverage relates to the amount of debt owed by a corporation in relation to the amount of its stockholders' equity. Highly leveraged companies have a higher proportion of debt compared to equity. Conservative investors tend to prefer companies that have low leverage (those that have relatively low amounts of debt). More aggressive investors often prefer highly leveraged companies. This situation would be advantageous for stockholders when the earnings are high, because once interest is paid on debt, they share in the remainder of the earnings. But because debt interest must be paid before common stockholders are entitled to dividends, high leverage works against stockholders when earnings decline.
- ***Return on Equity* (ROE)**—ROE can be useful, particularly when comparing several companies within one industry. ROE measures the rate of return on investors' capital. To derive ROE, divide earnings per share by book value per share. For example, a company that has earnings per share of $1.50 and a book value of $10 has an ROE of 15 percent ($1.50 divided by $10). ROE measures how efficiently company management uses stockholders' equity. Value investors

favor companies that have above-average ROEs, compared to companies that have below-average ROEs in the same industry.

- **Dividend yield**—A company's dividend expressed as a percentage of the stock's current market value is know as its dividend yield. Investors who are seeking current income prefer stocks that have higher dividend yields—as long as the high yield is not caused by a severely depressed and declining stock price. Value investors look for dividend-payment histories in order to determine strengths and weaknesses. Companies that have long histories of consistent dividend payments (and preferably, rising dividends) are favored by income investors.

Not all investors tend evaluate a company based on these fundamental indicators, so it is advisable to investigate other areas that might have more relevance to them.

1. **Industry dominance**—Are the company's products and services well known and used by the client? Is the company coming out with innovative concepts to change the way we live, and is it on the cutting edge of new technology? Is the company in a position to keep up or to stay ahead of its competition?
2. **Progressive management**—Do executives and top officers own large amounts of company stock? Is it available in their 401(k) plans? Does their compensation compare favorably to that of companies in the same industry? Are top executives overpaid in relation to their competition?
3. **Future volatility**—How volatile is the stock as compared to major market indices? Does it fluctuate more or less than the S&P 500 Index? Will future plans for business expansion make the stock more or less vulnerable to economic conditions? Will holding this stock jeopardize the client in achieving specific future goals?

The Popularity of Technical Analysis

This process of investment theory ignores the school of fundamental analysis and uses charts and graphs to make decisions. Technicians like to analyze price movements and chart patterns from the past in order to draw conclusions about future buying and selling. They believe that the market is much more psychological than logical when it comes to trading securities. You will find it easy to concur with their logic when we see the wild swings in technology stocks in 1999 and 2000.

In short, technical analysis tells us when to buy, whereas fundamental analysis tells us what to buy. More precisely, strict fundamental analysis ignores changes in price due to the perceptions and actions of buyers and sellers and only sells stocks when the fundamentals change. On the contrary, technical analysis ignores the fundamentals and focus on generating investment returns by predicting up-and-down trends in a stock's price.

With recent erratic market patterns showing validation for both schools of thought, we are beginning to see investment advisors using both theories to complement one another. Fundamental and technical analyses are being used to identify stocks to own and then to move in and out as either the fundamentals or price trends change. With more money moving into the stock market at an ever-increasing volume, we must take into account the psychological impact of the new American investor.

This point brings us to another controversial issue. By using charts and graphs to determine whether or not to be in or out of the market at any given time, we are actually practicing *market timing*. Conventional wisdom says to buy and hold for long-term appreciation and that market timing does not work. I would argue the case for technical analysis, however, in examining the actions of two indices during the first quarter of 2000.

Figure 6-16 shows the DJIA with 15- and 30-day moving average lines. When the 15-day line crossed the 30-day line in late January 2000, it signaled an exit from Dow stocks. Similarly, when the 15-day line crossed back over the 30-day line in mid-March, it signaled a re-entry into Dow stocks. An investor who followed the signals of these lines would have missed a major decline in the Dow Index or in individual Dow stocks.

Likewise, Figure 6-17 shows the NASDAQ Composite Index for the same period. These stocks kept making new highs during the first quarter of 2000, and the technician would have stayed in this market as long as the 15-day moving average line stayed higher than the 30-day moving average line. When the lines crossed in late March, the technician would

Figure 6-16 *The DJIA with 15- and 30-day moving average lines.*

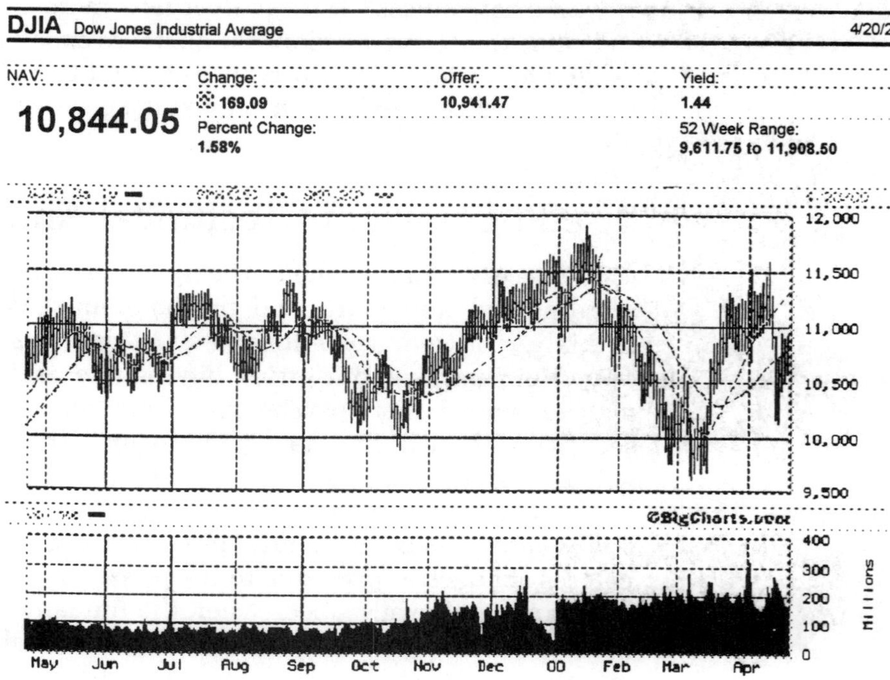

Figure 6-17 *The NASDAQ Composite Index for the same period.*

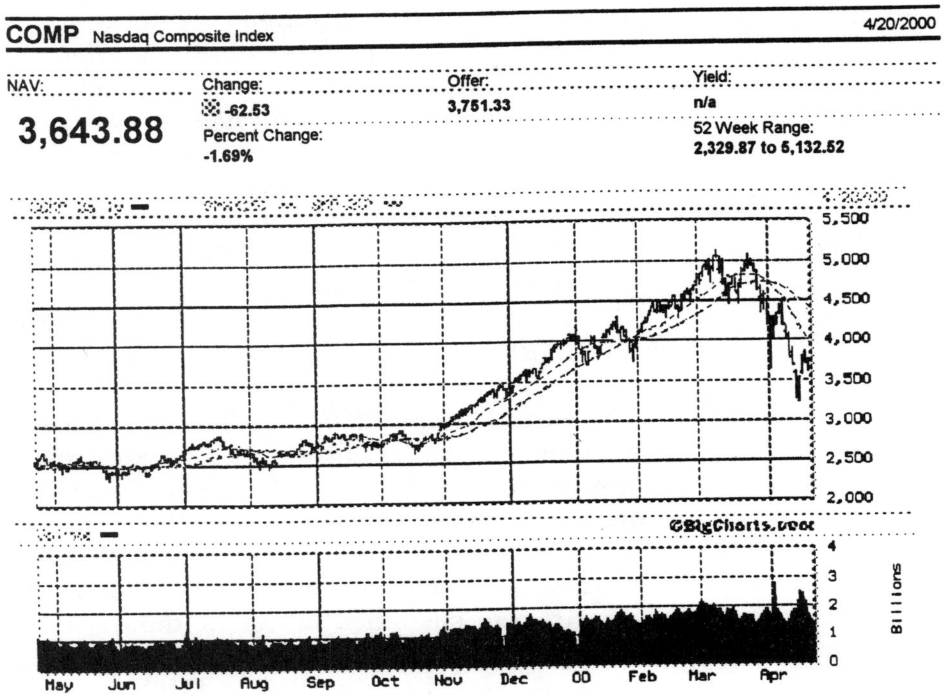

have moved out of these stocks and into cash—avoiding the major decline that followed in the spring of 2000.

Once the right stocks are selected for a portfolio, the case for using technical analysis has plenty of merit in today's investment environment. It can also be used to aid the investor or market trader with selecting the best time to execute security transactions. As more people become interested in the stock market, individual investors will find that they can gain more insight into investing by following various charting or technical methods.

The *breath-of-market index* is one of the popular techniques used to gauge major market movements. This index is calculated by dividing the net advances or declines in stock prices of a broad stock index by the number of issues traded. For simplicity, let's suppose that on any given trading day, the number of stocks traded on the NYSE was 1,500. Of that total, the share prices of 850 companies rose, 450 declined, and 200 remained unchanged. Net advances would have been 400 (850 minus 450), making the breadth index of that day 26.7 percent (400 divided by 1,500). Weekly breadth index ratios are combined into a moving average of 150 days (new days are added while old days are dropped).

These moving averages are then compared to the Dow averages. The resulting breadth index will support or fail to support the movement of the Dow. As with our analysis in Figure 6-16, it is a technical sign of market weakness when a broader index fails to support the Dow. In this case, failure to confirm the Dow averages indicates that the broader market is moving in a direction opposite to the 30 stocks in the Dow.

Volume-of-trading is another widely followed technical indicator. Simply put, price follows volume. If for example the market moves upward, accompanied by a large volume of trading, it is a sign of market strength. On the contrary, a movement of the market without higher volume is a sign of weakness. Also, if the number of new higher priced stocks does not correspond to the higher averages, it is a sign of technical weakness.

The volume of trading does not critically impact the financial markets and can be linked to an impending change in market direction. For example, if the broad market indices move higher but the rise is not accompanied by an equal increase in the volume of trading, we interpret this situation as technical weakness (despite a rise in the index). But, if the rise is accompanied by a corresponding increase in the volume of trading, it is interpreted as a sign of technical strength.

The Dow Theory. The Dow Theory is one of the best-known technical analysis systems for anticipating stock-price movements. The theory was developed by the founder of Dow Jones, who also gave us the key averages quoted in the financial pages: the *Dow Jones Industrial Average* (DJIA), the *Dow Jones Transportation Average* (DJTA), and the *Dow Jones Utility Average* (DJUA). If a move in the DJIA is confirmed by either of the other two in sustained uptrends, the market rise will continue. If the averages diverge, the market weakens.

As we stated previously, the DJIA is composed of 30 leading industrial companies that are chosen from sectors of the economy that represent America's lifeblood. The average is based on a formula that is computed daily, which results from the closing prices of these 30 major industrial companies. This formula adds the stock's daily closing prices and divides by a certain number in order to derive the average. Stocks that have a higher-priced average, such as Intel Corporation and IBM, have a much greater effect on the average when their prices change.

The Dow Theory is derived from three basic ideas:

1. If you want to make a profit in the stock market, you should take advantage of the primary market trend, which is the general upward movement of the market (taking from one to four years).
2. Whenever a primary trend is up, each secondary trend will produce a peak that is higher than the last one, or vice-versa for a down trend.
3. Any true indicator of a primary market trend will be confirmed relatively quickly by similar action of the different stock-price averages.

A recent study by Stephen Brown, William Goetzmann, and Alok Kumar supports the validity of the Dow Theory. For example, a portfolio that followed the signals to buy or sell identified by the Dow Theory software and that used a market index fund with no transaction costs would have outperformed a buy-hold strategy by about two percentage points per year. In addition, the Dow Theory portfolio would have incurred one-third less volatility. Will this approach work in the future? Only time will tell how well the Dow Theory will perform in the 21st century.

Modern Portfolio Theory

This strategy was developed in 1959 by two Nobel Prize-winning economists, Harry Markowitz and William Sharpe. They assumed that most people want to be cautious when investing and that they will take the smallest possible risk in order to obtain the greatest return. This theory is based on two assumptions:

1. The history of investment activity in major asset classes tends to repeat itself
2. Not all assets go up and down in tandem

This approach automatically diversifies a portfolio by using four main classes of investments: U.S. stocks, U.S. bonds, foreign stocks, and foreign bonds. This portfolio is designed for a time span of 15 years and works well with long-term investments such as mutual funds and variable annuities. Investors can use one family of funds or pick from a variety of top-performing funds that are run by different companies.

This strategy is well suited for a variety of investors, because they can choose the level of risk that is best suited for their comfort level. Three models are available for this purpose:

- **Conservative**—Designed for lower risk with a heavier concentration in bonds or equity income funds
- **Moderate**—Designed for medium risk with a balance between different types of stock and bond funds
- **Aggressive**—Designed for higher risk with a heavier concentration of stock or growth funds

Figure 6-18 illustrates the three models used by Money Concepts Capital Corporation as of August 2000. You will note that the conservative model has five options, which include 32 percent in international stock and bond funds. This situation shows that even a conservative investor should diversify internationally in today's expanding world market environment. The moderate model has four options, with approximately a $^{60}/_{40}$ stock-to-bond ratio. The aggressive model is marked by an increase in risk, with 34 percent in U.S. aggressive growth stocks and up to 38 percent in international stocks.

Figure 6-18 also illustrates the concept of rebalancing, which is the chief beneit of using the Modern Portfolio Theory. This strategy takes money out of assets that have risen in value and reinvests the money into assets that are relatively under-priced. In effect, investors are selling high and buying low, just as market gurus say that they should do. This practice reduces risk so that when the U.S. market experiences a decline, the investor will not have as many assets exposed to higher volatility. Furthermore, the investor makes money when the under-performing part of the portfolio starts moving up again.

Figure 6-18 *Conservative, moderate, and aggressive MPT models as of August 2000.*

MODERN PORTFOLIO THEORY

Current Asset Class Weightings as of August 2000

Asset Description	Portfolio Percentage
Conservative Model	
Aggressive Growth Fund	5.69%
Corporate Quality Bond	10.59%
Income Fund	52.00%
International Stock Fund	7.53%
International Bond Fund	24.19%
	100.00%
Moderate Model	
Aggressive Growth Fund	14.10%
Income Fund	52.00%
International Stock Fund	22.55%
International Bond Fund	11.35%
	100.00%
Aggressive Model	
International Stock Fund	38.24%
Income Fund	27.59%
Aggressive Growth Fund	34.11%
	100.00%

MODERN PORTFOLIO THEORY "REBALANCING" TECHNIQUE

Investment Class	Beginning Allocation	Qt Ending Allocation	Rebalancing Effect
U.S. Stocks	25%	35%	25%
Foreign Stocks	25%	30%	25%
U.S. Bonds	25%	20%	25%
Foreign Bonds	25%	15%	25%
Total Allocation	100%	100%	100%

As we will see in the next chapter, this strategy works particularly well with tax-deferred retirement plans. Rather than having to pay capital-gains taxes every time rebalancing takes place, investors get to keep all of the profits for future growth. Fortunately, investors can also rebalance within the stock portion of their portfolios. This situation helps maintain target percentages for blue-chip stocks, small-company shares, and foreign securities.

The Modern Portfolio Theory has five practical applications for client accounts:

1. *Reduces volatility in a portfolio of individual stocks*. This program is often used to reduce the volatility of individual U.S. securities. It balances the risk of a well-established portfolio by adding professional management found in mutual funds and variable annuities.
2. *Gives inflation protection for various life stages of an investor*. The program benefits both younger people who want to build a new investment portfolio and older people who are interested in more financial security before and after retirement.
3. *Builds capital in order to meet the expenses of a college education*. This program can be used for children and grandchildren to take a disciplined approach in order to meet the higher cost of future education.
4. *Saves more taxes through the use of variable annuities*. These investments are becoming extremely popular with people who want to keep more money for themselves. Variable annuities will compound interest on a tax-deferred basis indefinitely and do not require a mandatory withdrawal at age $70^1/_2$ (like traditional Individual Retirement Accounts do).
5. *Generates more income from IRA accounts after retirement*. As these accounts grow in value, more income can be taken each year in order to counter the higher cost of living. This concept is being used by more retirees to reduce stress and worry less about market volatility. It also creates a feeling of more control and security in the management of their assets.

In conclusion, this concept works well in a portfolio whose investors use a buy-and-hold approach for a portion of the assets. This strategy repositions cash in major asset classes in order to buy low and sell high. As we enter the 21st century, serious investors need to structure their portfolios in order to prepare for the challenges that lie ahead. The Modern Portfolio Theory concept is designed to strengthen existing assets and to help build more capital with confidence in the future.

Chapter 7

Goals and Guidelines: Setting Portfolio Parameters

Introduction

One of the first things that you *must* do as a professional financial planner is to make potential clients set goals and guidelines for achieving their dreams. This task can be extremely challenging, because many investors just want to see how much money they can make in the stock market within a short period of time. But focusing on achieving both short- and long-term goals with various amounts of money will help make the entire process of investing much more meaningful for everyone concerned.

To make investors want to use your services, you must immediately gain their confidence and trust, and offer value added services. Otherwise, they have no reason not to invest themselves, either by using a discount broker or by going to the Internet to purchase securities and manage their portfolios online. By perceiving you as someone who is interested in their financial well being and who wants to establish a long-term relationship, they will be more inclined to let you make recommendations and help invest their money. Remember, high quality personal service will never be replaced by a machine.

In this regard, you must distinguish between their "serious" and "play" money. First, you can define serious money as that which is targeted to grow over the long-term to meet specific future needs. For example, assume that we have a single male professional, age 25, who plans to marry in one year and make a down payment on a house in five years. His goals might be to accumulate $3,000 to pay for the honeymoon while building $30,000 to help pay for the new home later. In this case, he would need to save and deposit $250 per month, putting the money into a safe tax-free money-market account in order to meet his first goal. He would also need to immediately invest a lump sum of $18,627 into a balanced mutual fund, earning 10 percent for the next five years in order to meet the second goal.

Second, play money is used to take a gamble in areas of the market that are designed for higher risk. For example, our young professional might like to purchase new Internet stocks with the goal of making a killing in the market within a short period of time. In this case, he would put aside $10,000 in discretionary money (not intended to achieve his previously stated goals). Unless you are willing to watch his portfolio on a daily basis and give advice on when to buy and sell these individual stocks, he is not a suitable candidate for your services.

This chapter will focus on understanding various types of risks, how to avoid major investment mistakes, and how to achieve specific financial goals. A financial professional who has and applies knowledge gained in this area will build a successful practice within a shorter period of time. By understanding these goals and guidelines, you can immediately demonstrate your professionalism to prospects and gain more credibility in the eyes of your existing clients.

Investment Risks

Most investors will tend to ignore the possibility of risk during a raging bull-market environment. Instead, they only focus on making gains that they think are automatic. Your job is to point out the risk that they face in trying to achieve short, intermediate, and long-term goals. While this topic might not be the most pleasant subject to bring up during a planning session, you must remind your clients about market volatility. In fact, it is critical for you to discuss and document the subject of risk and save it in the client's file. In this way, he or she can never accuse you of having avoided the topic (or accuse you of not having warned them that something bad could negatively affect their portfolio in the future).

Furthermore, risk is a topic that might hinder you from making an investment sale. For this reason, many registered representatives or account executives tend to treat the subject lightly or avoid it altogether. This situation has become one of the biggest injustices in our industry today. In fact, Arthur Levitt, the current chairman of the *Securities and Exchange Commission* (SEC), has promised a crackdown by his agency on vendors and broker-dealers who avoid discussing the subject of risk and market volatility. "People must also be warned of the potential dangers of investing so they can make rational decisions before deciding what to do with their money," Levitt said recently.

Let's examine the various types of risks and put them into major categories when discussing future investment strategies with clients:

I. Domestic risk—Refers to what can happen when money is invested in various U.S. stock market securities. These risks can be subdivided into economic, interest rate, market, industry, and specific. Whether experienced or not, both young and old investors must understand what might happen to their money in our free and democratic society.

1. **Economic risk**—Takes place as we go through various stages of economic cycles. For example, the stock market is likely to perform well during periods of expansion, which are marked by low unemployment, rising wages, and high consumer confidence in regard to spending. Conversely, various equity markets will likely perform poorly during periods of contraction, which are marked by high unemployment, falling wages, and low consumer confidence (with a decrease in spending habits). In Chapter 2, "Economics Basics: Terms, Definitions, Trends, and Policies," we explained how the economy functions. Most importantly, you should try to give clients a feel for what is taking place in this environment each time you meet with them. Few other investment professionals will ever attempt to help clients understand this seemingly complicated area. However, your clients will

greatly appreciate any expression of helping them comprehend what is actually taking place.

2. **Interest-rate risk**—Takes place when the Federal Reserve attempts to regulate economic growth by holding down inflation. The Fed will usually implement a strategy to raise interest rates on money being loaned by member banks. As described in Chapter 2, this concept is called the Federal funds rate and will in turn cause the banks to pass the rate increase along to their loan customers. The higher interest rates go, the less attractive it is for individuals and businesses to borrow money. The stock market usually interprets this action as causing a slowdown in economic activity, which lowers corporate profits and reduces net earnings per share. Eventually, this situation will lead to lower market prices that reflect a decrease in the demand for business goods and services. In regard to bond investments, another way to explain interest-rate risk is to draw a seesaw, with interest rates on one end and bond prices on the other (see Figure 7-1). We are currently in a state where rates have risen in an attempt to control inflation. If the Fed decides to continue this policy, prices of fixed-rated bonds will continue to fall. For example, if you owned a 7 percent bond that matures in 20 years and new bonds with the same maturity are being issued for 8 percent, the value of your old 7 percent bond would drop as investors obviously seek the one that has a higher rate.
3. **Market risk**—Refers to possible negative activity within the overall U.S. stock market. For example, we will continue to expe-

Figure 7-1 *Seesaw representing interest-rate risk.*

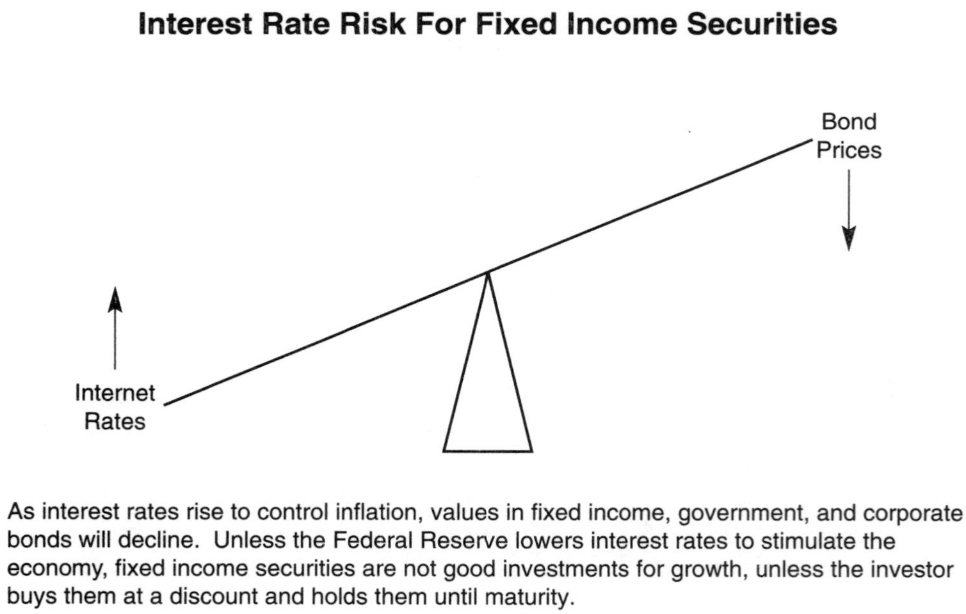
Interest Rate Risk For Fixed Income Securities
Bond
Prices
Internet
Rates
As interest rates rise to control inflation, values in fixed income, government, and corporate bonds will decline. Unless the Federal Reserve lowers interest rates to stimulate the economy, fixed income securities are not good investments for growth, unless the investor buys them at a discount and holds them until maturity.

rience a change in market leadership between old economy stocks, as represented by more mature blue-chip companies in the S&P 500 Stock Index, and the new economy stocks, as represented by technology companies in the NASDAQ index. As we saw in Chapter 6, "Analysis: Tools and Theories," one sector could be falling while the other is rising. One way to help reduce market risk in the United States is to encourage the addition of foreign stocks to a portfolio. Just because our markets decline here at home does not mean that other overseas markets will drop at the same time. For this reason, a proactive strategy to help clients diversify when establishing their portfolios is critically important.

4. **Industry risk**—Refers to individual industries or sectors that operate within our economy. As explained in Chapter 2, some industries will rise and fall with economic cycles (cyclical) while others will tend to resist these changes (defensive). Anything can happen to an industry and cause it to become out of favor with investors for any number of reasons. For example, the recent increase in the price of oil as reflected in fuel cost could be perceived as a big negative factor for the airline industry, causing even the most profitable companies to suffer a decline in stock prices. On the contrary, this situation would be very favorable for the energy industry, because industrial utilization at higher prices would increase earnings. This would be viewed as very positive by the markets, and many of these companies would benefited from higher stock prices in 2000.
5. **Specific risk**—Refers to individual companies whose stocks trade in the open market. As stated in our earlier example, on March 7, 2000, Proctor & Gamble, one of the Dow 30 stocks, suffered its greatest one-day decline when the company announced lower-than-expected earnings for the entire year. That day, its stock plunged 31 percent. An investor who had placed a lot of money in just this one security would have suffered a tremendous loss of capital and would require much patience to wait for the recovery to take place. This type of risk is also more prevalent in large institutional holdings of single-stock issues and in individual 401(k) plans, where matching contributions are sometimes only permitted for corporate stocks.

II. **Foreign risks**—Refers to what might happen when money is invested in various foreign stock market securities. These can be divided into currency, country, tax, confiscation, and company risks. Those investors who wish to diversify must understand that they are taking additional risks by placing money outside the U.S. mainland.

1. **Currency risk**—Refers to what might happen to a foreign currency if it falls in value relative to the investor's home currency. This situation might have a negative effect of devaluing overseas investments. Just as U.S. investors in foreign securities might gain from a decline in the value of the dollar, they might also sustain a

loss when selling foreign shares and reconverting back into dollars. This result would occur if the dollar appreciates relative to the currency in which that stock is denominated.

2. **Country risk**—Refers to the political risk that is inherent in doing business with a foreign country. While more developed countries that use private enterprise will tend to flourish, less-developed third-world countries are more likely to have political upheavals and change the rules in how companies can do business. In fact, the attitudes of both government and workers toward productivity, wage levels, and employee benefits all have an impact on equity values. For example, close cooperation between government, business, and labor in Japan has been a major factor in building a strong automobile industry. These products have achieved a dominant position in major world markets, resulting in higher equity prices for Japanese automobile makers.
3. **Tax changes**—Tax changes resulting in lower company profits might have a negative impact on stock prices. For example, Hong Kong provides an attractive environment for locally registered companies by taxing profits at 16.5 percent and by not taxing individual investors. This type of policy encourages foreign investors to buy stocks in that country, which can result in sharply rising equity prices.
4. **Confiscation threats**—This is one of the greatest concerns to international investors, where locally owned assets are left untouched while those held by foreigners are confiscated or devalued. For example, a policy change in Ottawa's petroleum industry in 1980 forced many U.S. oil companies to divest themselves of Canadian holdings at distressed prices. Foreign investors could also be prohibited from selling their shares (or, if they sell the shares, they could be denied conversion of their money into foreign currency).
5. **Corruption risk**—Refers to what might happen to an individual company that is operating in a foreign country. Corruption tends to take place in smaller companies operating in less-developed countries. They are also exposed to the previously mentioned risks, which can negatively affect their profitability. As with any U.S. company, sudden bad news will cause stock prices to fall, and tight liquidity can also result in not being able to sell shares and limit losses.

III. **Emotional risks**—Refers to our human makeup and how we feel at any point in time about our equity holdings. The way we react to national news or sudden changes in our personal lives has a tremendous impact on the value of stock prices on any given trading day. Our personalities will often be the deciding factors as to whether or not we buy and sell securities and how often these transactions take place.

1. **Aggressive personality**—An aggressive personality is characterized by someone who is more willing to take a risk and who wants to make quick decisions. This investor could be a day

trader who buys and sells stocks more frequently in an attempt to lock in quick profits and to avoid losses. An aggressive investor does not always need a lot of information to make decisions and will often use the Internet to save time in doing research. By making quicker judgments when executing trades, this type of investor will increase the volume of shares traded each day on various exchanges. As Americans become busier and have less time to conduct in-depth research, an increase in day trading will cause more market volatility in the years ahead.

2. **Passive personality**—A passive personality is characterized by an investor who is willing to stay the course during various market cycles. This individual will tend to do extensive research before deciding whether to purchase a security. But once the decision is made, the stock will tend to be in the portfolio for a long time. This investor typically favors a buy-and-hold approach with the goal of long-term capital accumulation and more favorable long-term capital gains tax treatment. Market fluctuations will not bother this type of personality, because he or she is classified as an investor who is striving to achieve specific goals in the future. A financial professional will have an opportunity to cultivate a solid and long-lasting relationship with this type of client. They are easier to work with and will be more inclined to use recommendations that fulfill their financial objectives.
3. **Risk adverse**—This personality type will tolerate very few losses in a portfolio. This investor might have had a bad experience with losing money in the past or might feel highly uncomfortable with market volatility. Generally, young investors who are unfamiliar with market risk might fall into this category. Also, investors who wish to minimize losses could well be retirees who do not want to continue taking unnecessary risk, especially with the possibility of losing the money they have worked so long and hard to accumulate. They will tend to purchase *certificates of deposit* (CDs) and short-term U.S. government securities with the goal of preserving capital and enjoying a comfortable retirement. As a financial professional, you should respect the emotions of anyone who is willing to invest money under your leadership, and create your investment plan centered around their tolerance for risk.

New Economy Risks

As we began the new millennium, many investors were focusing on returns rather than on risk. They wanted to get on board and not be left behind in making money on high-flying, new technology stocks. Despite the fact that it is not prudent to put all of your eggs in one basket, younger Americans in particular tend to be focused on making the most from dynamic changes that are taking place in the economy, and you can't blame them.

New studies from a host of research and government organizations confirm that the market of new economy stocks is drawing in new investors who are willing to pour in huge amounts of cash. While these securities might offer the temptation of higher rewards, they also present an ever-increasing amount of risk. The setback in spring 2000 is a reminder of what can happen to in over-extended market. Only time will tell how long this frame of mind will last. But as we enter 2001, more people will get back to the reality that earnings and profitability are what really matter.

Various organizations have conducted studies regarding recent investment trends. The *American Association of Individual Investors* reports that the average investor has now boosted stocks to 75 percent of his or her portfolio from 60 percent in 1994. According to data from the Federal Reserve, Figure 7-2 shows that 43 percent of American households owned stocks in 1999, up from 31 percent in 1995 and just 20 percent in 1990. Prior to that time, the previous peak was in December 1968, before the market began a 36 percent decline that lasted 18 months. Subsequently, the next decline of 45 percent began in January 1973 and lasted for 23 months. These two bear markets wiped out countless portfolios and brought the percentage of stock ownership back below 14 percent in the early 1980s. Today, however, individuals are leading the stampede, and for

Figure 7-2 *43 percent of American households owned stocks in 1999.*

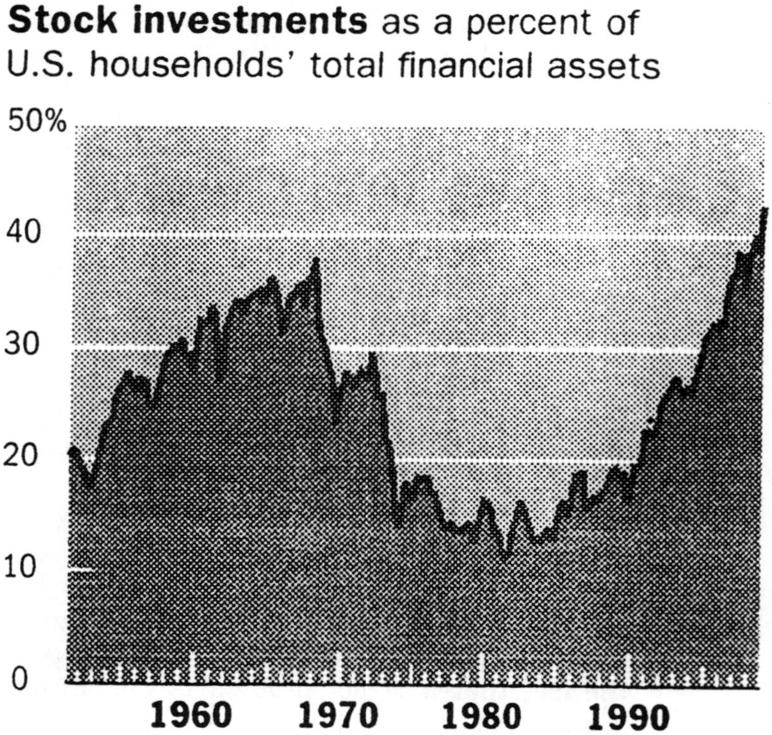

Figure 7-3 *In 1995, 8.9 percent of the value of the top 100 stocks held by investment clubs came from technology.*

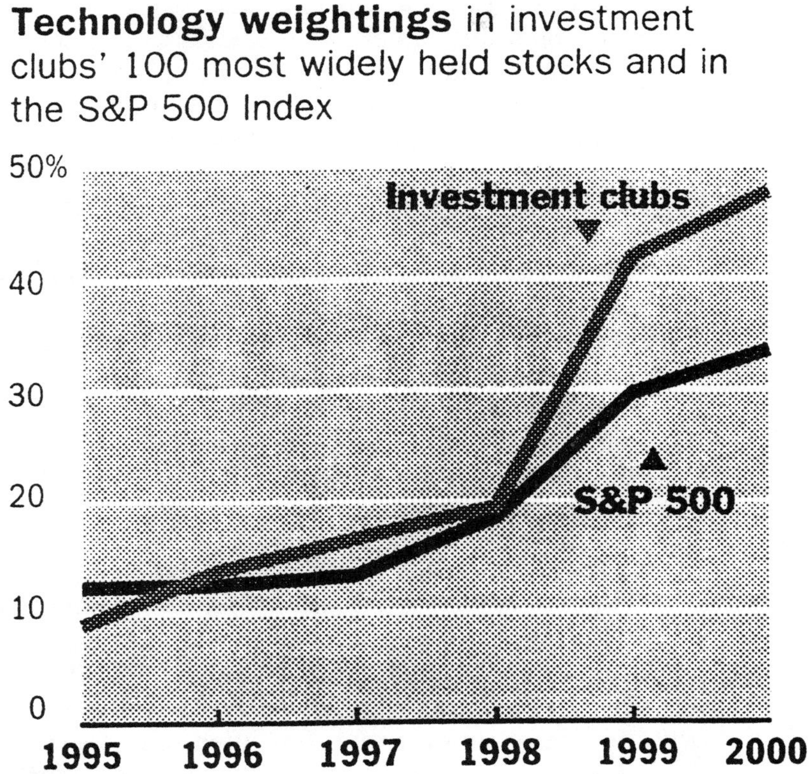

Source: *Federal Reserve Bank*

the first time in more than 10 years, ownership of the largest 1,000 U.S. companies has shifted back to individuals from institutions.

Investment clubs, once light in technology holdings, have also embraced this new-economy industry. Figure 7-3 shows that just 8.9 percent of the value of the top 100 stocks held by investment clubs came from technology in 1995, according to the Federal Reserve. Now, technology stocks make up 47.8 percent of the National Association of Investment Clubs Top 100 (versus 33.7 percent in the S&P 500).

What do all of these numbers mean? For optimists, it is a display of power generated by human emotion and a sign that significant demographic and technological changes will continue to boost stock prices in the future. For pessimists, these prizes glare like a blinking yellow traffic light at a dark crossing. For them, high values in these securities is a sign of a speculative and dangerous situation that is nothing to feel good about.

Distinguishing between a Stock Market Correction and a Bear Market

You must be able to distinguish between a regular correction and a bear market. A *correction* is generally defined as a 10 percent decline in the market over its previous high. A *bear market* is defined as a 20 percent decline in the market over its previous high. When the news media states that a market drop represents the beginning of a long-awaited decline, many investors will begin to focus on each single day of trading, rather than on solid fundamentals of a rising market trend and a strong economy.

History shows that declines of 10 percent and 20 percent are a normal part of market activity, and almost guaranteed to occur with some regularity. Furthermore, the market has historically shown great resiliency in bouncing back from declines. For example, Figures 6-2 through 6-5 illustrate the time it takes to bounce back to a previous peak.

How many 10 percent and 20 percent declines have we seen since 1925? According to Ibbotson Associates, there have been 22 declines of at least 10 percent since year-end 1925, which is roughly equal to one every $3^1/_2$ years. Their figures are based on monthly share-price changes and reinvested dividends for the Standard & Poor's 500 Index. You will also find it interesting to note that 11 of those 22 corrections turned into 20 percent declines, which equals one 20 percent decline every seven years.

As you will see in Table 7-1, we have had five declines of 20 percent or more since World War II.

Only one of those declines turned out to be significant. In the 1973–1974 bear market, stocks fell 42.6 percent from peak to low. The other four declines of 20 percent or more bottomed out at an average of 25.7 percent. This chart shows that unless we have tremendous economic turmoil or some major catastrophe, a decline below 20 percent or more will generally not last too long. More recently, they have been even shorter.

Unfortunately, investors often sell when we are in the depths of a bear market. Those who sold in October 1974, the low point of that massive decline, missed out on returns averaging 15 percent a year in the ensuing decade. Likewise, those who sold shortly after October 16, 1987, when the Dow went down 508 points and lost 23 percent of its value, lost out on returns of nearly 17 percent a year over the next five to 10 years.

Traditionally it takes anywhere from a matter of weeks to many years in order to fully recover from a bear market. Table 7-2 represents the bear markets of the DJIA since 1925. This table shows the number of months that it took to reach the trough and the number of months that it took to fully recover and return to its last peak.

This historical pattern shows that bear markets are a normal part of investing in the American stock market. Also, history shows that the market has great resiliency in bouncing back from these declines. However, a full recovery to its previous peak has had mixed results.

Table 7-1 *Major Market Declines since World War II*

June–November 1946	−21.8 percent
January–June 1962	−22.3 percent
December 1968–June 1970	−29.3 percent
January 1973–October 1974	−42.6 percent
September–November 1987	−29.5 percent

Table 7-2 *Bear markerts of the DJIA since 1925*

Date of Peak	Percent Decline	Months to Trough	Years to Return to Last Peak
7/16/90	−21.2 percent	3	.75
8/25/87	−36.1 percent	2	2.0
4/27/81	−24.1 percent	16	1.5
9/21/76	−26.9 percent	17	4.5
1/11/73	−45.1 percent	23	9.8
12/3/68	−35.9 percent	18	3.9
2/9/66	−25.2 percent	8	6.8
12/13/61	−27.1 percent	6	1.75
5/29/46	−23.2 percent	12	3.9
9/3/29	−47.9 percent	2	25.2

Major Investment Fears and Mistakes

In a volatile market environment, the average investor will not only fear making a purchase of stock at the wrong time but will also typically make a number of unnecessary mistakes. Let's examine 10 common fears that lead to avoidable mistakes:

1. **Possible loss of capital**—What is the best time to invest in the market and to buy common stocks? No one knows for sure, because crystal balls that predict the future is not for sale. When a client needs to invest in order to achieve future goals, anytime is the right time to invest. Historically, the longer your time horizon for investing in stocks, the greater your chances for producing positive returns. Figure 7-4 shows the growth of a $10,000 investment in three major classes over a 25-year period through September 1999. As we can readily see, the best growths achieved by investing in common stocks. This figure alone should convince most people that at least a portion of their capital should be committed to equities for the long term.
2. **Lack of knowledge**—Why do people hesitate to invest or end up buying the wrong type of investment? Very simply, they do not have the knowledge to pick the vehicle that is best suited for their needs. Remember, it is not their fault that they were not educated in school about the advantages and disadvantages of various types of investments. There is no excuse, however, to remain ignorant when it comes to making critical decisions about money. As dedicated financial professionals, it is our job to educate as many people as possible about the risks and rewards of investing. If we make the process

Figure 7-4 *Growth of a $10,000 investment in three major classes over a 25-year period.*

Growth of $10,000 Investment

Growth of $10,000 investment in U.S. Treasury bills, long-term government bonds and large-company stocks (as represented by the unmanaged Standard & Poor's 500 Stock Index) from Sept. 30, 1974 through Sept. 30, 1999.

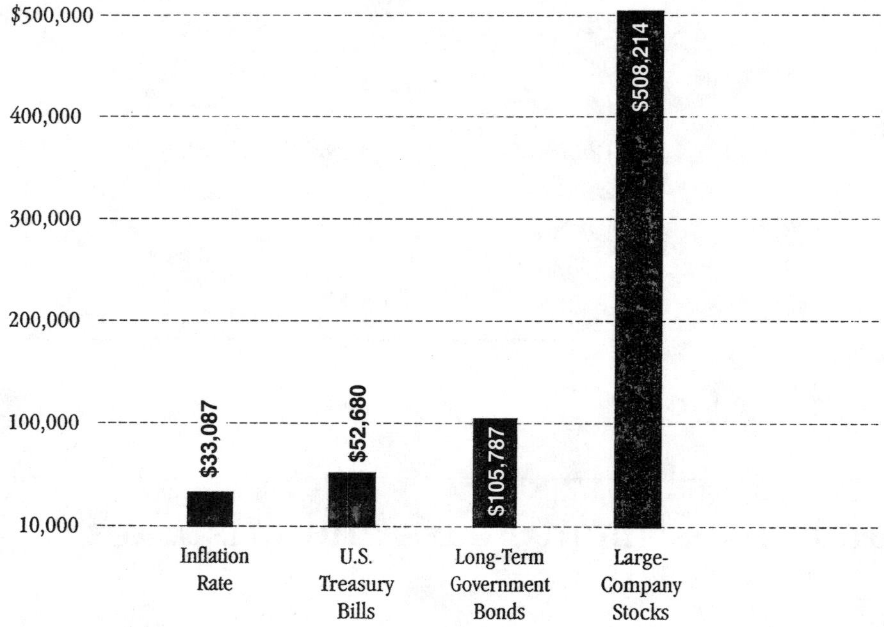

This hypothetical example is for illustrative purposes only and does not represent the actual performance of any particular fund, IRA or real investor. Results shown assume the reinvestment of dividends and capital gains.

Government securities, such as U.S. Treasury bonds and bills, offer a high degree of safety and are guaranteed as to the timely payment of principal and interest if held to maturity. Mutual fund shares are not insured and their value and yield will vary with market conditions. U.S. Treasury bills are short-term securities with maturities of one year or less. Long-term government bonds in this illustration have a maturity of approximately 20 years. Inflation is represented by the Consumer Price Index (CPI) and is a measure of change in consumer prices as determined by the U.S. Bureau of Labor Statistics. The Standard & Poor's Composite Index of 500 Stocks is a group of unmanaged securities widely regarded to be representative of large-company stocks in general. Index performance reflects the reinvestment of dividends. An investment cannot be made directly in an index.

easy to understand and do it in a sincere manner, we will continue to earn the trust and respect of more people who want our professional advice.

3. **Fear of making a change**—Why do investors want to hold a particular security forever? They might fear making a change for several reasons. First, by selling a security at a loss, it would confirm their guilt of making a wrong decision in the first place. Second, if they inherited a stock from a deceased family member, they might feel emotionally attached to it. Thus, selling it might make them feel even more guilty. Third, they might not want to pay taxes on a capital gain, despite knowing that the price of their stock might be near its peak. Our professional responsibility is to help investors work through these issues. For example, by giving them an easy-to-understand illustration and explaining some fundamental analysis data about

the company, they may be willing to part with a portion or all the stock. By structuring investment plans to achieve specific financial goals, we can show how repositioning these funds will work to make them more successful.

4. **Possible reoccurrence of past failures**—What would happen if an investor made another bad decision? This fear is not uncommon today, especially among short-term traders who might have suffered big losses during the spring 2000 correction. This situation is another good reason to encourage clients to fund their goals first with a solid investment strategy. Once they are on track with a workable financial plan, they can then speculate with dollars that they can afford to lose in the short term.
5. **Worry over what others might say or think**—If I commit money now, what will others say about my strategy to invest? Unfortunately, this fear can hold people back from making critical decisions to achieve long-term financial goals. As long as investors do their homework before investing, no one else has the right to criticize their actions. Second, they should be reminded it is no one else's business what they decide to do with their money. In the end, they are ultimately responsible for their final decisions, whether or not they seek advice from other people.
6. **Lack of self-confidence in decision-making abilities**—A combination of lack of knowledge or just not feeling comfortable with handling or managing money could cause this type of uneasiness. This situation could also reflect a problem in other areas of life (not being able to make important decisions). It is time to face the music and dance when it comes to managing money, and everyone must do it at one time or another. Increased knowledge in more of these matters will go a long way toward instilling confidence to become successful in making future decisions.
7. **Questionable investment performance**—How will current or future events affect the value of my new or existing portfolio? Should I wait until something bad happens and the market has dropped before making a move to invest? What classes of investments will perform best in the future? Dwelling on any of these questions could drive anyone crazy. We must be in a position to make decisions concerning when and where to invest so that we have confidence in our ability to become successful. Figure 7-4 shows what can happen if we don't invest. Because no one can predict the future, we must have a solid plan or strategy to follow during both good and bad times. Most importantly, that strategy must be flexible enough to give us a better chance to succeed.
8. **Being impatient with performance**—"If this stock or mutual fund does not perform like the rest of the market, I am going to sell and change to another investment." This trend of thought is bad unless it is used as a system for a day trader. Generally speaking, we must be patient and remain confident about our investment decision-making ability. If not, we will tend to get out of the market at the wrong time

(low end) and then re-enter the market at the wrong time (high end). Most importantly, we must resolve to be patient with increased market volatility that's in store for us in the future.

9. **Being negatively influenced by the news media**—Our American news media has a powerful influence over today's investment environment. Every time the market averages drop or rise significantly, we will be reminded about it immediately. Smart investors who already have a long-term plan in place will ignore short-term events and only focus on attaining their future goals. Only day traders who have a lot to lose from increased market volatility should focus on making decisions based on daily news events.
10. **Procrastination in knowing what to do**—This fear is probably the worst and often results in missed investment opportunities. The price of postponing the start of a retirement program could cost two or three times as much in monthly contributions. Figure 7-5 shows how much an investor needs to contribute monthly in order to reach a specific retirement goal. For example, if 25-year-old Andrea wants to retire at age 60 with a nest egg of $500,000, she will need to begin a savings and investment program as soon as possible. The key is to invest at a young age so that she will have an easier time reaching her goal. However, if she waits for 10 or 20 years to begin this program, it will take much higher monthly amounts in order to achieve her ultimate objective.

Figure 7-5 *Amount that an investor needs to contribute monthly in order to reach a specific retirement goal.*

The Price of Procrastination

What You May Have to Contribute Just to Catch Up

Here's an idea of how much you may need to contribute monthly to reach a $500,000 retirement goal. This hypothetical example assumes an estimate of a 10% average annual return.

Age	Average Monthly Investment Requirement	Age	Average Monthly Investment Requirement	Age	Average Monthly Investment Requirement
25	$131	37	$465	49	$2,076
26	145	38	520	50	2,421
27	161	39	582	51	2,849
28	178	40	653	52	3,392
29	198	41	734	53	4,100
30	219	42	826	54	5,054
31	244	43	932	55	6,403
32	271	44	1,054	56	8,444
33	301	45	1,196	57	11,868
34	335	46	1,363	58	18,750
35	374	47	1,560	59	39,462
36	417	48	1,794		

Smart Reasons for Selling a Stock

Buying a stock is easy, but deciding when to sell can be much harder. This process requires discipline, clear thinking, and a tight reign on one's emotions. Here are some guidelines to follow for considering when to sell a stock in a client's account:

1. **There is a radical change in company management**—If people in top management who are responsible for a company's success begin to leave, there might be some negative implications for the future outlook of that company. As an advisor, you should look into and find out why these changes are taking place. If there is an indication that the company might be weakening in its industry, you might want to recommend selling the stock and repositioning the funds into a similar company that has stronger and more stable management.
2. **What first attracted you to the stock no longer applies**—For example, let's assume that you purchased the stock of a health care company because of its innovative products in the pharmaceutical field. Suddenly, it loses a crucial patent for a life-saving drug. This situation could result in a decrease of market share in its industry, which might lead to a decrease in future profits (resulting in a decline in the value of its stock).
3. **The company has not kept up with its competition**—This situation usually applies to companies that are heavily competing in the same industry. For example, during the 1980s, Kmart stood by while Wal-Mart took away market share and set new standards for high-quality customer service. As a result, Kmart's stock grew cold and unattractive for investors, while Wal-Mart's stock grew in value and attracted many new investors.
4. **The stock has doubled or tripled in value**—This event can easily happen to a growth stock in a prolonged bull-market environment. A consistent rise in earnings will usually pull the value of a stock up to much higher levels. History shows, however, that investors can easily lose these profits from just one sudden market correction (for example, October 1987). If this type of company is still doing well fundamentally, one strategy is to lock in a profit on one-half the position. This move is not only wise, but the investor can also take advantage of lower long-term capital gains tax rates. The available funds can then be used to purchase another high-quality security using the same strategy.
5. **A company suddenly cuts dividends or lowers earnings estimates**—This event should be investigated thoroughly before making a decision to sell. For good reason, the board of directors might want to keep more profits for internal growth, rather than paying them out in dividends. A decrease in profits could be a sign of future trouble, however, and could result in securities analysts recommending a sell of

the stock to their institutional clients. Depending on the market environment or the number of shares outstanding, this situation could cause money managers to panic and unload their positions quickly.

6. **Refusing to sell because of paying taxes**—Some investors might know that their stock is already overvalued, but taking a profit will result in a huge tax liability to the government. Although no one likes to pay taxes, it does not make sense to lose profits in an unstable market environment. By selling a portion of the position, an investor can diversify—thereby lowering risk—and develop a better investment strategy. One famous Wall Street saying is, "You can never go broke taking a profit."
7. **Using newer concepts to prepare a portfolio for the future**—Sometimes a portfolio becomes out of balance when one or two issues of stock sharply increase in value. They suddenly represent an overweighting or higher percentage in the overall portfolio value. By using a strategy such as the Modern Portfolio Theory, an investor can automatically diversify between different classes of stock and build more security in order to lower risk in the future.
8. **Technical analysis shows an overvaluation**—Some investors like to employ technical analyses, which stated earlier uses charts and graphs to follow price movements of individual stocks. A breakdown in these indicators could signal a pending decline in the value of that security. Once more, a decrease in market momentum could cause a reversal in demand and signal a pending decline in share prices.
9. **A change in monetary policy**—We know that the Federal Reserve can change monetary policy if it perceives that inflation is heating up. By raising interest rates, it will contract the money supply and slow down the economy. Stocks generally react negatively to this type of action, and some are more volatile than others. Clients who are not comfortable with this type of risk should reposition a portion of their portfolio into securities that will not be as adversely affected. For example, during the spring 2000, utility stocks became a safe haven for investors fearing this type of problem.
10. **Implementing a financial plan to achieve more specific goals**—There might be stock positions in a portfolio that actually hinder an investor from achieving future financial goals, such as building capital for college or for retirement. In this case, an inactive or dormant stock should be sold, and the funds should be repositioned into better investments designed to attain these specific goals.

Lowering Risk with Equity Mutual Funds

While we have mainly focused on the risk of individual common-stock ownership, we must briefly mention a way to continue owning equities while attempting to reduce risk. The most popular way to accomplish this task is to own stock through mutual funds, or to own a diversified portfolio of many different securities. An experienced money manager will decide when to buy and sell stocks for the portfolio, which takes the emotional burden off the individual investor.

Needless to say, there are many different kinds of stock mutual funds that offer various degrees of risk and rewards. While we will treat this subject in greater detail in Chapter 8, "Diversifying with Mutual Funds," our point here is to emphasize that a combination of individual equities and mutual funds can be used together to achieve many financial objectives.

How to Tackle Specific Financial Goals

As we have stated, successful investment planning begins with setting financial goals. Clients must be reminded that having objectives to shoot for when investing makes more sense than just throwing darts. In markets where the bull is in charge, we tend to get off course or become lax in following a plan to achieve specific goals. The easier it is to make money, the greedier we become—and therefore think we need not follow any logical plan.

For example, between 1995 and 1999, the S&P 500 Index of leading stocks averaged more than 20 percent per year. With that kind of return, who needs to plan or even set goals? Unfortunately, history often shows that most who fail to plan ahead never have enough money when they need it later. Likewise, those who did plan their financial resources often ended up with enough or even more money to meet their goals. The old saying is, "We didn't plan to fail, we just failed to plan."

Let's examine some common profiles among 21st century American investors, the time horizon that they have set for achieving their dreams, and how you can recommend some equity investment strategies for structuring their portfolio.

1. **A young, married couple**—This recently married, dual-career couple are in their late 20s, have no children because they are focusing on building their working careers, and together earn an income of $70,000. Because they have just purchased a new home, they have little left in savings to invest. Solution: This couple must focus on the early stages of a capital-accumulation program. Assuming that they have little experience with stock-market investing, they should begin their program by diversifying their money. This busy couple should take advantage of professional management through mutual funds. Investments in some large companies or growth stocks should include a dividend-reinvestment program. Assuming they have more than enough income to pay monthly expenses, it is critical for them to set specific goals and begin a regular investment program in order to fund their future dreams. Until a systematic program has been established to save and invest on a regular basis, this couple should avoid significant risk taking with individual stocks.
2. **A young, single professional**—This person might be around age 35, have a high yearly income of $100,000, along with a bright and promising future. Let's assume that he or she does not need a home

at this time, is enrolled in a company 401(k) plan, and has already managed to accumulate a modest investment portfolio. Solution: A thorough review of his or her assets might reveal a major portion in cash equivalents or money-market securities. This is very inappropriate for a person of this age, with increasing income potential. After educating this client in the risks and rewards of investing, his or her cash should be redirected towards equity mutual funds and maybe toward some individual common stocks. It is also important to determine the risk tolerance of this client up front. Depending on his or her time horizon, a substantial portion of the client's future savings could gradually be put into equities as he or she becomes more comfortable with various types of investment risks.

3. **A two-earner, middle-aged family**—Lets assume this family of four has one child in college (oldest) and one in high school (second oldest). The couple's combined income of $80,000 is expected to keep up with inflation, despite being used to pay rising tuition bills. The family has a medium-size mortgage, and other investments have grown to $50,000. Solution: A review of the investment portfolio reveals that their individual stocks and mutual funds have good diversification. Therefore, they might want to reduce a large portion of the money being used for college out of equities and into some more conservative bonds or bond funds. This action would help protect against a sudden market reversal that would jeopardize the needed funds. A systematic investment program should be set up to fund college for the younger children, and the remainder of their money should be directed toward a future retirement program.
4. **Middle-income empty nesters**—The children of this early 50s-married couple have recently left home. The husband has worked more than 25 years for the same company and has accumulated a large balance in his pension and 401(k) retirement plan. The wife has recently gone back to work on a part-time basis. Their combined income is $65,000, and they have a moderate amount of debt to repay as a result of credit cards, their mortgage, and the children's college expenses. Solution: This couple has spent a lot of money raising their family and is now ready to do some serious planning for the future. A review shows that the husband has accumulated a large amount of company stock in his retirement 401(k)plan, which represents a major portion of their retirement assets. They can reduce future market risk by repositioning a portion of this company stock within the plan (no tax consequences) into other growth options, including mutual funds. A revised budget or mortgage refinancing at a lower rate could also produce more savings that can be earmarked for personal investments in order to help fund their future retirement program.
5. **High-income, self-employed pre-retiree**—The income of this successful 60-year-old business owner was $300,000 last year but fluctuates with changes in the economy. This client also owns rental property and has accumulated a large estate outside of his business. His 58 year-old wife has recently been diagnosed with cancer. Solution: This client is in a position to consider a wide range of equity alternatives. Because his business seems to be cyclical, he should con-

sider investing a portion of his money in industries that prosper when his company does not. He should also put away the maximum amount into a business retirement plan tailored to reduce current income taxes. He can also set up a more conservative personal account, using income securities to help pay for ongoing medical expenses related to his wife's illness. Assuming he can invest a major portion of his earnings, tax-free municipal bonds or a tax-efficient mutual fund can be used to reduce taxable income.

6. **Affluent retirees**—This couple, in their early 70s, have an income of $150,000—mostly from a combination of retirement plans, IRAs, and personal investments. The primary concern at this time is to transfer most of their estate to family heirs. Solution: The financial planner should contact an attorney to make sure that proper estate planning is implemented in order to help protect the total net worth of this couple. Their investments should be focused on high-quality, income-oriented common stocks. They might also want to own some tax-efficient mutual funds—those that pay little in capital-gains distributions—in order to reduce yearly income taxes. While stocks will provide them with inflation protection, they should also consider variable annuities to maximize tax-deferred growth and income for the future (refer to Chapter 9, "Tax Considerations: Equity-Related Vehicles").
7. **A recently widowed woman**—This 67-year-old woman's husband recently died, leaving her an estate of $1,200,000—including a $300,000 interest in their home. Her financial situation should be reviewed and updated, but only as soon as she is emotionally ready to consider financial alternatives. Her assets must be protected so that she can use them to derive a sufficient lifetime income. She also needs inflation protection, to generate even higher income for her later years. Solution: Various equity investments will play a significant role in funding her income needs. Assuming that she is still in good health, she could live another 20 years. She is probably unfamiliar with investments, however, and cannot afford a large amount of risk. Therefore, her portfolio should emphasize a diversified mixture of blue-chip stocks, large company mutual funds, and bond investments to balance her income payments from other sources (such as pension and Social Security).
8. **Recipients of an inheritance**—This family has recently received an inheritance of $650,000. Both spouses work and together earn $125,000. They would like to earmark half of the inheritance to fund college costs for their three children. Solution: These clients can afford a moderate amount of risk in view of their age, current income, and investment time horizon. Over the long term, equity investments will offer a good hedge against inflation. They should also consider investing in a combination of small-, medium-, and large-cap companies, both in individual securities and in mutual funds. Another way to diversify is to pick out some solid ADRs of foreign companies and use some zero-coupon bonds for tax-free college money. Minimizing taxes on their portfolio is also important in order to avoid paying unnecessary taxes on their inheritance.

A Word to the Wise

This chapter has given you an insight into various types of investment risks, how to avoid major mistakes, and how to structure portfolios for certain life situations. Generally speaking, you will find that young investors who have never experienced a market shakeout will not tend to worry about the market. The word *crash* is not in their vocabulary; rather, it only refers to their parent's stock market in a previous generation.

Most Wall Street veterans and Baby Boomers recall what it felt like when the stock market dropped 22.6 percent on October 19, 1987. But for many younger investors who are pointing and clicking their way to easy stock-market riches today, that Black Monday is nothing more than ancient history and is not likely to be repeated in their lifetime. What is scarier to them is not participating in a rising bull market.

Unfortunately, we are witnessing a deluge of television commercials trying to lure young investors into stocks without the proper evaluation techniques. Few of them barely mention the word *risk*. Also, competition for the business of individual investors' money has caused a rapid stampede of marketing campaigns among Internet companies. If these commercials had to be formally approved by the SEC before airing, we would not see many of them at all.

Here are some important lessons to keep in mind for the future.

- **Lesson 1: The market offers no free lunch—do your homework.** In the early years of the 20th century, people were encouraged to buy stocks for as little as 10 percent down in cash. The rest could be borrowed in anticipation of making huge profits—a practice we know as buying on margin. As with many young Americans today, the promise of easy riches attracted many middle-aged Americans in the 1920s. They bid up stock prices with little thought of the risk that they were taking or the real value of what they were actually buying. When the house of cards finally collapsed in the Great Crash of 1929, investors were forced to cover their debts by selling stocks in a market where prices were tumbling even lower. History repeated itself in the spring of 2000. Our lesson here is not to get caught up in a buying panic of speculative risk. Rather, as a financial industry professional, encourage investors to achieve their goals with discipline, patience, and realistic expectations about risk and returns.
- **Lesson 2: Ignorance and greed spell disaster—learn to spot important trends.** Sometimes, speculative excitement is masterminded by insiders who prey on the ignorance of others in order to benefit from their own selfishness. For example, a combination of ignorance and greed helped fuel the junk-bond debacle of the late 1980s. During this time, corporate raiders used lower-rated bonds to acquire public companies at highly inflated prices. Investors who had little understanding of the risk involved with these instruments were attracted by their astronomically high yields. Eventually, insider trading of the principal players came to the surface, but dozens of companies had already gone broke—and thousands of

investors were badly burned. In summary, the misuse of junk bonds contributed to the stock-market bubble and its subsequent collapse in October 1987. This experience taught us an important lesson: Not all investments are created equal. As a trusted financial professional, use the tool of fundamental analysis to help clients avoid unpleasant surprises.

- **Lesson 3: Don't be a sucker for someone else—avoid over-valued stock.** Today's Market fever is often characterized by investors who purchase company stocks that are already over-valued. Unscrupulous investors are confident of selling their shares at a higher price to someone who is even more foolish. We must be careful to avoid this type of frenzy, as witnessed in the technology sector during its recent run up in late 1999 and early 2000. A similar pattern happened in the early 1970s, when market euphoria sent stock prices of companies such as Avon, Coca-Cola, Disney, and Eastman Kodak out of sight. Investors who were caught up in that momentum continued to pour money into these securities, even as valuations reached unsustainable levels. When the market declined in 1973, these stocks fell particularly hard, and it took many of them a long time to recover. Does this sound familiar with what's happening in today's investment environment?

Finally, what we are experiencing now is a transition to a new economy that will propel us into a completely new kind of life. As we become more proficient, it will be harder to keep economic growth at sustainable levels. It is impossible to supress the excitement of investors and the stock market. In today's environment, as with riding a train, just be sure that your clients are on board for the long run and that they do not want to jump off during sudden market downturns. Diversify among different classes of stocks, and you will be rewarded with a loyal client base for many years to come.

Chapter 8

Diversifying with Mutual Funds

Introduction

Mutual funds are an essential part of any investment program. They complement a portfolio of individual stocks by giving the investor diversification to lower risk. Investing in a family of mutual funds can help achieve a number of financial goals, as indicated in the last part of Chapter 7, "Goals and Guidelines: Setting Portfolio Parameters." As a financial professional, you owe it to your clients to be well-versed on the benefits of using mutual funds, the types that are available for achieving specific goals, and how they can work to increase the size of an estate.

Speaking from experience, mutual funds have helped my clients to actually live better lives. For example, an automatic investment program makes it easier for someone to put away money on a monthly basis. A systematic withdrawal program enables others to receive extra cash to supplement retirement income. Most importantly, knowing that their money is diversified among many different securities gives clients peace of mind. Investors can also use mutual funds as a foundation for a highly successful financial future.

This chapter will review the benefits of using mutual funds in our changing market environment. We will focus on the types of equity mutual funds that are available for structuring both a beginning and an advanced portfolio. You will understand the terms and features of using professional money managers. Finally, we will show how risk and return work to complement each other and how advanced strategies can be implemented when structuring a mutual-fund portfolio for the 21st century.

Benefits of Using Mutual Funds

A *mutual fund*, also known as an investment company, is an arrangement in which thousands of people pool their money together so that a professional manager can invest the money according to specified goals. Mutual-fund portfolios are made up of various types of investments, the most popular being stocks, bonds, and money-market securities. Needless to say, the proliferation of mutual funds during the 1980s and 1990s has made them one of the most popular forms of equity investments.

According to a recent study by the Investment Company Institute, the number of U.S. households owning mutual funds rose 4.5 percent in 1999 to 50.6 million. This represents 49 percent of all households, up from 30.7 percent in 1994 and just 5.7 percent in 1980. Not surprisingly, stock funds are the most popular, owned by 35 percent of these households.

Another important statistic showed that fund ownership increased with income. For example, funds are owned by 32 percent of households with incomes under $50,000, but by a whopping 72 percent of households with incomes of $50,000 or higher.

As of mid 2000, there were about 7,000 mutual funds and out of this total there were around 4,200 stock funds. Is it any wander why investors are so confused when trying to pick the right funds for their portfolios? Over the last decade, the asstes held by mutual funds have soared to $5.76 trillion.

One reason for their popularity is that mutual funds have features similar to individual common stock ownership. They pay cash dividends to investors from the pool of securities held in their portfolios. They increase and decrease in value based on what is happening to these securities. But unlike a direct ownership in individual company stocks, they represent an indirect ownership—meaning that shareholders cannot vote on specific issues of each company that the portfolio holds.

Mutual funds can also make capital-gains distributions from yearly trading. These disbursements are made when the fund generates profits from the sale of individual stocks in its portfolio. While these payouts can be erratic and are not guaranteed from year to year, funds that have the objective of capital appreciation for shareholders will make every effort to generate an annual capital-gains distribution. Preferably, this distribution will be in the form of a long-term capital gain so that shareholders will be taxed on only 20 percent of the profit.

Investors can own mutual funds and use them for the same reasons they would use a portfolio of individual common stocks. Some examples include increasing their portfolio value, generating quarterly income, meeting a future investment goal, or providing liquidity. By using various types of equity mutual funds, financial advisors can help clients design a program to meet future financial needs. Most importantly, investors can obtain diversification and professional management at a very reasonable cost.

Let's examine some of the chief benefits of using mutual funds in a client's equity portfolio:

1. **Professional management**—Experts who are in touch with various markets on a daily basis select and manage the stocks in the portfolio so that mutual-fund owners can worry less about news that could adversely affect investment values. Top-quality management often enables investors to achieve a much higher return than they could on their own, especially if they are inexperienced. Professional management greatly increases the chance for long-term success by taking the emotions out of ordinary investing.
2. **Diversification**—A mutual-fund investor automatically buys into a large portfolio—typically from 50 to 100 different securities or even more. With this type of diversification, the risk of volatility is much lower compared to owning a few individual securities where a drop in value would mean a much greater loss of capital. This special feature makes mutual funds particularly attractive to both new and experienced investors who like to control their own portfolios.
3. **Simplicity**—The investment company that runs any mutual fund is committed to shareholder service. In other words, they will keep records of all transactions that take place during the year, mail out

monthly or quarterly statements, and reinvest any dividends or capital gains into new shares of the fund. For tax purposes, they will also send a year-end statement that shows all sales transactions and any taxable distributions. Computer programs calculate the cost basis of shares sold, making tax preparation for shareholders and their accountants much easier than in the past.

4. **Flexibility**—People who invest in one mutual-fund family can move money between various stock, bond, or money-market portfolios. If this system is set up in advance, investors can perform these exchanges with a quick telephone call before the market closes on any business day. Investors can also sell shares via the phone if they need cash within a short period of time. Most mutual funds will offer to reinvest earnings automatically, giving the opportunity for compounded growth. Shareholders can also make automatic deposits from checking or savings accounts and take advantage of dollar-cost averaging-buying shares with a set amount of money on a monthly basis.
5. **Controlled liquidity**—Investors can deposit a large sum into a money-market fund of an investment company of their choice. From there, they can transfer various sums into and out of other funds, in that fund family, based on their investment objectives. These objectives can include a combination of growth, income, tax savings, and safety. They can also set up check-writing privileges in a money market fund to pay for other personal expenses. This kind of liquidity makes it convenient to earn higher interest than paid on checking or savings accounts, and yet control the source of funds for each individual situation.

Reading the Prospectus

By definition, a *prospectus* is a legal document that contains specific information to help potential investors make a more informed decision. By law, each mutual fund must issue a prospectus to potential and current investors. The old type of prospectus was thick and boring to read, because it contained much legal and technical jargon that was difficult for most people to understand. The *Securities and Exchange Commission* (SEC) has recently enabled mutual-fund companies to begin printing newer versions (see Figure 8-1) that are more brief and user friendly. We will use the AIM Value Fund as our working example.

What are the key elements to look for when reading a prospectus?

1. **Make sure that the copy you receive is no more than one year old**—Because some of the information could be time sensitive, you should have the most recent or revised copy available for clients. Each copy will have a clause that states, "No dealer, salesperson, or any other person has been authorized to give any information or to make

Figure 8-1 *A newer version of a sample mutual fund company prospectus.*

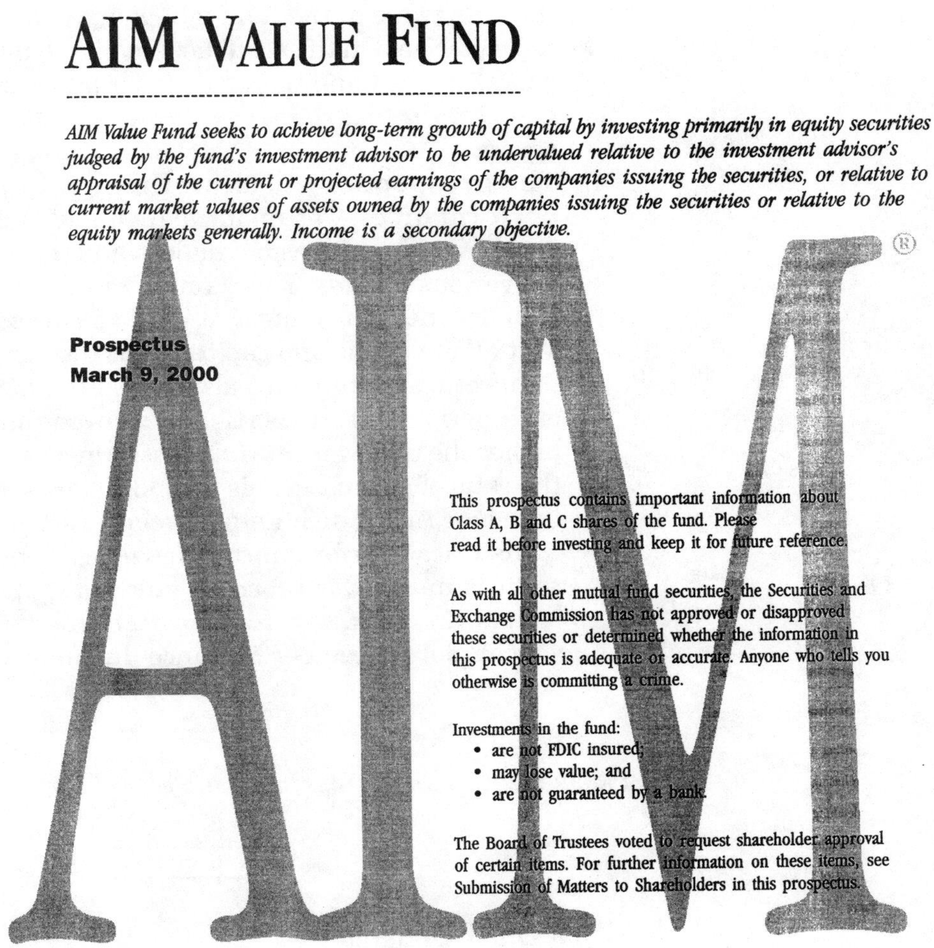

AIM VALUE FUND

AIM Value Fund seeks to achieve long-term growth of capital by investing primarily in equity securities judged by the fund's investment advisor to be undervalued relative to the investment advisor's appraisal of the current or projected earnings of the companies issuing the securities, or relative to current market values of assets owned by the companies issuing the securities or relative to the equity markets generally. Income is a secondary objective.

Prospectus
March 9, 2000

This prospectus contains important information about Class A, B and C shares of the fund. Please read it before investing and keep it for future reference.

As with all other mutual fund securities, the Securities and Exchange Commission has not approved or disapproved these securities or determined whether the information in this prospectus is adequate or accurate. Anyone who tells you otherwise is committing a crime.

Investments in the fund:
- are not FDIC insured;
- may lose value; and
- are not guaranteed by a bank.

The Board of Trustees voted to request shareholder approval of certain items. For further information on these items, see Submission of Matters to Shareholders in this prospectus.

any representations other than those contained in this prospectus, and you should not rely on such other information or representations."

2. **Each prospectus must carry a statement of the fund's declared investment objectives and strategies**—Most funds will focus on achieving one or more of the following goals: growth, income, or safety. The prospectus will state the investment parameters and types of investments that can be used in order to achieve the manager's stated objectives. Also, in anticipation of adverse market conditions, most funds can hold a portion of their assets in cash. Depending on how much can be held in this area, the fund might not achieve its investment objectives.
3. **Each prospectus will state the risks of investing in the fund**—For stock funds, these risks typically include the historical and prospective earnings of each individual company, the value of its assets, general economic conditions, interest rates, investor perceptions, and market liquidity. Any of these factors could cause an investor to lose all

or a portion of an investment, and the income generated from the portfolio might also vary with these conditions. The prospectus also states that the value of the fund will go up and down with the prices of the securities held in the portfolio. Finally, an investment in any fund is not a bank deposit and therefore is not insured or guaranteed by the *Federal Deposit Insurance Corporation* (FDIC) or any other government agency.

4. **The prospectus will show financial highlights and historical performance**—The financial highlights table, shown in Figure 8-2, is intended to help investors understand the fund's financial performance for various periods. This sample report covers a five-year period and includes the return rate that would have been earned or lost, assuming that all dividends and capital gains distributions were reinvested (see total return). The figure also shows the net assets held at the end of each period and the portfolio turnover rate. Generally speaking, the higher the turnover rate (expressed in a percentage), the higher will be the ratio of expenses. This example shows a decrease in the portfolio turnover rate which help to keep expenses down.

   Historical performance, shown in Figure 8-3, illustrates annual returns in bar chart format which gives potential investors an idea of volatility risk. The further back this information goes, the better we can determine performance during both up and down economic

Figure 8-2 *Financial highlights table.*

AIM VALUE FUND

Financial Highlights

The financial highlights table is intended to help you understand the fund's financial performance. Certain information reflects financial results for a single fund share.

The total returns in the table represent the rate that an investor would have earned (or lost) on an investment in the fund (assuming reinvestment of all dividends and distributions).

This information has been audited by KPMG LLP, whose report, along with the fund's financial statements, is included in the fund's annual report, which is available upon request.

	Class A				
	Year Ended December 31,				
	1999	**1998**	**1997**	**1996(a)**	**1995**
Net asset value, beginning of period	$ 40.19	$ 32.42	$ 29.15	$ 26.81	$ 21.14
Income from investment operations:					
Net investment income (loss)	(0.04)	0.09	0.17	0.43	0.14
Net gains on securities (both realized and unrealized)	11.93	10.38	6.78	3.42	7.21
Total from investment operations	11.89	10.47	6.95	3.85	7.35
Less distributions:					
Dividends from net investment income	—	(0.09)	(0.04)	(0.41)	(0.09)
Distributions from net realized gains	(3.25)	(2.61)	(3.64)	(1.10)	(1.59)
Total distributions	(3.25)	(2.70)	(3.68)	(1.51)	(1.68)
Net asset value, end of period	$ 48.83	$ 40.19	$ 32.42	$ 29.15	$ 26.81
Total return(b)	29.95%	32.76%	23.95%	14.52%	34.85%
Ratios/supplemental data:					
Net assets, end of period (000s omitted)	$12,640,073	$8,823,094	$6,745,253	$5,100,061	$3,408,952
Ratio of expenses to average net assets(c)	1.00%(d)	1.00%	1.04%	1.11%	1.12%
Ratio of net investment income (loss) to average net assets(e)	(0.09)%(d)	0.26%	0.57%	1.65%	0.74%
Portfolio turnover rate	66%	113%	137%	126%	151%

(a) Calculated using average shares outstanding.
(b) Does not deduct sales charges.
(c) After fee waivers and/or expense reimbursements. Ratios of expenses to average net assets prior to fee waivers and/or expense reimbursements were 1.02%, 1.02%, 1.06%, 1.13% and 1.13% for 1999-1995, respectively.
(d) Ratios are based on average net assets of $10,456,191,563.
(e) After fee waivers and/or expense reimbursements. Ratios of net investment income to average net assets prior to fee waivers and/or expense reimbursements were (0.11%), 0.24%, 0.55%, 1.63% and 0.73% for 1999-1995, respectively.

Figure 8-3 *Historical performance.*

AIM VALUE FUND

Performance Information

The bar chart and table shown below provide an indication of the risks of investing in the fund. The fund's past performance is not necessarily an indication of its future performance.

ANNUAL TOTAL RETURNS

The following bar chart shows changes in the performance of the fund's Class A shares from year to year. The bar chart does not reflect sales loads. If it did, the annual total returns shown would be lower.

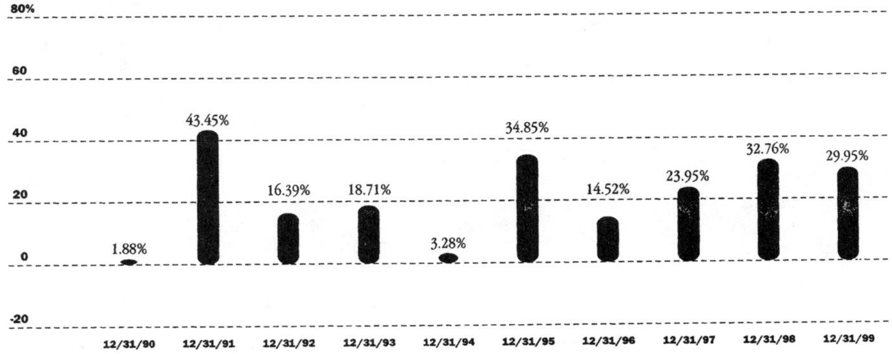

During the periods shown in the bar chart, the highest quarterly return was 27.35% (quarter ended December 31, 1998) and the lowest quarterly return was -20.11% (quarter ended September 30, 1990).

PERFORMANCE TABLE

The following performance table compares the fund's performance to that of a broad-based securities market index. The fund's performance reflects payment of sales loads.

Average Annual Total Returns

(for the periods ended December 31, 1999)	1 Year	5 Years	10 Years	Since Inception	Inception Date
Class A	22.80%	25.56%	20.60%	19.38%	05/01/84
Class B	23.94%	25.80%	—	20.78%	10/18/93
Class C	27.92%	—	—	24.55%	08/04/97
S&P 500[1]	21.03%	28.54%	18.19%	18.60%[2]	04/30/84[2]

[1] The Standard & Poor's 500 Index is an unmanaged index of common stocks frequently used as a general measure of U.S. stock market performance.
[2] The average annual total return given is since the date closest to the inception date of the class with the longest performance history.

periods. Other meaningful information shows average returns stated in percentages for different classes of shares which are compared to the *Standard & Poor's 500* (S&P 500) Index.

5. **Each prospectus will have a fee and expense table**—This table, illustrated in Figure 8-4, describes the fees and expenses that an investor would pay if purchasing and holding shares of the AIM Value Fund. For example, the AIM Mutual Fund Family offers Class A, Class B, and Class C shares. The purchase of Class A shares includes paying a maximum up-front sales charge of 5.50 percent for the AIM Value Fund, with no back-end charge to sell shares. With Class B shares, there is no up-front charge to purchase, but a

Figure 8-4 *Fee and expense table.*

AIM VALUE FUND

Fee Table and Expense Example

FEE TABLE

This table describes the fees and expenses that you may pay if you buy and hold shares of the fund:

Shareholder Fees

(fees paid directly from your investment)	Class A	Class B	Class C
Maximum Sales Charge (Load) Imposed on Purchases *(as a percentage of offering price)*	5.50%	None	None
Maximum Deferred Sales Charge (Load) *(as a percentage of original purchase price or redemption proceeds, whichever is less)*	None[1]	5.00%	1.00%

Annual Fund Operating Expenses

(expenses that are deducted from fund assets)	Class A	Class B	Class C
Management Fees	0.63%	0.63%	0.63%
Distribution and/or Service (12b-1) Fees	0.25	1.00	1.00
Other Expenses	0.14	0.18	0.18
Total Annual Fund Operating Expenses	1.02	1.81	1.81
Fee Waiver[2]	0.02	0.02	0.02
Net Expenses	1.00	1.79	1.79

[1] If you buy $1,000,000 or more of Class A shares and redeem these shares within 18 months from the date of purchase, you may pay a 1% contingent deferred sales charge (CDSC) at the time of redemption.

[2] The investment advisor has contractually agreed to waive 0.025% of the management fee on average net assets in excess of $2 billion.

As a result of 12b-1 fees, long-term shareholders in the fund may pay more than the maximum permitted initial sales charge.

EXPENSE EXAMPLE

This example is intended to help you compare the costs of investing in different classes of the fund with the cost of investing in other mutual funds.

The example assumes that you invest $10,000 in the fund for the time periods indicated and then redeem all of your shares at the end of those periods. The example also assumes that your investment has a 5% return each year and that the fund's gross operating expenses remain the same. To the extent fees are waived or expenses are reimbursed, the expenses will be lower. Although your actual returns and costs may be higher or lower, based on these assumptions your costs would be:

	1 Year	3 Years	5 Years	10 Years
Class A	$648	$857	$1,082	$1,729
Class B	684	869	1,180	1,919
Class C	284	569	980	2,127

You would pay the following expenses if you did not redeem your shares:

	1 Year	3 Years	5 Years	10 Years
Class A	$648	$857	$1,082	$1,729
Class B	184	569	980	1,919
Class C	184	569	980	2,127

back-end deferred charge to sell shares over a stated period of years. Class C shares involve no up-front charge but usually have a 1 percent fee to redeem during the first year only. Management fees and other expenses pertaining to each share class are also stated here in percentages. Finally, an example of actual expenses based on a sample $10,000 deposit will show the costs of these classes which an investor can compare with the cost of investing in other mutual funds.

6. **Other shareholder information is invaluable in making a final decision**—This section will help potential investors by describing in more detail the features of each share class, including (12b-1) fees and sales charges (see Figure 8-5). The prospectus will also state the minimum amount needed to invest in that particular fund and amounts of additional investments that are allowed. Potential

Figure 8-5 *Features of each share class.*

THE AIM FUNDS

Shareholder Information

In addition to the fund, A I M Advisors, Inc. serves as investment advisor to many other mutual funds (the AIM Funds). The following information is about all the AIM Funds.

CHOOSING A SHARE CLASS

Many of the AIM Funds have multiple classes of shares, each class representing an interest in the same portfolio of investments. When choosing a share class, you should consider the factors below:

Class A	Class B	Class C
• Initial sales charge	• No initial sales charge	• No initial sales charge
• Reduced or waived initial sales charge for certain purchases	• Contingent deferred sales charge on redemptions within six years	• Contingent deferred sales charge on redemptions within one year
• Lower distribution and service (12b-1) fee than Class B or Class C shares (See "Fee Table and Expense Example")	• 12b-1 fee of 1.00%	• 12b-1 fee of 1.00%
	• Converts to Class A shares after eight years along with a pro rata portion of its reinvested dividends and distributions[1]	• Does not convert to Class A shares
• Generally more appropriate for long-term investors	• Purchase orders limited to amounts less than $250,000	• Generally more appropriate for short-term investors

[1] AIM Money Market Fund: Class B shares convert to AIM Cash Reserve Shares.
AIM Global Trends Fund: If you held Class B shares on May 29, 1998 and continue to hold them, those shares will convert to Class A shares of that fund seven years after your date of purchase. If you exchange those shares for Class B shares of another AIM Fund, the shares into which you exchanged will not convert to Class A shares until eight years after your date of purchase of the original shares.

Distribution and Service (12b-1) Fees

Each AIM Fund (except AIM Tax-Free Intermediate Fund) has adopted 12b-1 plans that allow the AIM Fund to pay distribution fees to A I M Distributors, Inc. (the distributor) for the sale and distribution of its shares and fees for services provided to shareholders, all or a substantial portion of which are paid to the dealer of record. Because the AIM Fund pays these fees out of its assets on an ongoing basis, over time these fees will increase the cost of your investment and may cost you more than paying other types of sales charges.

Sales Charges

Generally, you will not pay a sales charge on purchases or redemptions of Class A shares of AIM Tax-Exempt Cash Fund and AIM Cash Reserve Shares of AIM Money Market Fund.
You may be charged a contingent deferred sales charge if you redeem AIM Cash Reserve Shares of AIM Money Market Fund acquired through certain exchanges. Sales charges on all other AIM Funds and classes of those Funds are detailed below.
As used below, the term "offering price" with respect to all categories of Class A shares includes the initial sales charge.

Initial Sales Charges

The AIM Funds are grouped into three categories with respect to initial sales charges. The "Other Information" section of your prospectus will tell you in what category your particular AIM Fund is classified.

Category I Initial Sales Charges

Amount of investment in single transaction	Investor's Sales Charge: As a % of offering price	Investor's Sales Charge: As a % of investment
Less than $ 25,000	5.50%	5.82%
$ 25,000 but less than $ 50,000	5.25	5.54
$ 50,000 but less than $ 100,000	4.75	4.99
$100,000 but less than $ 250,000	3.75	3.90
$250,000 but less than $ 500,000	3.00	3.09
$500,000 but less than $1,000,000	2.00	2.04

investors will learn how to purchase new shares and will learn how old shares can be redeemed. Finally, they will learn about transfers between other funds run by the same company, reinvestment privileges, and other redemption features.

Open-End and Closed-End Funds

Mutual funds can be classified into two main types: open-end and closed-end. They differ mainly in the way in which they are capitalized and how their shares are priced.

- **Open-end funds**—These funds have an open capital structure, meaning that when investors want to buy shares, the fund simply issues new ones. The purchase is made directly from the fund, rather than from another investor. The price is determined after each trading day by dividing the fund's net assets by its number of shares outstanding. The result is referred to as the *Net Asset Value* (NAV). For example, if an open-end fund has net assets of $20 million and has two million outstanding shares, its NAV is $10 per share.
- **Closed-end funds**—These funds have a fixed capital structure, meaning that a fixed number of shares are issued and are then publicly traded among investors in the open market (usually on the *New York Stock Exchange* [NYSE]). An investor who trades shares in a closed-end fund is trading with another investor, rather than with the fund itself. The price is determined by the forces of supply and demand and behaves just like the prices of a regular stock. For example, a closed-end fund that has total net assets of $300 million might have an NAV of $30 per share (with 10 million shares outstanding) but might sell at a 15 percent discount, or $25.50 per share. Therefore, for every share purchased at $25.50, the investor acquires $30 worth of earning assets.
- **Listings**—Open-end mutual funds are listed daily in *The Wall Street Journal*, but the comprehensive listing once each month can be used for a better analysis (see Figure 8-6). Included here is the net asset value, fund objective, total return performance over the past 10 years, maximum sales charge, and annual expenses. The report also gives rankings to compare performance among funds with the same investment objective (A through E). I particularly like this section, as you can quickly check the performance of other mutual funds the client may own. The activity of closed-end funds is listed daily on their respective exchanges and is also listed every Monday in Section C under Closed-End Funds (see Figure 8-7). This small sampling shows a breakdown by fund type (including the 52-week return). The more information that is available for your analysis, the better recommendations that can be made for prospects and clients.

Types of Mutual Funds

The following categories of mutual funds are classifications that are used by various professional services, including CDA/Weisenberger, Value Line, and Morningstar. Keep in mind that each service has its own specific style of measuring fund performance.

- **Aggressive growth**—These funds mainly buy speculative stocks of companies that pay low or no dividends. They seek maximum capital gains or appreciation of the stocks in the portfolio. Although these funds offer high potential returns during bull markets, they are equally as risky in bear markets. Some characteristics that you will likely find in these funds include the following:

Figure 8-6 *Listing of open-end mutual funds.*

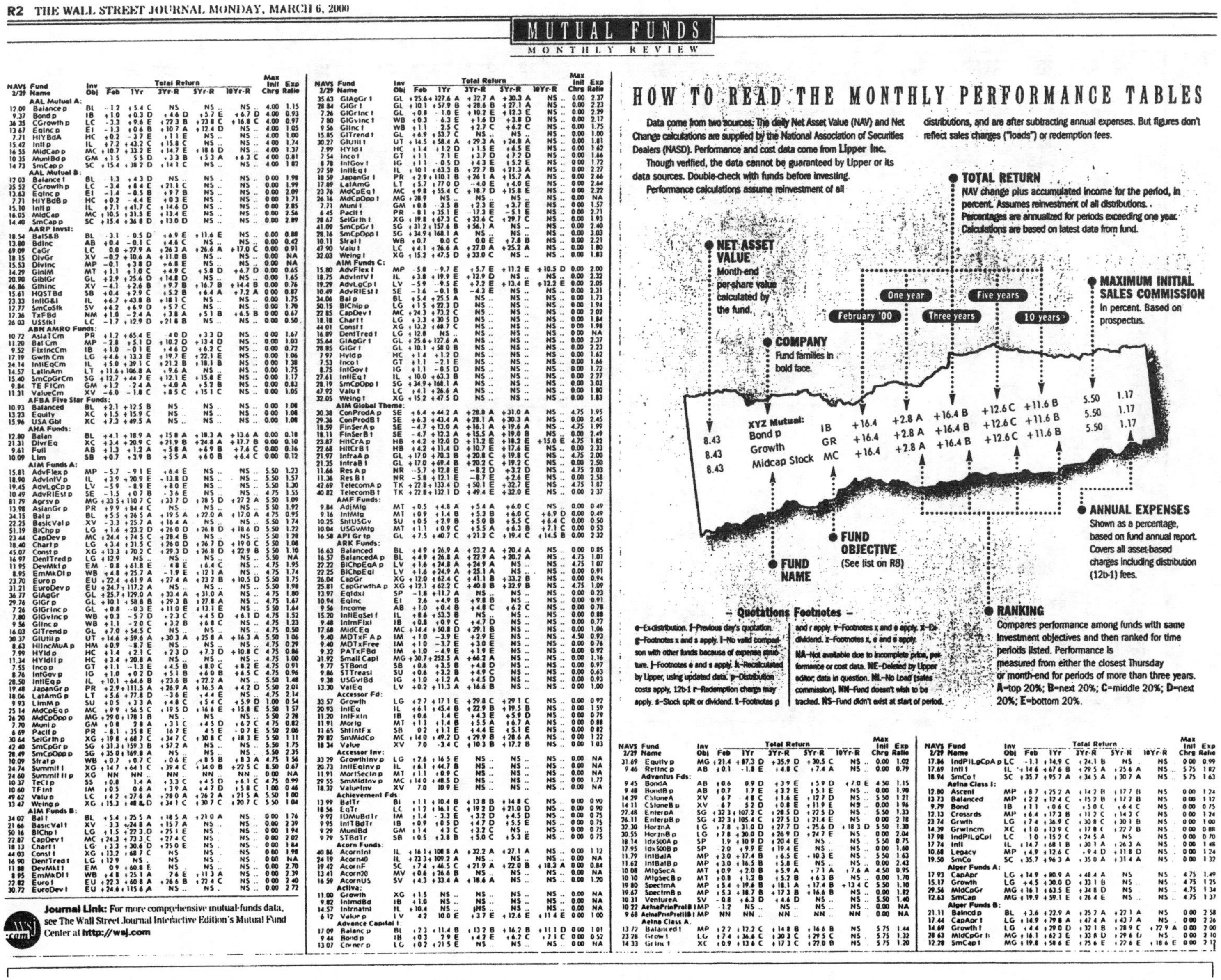
R2 THE WALL STREET JOURNAL MONDAY, MARCH 6, 2000

MUTUAL FUNDS

MONTHLY REVIEW

HOW TO READ THE MONTHLY PERFORMANCE TABLES

Data come from two sources: The daily Net Asset Value (NAV) and Net Change calculations are supplied by the National Association of Securities Dealers (NASD). Performance and cost data come from Lipper Inc.

Though verified, the data cannot be guaranteed by Lipper or its data sources. Double-check with funds before investing.

Performance calculations assume reinvestment of all distributions, and are after subtracting annual expenses. But figures don't reflect sales charges ("loads") or redemption fees.

TOTAL RETURN
NAV change plus accumulated income for the period, in percent. Assumes reinvestment of all distributions. Percentages are annualized for periods exceeding one year. Calculations are based on latest data from fund.

MAXIMUM INITIAL SALES COMMISSION
In percent. Based on prospectus.

ANNUAL EXPENSES
Shown as a percentage, based on fund annual report. Covers all asset-based charges including distribution (12b-1) fees.

– Quotations Footnotes –

e-Ex-distribution. f-Previous day's quotation. g-Footnotes x and s apply. j-No valid comparison with other funds because of expense structure. k-Footnotes e and s apply. k-Recalculated by Lipper, using updated data. p-Distribution costs apply, 12b-1 r-Redemption charge may apply. s-Stock split or dividend. t-Footnotes p and r apply. v-Footnotes x and e apply. x-Ex-dividend. z-Footnotes x, e and s apply. NA-Not available due to incomplete price, performance or cost data. NE-Deleted by Lipper editor; data in question. NL-No Load (sales commission). NN-Fund doesn't wish to be tracked. NS-Fund didn't exist at start of period.

RANKING
Compares performance among funds with same investment objectives and then ranked for time periods listed. Performance is measured from either the closest Thursday or month-end for periods of more than three years. A-top 20%; B-next 20%; C-middle 20%; D-next 20%; E-bottom 20%.

Journal Link: For more comprehensive mutual-funds data, see The Wall Street Journal Interactive Edition's Mutual Fund Center at **http://wsj.com**

Figure 8-7 *Closed-end funds in* The Wall Street Journal.

Friday, April 7, 2000

Closed-end funds sell a limited number of shares and invest the proceeds in securities. Unlike open-end funds, closed-ends generally do not buy their shares back from investors who wish to cash in their holdings. Instead, fund shares trade on a stock exchange. The following list, provided by Lipper, shows the ticker symbol and exchange where each fund trades (A: American; C: Chicago; N: NYSE; O: Nasdaq; T: Toronto; z: does not trade on an exchange). The data also include the fund's most recent net asset value, share price and the percentage difference between the market price and the NAV (often called the premium or discount). For equity funds, the final column provides 52-week returns based on market prices plus dividends. For bond funds, the final column shows the past 12 months' income distributions as a percentage of the current market price. Footnotes appear after a fund's name. a: the NAV and market price are ex dividend. b: the NAV is fully diluted. c: NAV is as of Thursday's close. d: NAV is as of Wednesday's close. e: NAV assumes rights offering is fully subscribed. v: NAV is converted at the commercial Rand rate. w: Convertible Note-NAV (not market) conversion value. y: NAV and market price are in Canadian dollars. All other footnotes refer to unusual circumstances; explanations for those that appear can be found at the bottom of this list. N/A signifies that the information is not available or not applicable.

Fund Name (Symbol)	Stock Exch	NAV	Market Price	Prem /Disc	52 week Market Return
General Equity Funds					
Adams Express (ADX)	♣N	43.20	36 11/16	− 15.1	42.6
Alliance All-Mkt (AMO)	N	51.15	42 1/4	− 17.4	6.3
Avalon Capital (MIST)	O	16.41	15 1/2	− 5.6	−15.1
Bergstrom Cap (BEM)	A	294.37	265	− 10.0	49.9
Blue Chip Value Fd (BLU)	♣N	9.18	8 5/16	− 9.5	0.7
Boulder Tot Rtn (BTF)	♣N	13.31	9 7/8	− 25.8	−11.3
Brantley Capital Corp (BBDC)	O	NA	10 1/2	NA	54.1
Central Secs (CET)	A	41.90	33 13/16	− 19.3	54.9
Engex (EGX)	A	25.63	35	+ 36.6	374.6
Equus II (EQS)	♣N	17.01	10 7/16	− 38.6	−1.9
Gabelli Equity Tr (GAB)	N	12.71	12	− 5.6	17.7
General American (GAM)	♣N	43.92	40	− 8.9	45.0
Librty AllStr Eq (USA)	♣N	14.64	11 3/8	− 22.3	−1.1
Librty AllStr Gr (ASG)	♣N	14.46	11 5/16	− 21.8	21.0
MFS Special Value (MFV)	N	14.55	14 1/16	− 3.4	6.8
Morgan FunShares (MFUN)-c	O	7.44	7 1/4	− 2.6	−20.0
Morgan Gr Sm Cap (MGC)	♣N	18.34	15 9/16	− 15.2	77.8
NAIC Growth (GRF)-c	C	14.10	10 1/4	− 27.3	−7.7
Royce Focus Trust (FUND)	O	6.01	5 1/16	− 15.8	47.5
Royce Micro-Cap Tr (OTCM)	O	11.98	10 1/16	− 16.0	47.9
Royce Value Trust (RVT)	N	16.37	13 11/16	− 16.4	33.9
Salomon Brothers (SBF)	N	20.99	19 5/16	− 8.0	28.6
Source Capital (SOR)	N	52.47	49 5/8	− 5.4	29.0
Tri-Continental (TY)	♣N	33.17	25 5/16	− 23.7	−1.9
Zweig (ZF)-a	♣N	11.76	9 3/4	− 17.1	4.6
Specialized Equity Funds					
ASA Limited (ASA)-c	N	19.24	17 3/16	− 10.7	9.0
C&S Realty Inc (RIF)	♣A	6.51	6 7/16	− 1.1	−9.9
Centrl Fd Canada (CEF)-cl	♣A	3.77	3 1/2	− 7.2	−12.3
Cohen&Steers TotRet (RFI)-a	♣N	10.75	11 1/4	+ 4.7	6.2
Duff&Ph Util Inc (DNP)	N	NA	9	NA	−7.1
Dundee Prec Mtls (DPM.A)-cy	T	13.01	8 3/16	− 37.0	−9.4
First Financial (FF)	N	8.79	7 15/16	− 9.7	13.5
Gabelli Gl MltiMed (GGT)-g	N	20.40	17 1/4	− 15.4	65.9
Gabelli Utility (GUT)	N	7.68	8 1/8	+ 5.9	NS
H&Q Health Inv (HQH)	♣N	37.29	29 3/4	− 20.2	153.1
H&Q Life Sci Inv (HQL)	♣N	31.23	30 15/16	− 0.9	214.4
INVESCO GloblHlth (GHS)	♣N	19.52	16 15/16	− 13.2	12.6
J Han Bank (BTO)	♣N	8.35	7 3/16	− 13.9	−17.3
LCM Internet Growth (FND)	A	14.18	11 5/8	− 18.0	NS
Petroleum & Res (PEO)	♣N	42.75	34 5/8	− 19.0	16.9
Seligman New Tech (N/A)	z	43.14	NA	NA	NS
SthEastrn Thrift (STBF)	♣O	16.61	14 5/16	− 13.9	−6.7
Thermo Opprtunty (TMF)	A	13.27	12 1/2	− 5.8	92.3
Income & Preferred Stock Funds					
Chartwell Div&Inc (CWF)	♣N	12.87	10 9/16	− 18.0	−11.9
Delaware Gr Div (DDF)	N	12.51	10 11/16	− 14.6	−18.8
Delaware Grp Gl (DGF)	N	13.45	10 7/8	− 19.1	−13.0
J Han Pat Globl (PGD)-a	♣N	12.42	10 1/2	− 15.5	−7.1
J Han Pat Pref (PPF)-a	♣N	11.92	10 1/2	− 11.9	−5.2
J Han Pat Prm (PDF)	♣N	9.56	8	− 16.3	−9.6
J Han Pat Prm II (PDT)	♣N	11.58	9 3/8	− 19.0	−9.2
J Han Pat Sel (DIV)-a	♣N	14.48	12 9/16	− 13.3	−13.3
Preferred Inc Op (PFO)	♣N	10.75	9 5/8	− 10.4	−3.5
Preferred Income (PFD)	♣N	13.56	12 1/2	− 7.8	−0.6
Putnam Divd Inc (PDI)	N	10.65	9 1/4	− 13.2	−0.7
Convertible Sec's. Funds					
Bancroft Conv (BCV)	♣A	28.23	22 1/4	− 21.2	13.5
Castle Conv (CVF)	A	28.06	20 5/8	− 26.5	3.3
Ellsworth Conv (ECF)	♣A	12.02	9	− 25.1	10.6
Gabelli Conv Sec (GCV)	N	11.36	9 11/16	− 14.7	1.5
Lincoln Conv (LNV)-c	♣N	24.21	18 5/16	− 24.4	50.6
Putnam Conv Opp (PCV)	N	23.75	19 3/8	− 18.4	3.2
Putnam Hi Inc Cv (PCF)	N	8.27	7 1/8	− 13.8	−8.4
Ren Cap G&I III (RENN)	O	18.31	13 1/16	− 28.7	126.3
TCW Conv Secs (CVT)	♣N	13.19	10 3/8	− 21.3	19.6
VK Conv Sec (VXS)	N	38.88	29 7/8	− 23.2	51.2
World Equity Funds					
Argentina (AF)	N	16.82	11 7/16	− 32.0	20:5
Asia Pacific (APB)	N	14.57	10 7/16	− 28.4	38.7
Asia Tigers (GRR)	N	14.03	10 1/16	− 28.3	34.0
Austria (OST)	♣N	17.75	12 1/2	− 29.6	39.7
Brazil (BZF)	N	23.78	17 1/8	− 28.0	23.9
Brazilian Equity (BZL)	♣N	8.28	6 1/16	− 26.8	25.9
Cdn Genl Inv (CGI)-y	♣T	19.41	12 11/16	− 34.6	14.3
Cdn Wrld Fd Ltd (CWF)-cy	♣T	8.36	5 11/16	− 31.8	39.0
Central Eur Eqty (CEE)	♣N	23.11	16 1/8	− 30.2	27.1
Central Eur Value (CRF)	N	15.32	12 1/16	− 21.3	28.6
Chile (CH)	♣N	15.45	10 9/16	− 31.7	0.2
China (CHN)	N	14.09	10 1/8	− 28.1	22.2
China, Greater (GCH)	♣N	12.27	8 1/4	− 32.8	23.4
Clemente Strat Val (CLM)	N	15.89	13 3/4	− 13.5	33.6
Economic Inv Tr (EVT)-cy	T	158.54	87 1/2	− 44.8	NA
Emer Mkts Grow (N/A)	z	76.90	NA	NA	NA
Emer Mkts Infra (EMG)	♣N	16.57	12 1/2	− 24.6	53.1
Emer Mkts Tel (ETF)	♣N	22.58	17 3/8	− 23.0	79.4
Europe Fd (EF)	♣N	21.08	17 15/16	− 14.9	18.2
European Warrant (EWF)-c	N	22.19	17 1/16	− 23.1	35.5
F&C Middle East (EME)-c	N	20.56	18 3/8	− 10.6	42.7
Fidelty Ad Korea (FAK)	♣N	13.06	11 7/16	− 12.4	64.9
First Australia (IAF)	A	8.35	6 7/8	− 17.6	−0.4
First Israel (ISL)	♣N	20.36	16 5/8	− 18.3	38.5
First Philippine (FPF)	N	6.31	4 3/4	− 24.7	−27.6
France Growth (FRF)-a	N	17.21	14 15/16	− 13.2	45.8
Germany Fund (GER)	♣N	17.29	15 7/16	− 10.7	27.3
Herzfeld Caribb (CUBA)	O	5.94	5 5/32	− 13.1	−15.8
India Fund (IFN)	N	24.43	17 11/16	− 27.6	106.6
India Growth (IGF)-d	N	20.93	15 3/8	− 26.5	61.9
Indonesia (IF)	♣N	3.17	4 1/4	+ 34.1	6.2
Irish Inv (IRL)	N	21.81	15 1/8	− 30.6	−12.9
Italy (ITA)	N	22.21	18 11/16	− 15.9	51.8
Jakarta Growth (JGF)	N	2.16	2 3/16	+ 1.4	−20.4
Japan Equity (JEQ)-c	♣N	10.25	8 3/16	− 20.1	−11.5
Japan OTC Equity (JOF)	N	14.71	10 5/8	− 27.7	35.2
Jardine Fl China (JFC)	♣N	12.20	8 5/8	− 29.3	36.7
Jardine Fl India (JFI)-c	♣N	18.46	14 1/2	− 21.5	127.5
Korea (KF)	N	20.92	14 3/8	− 31.3	27.8
Korea Equity (KEF)	N	5.92	4	− 32.4	1.6
Korean Inv (KIF)	N	10.62	7 5/16	− 31.2	40.9
Latin Amer Disc (LDF)	N	15.19	11 1/4	− 25.9	25.3
Latin Amer Eq (LAQ)	♣N	18.08	13 1/8	− 27.4	38.2
Latin Amer Inv (LAM)	♣N	18.43	13 5/16	− 27.8	28.8
MSDW Emg Mkts (MSF)	N	22.75	16 3/4	− 26.4	67.5
MSDW Africa (AFF)	N	13.03	8 13/16	− 32.4	−4.6
MSDW Asia-Pac (APF)	N	15.18	10 13/16	− 28.8	28.6
MSDW E Europe (RNE)	N	23.74	18 15/16	− 20.2	77.2
MSDW India (IIF)	N	20.77	15 1/8	− 27.2	87.5
Malaysia (MF)	N	6.73	6 1/4	− 7.1	25.0
Mexico (MXF)-m	♣N	24.74	17 3/16	− 30.5	10.8
Mexico Eqty&Inc (MXE)-c	N	12.32	11 3/8	− 7.6	61.9
New Germany (GF)	♣N	18.87	14 3/8	− 23.8	28.4
Pakistan Inv (PKF)	N	4.57	2 15/16	− 35.7	51.0
Portugal (PGF)	♣N	16.26	13 9/16	− 16.6	10.9
ROC Taiwan (ROC)	N	12.70	10 1/16	− 20.8	41.2
Scudder New Asia (SAF)	N	23.64	17 1/16	− 27.8	51.6
Singapore (SGF)-c	♣N	9.12	7 5/8	− 16.3	−0.7
Southern Africa (SOA)	N	19.31	14 9/16	− 24.6	33.6
Spain (SNF)	N	16.15	14 7/16	− 10.6	24.4
Swiss Helvetia (SWZ)	♣N	17.64	13 13/16	− 21.7	0.3
Taiwan (TWN)	N	28.17	23 1/2	− 16.6	50.4
Taiwan Equity (TYW)-c	♣N	21.42	20 1/4	− 5.5	98.8
Templeton China (TCH)-cl	N	11.00	7 3/4	− 29.6	20.4
Templeton Dragon (TDF)	N	12.59	8 7/8	− 29.5	18.5
Templeton Em App (TEA)-cl	N	14.24	10 5/16	− 27.6	7.0
Templeton Em Mkt (EMF)	N	12.94	10 5/8	− 17.9	−7.2
Templeton Russia (TRF)-cl	N	19.25	17 5/8	− 8.4	76.4
Templeton Vietnm (TVF)	N	11.54	8 3/16	− 29.0	9.2
Thai (TTF)	N	4.94	5 15/16	+ 20.2	−15.9
Thai Capital (TC)-c	♣N	2.74	3 13/16	+ 39.1	−14.1
Third Canadian (THD)-cy	T	21.60	16 3/32	− 25.5	−0.4
Turkish Inv (TKF)	N	23.17	18	− 22.3	185.7
United Corps Ltd (UNC)-cy	T	80.84	44	− 45.6	NA
Z-Seven (ZSEV)	O	7.52	7 1/2	− 0.3	7.9

Fund Name (Symbol)	Stock Exch	NAV	Market Price	Prem /Disc	12 Mo Yield 3/31/00
U.S. Gov't. Bond Funds					
ACM Govt Incm (ACG)-a	N	8.17	7 1/16	− 13.6	11.3
ACM Govt Oppty (AOF)-a	N	7.95	7 7/16	− 6.4	8.2
ACM Govt Sec (GSF)-a	N	8.14	6 3/4	− 17.1	11.8
ACM Govt Spectrum (SI)-a	N	6.68	5 7/8	− 12.0	9.0
Excelsior Income (EIS)-c	♣N	18.00	14 3/8	− 20.1	6.9
Kemper Int Govt (KGT)	♣N	7.18	6 3/8	− 11.1	8.9
MFS Govt Mkts (MGF)	N	7.04	6	− 14.8	7.8
MSDW Govt Inc (GVT)-a	♣N	9.02	8 1/16	− 10.6	6.8

- A high rate of turnover (sales) in the portfolio
- Little yield or dividend income from the stock holdings
- A concentration of the portfolio in a relatively limited number of stocks
- A focus on technical analysis when choosing securities

- **Small cap; emerging growth**—The assets of these funds are focused on stocks of publicly traded companies that have market capitalizations of $250 million or less. Similar to aggressive growth funds, they invest in stocks that pay few dividends and that depend on capital gains in order to generate good investment returns.
- **Mid-cap**—Managers of these funds focus on purchasing stocks of companies that have market capitalizations of between $250 million and $5 billion. This wide range enables some higher-dividend payouts, but the emphasis is still on capital appreciation.
- **Large cap; blue chip**—Structured to focus primarily on larger companies that have $5 billion or more in market capitalization. They are characterized by global brand names, strong franchises, and accelerating earnings. These stocks will also pay higher dividends than mid- or small-cap company stocks.
- **International**—These funds invest only in stocks of foreign companies. While some are quite diversified geographically, others focus only on a single country or region. These specialized funds can provide high returns but are riskier than more diversified global funds. For example, if a country's economy deteriorates, all of the companies in that country or region are likely to be negatively affected. Clients who can afford to invest internationally are usually better off buying shares in more geographically diversified funds. All international funds are subject to currency risk. When the value of the dollar rises, a handsome return can be wiped out quickly. Conversely, a fall in the value of the dollar could turn a lackluster portfolio into a top performer. Sometimes, the portfolio manager will hedge currencies in order to reduce the portfolio's exposure to currency risk.
- **Global**—These funds are similar to international funds because they can purchase foreign stock, but they can also invest in U.S. equities. There is more flexibility because they can move in and out of world markets based on economic and market conditions. Likewise, the inclusion of U.S. stocks in the portfolio provides a hedge against currency risk. These fund managers have the discretion to structure their portfolios any way they want in any part of the world, based on current economic and political conditions.
- **Growth**—These fund managers purchase stocks of U.S. companies that they feel have a tremendous opportunity for growth in the future. They conduct extensive fundamental analyses and usually pick companies that have good track records with consistent growth in sales and earnings. Chosen companies in this area can involve a combination of small-, mid-, or large-cap stocks.
- **Value**—Some professional money managers like to pick stocks that are under-valued in relation to the rest of the market. These companies might have fallen out of favor due to lower earnings, no previous dividend payments, lackluster sales, or operation in an unfavorable industry. But unlike growth companies, they are expected to turn around and produce much better results, which would cause their stock prices to soar. Between 1995 and 1999, these companies were out of favor and turned in poor returns while growth company stocks showed excellent

performance. As growth stocks become more over-valued, value mutual funds might very well become popular once again.

- **Balanced**—These funds contain a mixture of common stocks, bonds, and sometimes preferred stocks. Their primary objective is usually a combination of growth and income. They are less risky than growth funds because the income from dividend-paying stocks and the interest from corporate bonds tends to put a cushion under their value in down market conditions. For beginning investors, this approach is an excellent way to diversify their portfolios with a single investment.
- **Equity income**—About half of this portfolio will be invested in dividend-paying stocks, while remaining fund assets will be invested in convertible securities and bonds. These funds focus on providing the investor with a steady cash flow from dividends of high-quality stocks. Many funds in this category have capital growth as a secondary objective.
- **Sector**—These funds concentrate their assets in stocks on one particular industry. Due to the lack of diversification across industry classes, sector funds are much more speculative—and their prices are more volatile. Thus, they behave more like individual stocks than typical diversified mutual funds. These funds can be useful for clients who want to invest in a diversified stock portfolio within a particular industry. The performance of sectors funds that are often quoted in *The Wall Street Journal* includes health and biotechnology, financial services, natural resources, science and technology, utilities, and telecommunications.
- **Index**—Funds in this category attempt to duplicate the composition of a given stock-market index: the S&P 500, the DJIA, the Russell 2000, and the NASDAQ 100. These funds have become more popular during the 1990s due to lower management expenses and portfolio turnover, reduced brokerage commissions, and the ability to follow one particular market. The returns of these funds were higher during the later part of the 1990s and beat many actively managed equity funds. This statement does not mean, however, that they will continue to do so as we embark on the 21st century.
- **Convertible**—These funds contain bonds or preferred stock that can be converted into their underlying common stock. They give a risk adverse investor the opportunity to participate in stock market growth without having to own common stock. They are often used to balance risk in a pure equity portfolio.

Paying Commissions and Fees

As illustrated previously, the prospectus will explain any charges and ongoing fees involved in the purchase or sale of mutual-fund shares. There has been a controversy for years as to the best way to buy this type of investment. Fee-only investment advisors advocate the use of no-load funds, which can be bought without paying any up-front or back-end sales charges. In this case, the investor deals directly with the fund company and avoids using the services or advice of a registered broker or financial planner. The idea here is to save commission charges if advice is not needed, and the investor can make his or her own decision. However, there are still internal operating expenses and management fees deducted from the accounts of no-load funds.

Many mutual-fund companies build business by establishing relationships with broker-dealers and with their licensed securities representatives. Despite initial screening and due-diligence from the home office, investment professionals should evaluate various fund companies on their own and then pick those that are best suited for their clients. When using a professional advisor, there are a number of ways in which investors can purchase shares of popular open-end mutual funds:

	A Shares	B Shares	C Shares
Initial sales charge	Yes*	No	No
Annual expenses	Lower	Higher	Higher
Redemption fees	None	Yes**	None***
Investor objective	Has a long-term horizon	Has a short-term horizon of at least six years	Has a time horizon
	Wants lower management fees	Is not concerned by higher expenses	Wants to be free to sell shares
	Can invest larger	Prefers to spread the amounts over several years in order to reduce the cost of investing	Prefers the simple "pay as I go" pricing structure

*The Class A shares initial sales charge can be reduced with higher investment amounts.
**Class B shares have a sliding scale of redemption fees and free redemptions after conversion to Class A shares, often after five to eight years.
***Class C shares have a 1 percent contingent deferred sales change (CDSC) on redemptions within 12 months of investing.

Mutual-Fund Investment Strategies

One reason why mutual funds have become so popular is the ease at which money can be made in order to achieve various financial goals. Investors can use two strategies that make it convenient so that they do not have to constantly watch values on a daily basis. By understanding how each works, you can make specific recommendations to use either one as the situation warrants.

1. **Dollar cost averaging**—A system in which the investor makes a commitment to put a certain dollar amount into an investment program over a period of time. This method is a popular way to avoid

becoming a victim of volatile markets and enables the investor to ignore market fluctuations. Numerous studies have shown that the use of dollar cost averaging benefits most mutual-fund investors. By investing the same amount of money each time at various prices, the average price paid for a stock fund will be lower than the average market price for the same given period. For example, let's say that John Smith signs a letter of intent to invest $25,000 into a blue-chip stock fund over a 13-month period. His goal is to reach the higher purchase limit on A shares in order to receive a lower initial sales charge. His investment strategy is summarized as follows:

	Amount Invested	Price	Number of Shares Bought
January 1, 2000	$5,000	$25	200
April 1, 2000	$5,000	$20	250
July 1, 2000	$5,000	$15.375	325
October 1, 2000	$5,000	$22.50	222
January 1, 2001	$5,000	$28.25	177

Total amount invested over five periods: $25,000

Number of shares purchased: 1,174

Average market price: $22.23

Average cost ($25,000/1,174 shares): $21.30

Under this strategy, the investor buys more shares as the dollar price drops and fewer shares as the dollar price rises. The advantage of dollar cost averaging becomes apparent when the fund's average market price for the period is contrasted with the average cost paid. In this example, the fund traded at an average price per share of $22.23 during the period, while the investor paid an average price of only $21.30. As the price of the fund goes higher in the future, these advantages will be even more apparent.

In addition to being an effective investment strategy, dollar cost averaging is also an easy system to implement and follow. This concept can be combined with an automatic direct-deposit investment program or dividend reinvestment plan to become almost automatic. This technique is ideal for investors who are too busy to review their fund performance and who want a systematic way to fund their future goals.

2. **Modern Portfolio Theory**—As explained previously, this technique divides funds between four asset classes which are periodically rebalanced to reduce risk and seek higher returns. As mentioned in Chapter 6, this concept was developed in 1959 by two Nobel Prize-winning economists: Harry Markowitz and William Sharpe. This theory uses four classes of investments, including U.S. stocks and bonds and foreign stocks and bonds. Mutual funds are used to diversify between the asset classes that tend to be negatively correlated. For example,

when U.S. stocks are going up, foreign bonds might be going down (and vice-versa). Let's examine more closely how this concept works:

	Jan. 1 Allocation	Mar. 31 Allocation	Apr. 1 Reallocation
U.S. Stock Fund	$25,000	$38,500	$27,500
U.S. Bond Fund	$25,000	$22,000	$27,500
Foreign Stock Fund	$25,000	$33,000	$27,500
Foreign Bond Fund	$25,000	$16,500	$27,500
Totals	$100,000	$110,000	$110,000

We began our allocation by dividing $100,000 into four equal parts of 25 percent into each of the four asset classes. During the first six months, some markets went up while others went down, but overall the total value of our portfolio was increasing. At the end of the period, the U.S. and Foreign Stock Funds had increased in value while the U.S. and Foreign Bond Funds had decreased in value. By rebalancing back to the original allocation of 25 percent for each asset class, we are taking money from the winners and reallocating back to the losers. This strategy is also known as selling high and buying low and has been touted as the best way to make money in the markets. This system works particularly well with mutual funds, whose management in these asset classes has shown favorable results over longer periods of time.

Redeeming and Exchanging Shares

Open-end mutual-fund families make it easy to sell shares. If this privilege is set up in advance, investors can redeem via the Internet or can call and sell shares by telephone during one business day, and a check will be sent out the following day to the address on record. The proceeds can also be transmitted electronically to a pre-authorized bank account. Expedited redemptions for transmittal on the same business day are available for most money-market accounts if ordered before 11:30 A.M. Eastern time.

Systematic withdrawals are a popular way for retirees to receive monthly or quarterly income from their mutual fund. For example, a shareholder must have an account balance of at least $5,000 and make a minimum payment of $50 in order to establish this type of plan. This action can also be stopped at any time or changed to a different amount by giving written instructions to the transfer agent.

Sometimes, a signature guarantee is required when an investor redeems by mail and

1. the amount is greater than $50,000;
2. the owner requests for payment to be made to someone other than the name registered on the account;

3. the owner requests for payment to be sent somewhere other than the address on record on the account; and
4. the owner requests for payment to be sent to a new address or to an address that changed in the last 90 days

An investor who owns Class A shares can also use a reinstatement privilege. This privilege enables the owner to reinvest all or part of the redemption proceeds back into any fund in that mutual-fund family at NAV (without sales charge) within 90 days of the sale. The transfer agent must be notified in writing at the time of reinstatement, explaining how this procedure is to be done. This privilege can only be exercised once per year.

An investor can exchange shares into one or more funds of the same mutual-fund family. However, the shares must be kept within the same class of shares (A, B, or C). If redeeming and purchasing another fund in an entirely different fund family, the investor would pay an appropriate charge for going into that new class of shares.

The following conditions apply to all exchanges:

- Minimum purchase requirements must be met for the fund into which the exchange is being made.
- Shares of the fund to be acquired must be available in the state of residence.
- Exchanges must be made between accounts that have identical registration information.
- Shares must have been held for at least one day prior to the exchange.
- Any certificate of shares held by the owner must be returned to the transfer agent prior to the exchange.
- There is a maximum of 10 exchanges per calendar year, because excessive short-term trading or market-timing activity can hurt fund performance.

Terms of the exchange can include giving the mutual fund up to five business days to process the request. There is usually no fee for this privilege. An exchange request by mail must include original signatures of each registered owner. Exchanges by phone must be received during the hours that the NYSE is open for business. Investors can exchange by Internet if 1) their shares are held at the fund; 2) they can provide proper identification information; and 3) they have established the Internet trading option in advance.

Determining NAV

The price listed in the newspaper or in *The Wall Street Journal* is the fund's NAV per share. It is determined at the close of business on each trading day. The value of all the securities represented in the portfolio are added in order to arrive at a grand total. This figure is then divided by the total number of shares outstanding, or held in the hands of shareholders, at the end of that day. The resulting figure is the NAV.

This figure is critical when determining the unit value of mutual-fund shares for individual investors. For example, shares bought at $10 that are now valued at $10.50 mean that the investment has increased in value by 5 percent. However, the performance gauge will vary greatly with the type of fund and the holdings in the portfolio. While some funds are more volatile than others, their NAVs will always reflect the holdings of individual stocks in their respective portfolios.

Many mutual-fund services and reports use the NAV to calculate the percentage of change in annual rates of return. This procedure is done by taking the NAV at the end of the year and subtracting it from the NAV at the beginning of the year. The difference is divided by the beginning NAV to get a positive or negative return for the previous 12 months. Investors are also interested in the return figures for three, five, and 10 years when doing their comparisons.

Some mutual funds that have been in existence for a longer time will provide the return figures going back to inception. For example, the Investment Company of America from the American Funds family provides information in its sales literature going back to its founding in 1934. Stock funds of this type that have a proven record of positive performance from experienced management should not be ignored by potential investors. A long history of increases in the NAV shows that a mutual fund has been run and managed successfully during both good and bad times.

How to Review the Fund Company

Gauging the quality of a fund company is not always easy. Because most are private, accurate financial information about profits and losses can be hard to obtain. Here are some details to consider during your review:

- **Reputation**—Consider how they rank in the financial services industry and the relative performance of their individual funds. Try to seek a fund family with a consistent history of top-performing funds in different categories. Some might be known for their equity funds, while others will have a strong reputation for income funds. Most importantly, have the flexibility to pick and use those fund families that will work for the client's best interest and will give good service.
- **Assets under management**—While lots of money under management shows that investors have confidence in that particular company, it does not necessarily indicate good performing mutual funds. In such a competitive industry, a fund family with spotty achievement records, poor service, and high management turnover will have a hard time attracting new money. Generally speaking, the more assets that a fund has, the harder it can be to manage effectively. For this reason, some funds that attract a large amount of money will be closed to new investors for a period of time.
- **Longevity**—Find out how long a fund family has been in existence. Has it withstood the test of time in both bull and bear markets? Has there been a merger that has benefited both companies (i.e., Franklin-Templeton). The longer a company has been in existence, the better it will indicate solid management and quality shareholder service.

How to Evaluate the Fund Manager

While some funds use a multi-manager approach, most are still managed by one person whose name should be easily obtainable from the prospectus. The following key points should be examined in determining a manager's qualifications:

- **Experience**—After checking how long the fund has been in existence, find out how long the current manager has been at the helm. While longer tenure does not always guarantee good performance, it helps to have someone who has experience in both good and bad market environments. Fund families today want managers who make the right decisions and who can be competitive with performance numbers. In other words, they usually do not keep poor managers on staff for very long. Because there has been a proliferation of new funds created during the 1990s, there are also many new managers running them. If this situation is the case for a fund that you might be recommending, explain it to the client and reassure him or her of your commitment to monitoring this situation.
- **Education**—While it is true that many of the top managers did not go to the most famous schools, it does not hurt to see some top-quality universities in a biography. Besides having completed a graduate business program, also look for a designation such as a *Certified Financial Analyst* (CFA). This is the highest designation in that career field, just as a *Certified Public Accountant* (CPA) is the highest designation for an accountant. It will also be a plus if the manager has a law degree.
- **Performance and consistency**—It is nice to have a manager whose track record shows consistently good performance. It takes more than luck to pick the right stocks over a period of time, and the really great managers stay on top of their ranks. If your client is considering a fund that consistently ranks in the bottom with its competition, it is critical to point out that the manager is not very good or that the fund company will probably hire someone better in the future. This situation would warrant waiting for a purchase, or looking at other funds that show a better performance history. Your goal is to help the prospect or client achieve his or her stated investment objectives with the best money managers in the business.

Determining Portfolio Objectives

Growth-oriented investors have different financial goals based on age. Let's examine various age brackets to determine how a client might invest in order to establish a portfolio of mutual funds.

1. **Young investor**—Might be someone just beginning a career in their 20s. Assuming that they understand the risk of investing, they will tend to strive for maximum growth of their money because they have time to make up for any losses incurred along the way. One investment that I always recommend is a Roth IRA as part of their

new program. Because most people are not focused on retirement planning in their younger years, funding a Roth IRA with the $2,000 maximum yearly contribution is the least they can do to get a head start on retirement. This procedure can be done painlessly by setting up an investment program to make automatic deposits into a small-cap value or growth mutual fund of their choice. Figure 8-8 illustrates the power of an annual contribution for this purpose. It shows that the earlier an investment program begins, the more money will be accumulated at various rates of return. The younger an investor and the higher rate of return that he or she can earn, the more that will be available for retirement. To add icing on the cake, if this deposit was made into a Roth IRA account, all accumulated earnings will be available for withdrawal on an income tax-free basis at retirement.

2. **Middle-age investors**—Can be a married couple in their mid-30s. Goals might include beginning a family or accumulating money for college educations. Let's assume that both spouses have worked for 10 years, have two children ages five and 10, and have accumulated $50,000 in savings to invest. These funds could be earmarked for education accounts, each going into a mid-cap value or growth fund for college. If they could average a return of just 12 percent per year, these funds would grow as follows:

   a. Child 1 (age 10) will start college in eight years; invest $30,000 at 12 percent for eight years = $74,280
   b. Child 2 (age 5) will start college in 13 years; invest $20,000 at 12 percent for 13 years = $87,270

   For this family, the cost of college will be higher for Child 2, so we need more money to account for higher inflation. Another investment strategy could be as follows:

   a. **Child 1**—Divide $30,000 into three mutual funds of $10,000 each: one into large cap, one into global, and one into balanced.
   b. **Child 2**—Divide $20,000 into four mutual funds of $5,000 each: one into small cap, one into large cap, one into international, and

Figure 8-8 *Compounding annual contributions in a Roth IRA.*

The Importance of Investing For Growth

By investing $ 2,000 per year at these average rates of return:

Age Investment Program Begins	**8%**	**10%**	**12%**	**14%**
	At age 65 you will accumulate:			
20	**$ 834,852**	**$ 1,581,590**	**$ 3,042,435**	**$ 5,906,488**
25	**559,562**	**973,704**	**1,718,285**	**3,059,817**
30	**372,204**	**596,254**	**966,926**	**1,581,345**
35	**244,692**	**361,886**	**540,585**	**813,474**
40	**157,908**	**216,364**	**298,668**	**414,665**
45	**98,846**	**126,005**	**161,397**	**207,536**
50	**58,648**	**69,899**	**83,506**	**99,089**
55	**31,291**	**35,062**	**39,309**	**44,089**

one into equity income. This approach shows that we can be even more aggressive with funds for Child 2, because we have more time to make up for losses but have more capital appreciation potential.

3. **Pre-retired investors**—Might be in their early 50s and concerned with having enough money for retirement at age 62. Hopefully, they have already invested their company 401(k) retirement plans in growth options over the years and are now concerned with the amount of income that their personal portfolios will provide. They can invest extra funds in higher-quality mutual funds with a portfolio of more conservative blue-chip stocks. They should also use Modern Portfolio Theory with their mutual funds to help guard against market volatility. Assuming that they had extra money of $100,000 to invest at this time, they would pick one family of funds and divide the money between four asset classes (as illustrated previously). This strategy would work well to give them sustained growth for the next 12 years, with the goal of beginning systematic withdrawals from their mutual funds in order to supplement other retirement income sources.
4. **Retired investor**—In her mid-60s, wanting to maintain a steady stream of income with limited risk. This investor is focused on risk-reduction strategies, which could include balanced and equity income mutual funds along with more stable bond-type funds. The first step is to analyze various income sources so that she can maintain her standard of living. Her investment plan must be monitored carefully so that she does not withdraw too much income that would dip into her capital. Because she will be living longer during retirement, she must have a portion of her assets in stock mutual funds for inflation protection. A sample of her $100,000 portfolio allocated for growth might look like the following:

Type of Fund	Amount
Large Cap Growth and Value Fund	$20,000
Global Fund	$20,000
Balanced Fund	$20,000
Equity Income Fund	$20,000
Index Fund	$20,000
Total Investment	$100,000

Conclusion

Mutual-fund investing can be fun and challenging at the same time. You must find out as much about investors as possible before making recommendations. This includes knowing their tolerance for risk and about any past investment experiences. Most people are familiar with mutual funds but might not know all of the flexible features they offer. By understanding the information in this chapter, your job is to explain and educate potential clients about the pros and cons of mutual-fund investing before they make a commitment.

With equity markets becoming even more volatile in the 21st century, a portfolio of mutual funds diversified by the type described in this chapter should work extremely well in helping clients achieve their financial objectives. They will respect your professionalism if you lay out a plan that will recommend only high-quality investment managers, along with a follow-up program to review their performance on a regular basis. Whether choosing load or no-load funds, flexibility is the key to using mutual funds in a growth or income program that is set up for the client's benefit.

The 21st century will feature "value added" investment services for clients. This includes the accumulation of assets under management using no load funds along with Modern Portfolio Theory. A portfolio set up using this strategy is almost certain to make money. We can now pick tax efficient mutual funds to help minimize taxes and reduce risk to an acceptable level.

This is an ideal way to structure your practice for the future.

Chapter 9

Tax Considerations: Equity-Related Vehicles

Introduction

Up to this point, you have learned a lot about how to make money on equity-related investments. We have discussed the overall market environment, types of equity vehicles, and various risk-reduction strategies. Another important element which the financial professional must be aware of is taxation. Making intelligent decisions is one thing when it comes to picking the right equity investments for clients, but our goal is to help them keep as much money as possible after they have made it. This chapter will focus specifically on this issue.

Through various legislative acts, the government is making progress toward giving investors some much-needed tax relief. From lower capital gains rates to newer *Individual Retirement Accounts* (IRA), we can now structure client portfolios to take advantage of these special opportunities. It is often easy for clients to forget that recommendations can be implemented that will help them keep more of the money they make in their investment programs. Likewise, we should make every effort to shelter as much money as possible so that clients can keep earning interest on the money they make on their investments. In this way, we are actually helping them build a greater amount of wealth for the future.

Let's take a serious look at how investment vehicles are taxed, the provisions of recent legislation, and how to structure portfolios in order to maximize tax savings.

Taxes and Capital Gains

As part of the Taxpayer Relief Act of 1997, the *Internal Revenue Service* (IRS) unveiled a new capital gains tax schedule with some rates considerably lower than before. What rates apply to investors? This situation depends on the following:

- The type of asset that is sold
- The cost basis
- The length of time that the asset was held before it was sold
- The taxpayer's income level

Qualifying for the lowest new rates are stocks, bonds, mutual funds, and many other capital assets. Taxed at a slightly higher rate are business or rental real estate, collectibles, depreciation, and some other items.

For investment purposes, there are two holding periods for capital assets:

- Those that are held for one year or less are considered short term and receive no preferred tax treatment. Taxes are paid at the normal tax rate on those gains.
- Those that are held for more than one year are considered long term and receive a special tax break on the sale of those assets.

If the taxpayer is in the 15 percent tax bracket, then

- Gains on assets held for a year or less are taxes at the ordinary income tax rate (15 percent in most cases).
- Gains on assets held for more than one year are taxed at a reduced rate of 10 percent.

If the taxpayer's ordinary income tax bracket is greater than 15 percent, then

- Gains on assets held for a year or less are taxed at the ordinary income tax rate (anywhere from 28 percent up to as high as 39.6 percent, depending on the ordinary tax rate).
- Gains on assets held for more than one year are taxed at a reduced rate of 20 percent.

When an order is placed to buy or sell a security, there will be a trade date and a settlement date recorded for the order. The *trade date*, which is the date that the order was actually executed, counts for tax purposes. The settlement date, usually three days later, is now immaterial for tax-reporting purposes.

Computing Your Tax Bracket

For many investors, it is not easy to figure out the tax rate on their last dollar of earned income. We begin by paying 15 percent federal income tax on the first chunk of annual income. Then, depending on earnings, we pay successively higher rates on additional income. The top or *marginal rate* is based on your taxable income, which is income after all sorts of deductions and adjustments are taken from the gross income. Knowing the client's marginal rate is essential for good tax planning and for making rational investment recommendations.

For example, what types of mutual funds should you buy, and how much money should be put into tax-deferred or tax-exempt accounts (such as traditional IRAs and Roth IRAs)? Many taxpayers who hire accountants or use tax software never get a real fix on their top bracket. This situation is not surprising, because there are so many brackets and deductions for state and local taxes that can end up changing a client's effective federal tax rate.

Figure 9-1 *Five federal brackets.*

YOUR 2000 TAX BRACKET

FEDERAL BRACKET	SINGLE	MARRIED FILING JOINTLY	MARRIED FILING SEPARATELY	HEAD OF HOUSEHOLD
	APPLIES TO TAXABLE INCOME UP TO:			
15%	$26,250	43,850	21,925	35,150
	APPLIES TO TAXABLE INCOME BETWEEN:			
28%	$26,250–63,550	43,850–105,950	21,925–52,975	35,150–90,800
31%	$63,550–132,600	105,950–161,450	52,975–80,725	90,800–147,050
36%	$132,600–288,350	161,450–288,350	80,725–144,175	147,050–288,350
	APPLIES TO TAXABLE INCOME ABOVE:			
39.6%	$288,350	288,350	144,175	288,350

Currently, there are no fewer than five federal brackets, ranging from 15 percent to 39.6 percent, for ordinary income and short-term capital gains (see Figure 9-1), plus another two for long-term capital gains. As you can see, single taxpayers pay a higher amount of taxes in comparison to married couples who file jointly. Likewise, the head of household will pay a higher amount in comparison to someone who is married and filing separately. Equity investors should realize that a long-term capital gains rate of 20 percent applies to taxpayers in the 28 percent to 39.6 percent bracket, while a rate of 10 percent applies to taxpayers in the 15 percent income-tax bracket.

You will find that an alarmingly high number of clients do not know the difference between *adjusted gross income* (AGI) and taxable income. These terms are used often in financial circles, and you must know the difference between them. *Taxable income* is the last number you arrive at (after taking deductions) before looking up the amount of tax to pay Uncle Sam. Start with your gross income and the amount reported on your W-2 forms from employers and on 1099 statements from banks, fund companies, and brokerage firms. Add business income, capital gains, and all other income in order to arrive at your total income.

To figure *AGI*, apply certain deductions (such as money contributed to traditional IRAs, student-loan interest, and moving expenses). Small-business owners can deduct one-half of their self-employment tax, health insurance premiums, and retirement plan contributions. These deduc-

Figure 9-2 *How to compute AGI.*

Form **1040** Department of the Treasury—Internal Revenue Service
U.S. Individual Income Tax Return **1999** (L) IRS Use Only—Do not write or staple in this space.

For the year Jan. 1–Dec. 31, 1999, or other tax year beginning , 1999, ending , 19 OMB No. 1545-0074

Label (See instructions on page 18.) **Use the IRS label.** Otherwise, please print or type.

LABEL HERE

- Your first name and initial | Last name | **Your social security number**
- If a joint return, spouse's first name and initial | Last name | **Spouse's social security number**
- Home address (number and street). If you have a P.O. box, see page 18. | Apt. no.
- City, town or post office, state, and ZIP code. If you have a foreign address, see page 18.

▲ **IMPORTANT!** ▲ You **must** enter your SSN(s) above.

Presidential Election Campaign (See page 18.)
Do you want $3 to go to this fund? . . . Yes No
If a joint return, does your spouse want $3 to go to this fund? . . . Yes No
Note. Checking "Yes" will not change your tax or reduce your refund.

Filing Status

Check only one box.

1 ☐ Single
2 ☐ Married filing joint return (even if only one had income)
3 ☐ Married filing separate return. Enter spouse's social security no. above and full name here. ▶
4 ☐ Head of household (with qualifying person). (See page 18.) If the qualifying person is a child but not your dependent, enter this child's name here. ▶
5 ☐ Qualifying widow(er) with dependent child (year spouse died ▶ 19). (See page 18.)

Exemptions

6a ☐ **Yourself.** If your parent (or someone else) can claim you as a dependent on his or her tax return, **do not** check box 6a . . .
b ☐ **Spouse** . . .
c **Dependents:**

(1) First name Last name	(2) Dependent's social security number	(3) Dependent's relationship to you	(4) ✓ if qualifying child for child tax credit (see page 19)
			☐
			☐
			☐
			☐
			☐
			☐

If more than six dependents, see page 19.

d Total number of exemptions claimed . . .

No. of boxes checked on 6a and 6b ____
No. of your children on 6c who:
• **lived with you** ____
• **did not live with you due to divorce or separation (see page 19)** ____
Dependents on 6c not entered above ____
Add numbers entered on lines above ▶ ☐

Income

Attach Copy B of your Forms W-2 and W-2G here. Also attach Form(s) 1099-R if tax was withheld.

If you did not get a W-2, see page 20.

Enclose, but do not staple, any payment. Also, please use **Form 1040-V.**

7 Wages, salaries, tips, etc. Attach Form(s) W-2 . . . 7
8a **Taxable** interest. Attach Schedule B if required . . . 8a
b **Tax-exempt** interest. DO NOT include on line 8a . . . 8b
9 Ordinary dividends. Attach Schedule B if required . . . 9
10 Taxable refunds, credits, or offsets of state and local income taxes (see page 21) . . 10
11 Alimony received . . . 11
12 Business income or (loss). Attach Schedule C or C-EZ . . . 12
13 Capital gain or (loss). Attach Schedule D if required. If not required, check here ▶ ☐ 13
14 Other gains or (losses). Attach Form 4797 . . . 14
15a Total IRA distributions . 15a | b Taxable amount (see page 22) 15b
16a Total pensions and annuities 16a | b Taxable amount (see page 22) 16b
17 Rental real estate, royalties, partnerships, S corporations, trusts, etc. Attach Schedule E 17
18 Farm income or (loss). Attach Schedule F . . . 18
19 Unemployment compensation . . . 19
20a Social security benefits . 20a | b Taxable amount (see page 24) 20b
21 Other income. List type and amount (see page 24) 21
22 Add the amounts in the far right column for lines 7 through 21. This is your **total income** ▶ 22

Adjusted Gross Income

23 IRA deduction (see page 26) . . . 23
24 Student loan interest deduction (see page 26) . . . 24
25 Medical savings account deduction. Attach Form 8853 . 25
26 Moving expenses. Attach Form 3903 . . . 26
27 One-half of self-employment tax. Attach Schedule SE . 27
28 Self-employed health insurance deduction (see page 28) 28
29 Keogh and self-employed SEP and SIMPLE plans . . 29
30 Penalty on early withdrawal of savings . . . 30
31a Alimony paid b Recipient's SSN ▶ 31a
32 Add lines 23 through 31a . . . 32
33 Subtract line 32 from line 22. This is your **adjusted gross income** . . . ▶ 33

For Disclosure, Privacy Act, and Paperwork Reduction Act Notice, see page 54. Cat. No. 12600W Form **1040** (1999)

tions are added together and then subtracted from the total income to arrive at the AGI as shown on the bottom of page one of Form 1040 (see Figure 9-2).

To turn AGI into taxable income, factor in dependency exemptions ($2,800 for you and for each dependent in the year 2000) and all itemized deductions. These deductions include mortgage-interest expense, state and local taxes, charitable donations, and some medical expenses. If you do not itemize deductions, take the standard deduction instead. These

Figure 9-3 *Determining taxable income.*

Form 1040 (1999) Page **2**

Tax and Credits

34 Amount from line 33 (adjusted gross income) 34

35a Check if: ☐ **You** were 65 or older, ☐ Blind; ☐ **Spouse** was 65 or older, ☐ Blind.
Add the number of boxes checked above and enter the total here . . . . ▶ 35a

b If you are married filing separately and your spouse itemizes deductions or you were a dual-status alien, see page 30 and check here . . . . . . ▶ 35b ☐

Standard Deduction for Most People
Single: $4,300
Head of household: $6,350
Married filing jointly or Qualifying widow(er): $7,200
Married filing separately: $3,600

36 Enter your **itemized deductions** from Schedule A, line 28, **OR standard deduction** shown on the left. **But** see page 30 to find your standard deduction if you checked any box on line 35a or 35b **or** if someone can claim you as a dependent 36

37 Subtract line 36 from line 34 37

38 If line 34 is $94,975 or less, multiply $2,750 by the total number of exemptions claimed on line 6d. If line 34 is over $94,975, see the worksheet on page 31 for the amount to enter . 38

39 **Taxable income.** Subtract line 38 from line 37. If line 38 is more than line 37, enter -0- . 39

40 **Tax** (see page 31). Check if any tax is from **a** ☐ Form(s) 8814 **b** ☐ Form 4972 . . ▶ 40

41 Credit for child and dependent care expenses. Attach Form 2441 41

42 Credit for the elderly or the disabled. Attach Schedule R . . 42

43 Child tax credit (see page 33) 43

44 Education credits. Attach Form 8863 44

45 Adoption credit. Attach Form 8839 45

46 Foreign tax credit. Attach Form 1116 if required 46

47 Other. Check if from **a** ☐ Form 3800 **b** ☐ Form 8396
c ☐ Form 8801 **d** ☐ Form (specify) ______ 47

48 Add lines 41 through 47. These are your **total credits** 48

49 Subtract line 48 from line 40. If line 48 is more than line 40, enter -0- . . . . ▶ 49

Other Taxes

50 Self-employment tax. Attach Schedule SE 50

51 Alternative minimum tax. Attach Form 6251 51

52 Social security and Medicare tax on tip income not reported to employer. Attach Form 4137 . 52

53 Tax on IRAs, other retirement plans, and MSAs. Attach Form 5329 if required 53

54 Advance earned income credit payments from Form(s) W-2 54

55 Household employment taxes. Attach Schedule H 55

56 Add lines 49 through 55. This is your **total tax** . . . . ▶ 56

Payments

57 Federal income tax withheld from Forms W-2 and 1099 . . 57

58 1999 estimated tax payments and amount applied from 1998 return . 58

59a **Earned income credit.** Attach Sch. EIC if you have a qualifying child
b Nontaxable earned income: amount . . ▶
and type ▶ ______ 59a

60 Additional child tax credit. Attach Form 8812 60

61 Amount paid with request for extension to file (see page 48) 61

62 Excess social security and RRTA tax withheld (see page 48) 62

63 Other payments. Check if from **a** ☐ Form 2439 **b** ☐ Form 4136 63

64 Add lines 57, 58, 59a, and 60 through 63. These are your **total payments** . . . . ▶ 64

Refund

65 If line 64 is more than line 56, subtract line 56 from line 64. This is the amount you **OVERPAID** 65

66a Amount of line 65 you want **REFUNDED TO YOU** . . . . ▶ 66a

Have it directly deposited! See page 48 and fill in 66b, 66c, and 66d.

▶ b Routing number ▶ c Type: ☐ Checking ☐ Savings

▶ d Account number

67 Amount of line 65 you want **APPLIED TO YOUR 2000 ESTIMATED TAX** ▶ 67

Amount You Owe

68 If line 56 is more than line 64, subtract line 64 from line 56. This is the **AMOUNT YOU OWE**. For details on how to pay, see page 49 . . . . ▶ 68

69 Estimated tax penalty. Also include on line 68 69

Sign Here

Under penalties of perjury, I declare that I have examined this return and accompanying schedules and statements, and to the best of my knowledge and belief, they are true, correct, and complete. Declaration of preparer (other than taxpayer) is based on all information of which preparer has any knowledge.

Joint return? See page 18. Keep a copy for your records.

Your signature	Date	Your occupation	Daytime telephone number (optional) ( )
Spouse's signature. If a joint return, BOTH must sign.	Date	Spouse's occupation	

Paid Preparer's Use Only

Preparer's signature	Date	Check if self-employed ☐	Preparer's SSN or PTIN
Firm's name (or yours if self-employed) and address			EIN
			ZIP code

Form **1040** (1999)

Printed on recycled paper

*U.S.GPO:1999-456-060

two items are subtracted from AGI to determine taxable income on page two of Form 1040 (see Figure 9-3). From there, you have the privilege of figuring your federal income tax.

Most taxpayers fall into the lowest bracket of 15 percent, referring to taxable income (for the year 2000) of no more than $26,250 for single people or $43,850 for couples who are filing jointly. If we add people who fall into the next 28 percent bracket (taxable income between $26,250 and $63,550 for single people or between $43,850 and $105,950 for married couples), we have accounted for 94 percent of the households in America (according to tax information published by Commerce Clearing House, Inc).

For those clients who fall into a higher bracket, such as 31 percent or 36 percent, you should know that the true top rates for them often exceed these official rates. The marginal rates for these people are boosted by carefully disguised tax hikes that work in one of two ways. The government gradually reduces or phases out personal exemptions or limits most kinds of itemized deductions based on the amount of their AGI.

Whether working for yourself or helping a client in this area, there is one important point to understand with respect to capital-gains income. To determine your normal tax bracket, capital-gains income is added to regular income—and you use that total, not just the portion related to earned income. This procedure enables you to use *Schedule D* in order to compute the tax with a preferred tax rate on the long-term capital gain.

While some gains would be taxed at a lower, preferred rate, the vast majority of the income would be taxed at the 20 percent long-term capital gain rates. In effect, once you fill up the 15 percent normal tax bracket bucket with income (either regular income, capital gain income, or a combination of both), you will move to the next-higher tax bracket—and your preferred capital gain tax rate will move from 10 percent to 20 percent. This rate is still better than the normal rate of 28 percent (the next bracket higher than the 15 percent bracket) and is much better than the 39.6 percent rate (the highest bracket).

Trading versus Buy and Hold: Foolishness versus Tax Savvy

One bone of contention between fools and the wise is the value of holding stocks for the long term. In short, the longer the holding period for investors, the fewer taxes that they are probably going to pay. For example, if a security is held for longer than a year, they are likely to pay only 20 percent of the gain in taxes. But if their holding period is less than a year, the gain could be taxed as high as 39.6 percent. For every $1,000 worth of gain, that is a difference of $196 (or 19.6 percent).

The all-important question to ask a client is, "Are your short-term trading profits going to be substantial enough to compensate for the fact that you will be paying nearly twice as much in taxes?" The answer is "Probably not." Unfortunately, traders usually end up paying large amounts of ordinary income taxes. To add insult to injury, they are likely to be in the market at the wrong time when a correction hits, and they end up with less capital than they initially invested. Thus, they pay ordinary income taxes on non-existent profits.

In a raging bull-market environment, it is all too tempting to become a trader and dream of making quick profits while ignoring the payment of taxes. Instead, encourage clients to find great companies that are worthy of investment, with the idea of holding the stock for at least several years. This theory will remain valid as long as the reasons for buying the stock remain unchanged. Most importantly, long-term capital gains enable the investor to keep more profits and to attain their financial goals within a shorter period of time.

How to Lower Taxes with Individual Stocks

It is possible to build a superior portfolio for clients by using individual stocks. While it might be hard to pick consistent winners, it is relatively easy to hold down investment costs (commissions) and the payment of taxes. Although stock mutual funds tend to distribute large capital gains each year that are taxed, appreciated individual stocks, other than paying dividends, will not be taxable unless they are actually sold. This means that investors can gloat over paper profits without having to pay a penny in taxes to Uncle Sam.

To lay the foundation for a successful portfolio, large company stocks, for example, can be chosen from the *Standard & Poor's 500* (S&P's 500) Index. Our goal here is to capture the historical return of the S&P 500 with maximum tax efficiency. First, find out how this index is divided among technology, health care, financials, and other sectors. Next, pick some high quality stocks from each sector, setting up a trading account and holding the securities at your broker-dealer. This strategy enables you to sell losers quickly while keeping winners for as long as possible.

What should you do about losses? Suppose that you had one stock that took a big hit. Depending on the client's tax bracket, it could be sold in order to reduce taxable income or to offset other capital gains that year in order to lower the total tax bill. To take advantage of the loss, sell that company's stock and immediately replace it with another one from the same industry.

What if a client has a big position in one stock with a large, built-in profit? You can build a new portfolio around this position, purchasing stocks from every other sector except from that industry. Thereafter, whenever a loss is realized, sell a little of the big position in order to reduce it without generating a big tax bill. The proceeds can then be used to better diversify the new portfolio.

This type of approach will often end up with more winners than losers. In fact, there might be some superstars that turn into highly appreciated stock. According to Modern Portfolio Theory, discussed in Chapter 6 ("Analysis: Tools and Theories"), these runaway winners could actually cause an undiversified portfolio. This stock could gradually be given away to charity or to children in a much lower tax bracket.

One final tip: If a client dies while holding a number of winners, their cost basis will be stepped up to the valuation on date of death. In other words, heirs can then sell the positions without triggering capital-gains taxes. By sharing your knowledge with clients in this area, they will perceive you as an expert and will be inclined to let you manage more of their individual stocks. This situation, in turn, should lead to other business in the form of retirement planning with IRAs.

IRAs: Rules and Regulations

Anyone who is working and earning W-2 income *must* make a contribution to some type of IRA. The Taxpayer Relief Act of 1997 gave us new planning tools to help clients in this area. Besides traditional IRAs, we can use a new type called the Roth IRA that gives even better tax-deferred advantages. Let's look at each one to get a better understanding.

Traditional IRAs. These types of IRAs have been around for a long time. Their special feature is to grant a direct deduction from taxable income if the worker qualifies. Figure 9-4 summarizes the new types of IRAs available for clients. Basically, anyone who works for a company that does not offer a pension plan or qualified retirement plan can take a full deduction by using a traditional IRA. The maximum amount that can be contributed each year is up to $2,000 per person.

On the other hand, those who work for companies that offer qualified retirement plans can only deduct their IRA contribution if their AGI does not exceed specified limits. There are phase-out limits for active participants who want to take a partial IRA deduction (see bottom of Figure 9-4). In 2001, for example, singles who earn between $33,000 and $43,000, and joint filers who earn between $53,000 and $63,000 would qualify for a partial deduction. By 2007, these income levels will be increased to much higher levels. Unless these rules are changed by Congress, more Americans will be eligible to open and benefit from deductible IRA accounts.

There is a special rule for any spouse who works outside the home but is not covered by an employee retirement plan at any time during the year. The spouse who is not covered can make a $2,000 IRA-deductible contribution if the joint AGI is less than $150,000. Contributions are partially deductible if the joint AGI is $150,000 to $160,000. Contributions are not deductible if the joint AGI exceeds $160,000.

In addition, the new tax rules permit a spouse who does not work outside the home to contribute up to $2,000 into an IRA. Therefore, married couples can contribute up to $4,000 even if one spouse does not work, as long as the IRA contribution does not exceed the total family work-related income. This feature gives planners an excellent opportunity to make sure that both spouses are enrolled in a retirement savings plan.

Whether or not the contributions are deductible, tax on the earnings is deferred in a traditional IRA until a taxpayer begins to withdraw funds. As of this writing, there is a 10 percent income tax penalty on amounts withdrawn from this type of IRA before the owner reaches age 59 $^1/_2$ (with some exceptions). In general, investors who envision having to tap into their IRA accounts before they can make a penalty-free withdrawal should keep their investments outside a traditional IRA.

Roth IRAs. The Roth IRA is a savings vehicle that presents a unique opportunity to receive tax-free income at retirement. The Roth IRA actually offers more flexibility than the traditional IRA discussed previously. Although the $2,000 contribution is not deductible, other features of the Roth IRA outweigh this disadvantage. The benefits are as follows:

Figure 9-4 *IRA options available to investors.*

Key Provisions: Traditional & Roth IRAs

FEATURES	TRADITIONAL IRA — DEDUCTIBLE	TRADITIONAL IRA — NONDEDUCTIBLE	ROTH IRA
MAXIMUM ANNUAL CONTRIBUTIONS	$2,000 single; $4,000 married (@ $2,000 per account)		
CONTRIBUTION PERIOD	Up to tax year in which age 70½ is attained		For as long as you have earned income (no age limit)
CONTRIBUTION DEADLINE	April 15th of the year following the tax year for which the contribution is made		
INCOME ELIGIBILITY	Must have earned income		
	Income limits apply only to individuals (including spouses) who are active participants in an employer's retirement plan, as follows: (see below)	No income limits	(see below)
CONTRIBUTIONS	Tax-deductible	Not deductible	
TAX TREATMENT OF EARNINGS	Tax-deferred		
TAXATION OF CONTRIBUTIONS UPON WITHDRAWAL	Subject to income tax	Not subject to income tax	
TAXATION OF EARNINGS UPON WITHDRAWAL	Subject to income tax		Not subject to income tax (after age 59½ and five years in the Roth IRA)
10% PENALTY ON PREMATURE WITHDRAWALS	Yes	Yes, applicable to earning only. Roth–contributions are withdrawn first, without penalty. Nondeductible IRA–withdrawals prorated between contributions and earnings.	
EXCEPTIONS TO 10% PENALTY	Age 59½, first time homebuyer expenses, certain medical and unemployment expenses, disability, death		
	Higher education expenses		
MINIMUM DISTRIBUTIONS	Must begin at age 70½		None (only upon death for beneficiaries)

Traditional IRA — Deductible, income limits:

	Individuals	Joint Filers
Fully Deductible	< $30,000	< $50,000
Partial Deduction (phase out range)	$30,000-$40,000	$50,000-$60,000 and $150,000-$160,000*
Not Deductible	> $40,000	> $60,000 and > $160,000*

* applies only if one spouse is not participating in an employer's retirement plan

Roth IRA, income limits:

	Individuals	Joint Filers
Fully Eligible	< $95,000	< $150,000
Partial Contribution (phase out range)	$95,000-$110,000	$150,000-$160,000
Not Eligible	> $110,000	> $160,000

TRADITIONAL IRA INCOME "PHASE OUT" LIMITS FOR "ACTIVE PARTICIPANTS" MAKING DEDUCTIBLE IRA CONTRIBUTIONS: 1998-2007

YEAR	1998	1999	2000	2001	2002	2003	2004	2005	2006	2007
JOINT FILERS	$50,000-$60,000	$51,000-$61,000	$52,000-$62,000	$53,000-$63,000	$54,000-$64,000	$60,000-$70,000	$65,000-$75,000	$70,000-$80,000	$75,000-$85,000	$80,000-$100,000
INDIVIDUALS	$30,000-$40,000	$31,000-$41,000	$32,000-$42,000	$33,000-$43,000	$34,000-$44,000	$40,000-$50,000	$45,000-$55,000	$50,000-$60,000	$50,000-$60,000	$50,000-$60,000

Individuals under 70½ not covered by an employer-sponsored plan can make traditional IRA contributions regardless of income, otherwise, contributions are fully deductible if income is below the phase out range. A spouse (whether working or non-working) can make a maximum $2,000 deductible contribution to an IRA, even if the other spouse is participating in an employer-sponsored retirement plan, as long as the couple's total income is less than $150,000.

- Contributions, not earnings, can be withdrawn at any time and for any reason, without penalty.
- The account allows for tax-free earnings and distributions if held in the account for five years. In other words, withdrawals can be totally tax-free for the client in retirement.
- Roth IRAs permit penalty-free withdrawals for higher-education expenses and first-time home purchases.
- Unlike traditional IRAs, contributions can be made past age $70^1/_2$ if there is work-related income.
- Unlike traditional IRAs, distributions are not required after age $70^1/_2$.

The combination of tax-free build-up and tax-free distributions make the Roth IRA a powerful planning tool. Because of its flexibility, a Roth IRA is worth considering—even for those clients who qualify for a tax-deductible IRA. Because this type of savings vehicle will probably be the only source of tax-free income for the client at retirement, you should use it in most planning situations.

If the money in a Roth IRA is invested for at least five years, there will be no income taxes on distributions if any of the following requirements are met:

- Withdrawals are made after age $59^1/_2$.
- Withdrawals made prior to age $59^1/_2$ are for first-time home purchases (up to a maximum of $10,000) or for qualifying educational costs.
- Withdrawals are made due to disability.
- Withdrawals are made by a beneficiary after the Roth IRA owner's death.

If none of these requirements are met, the portion of the withdrawal that represents earnings will be subject to income tax plus a 10 percent penalty.

There is generally a catch to watch out for with any government program. In this case, a person must meet income requirements in order to be eligible to make contributions to a Roth IRA. As shown in Figure 9-4, a full $2,000 annual contribution is allowed for an AGI of less than $95,000 for individuals and less than $150,000 for joint filers. The $2,000 contribution is phased out between $95,000 to $110,000 for individuals and $150,000 to $160,000 for joint filers. Any AGIs over these limits will disqualify the taxpayer from making any contribution into a Roth IRA.

As a professional planner, you should be aware that the Roth IRA often produces much better results than a deductible IRA. You must consider the following factors in deciding which type of Roth IRA is best for each client: the investment time horizon until retirement, the current income-tax bracket at time of contribution, and the expected tax bracket at the time of withdrawal. Because there is no mandatory requirement for withdrawals, the Roth IRA permits tax-free compounding of retirement funds well into the future.

Traditional IRA Conversions to Roth IRAs. The Taxpayer Relief Act of 1997 also enabled the conversion of old IRAs into new Roth IRAs. Many investors who contributed to traditional IRAs in the past in order to get the tax deduction are wondering now whether or not it makes sense to convert these old IRAs into a new Roth IRA. Keep in mind, however, that an investor who converts this money into a Roth IRA must pay ordinary inome tax on the amount converted. In other words, for the privilege of earning tax-free income in the future, the IRS wants your tax dollars now that had been withheld from them in the old IRA. What the IRS giveth, the IRS taketh away. Also, AGI (must be less than $100,000) in the year of conversion.

For example, Jane has traditional IRAs worth $75,000 that she wants to convert to a new Roth IRA. This $75,000 includes $10,000 that came from nondeductible IRA contributions that Jane had made over the years. Therefore, only $65,000 will be eligible for conversion and is subject to her regular tax rate. If Jane is in the 28 percent tax bracket, her tax on the conversion will be $18,200 ($65,000 × .28). This tax is due in the year in which the conversion takes place.

The next question is how will she pay the $18,200 tax bill. Two possibilities exist—from the IRA itself or from other funds that she has outside the IRA. If Jane pays the tax out of the converted IRA money, this procedure reduces the amount that she actually rolls over from $65,000 to only $46,800 ($65,000 − $18,200). To add insult to injury, if Jane is younger than age 59½ and decides that she wants to keep some money for spending purposes, the portion that she does not roll over is subject to a 10 percent early-withdrawal penalty.

To avoid having to pay such a large tax in any one year, Jane could convert $13,000 per year over the next five years to spread out her tax liability. Before making any decision, she should also consider her projected income and tax bracket in future years. If she is still working and earns higher income in subsequent years, it might be better to convert more money earlier. In general, the younger the IRA owner, the more sense it makes to convert so more tax-free income can accumulate for retirement. Also, it is much better to pay the taxes from other funds outside the IRA so that all converted funds can begin to compound tax free for the future.

Rollovers from an Employer's Retirement Plan. Employer retirement plans come in many shapes and sizes and are generally divided into defined benefit and defined contribution plans. You *must* distinguish between these plans, because their sources of income will differentiate greatly at retirement.

- **Defined benefit plans**—Often referred to as a pension plan, they are designed to provide monthly income for retirees who have worked for an employer for a specified number of years. While it is always a good idea to check how a payment is calculated, a typical formula might state an employee is entitled to a pension that is equal to 1 percent of the final salary for every year that he or she worked for the company. These funds come strictly from contributions made by the employer and are managed by a plan administrator. More flexibility today might allow the accumulated value, or a portion thereof, to be rolled over at retirement. However, an employee who leaves early or changes jobs frequently might not have accumulated enough time to be entitled to any pension income.
- **Defined contribution plans**—Separate accounts that are set up for each employee who is eligible to contribute to the plan. Some of the more popular plans include the following: 401(k)s, profit-sharing plans, SEP-IRAs, simple IRAs, and money purchase plans. The employer turns over the responsibility of making investment decisions to each employee, and there are usually a number of investment options from

which to choose. These typically include various types of stock and bond funds, along with the employer's stock if it is publicly traded. The value of each account is easily determined by adding all prior contributions plus all the accumulated earnings. By law, statements are frequently sent to each participant.

Funds accumulated in both defined benefit and defined contribution plans are mostly tax deferred, so any direct distribution or payout to an employee will incur taxes at ordinary income tax rates. However, more plans today permit the transfer of these funds into the qualified plan of another employer or directly into a personal IRA rollover account. This special feature enables the owner to preserve the tax-deferred treatment of these funds until withdrawn at a later date. A financial planner must also keep these accounts separate from traditional or Roth IRA accounts that were made from regular yearly contributions. That way, an employee can take the funds back out of the IRA rollover account and put them into a new employer's qualified plan later on if permissible.

Figure 9-5 explains why, when leaving a company, it is most often better to choose an IRA rollover than to keep funds with an old employer. The client should maintain control of these funds in order to keep the pretaxed dollars working for as long as possible. By keeping this tax money working on the client's behalf, the financial planner builds more capital for the client's retirement. In reality, Uncle Sam is making a loan of his tax dollars so that the client can use them to build future financial security.

Likewise, IRA rollovers permit a wide choice of equity investments. A self-directed rollover permits the client to buy individual stocks and to maintain direct control over the assets. More popular vehicles include a wide variety of equity mutual funds, as described in Chapter 8 ("Diversifying with Mutual Funds"). Most importantly, clients can defer paying taxes up to age $70^1/_2$, which is when mandatory distributions must begin (according to current IRS regulations).

The Benefits of Variable Annuities

Most Americans look forward to enjoying their retirement years, but a comfortable retirement does not happen automatically. Careful planning is needed to ensure that enough income is available to enjoy this special time of life. When considering financial products for clients, you will want to examine those that offer a wide variety of investment options (including stocks) to help beat inflation. One solution for many retirement-planning needs might be a variable annuity.

By definition, an annuity is a contract issued by an insurance company that generally provides for two stages:

- The *accumulation period*, during which contract values are built by using fixed or variable investment options. Also during this period, the earning of income is deferred from taxation as long as it stays inside the annuity.

Figure 9-5 *The importance of using an IRA rollover.*

■ *Making Choices*

If an individual has a choice between keeping retirement funds in a company pension plan or in an IRA, he or she is almost always better off choosing the IRA, which provides more flexibility than most company plans. Here are some reasons why:

- Distributions

  Many company plans offer a participant annuity distributions on a fixed schedule. An IRA gives a participant many more alternatives. Of course, the participant may acquire an annuity contract within the framework of the IRA and thus take the same type of annuity payout from the IRA that generally would be available from the typical employer retirement plan.

  However, the participant may be more concerned with continuing to defer taxes than receiving a life income. With an IRA, an individual may take only minimum distributions to keep as much money as possible in the IRA for as long as possible to let tax-deferred investment returns keep growing.

- Investments

  An IRA lets a participant make almost any type of investment that he or she chooses. Because the plan trustee controls the funds left in an employer-qualified plan, an employee may have limited control over how the funds are invested, or, worse, he or she may have no control at all.

- Withdrawals

  IRA owners can withdraw their money early, even if it means paying a penalty. The decision belongs to them. Qualified plans are much more stringent.

- Beneficiaries

  Employees are required legally to name their spouses as the beneficiaries of their companies' qualified retirement plans unless the spouses agree, in writing, to different beneficiaries.

  However, with an IRA, a participant can name a child or grandchild as the beneficiary so that the child inherits the account. (The IRA must be maintained in the deceased IRA owner's name for the benefit of the child.)

- Security

  Unfortunately, many of today's company pension plans are underfunded. Even if employers and their qualified plans are healthy now, it's risky to assume that such plans will not falter years from now when participants must depend on them for retirement income. With an IRA, participants know that the money is available. It remains under the participants' control.

- The *payout period* occurs when accumulated values are distributed. Each contract offers a number of options for the payment of income. During this time, the receipt of income is taxed as ordinary income.

In a variable annuity, capital is accumulated by investing in various portfolios. As opposed to a fixed annuity, where funds compound at a guaranteed rate of interest, variable means that the return on assets is not guaranteed by the insurance company. In other words, the contract value will fluctuate over time, reflecting the performance of the options chosen for the underlying portfolio. To provide a margin of safety, most variable annuities will also offer several fixed interest-rate accounts, providing a set return guaranteed by the insurance company. Funds can be transferred between both the fixed and variable side of the contract, depending on limitations set forth by each insurance company.

The Accumulation Period. When a deposit is made, the accumulation period in the annuity begins. During this time, funds grow tax-deferred in an investment for the purpose of building more capital that can be withdrawn at a later date. Today's annuities are considered very special because the IRS has not disqualified them from receiving tax-deferred treatment. Thus, many investors like to use annuities to complement their tax-deferred company retirement plans or IRAs. Other benefits of using variable annuities include the following:

- Professional management in each sub-account chosen by the investors
- Diversification within each portfolio to help reduce market risk
- The ability to move money between investment options without incurring a tax liability
- The opportunity to indirectly participate in stock investments (similar to mutual funds) in an instrument designed to be held over a long period of time, reducing concerns about short-term market fluctuations
- The ability to allocate money in different proportions to both a fixed interest-rate account (offered in many contracts) and stock and bond investment options—all within one product
- Tax-deferred growth of earnings until withdrawn at a later date (withdrawals prior to age $59^1/_2$ might be subject to a 10 percent IRS premature penalty)
- No IRS annual limit on the amount invested, and no mandatory withdrawal requirement at age $70^1/_2$
- A special death benefit guaranteed to insure that beneficiaries will receive at least the full amount of money that has been invested, less any withdrawals, in case of death during the accumulation period. This benefit is often raised by the insurance company over time in order to help lock in any investment gains to increase the benefit.

During the accumulation period, the investor receives a wide variety of options from which to choose. Figure 9-6 illustrates a sample from the Manulife Financial Venture annuity portfolio. Note how these options are listed in terms of risk and reward. For example, there are fifteen choices in the higher-risk area (classified as aggressive growth). Similarly, there are ten options for growth and eight options for growth and

Figure 9-6 *A sample from the Manulife Financial Venture annuity portfolio.*

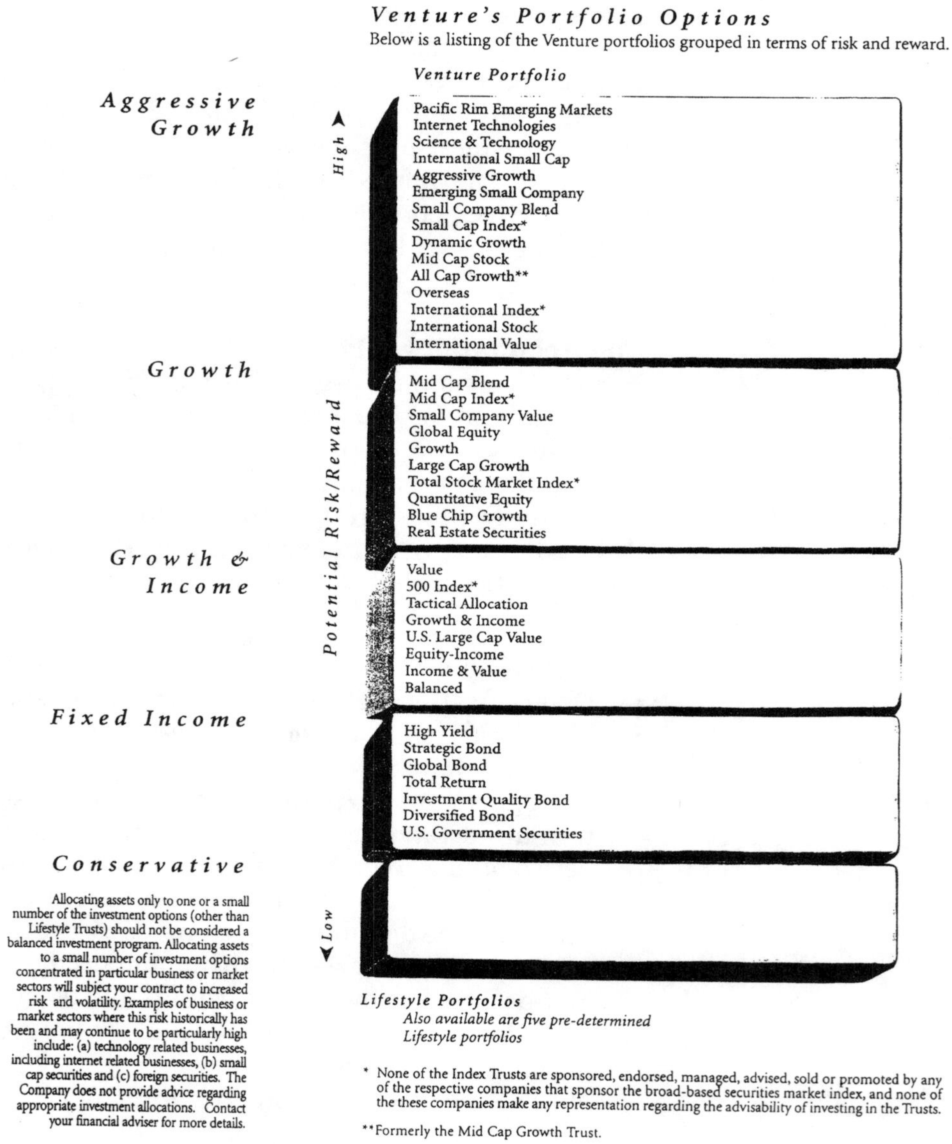

income. Chosen money managers will invest mostly in stocks, while those in the fixed income classification might purchase a combination of corporate or government bonds. As we go down the scale of potential risks/rewards, various options are offered to investors, including low-risk money market and fixed income accounts that are classified as conservative.

Venture's Portfolio Options
Below is a listing of the Venture portfolios grouped in terms of risk and reward.
Venture Portfolio
Aggressive Growth
Pacific Rim Emerging Markets
Internet Technologies
Science & Technology
International Small Cap
Aggressive Growth
Emerging Small Company
Small Company Blend
Small Cap Index*
Dynamic Growth
Mid Cap Stock
All Cap Growth**
Overseas
International Index*
International Stock
International Value
Growth
Mid Cap Blend
Mid Cap Index*
Small Company Value
Global Equity
Growth
Large Cap Growth
Total Stock Market Index*
Quantitative Equity
Blue Chip Growth
Real Estate Securities
Growth & Income
Value
500 Index*
Tactical Allocation
Growth & Income
U.S. Large Cap Value
Equity-Income
Income & Value
Balanced
Fixed Income
High Yield
Strategic Bond
Global Bond
Total Return
Investment Quality Bond
Diversified Bond
U.S. Government Securities
Conservative
High
Potential Risk/Reward
Low
Allocating assets only to one or a small number of the investment options (other than Lifestyle Trusts) should not be considered a balanced investment program. Allocating assets to a small number of investment options concentrated in particular business or market sectors will subject your contract to increased risk and volatility. Examples of business or market sectors where this risk historically has been and may continue to be particularly high include: (a) technology related businesses, including internet related businesses, (b) small cap securities and (c) foreign securities. The Company does not provide advice regarding appropriate investment allocations. Contact your financial adviser for more details.
Lifestyle Portfolios
Also available are five pre-determined Lifestyle portfolios
* None of the Index Trusts are sponsored, endorsed, managed, advised, sold or promoted by any of the respective companies that sponsor the broad-based securities market index, and none of the these companies make any representation regarding the advisability of investing in the Trusts.
**Formerly the Mid Cap Growth Trust.

Figure 9-7 shows once again the investment options of the Venture annuity. This figure, however, is organized by major asset classes for the equity and bond portfolios (top to bottom) and generally recognized investment styles (left to right). The style analysis is important because it provides finer distinctions between the portfolios than would be gained by looking at them only in terms of risk and reward. By understanding these

Figure 9-7 *Investment options of the Venture annuity.*

Equity Portfolios

	Value	*Blend*	*Growth*
Large Company U.S. Stocks *(Generally larger than $11 billion)*	Equity-Income U.S. Large Cap Value	Total Stock Market Index Growth & Income Blue Chip Growth Quantitative Equity Tactical Allocation 500 Index	Large Cap Growth Growth
Medium Company U.S. Stocks *(Generally between $2–$11 billion)*	Value	Mid Cap Blend Mid Cap Index	Dynamic Growth Mid Cap Stock
Small Company U.S. Stocks *(Generally smaller than $2 billion)*	Small Company Value	Small Company Blend Small Cap Index	Aggressive Growth Emerging Small Company
Specialty Stocks	Real Estate Securities		Science & Technology Internet Technologies All Cap Growth
International Stocks	International Value	Pacific Rim Emerging Markets Overseas International Index	International Stock International Small Cap
Global Stocks	Global Equity		

Hybrid Portfolios

	Income & Value		Balanced

Fixed Income Portfolios

	Short-Term *Less than 3.5 years*	*Intermediate-Term* *3.5 years to 6 years*	*Long-Term* *Greater than 6 years*
High Quality *(Rated AA to AAA)*	U.S. Government Securities Money Market	Total Return	Investment Quality Bond
Medium Quality *(Rated BBB to A)*		Diversified Bond Strategic Bond	
Low Quality *(Rated BB or lower)*		High Yield	
Global		Global Bond	

These ratings, as set forth by Standard & Poor's, pertain to the type of securities a Venture portfolio may purchase and not to the Venture portfolios themselves.

Both charts illustrate the principle investment style of each portfolio, but they may also invest, to a limited extent, in other types of securities.

additional layers of diversification, the client can use the annuity to better exploit the relationships between classes and styles. This enhances the investor's opportunity to select and build a much better portfolio.

The Payout Period. When an investor is ready to start using the savings that have accumulated, variable annuities offer a number of payout plan options. Each has tax implications that you should understand before making a final recommendation. The three primary payout options are as follows:

- **Lump sum**—When all funds are withdrawn and all of the taxes are paid on the accumulated earnings. This option will incur the highest tax liability, and for that reason, most recipients do not usually choose to take a lump sum all at once.
- **Systematic withdrawal**—Pays a preset amount at regular intervals until all assets have been withdrawn. This option enables the

investor to spread out the tax liability and provides flexibility in the payment amount. This option must be monitored closely, however, so that assets are not exhausted before the death of the recipient.

- **Annuitization**—Provides for a steady stream of income payments through which the insurance company guarantees to provide an income for a certain period of time or for the rest of the investor's life. While changes to these payments can be limited, the options can be initially customized in order to suit personal needs. In addition to spreading out the tax liability, a portion of each payment received by the investor is treated as a return of principal.

The flexibility in annuities allows for a number of ways to receive income payments. Some common annuitization options include the following:

- **Lifetime income for one person**—The insurance company guarantees that income payments will be received by the annuitant for the rest of his or her life, then payments will cease upon death.
- **Lifetime income with a guarantee period**—The annuitant will receive an income for life. If death occurs before this period is over, the beneficiaries will receive the remaining specified number of payments.
- **Lifetime income for two people**—Income payments will be received as long as one of two designated people are still alive. Upon the death of either person, income to the survivor will continue until his or her death.

Payout periods will reflect two types of annuities: fixed (in which each payment is a fixed dollar amount) or variable (in which the amount of each payment reflects changes in market value of the underlying portfolio). If the insurance company offers both, the annuitant has the option of selecting a combination of the two.

1. **Fixed-income payments**—The annuitant receives a fixed dollar amount at regular intervals. The amount will depend on the annuitization option selected. While the recipient knows the amount of each payment, this choice might be inadequate if the money does not keep pace with inflation.
2. **Variable-income payments**—Payments will vary based on the performance of the underlying investment options. In other words, income payments might be reduced in periods of market decline. There is also the possibility of increased payments in rising markets, however, which might provide the opportunity for income to keep pace with inflation during retirement.

Monitoring Variable-Annuity Performance. In addition to understanding the structure of these special tax-deferred investments, you must know about the issuing insurance company and its management performance. By contacting the company directly, you can obtain the sales literature (including a current prospectus) on the annuity of your choice. As with mutual funds, all current and relevant data will be available, including the options that investors can use to buy and sell the annuity. In addition, ratings by different services such as A. M. Best, Duff & Phelps, and Standard & Poor's will comment on the current financial strength of each company along with the capability to pay claims of policyholders.

Another way to keep track of current performance is to examine the annuity section of *The Wall Street Journal* each Monday morning in Section C. However, quarterly reviews have more pertinent data, as shown in Figure 9-8. Here, we see another example of Manulife's Venture Variable Annuity, with sample results at the end of the first quarter of 2000. This annuity has no up-front sales charge; rather, it has a maximum surrender charge starting at 6 percent that declines over a seven-year period. Also, expenses are divided into three areas: mortality and expense (1.40 percent for all options), fund-management expenses (varies for each portfolio), and the total expense for each option. Finally, we have average total returns listed for the current (previous) quarter, one-year, three-year, and five-year periods.

As with any investment, it is critical to know how a variable annuity will fit into a portfolio based on the client's age, goals, and objectives. These are not short-term investments; rather, they are vehicles for the serious investor who wants to build long-term financial security. Most importantly, they can be used to generate a steady stream of income during retirement (along with other income sources). During the coming years, we will see more choices in the variety of variable annuities being offered to the public, along with expanding investment options as more investors realize the importance of tax-deferred savings.

Variable Annuities: A Strategic Asset-Allocation Tool

Variable annuities are ideally suited for clients who want diversification through the use of multiple money managers. Benefits include the following:

1. **Tax-free investment exchanges**—Funds can be switched from one investment portfolio to the next by phone without paying taxes or trading costs. A 1999 study conducted by Price Waterhouse Coopers found that investors who used dollar-cost averaging and asset allocation would have received "significantly higher after-tax payouts from variable annuities as compared to mutual funds" over a holding period from 10 to 25 years.
2. **Diversification**—Variable annuities today offer well-designed diversification opportunities—not only across asset classes, buy also across money managers. This multi-manager approach can be especially beneficial for clients, because the annuity provider has already chosen each money management firm for its expertise in a particular asset class or style of investing.

Figure 9-8 *Annuity quarterly review.*

THE WALL STREET JOURNAL MONDAY, APRIL 10, 2000

VARIABLE ANNUITIES

QUARTERLY REVIEW

Policy	----Expenses---- Ins	Fund	Tot	-------Tot. Returns-------- Cur Qtr	One Year	Three Year	Five Year
Manulife Venture Variable Annuity							
Maximum surrender charge: 6.0%, over 7 years-R							
ManInTr Aggr Gr	1.40	1.14	2.54	25.46	72.07	25.42	NA
ManInTr BlueChl	1.40	0.97	2.37	5.78	20.61	25.80	23.33
ManInTr DivBond	1.40	0.89	2.29	0.76	-0.59	6.39	7.24
ManInTr Eq Inc	1.40	0.85	2.25	-3.33	-0.36	9.71	12.66
ManInTr G & I	1.40	0.79	2.19	3.34	15.35	24.69	23.53
ManInTr Gbl Eq	1.40	1.01	2.41	-0.40	6.33	9.75	10.09
ManInTr GblBond	1.40	0.94	2.34	-0.95	-3.91	0.62	4.75
ManInTr Growth	1.40	0.90	2.30	7.47	33.12	30.05	NA
ManInTr High Yd	1.40	0.84	2.24	-1.12	3.11	6.31	NA
ManInTr Inc&Val	1.40	0.84	2.24	2.66	7.58	12.80	12.08
ManInTr Intl SC	1.40	1.25	2.65	15.54	105.25	31.01	NA
ManInTr Inv Bd	1.40	0.72	2.12	1.80	-0.27	4.97	5.47
ManInTr Lfs 280	1.40	0.00	1.40	1.20	3.43	7.59	NA
ManInTr Lfs 460	1.40	0.00	1.40	2.33	8.43	9.69	NA
ManInTr Lfs 640	1.40	0.00	1.40	3.50	15.74	10.88	NA
ManInTr Lfs 820	1.40	0.00	1.40	3.46	20.12	12.61	NA
ManInTr Lfs1000	1.40	0.00	1.40	3.83	20.27	11.64	NA
ManInTr MC Blnd	1.40	0.80	2.20	7.02	36.76	21.60	21.72
ManInTr MidCpGr	1.40	1.04	2.44	13.50	58.42	35.78	NA
ManInTr Oversea	1.40	1.16	2.56	-0.54	32.79	13.46	11.07
ManInTr Sc&Tech	1.40	1.21	2.61	10.76	94.08	53.41	NA
ManInTr Str Bd	1.40	0.85	2.25	1.53	2.09	3.76	8.19
ManInTr US Govt	1.40	0.72	2.12	1.31	0.02	4.23	4.74
ManInTr Value	1.40	0.85	2.25	0.56	-1.95	3.63	NA
ManInvTr Balncd	1.40	0.87	2.27	5.80	5.30	9.96	NA
ManInvTr EmSmCo	1.40	1.10	2.50	16.82	100.44	36.21	NA
ManInvTr Intl	1.40	1.25	2.65	-0.03	28.02	13.68	NA
ManInvTr LC Gr	1.40	0.88	2.28	3.82	24.54	21.15	18.03
ManInvTr PacRim	1.40	1.21	2.61	-2.09	46.83	-0.35	NA
ManInvTr QuantE	1.40	0.76	2.16	10.87	25.84	27.97	NA
ManInvTr RealE	1.40	0.76	2.16	0.04	-3.09	-4.37	NA
ManInvTr Sm Co	1.40	1.23	2.63	2.66	19.47	NA	NA

Source: *Republished with permission of Dow Jones from WSJ Market Data Group Year 2000; Permission conveyed through Copyright Clearance Center.*

3. **Convenience**—Annuities offer rebalancing options that will automatically restore assets to their original target allocations on a quarterly, semi-annual, or annual basis. Also, there is no need to keep records of purchases and sales, because clients have no tax-reporting requirements associated with these transactions until withdrawals begin.

4. **Guaranteed minimum death benefits**—Annuities have death benefits that enable individuals to invest aggressively, without jeopardizing what they leave to their heirs. This feature guarantees that beneficiaries will receive the amount that the investor contributed to the account (less withdrawals), or the account's market value, whichever is greater. Many annuities also step up the minimum death benefit every year in order to lock in any increases in market value for the beneficiaries.
5. **Living benefits**—Variable annuity holders have the option of annuitizing, or converting the annuity into a steady income stream that is guaranteed to last for life (or the lifetime of both spouses). Some even offer more by ensuring a minimum future income stream no matter how the investments perform during the accumulation period.
6. **Avoidance of probate**—A key advantage of annuities is that death benefits paid out directly to a named beneficiary are not subject to probate. This avoids unnecessary costs and delays at the time of the owner's death.
7. **Special retiree benefits**—Most retirees with IRA accounts are required to take mandatory distributions beginning at age 70½. This rule does not apply to annuities set up in personal accounts (outside of IRAs). Also, earnings which accumulate inside an annuity are not counted in the formula for taxing income from Social Security benefits.
8. **Continued tax benefits**—Unlike with traditional IRAs, investors can continue to open accounts in tax deferred annuities to save unnecessary money from going to the government, even after age 70½. Some companies even offer *bonus* annuities, which pay an extra credit for opening the account. Sometimes, back-end fees will be waived if funds are used for long-term care expenses.

In summary, we can see why the variable annuity has increased in popularity over recent years, because people have begun to understand its value as a strategic planning tool. The ability to optimize an investment portfolio without taxes, trading costs, or hassles is an extraordinary benefit. At some point, the stock market's unprecedented surge will slow. When it does, many people will be reminded of the value that diversification brings to an investment program. Furthermore, investors will be more interested than ever in using the benefits of variable annuities.

Gifts and Inheritances. Equity securities, whether held in individual shares or in mutual funds, can be given to recipients each year. Under current law, an individual donor can give up to $10,000 in cash or securities to anyone without incurring a gift tax. The federal gift tax is an excise tax that is charged on the transfer of property. This tax is coupled with an estate tax; otherwise, an investor would be able to transfer an unlimited amount of wealth in order to lower a taxable estate.

A husband and wife together can give someone up to $20,000 per year in cash or securities without incurring a gift tax. Because it is classified as a gift, the money is not taxed as such to the recipient. However, any future earnings on these invested funds will become income of the recipient. For example, if clients are interested in providing funds for their children's college education, it is easy to set up a custodial account at a bank or financial institution and make a gift each year. The gift becomes the property of each minor child and can be used for his or her benefit later.

For minors under the age of 14, up to $1,400 of unearned income is taxable at the child's own rate, with the first $650 fully offset by the standard deduction. The child's unearned income over $1,650 is taxed at the higher of the parents' or child's rate. It might not seem like much, because only $1,400 of income receives favorable tax treatment. But any time we can shift income into a lower bracket, we should take advantage of substantial tax savings.

In planning ahead for a major expense (such as college), the sooner a gifting program to fund an investment account is started, the better. This planning ahead gives more time for invested securities to grow and to help cover the higher cost of tuition, books, room and board. Also, for minors who are age 14 years or older, all income from gifted securities is taxed at their rates only. Thus, it makes even more sense to increase gift amounts for these individuals.

We must, however, be careful in setting up these types of accounts for minors, especially because they become the property of the recipient. The donor loses control of the money and cannot legally get it back. Because custodian accounts are set up with the minor's Social Security number, any sale of securities are taxable to the minor (who is usually in a lower-income tax bracket). Two drawbacks to these accounts are that they are considered assets of minors and are therefore counted against the amount of financial aid given by the educational institution. The other drawback is that when the minor reaches legal age (18 in most states), he or she could take the money and blow it on frivolous spending.

In 1976, Congress passed a unified rate schedule that applies identical tax rates to taxable gifts and estates. The tax-rate structure shown in Figure 9-9 is progressive, with a maximum rate of 55 percent on taxable estates of more than $3 million. These rates seem high when you consider that the income that generates this wealth has already been subject to income tax. However, they only apply after exclusions and exemptions, along with a reduction by the unified credit.

Under the Taxpayer Relief Act of 1997, the unified tax credit will progressively increase until the year 2006. As shown in Figure 9-10, this process effectively eliminates the tax on estates of less than $675,000 in 2000 and 2001 and is scheduled to increase up to $1,000,000 by 2006. Taxable gifts equal the total value of gifts made during the year less the annual exclusion for each recipient. These include gifts to charitable institutions, amounts paid to medical and educational institutions for services provided to the recipient, and amounts given to a spouse.

For example, the annual exclusion per recipient in 1998 was $10,000. For 1999 and beyond, this amount will be indexed for inflation. When a donor applies this exclusion each year, a good part of his or her estate can be transferred tax free during life. Let's suppose that a client had two children and transferred $10,000 to each one during 1998. In other words, $20,000 could be transferred out of the estate each year without incurring

Figure 9-9 *Tax-rate structure.*

Federal Estate and Gift Tax Rates

If the Amount Is:		*The Tenative Tax Is:*			
From	*To*	*Tax*	*+*	*%*	*On Excess Over*
0	$10,000	0		18	0
$10,000	20,000	$1,800		20	$10,000
20,000	40,000	3,800		22	20,000
40,000	60,000	8,200		24	40,000
60,000	80,000	13,000		26	60,000
80,000	100,000	18,200		28	80,000
100,000	150,000	23,800		30	100,000
150,000	250,000	38,800		32	150,000
250,000	500,000	70,800		34	250,000
500,000	750,000	155,800		37	500,000
750,000	1,000,000	248,300		39	750,000
1,000,000	1,250,000	345,800		41	1,000,000
1,250,000	1,500,000	448,300		43	1,250,000
1,500,000	2,000,000	555,800		45	1,500,000
2,000,000	2,500,000	780,800		49	2,000,000
2,500,000	3,000,000	1,025,800		53	2,500,000
3,000,000 or more		1,290,800		55	3,000,000

Figure 9-10 *Tax credit progressively increasing.*

Death in	Credit	Equivalent exemption*
1998	$202,050	$625,000
1999	211,300	650,000
2000 & 2001	220,550	675,000
2002 & 2003	229,800	700,000
2004	287,300	850,000
2005	326,300	950,000
20006 & after	345,800	1,000,000

*Indicates the value of an estate that may pass to beneficiaries without an estate tax due.

a gift tax. Once more, for a married couple, each spouse can transfer $10,000 to each recipient, so in this case a total of $40,000 in yearly transfers would escape gift taxes. This is an invaluable strategy for high net worth individuals.

The federal government does not impose an inheritance tax. However, eighteen states do, and in all of them, the rates are structured so that the larger the estate, the higher the tax rate. The exact tax rate and exemption accorded each beneficiary from the tax differ from state to state and should be checked accordingly.

Inheritance tax statutes generally segregate beneficiaries into classes similar to the following:

- **Class 1**—Spouse
- **Class 2**—Parents, children, grandparents, and lineal descendants
- **Class 3**—Brothers and sisters, aunts and uncles
- **Class 4**—Children of brothers and sisters, and children of aunts and uncles
- **Class 5**—All others

Inheritance taxes should play a major role in both investment and estate planning by providing an incentive to leave more property to immediate family members and to close relatives. Furthermore, because exemptions are low (in one state, only $5,000 for a spouse) and because rates can be high on large estates (approaching 30 percent), the threat of inheritance taxes also provide an incentive for lifetime gifts of appreciated securities.

Tax Swapping. The reasons for selling securities vary with each investor. Sometimes a perception of overvaluation will cause a sale, while another reason might be a change in investment objectives. More recently, a highly volatile market will force traders to be in and out of stocks more frequently. Those who buy on margin might be forced to cover their margin calls in a down market, which can result in the sale of a large number of shares.

No matter the reason, tax laws come into play with every transaction. For example, suppose that you had bought shares in Intel Corporation stock, which subsequently declined in value. You now have a $3,000 loss. Would it be a good idea to sell? This decision depends on your tax bracket and whether or not you have other gains to offset. Should you decide to sell, this loss would be used to offset other income on your tax return (which will save you taxes). The actual amount saved depends on your marginal tax rate. For example, at 28 percent, you would immediately save $840 ($3,000 ×.28).

In general, most investors do not sell just to save taxes (unless they are in higher tax brackets and it is subsequently recommended by their tax advisors). Another example would be that if you thought Cisco Systems and Microsoft were just as attractive as your Intel Corporation stock, you can sell the latter and buy stock in one of the former companies.

In this situation, you will save enough in taxes to enable you to buy more shares of the new company. Changing investments for tax reasons is referred to as a *tax swap*, and they have become more popular with short-term traders.

Conclusion

The issue of taxes as they relate to equity investments will become more of a critical factor in the next century. Assuming that Congress never votes to have a flat tax during our lifetime, it is critical to include some planning for client tax savings. Most people fail to realize how tax planning can benefit them when preparing for the future. While no one likes to sell securities for a loss, it can be beneficial—as this chapter illustrated.

The key principal to embrace here is that the more we can save in taxes during our working years, the more capital we can accumulate for spending and enjoying during our retirement years. For example, by using more of Uncle Sam's tax dollars with tax-deferred investment vehicles such as IRAs and company retirement plans, we can help strengthen our future financial security. Similarly, we should strive to minimize taxes in personal investment programs by focusing on long-term capital gains, which are taxed at more favorable rates. Finally, variable annuities are a tremendous vehicle to use for personal accounts in order to maximize tax savings during the accumulation period. A thorough knowledge of useful tax strategies for clients will help you become a more successful financial professional as we embark on the new millennium.

Chapter 10

Brokers: Investment Companies and Services

Introduction

This concluding chapter will focus on the major sources from which to purchase stocks and equity investments. The evolution of our financial system today has led to increased competition among financial institutions for the investment dollars of individuals. As we stated in Chapter 1, "Origins: The Markets and Major Indices," the markets evolved strictly through the development of a specialized industry in which stocks were traded only on designated exchanges. Various governmental acts were passed during the 1900s to help regulate the securities industry.

As our free market system expanded during the mid to late 1900s, there was an increased demand for financial services to be offered by a variety of financial intermediaries. Besides traditional full-service brokerage firms, we now have banks, discount brokers, financial planners, and even Internet providers to satisfy the needs of American investors. We will conclude our journey through stock market fundamentals by describing the services of these companies, and the functions of the individuals who offer us an opportunity to realize in the dream of ownership in corporate America.

Bank Investment Services

Bank-managed accounts are trust funds that are generally divided into three forms: commingled (pooled) funds for the exclusive use of the bank's employee-benefit clients; common trust funds, available for the trusts of estates and individuals; and individually invested accounts, which are owned exclusively by an individual or by corporate investors. Unlike mutual funds, these accounts have no board of directors, no prospectus, and generally have lower management fees.

A *commingled fund* is established by a trust company solely for the use of bank clients and cannot be legally used by people outside an established trust relationship. In this respect, these accounts differ from mutual funds, which are designed for investors at large to pool their resources. While banks can employ registered representatives to sell outside mutual funds to the investing public, commingled funds are special vehicles that are usually offered in conjunction with services of the bank's trust department.

The technique known as commingling involves the pooling of securities to create a fund of a certain type or classification of security. The commingling technique applies to both commingled funds and common trust funds. In a broad sense, the idea of commingling or pooling securities can be compared with the mutual fund concept. In each instance, participants share in the total returns of stocks that pay dividends and appreciate in value.

The Pooling Concept

Asset management is greatly enhanced by the use of a *pooling concept*. Here, the element of timing is critical to the successful execution of security trades. For example, the pooled fund manager has immediate access to each holding in the fund and has easy reference to the weighted effect of each security in the portfolio. The individually invested account manager must consider each account profile in order to determine the advisability of a purchase or a sale.

Another advantage of this concept is that individual trusts can share in attractive investments in a number of companies. Thus, the investor can participate in a composite fund of securities that consists of many small- to medium-sized companies, which otherwise would have been impractical to invest directly on behalf of the individual trust.

The degree to which assets are invested on a pooled basis depends on the participating client and his or her trustee. For example, when a trust is established for an individual and his or her beneficiaries, parameters are set so the emphasis is placed on current and future income, growth and capital appreciation, tax-free return, and risk tolerance. When a decision is made to use a common fund vehicle, a selection is subsequently made from the various equity, convertible, fixed-income, and tax-exempt funds in order to satisfy the needs of the client and beneficiary.

When designing an equity portfolio, the account manager might review each industry with an in-house or outside research group in order to determine which sectors of the economy should be included and which should be eliminated from consideration. A selection of individual stocks is then made on the basis of their short- or long-term attractiveness, as well as risk tolerance and anticipated total return (dividend payment plus potential appreciation).

Sometimes, the choice of specific companies might take precedence over industry considerations. However, the turnover, or trading in and out of securities, is generally based on long-range considerations and fundamental analysis—using a two- to three-year time horizon. In an overvalued situation, a stock can be sold and then repurchased at a later date when its price is judged to be more in line with researched criteria peculiar to its industry or to the company itself.

A Variety of Investments

Commingled Funds. This commingled concept is used for the investment of pension, profit sharing, and thrift-fund assets. Commingling evolved from the establishment of the basic common stock and bond funds to the creation of a profusion of funds aimed at designated areas of investment opportunity:

- **Common stock funds**—Portfolios are usually invested in a diverse group of **large capitalized stocks** (more than $1 billion in market value) with 50 or more issues held in a fund. For diversification purposes, investments are made in a broad class of industry sectors so that the fund is not adversely affected by economic events that would negatively impact one sector. The funds will usually be 80 or 90 percent invested in common stocks, with the remainder invested in money-market securities. Unless the fund's objective includes the use of market timing, it would be rare to find a cash reserve ratio higher than 20 percent. A common stock fund with the objective of capital appreciation will usually have some high quality equities that pay consistent dividends. However, if the fund has the objective of providing a generous income, the equity portfolio will usually consist of higher-yielding stocks.

- **Intermediate capitalization stocks ($500 to $1 billion in market value)—**Will be used mainly for their prospective growth in sales and earnings. **Small capitalization companies** (less than $500 million) can also be used for their higher potential rewards. There is more risk in owning these companies, however, due to their need for new capital in order to finance growth as well as a thinner layer of management. These risks can be spread more for the investor by owning a large number of small companies.
- **International equities**—Classified as stocks of foreign companies traded on foreign exchanges. Country weightings in an international equity fund are extremely important to that fund's performance at any given time. These weightings are periodically changed in order to reflect world financial, political, and economic conditions. As we discussed in Chapter 5, the market volatility of a U.S. equity portfolio can be lowered considerably by a representative holding of international equities.
- **Fixed-income funds**—Money-market funds are used by bank trustees as temporary vehicles for money that is earmarked for more permanent investments. This money can also be distributed to employees as retirement benefits, profit sharing, or thrift payments. These instruments typically include *certificates of deposit* (CDs), *banker's acceptances*, *commercial paper*, and *Treasury bills* (T-bills). These funds can also include a combination of debt instruments. For example, a bond portfolio might consist of varying amounts of intermediate and long-term maturities that are tailored to fit the risk factor of the portfolio. Maturity structure can fluctuate, depending on the forecast for interest rates, market opportunities, and the need for cash. More recently, in response to inflationary pressures and rising interest rates, there has been more active trading of public-market bond issues.
- **Common trust funds**—The common trust vehicle for the pooling of personal trust assets was originally formed to give individual trusts the advantage of diversified investing. This broadening of participation in equity and fixed-income markets permitted individual trusts to have representative holdings in a greater number of issues (without the expense involved in odd-lot trading of smaller holdings). Types of common trust funds can be classified as follows:

  - **Common trust equity fund**—This fund can include common stocks of domestic, multi-national, and foreign-based companies, or it can be a specialized fund consisting mainly of emerging growth companies and small companies that have superior growth potential.
  - **Convertible common trust fund**—This kind of fund invests in fixed-income and preferred issues that are convertible into common stock. A representative holding in this type of fund tends to lower a portfolio's volatility and pay more income.
  - **Fixed-income fund**—A fixed-income fund for the common trust investor can include not only public issues of U.S. companies, but also private placements, government bonds, and dollar-denominated international bonds. Other refinements could include short- and intermediate-term maturities of public, private, government, and international issues.

- **Individually invested accounts**—An individually managed trust account contains a selection of individual stock and bond issues. For example, a hypothetical trust of less than $1 million in size would not have a diversification as broad as that of a larger trust. That is, the number of issues would be smaller. On the other hand, the allocation of assets between equity and fixed income for any size trust depends to a large extent on the account profile, growth orientation, yield emphasis, and payout requirements. The minimum account size generally ranges from $250,000 to $1 million, although some banks might have a lower minimum.

Brokerage Companies

Historically, investors found it easy to differentiate one financial intermediary from another, because each offered its own specialized products and services. For example, consumers bought life and health insurance from life-insurance companies; banks offered checking and savings accounts and other services to depositors; and stock brokerage firms bought and sold stocks and bonds for their customers. However, those days of specialization are gone forever.

Today, bankers, stock brokers, and insurance salespeople offer a wide spectrum of financial products and services. Besides special trust accounts offered by banks (described in the previous section), banks also offer discount brokerage services to compete with stock brokers, money-market accounts to compete with money-market mutual funds, and pension plans to compete with insurance companies.

Likewise, to stay competitive with banks, brokerage firms now offer cash management accounts. They combine traditional brokerage custodial services with check writing privileges, a credit card such as Mastercard or Visa, and higher money-market interest on funds that are held in reserve accounts. A brokerage firm can even search for the highest rates available on CDs from a variety of banks, for their customers who do not want to invest in the securities markets.

Likewise, as a result of the merging of various financial institutions, such as banks, brokerage firms, and insurance companies, we have "financial supermarkets" that encompass a variety of services now being offered to the public. This concept literally encompasses the theme of one-stop shopping for all financial products and services from one provider. This shows the financial services industry is becoming more competitive every day.

For example, Figure 10-1 shows three classes of brokerage services that are currently being offered to the investing public. While traditional full-service brokerage firms were once thought of as the only place in which purchase individual stocks, they have spent millions of dollars to maintain their reputation as leaders in the investment world. The emphasis here is on registered representatives who can work directly with clients to solve their investment needs. They also offer comprehensive financial planning, along with access to in-depth research reports, and the opportunity to purchase IPOs at their initial offering price.

The investor should realize that brokers make their living through transactions such as buying and selling for their customers' accounts. There are two types of relationships between the brokerage firm and its salespeople. In one case, the firm pays a basic salary with the broker bringing in a specified amount of commissions that go to the firm. After the minimum has been met, the salary is increased in proportion to the amount of additional commissions generated. In the second type of relationship, the broker's income is related entirely to the amount of commissions generated from selling investment products.

In either case, the broker's livelihood depends on the sale of securities. In other words, the advice given might at times be tinted by the desire to receive more commissions. However, the ultimate decision rests on the shoulders of the investor. Most importantly, he or she must weigh the impact of a decision in terms of fulfilling specific financial goals.

The challenge in selecting a full-service firm that gives investment advice can be a difficult task. Some might specialize in debt securities, while others may focus in stock offerings of companies located in a particular geographic region. Sometimes, regional brokerage firms can be an excellent source of information concerning companies of local interest, and might even publish special reports about the performance of a select group of stocks.

For example, Figure 10-2 illustrates a statistical summary from the *Regional Bank Monthly Monitor* as followed by Stifel, Nicolaus, & Company, Inc. in St. Louis. Banks are broken down according to asset size and investment rankings. Price information includes the close at month's end, the 52-week high and low price, and price change since the beginning of the year. Other fundamental data includes book value, price to book value, yearly dividends, and stated yields. Actual and estimated earnings per share are also listed, along with price earnings multiples. Finally, data is given on shares outstanding along with market capitalization. Although a number of professional analysts were responsible for putting this data together, they cannot guarantee the future performance of any securities listed in the report.

Other brokerage firms offer a variety of services, including estate planning and life insurance as well as traditional trading of stocks and bonds. Still other firms offer virtually no services other than executing

Figure 10-1 *Three classes of brokerage services.*

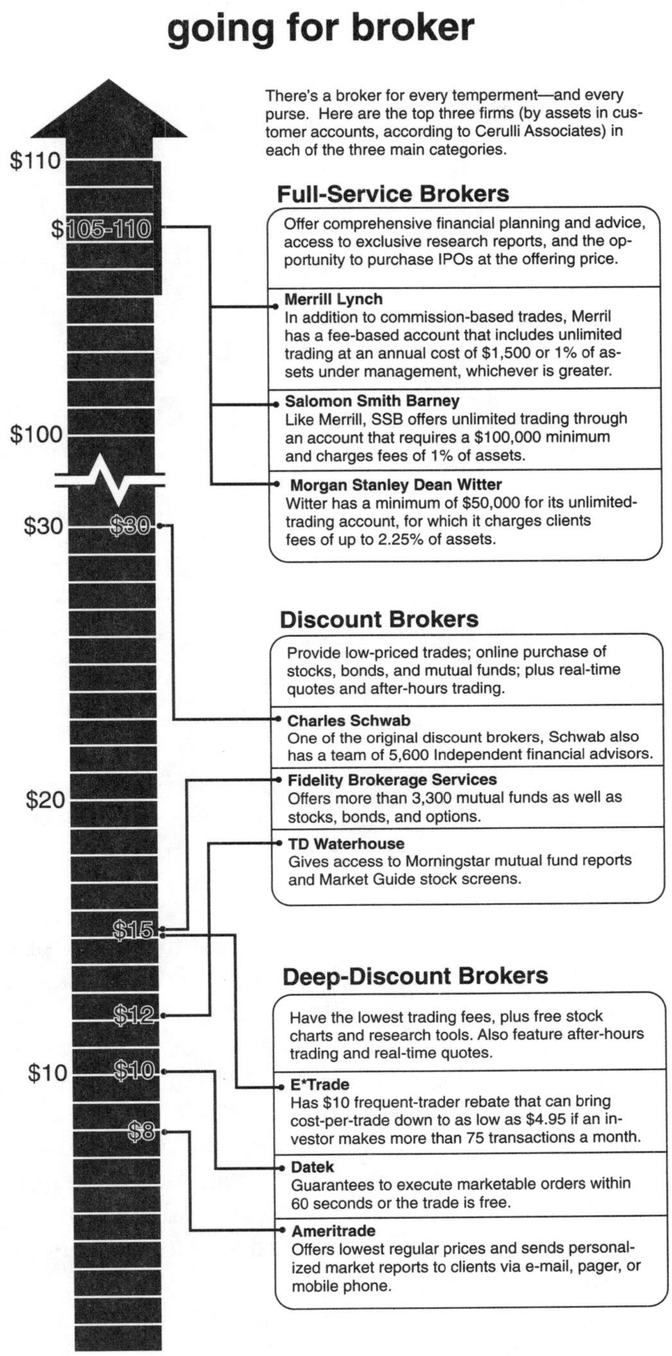

going for broker
There's a broker for every temperment—and every purse. Here are the top three firms (by assets in customer accounts, according to Cerulli Associates) in each of the three main categories.
$110
$105-110
$100
$30
$30
$20
$15
$12
$10
$10
$8
Full-Service Brokers
Offer comprehensive financial planning and advice, access to exclusive research reports, and the opportunity to purchase IPOs at the offering price.
Merrill Lynch
In addition to commission-based trades, Merril has a fee-based account that includes unlimited trading at an annual cost of $1,500 or 1% of assets under management, whichever is greater.
Salomon Smith Barney
Like Merrill, SSB offers unlimited trading through an account that requires a $100,000 minimum and charges fees of 1% of assets.
Morgan Stanley Dean Witter
Witter has a minimum of $50,000 for its unlimited-trading account, for which it charges clients fees of up to 2.25% of assets.
Discount Brokers
Provide low-priced trades; online purchase of stocks, bonds, and mutual funds; plus real-time quotes and after-hours trading.
Charles Schwab
One of the original discount brokers, Schwab also has a team of 5,600 Independent financial advisors.
Fidelity Brokerage Services
Offers more than 3,300 mutual funds as well as stocks, bonds, and options.
TD Waterhouse
Gives access to Morningstar mutual fund reports and Market Guide stock screens.
Deep-Discount Brokers
Have the lowest trading fees, plus free stock charts and research tools. Also feature after-hours trading and real-time quotes.
E*Trade
Has $10 frequent-trader rebate that can bring cost-per-trade down to as low as $4.95 if an investor makes more than 75 transactions a month.
Datek
Guarantees to execute marketable orders within 60 seconds or the trade is free.
Ameritrade
Offers lowest regular prices and sends personalized market reports to clients via e-mail, pager, or mobile phone.

Source: *Individual Investor Magazine*

orders at a discount (lower commissions). Therefore, it is critical that each investor identify his or her personal investment goals, and decide the best strategies to attain them in order to select the brokerage firm that best suits their individual needs. For investors who wish to trade securities without the advice or help of a full-service broker-dealer, discount brokerage firms will fit the bill. Figure 10-1 shows some examples of firms

Figure 10-2 *Regional Bank Monthly Monitor as reported by Stifel, Nicolaus & Company.*

STIFEL, NICOLAUS REGIONAL BANKING STATISTICAL SUMMARY

	State	Sym./Exch.	Invest. Rating	Current Price 5/31/00	52 Week Hi	52 Week Lo	Price Change Since 12/31/99	Book Value 3/31/00	Price to Book Value	Ind. Div.	Div. Yld.	GAAP EPS 2001E	GAAP EPS 2000E	GAAP EPS 1999A	GAAP P/E 2001E	GAAP P/E 2000E	Adjusted Cash 4/ EPS 2001E	Adjusted Cash 4/ EPS 2000E	Adjusted Cash 4/ P/E 2001E	Adjusted Cash 4/ P/E 2000E	Shares Out. (000s)	Market Cap. (Million)
Bank of the Ozarks 1/	AR	OZRK / OTC	2	$16.50	$22	$14	-15.4%	$11.93	138.3%	$0.40	2.4%	$2.25	$2.00	$1.75	7.3 x	8.3 x	$2.30	$2.05	7.2 x	8.0 x	3,780	$62.4
Cass Commercial Corp. 1/	MO	CASS / OTC	3	20.75	26	19	2.5	15.22	136.3	0.80	3.9	2.15	2.00 ↑	1.61	9.7	10.4	2.15	2.00 ↑	9.7	10.4	3,543	73.5
CNBT Bancshares, Inc. 1/	TX	CNBT / OTC	N	12.31	13	9	14.5	6.37	193.3	0.48	3.9	1.15	1.05	1.00	10.7	11.7	1.15	1.05	10.7	11.7	4,927	60.7
Colorado Business Bankshares	CO	COBZ / OTC	N	12.94	15	11	1.5	6.21	208.3	0.20	1.5	1.15	0.95	0.72	11.3	13.6	1.15	0.95	11.3	13.6	6,705	86.7
CoVest Bancshares 1/	IL	COVB / OTC	2	10.38	16	9	-22.1	11.36	91.3	0.32	3.1	1.20	1.10	0.93	8.6	9.4	1.22	1.12	8.5	9.3	4,076	42.3
Great Southern Bancorp 1/	MO	GSBC / OTC	2 ↑	16.75	28	17	-23.9	9.20	182.1	0.50	3.0	2.15	1.95 ↑	1.76	7.8	8.6	2.15	1.95 ↑	7.8	8.6	7,277	121.9
Independent Bankshares, Inc. 2/	TX	IBK / ASE	4	19.00	21	10	36.9	11.47	165.6	0.24	1.3	1.35	1.23 ↓	1.08	14.1	15.4	1.59	1.47 ↓	11.9	12.9	2,262	43.0
Indiana United Bancorp 1/ 2/	IN	IUBC / OTC	3	16.00	23	16	-14.7	12.35	129.6	0.66	4.1	1.85	1.65	1.47	8.6	9.7	2.05	1.86	7.8	8.6	4,856	77.7
Macatawa Bank Corporation 1/	MI	MCBC / OTC	N	12.75	16	12	-12.1	9.75	130.8	0.00	0.0	1.05	0.75	0.22	12.1	17.0	1.05	0.75	12.1	17.0	3,589	45.8
Mercantile Bank Corp. 1/ 2/	MI	MBWM / OTC	2	10.13	17	10	-20.6	11.48	88.2	0.00	0.0	1.15	1.00	0.85	8.8	10.1	1.15	1.00	8.8	10.1	2,473	25.0
PrivateBancorp, Inc. 1/ 2/	IL	PVTB / OTC	2	12.63	36	10	-5.6	10.57	119.4	0.10	0.8	1.30	1.00	0.69	9.7	12.6	1.30	1.00	9.7	12.6	4,590	58.0
S.Y. Bancorp, Inc.	KY	SYI / ASE	3	21.94	25	19	0.3	7.80	281.3	0.40	1.8	1.85	1.60	1.41	11.9	13.7	1.85	1.60	11.9	13.7	6,635	145.6
Southside Bancshares Corp.	MO	SBCO / OTC	N	8.25	12	7	-5.7	7.58	108.8	0.32	3.9	**0.95**	0.85	0.72	8.7	9.7	0.98	0.88	8.4	9.4	8,594	70.9
Summit Bancshares 1/	TX	SBIT / OTC	2	17.00	20	15	-8.1	7.77	218.8	0.40	2.4	1.75	1.55	1.39	9.7	11.0	1.75	1.55	9.7	11.0	6,380	108.5
Assets less than $1.0 Billion:							**-7.1**		**151.9**		**2.3**				**9.8**	**11.3**			**9.7**	**11.0**		**70.9**
BancFirst Corporation 1/	OK	BANF / OTC	2	$32.00	$38	$25	-5.7%	$20.74	154.3%	$0.64	2.0%	$3.40	$3.10 ↑	$2.75	9.4 x	10.3 x	$3.70	$3.40 ↑	8.6 x	9.4 x	8,098	$259.1
Brenton Banks 1/	IA	BRBK / OTC	3	10.00	17	7	-1.2	6.55	152.7	0.32	3.2	1.00	0.90	0.80	10.0	11.1	1.02	0.92	9.8	10.9	20,357	203.6
Capitol Bancorp Ltd. 1/ 2/	MI	CBCL / OTC	4	11.19	19	8	7.8	8.26	135.4	0.36	3.2	1.20	1.05	0.83	9.3	10.7	1.23	1.08	9.1	10.4	6,900	77.2
First Banks America 2/	MO	FBA / NYSE	3	17.38	18	17	-4.8	13.42	129.5	0.00	0.0	2.20	1.95 ↑	1.66	7.9	8.9	2.45	2.20 ↑	7.1	7.9	5,601	97.3
First Busey Corp. 1/	IL	BUSE / OTC	4	20.00	27	18	-11.6	6.08	328.9	0.48	2.4	1.15	1.00	0.90	17.4	20.0	1.21	1.06	16.5	18.9	13,475	269.5
First Financial Bankshares 1/	TX	FFIN / OTC	3	29.25	35	24	-4.9	18.29	159.9	1.32	4.5	3.10	2.85	2.58	9.4	10.3	3.22	2.97	9.1	9.8	9,974	291.7
First Oak Brook Bancshares 1/	IL	FOBB / OTC	1	15.13	21	15	-18.2	12.31	122.9	0.44	2.9	1.80	1.65 ↓	1.57	8.4	9.2	1.80	1.65 ↓	8.4	9.2	6,442	97.4
Independent Bank Corp. 1/ 2/ 3/	MI	IBCP / OTC	1	13.00	17	10	-10.0	10.38	125.2	0.60	4.6	1.85	1.65	0.75	7.0	7.9	1.97	1.77	6.6	7.3	11,222	145.9
Integra Bank Corp. 1/	IN	IBNK / OTC	3	20.00	33	19	-20.4	13.08	152.9	0.84	4.2	2.10	1.85 ↓	1.27	9.5	10.8	2.25	2.00 ↓	8.9	10.0	17,459	349.2
Irwin Financial 1/	IN	IRWN / OTC	2	14.44	25	14	-18.9	7.83	184.4	0.24	1.7	1.80	1.65	1.51	8.0	8.8	1.82	1.67	7.9	8.6	20,936	302.3
IBERIABANK Corporation 1/	LA	IBKC / OTC	1	14.50	22	11	5.5	17.94	80.8	0.64	4.4	2.25	2.05	1.53	6.4	7.1	2.60	2.40	5.6	6.0	6,537	94.8
Lakeland Financial 1/ 2/	IN	LKFN / OTC	2	12.50	20	11	-16.3	9.51	131.4	0.52	4.2	1.75	1.60	1.43	7.1	7.8	1.90	1.76	6.6	7.1	5,814	72.7
Local Financial Corp. 1/	OK	LFIN / OTC	2	8.56	11	7	-17.5	6.39	134.0	0.00	0.0	1.35	1.20	1.08	6.3	7.1	1.42	1.27	6.0	6.7	20,537	175.8
Mississippi Valley 1/	MO	MVBI / OTC	2	22.75	35	21	-15.7	12.63	180.1	0.40	1.8	2.60	2.30	2.25	8.8	9.9	2.60	2.30	8.8	9.9	9,353	212.8
Simmons First National 1/ 2/	AR	SFNCA / OTC	2	19.16	34	19	-23.4	22.21	86.3	0.80	4.2	2.85	2.65 ↓	2.33	6.7	7.2	3.10	2.90 ↓	6.2	6.6	7,330	140.4
Southside Bancshares	TX	SBSI / OTC	2	8.88	14	8	-4.1	5.39	164.7	0.20	2.3	1.35	1.25 ↑	1.05	6.6	7.1	1.35	1.25 ↑	6.6	7.1	7,231	64.2
Southwest Bancorp 1/ 2/ 3/	OK	OKSB / OTC	1	16.38	25	14	-18.1	16.96	96.6	0.44	2.7	2.80	2.55 ↑	2.19	5.8	6.4	2.80	2.55 ↑	5.8	6.4	3,855	63.1
Sterling Bancshares 1/ 2/	TX	SBIB / OTC	2	11.06	15	9	-1.1	5.27	209.9	0.20	1.8	1.10	0.98	0.81	10.1	11.3	1.12	1.00	9.9	11.1	26,085	288.6
Texas Regional Bancshares	TX	TRBS / OTC	3	26.94	30	22	-7.1	13.25	203.3	0.56	2.1	2.65	2.35	2.11	10.2	11.5	2.90	2.60	9.3	10.4	14,525	391.3
Assets $1.0 - $2.5 Billion:							**-10.0**		**148.4**		**2.8**				**8.3**	**9.2**			**7.9**	**8.8**		**184.9**
1st Source Corporation 1/	IN	SRCE / OTC	2 ↓	$17.75	$33	$18	-29.0%	$13.01	136.4%	$0.36	2.0%	$2.15	$1.95 ↓	$1.86	8.3 x	9.1 x	$2.17	$1.97 ↓	8.2 x	9.0 x	18,900	$335.5
AMCORE Financial 1/	IL	AMFI / OTC	2	19.38	25	17	-19.3	10.44	185.6	0.64	3.3	1.90	1.70 ↓	1.40	10.2	11.4	1.97	1.77 ↓	9.8	10.9	27,113	525.3
BancorpSouth, Inc.	MS	BXS / NYSE	2	15.38	19	14	-5.7	8.74	175.9	0.52	3.4	1.45	1.35	1.20	10.6	11.4	1.46	1.36	10.5	11.3	56,516	868.9
First Financial Bancorp	OH	FFBC / OTC	N	17.75	24	16	-17.0	8.01	221.6	0.60	3.4	1.40	1.30	1.07	12.7	13.7	1.45	1.35	12.2	13.1	46,617	827.5
First Midwest 1/	IL	FMBI / OTC	3	25.00	30	21	-5.7	9.34	267.7	0.72	2.9	2.05	1.85	1.67	12.2	13.5	2.12	1.92	11.8	13.0	41,129	1,028.2
First United Bancshares 1/	AR	UNTD / OTC	2	16.88	19	10	26.2	10.44	161.6	0.58	3.4	1.50	1.40	1.32	11.3	12.1	1.58	1.48	10.7	11.4	25,297	426.9
National Commerce Banc.	TN	NCBC / OTC	2 ↑	19.00	27	15	-16.3	5.21	364.7	0.42	2.2	1.55	1.15	0.99	12.3	16.5	1.55	1.15	12.3	16.5	108,106	2,054.0
Old National Bancorp 2/	IN	OLDB / OTC	N	29.44	35	23	-4.7	10.05	292.9	0.68	2.3	2.00	1.55 ↓	1.67	14.7	19.0	2.05	1.60 ↓	14.4	18.4	56,047	1,649.9
Republic Bancorp 1/	MI	RBNC / OTC	2	9.75	14	7	-19.7	6.03	161.7	0.34	3.5	1.20	1.10	0.33	8.1	8.9	1.22	1.12	8.0	8.7	45,135	440.1
Southwest Bancorp of TX 1/	TX	SWBT / OTC	3	19.75	21	15	-0.3	7.09	278.6	0.00	0.0	1.45	1.25 ↑	0.93	13.6	15.8	1.45	1.25 ↑	13.6	15.8	28,141	555.8
UMB Financial	MO	UMBF / OTC	2	37.00	42	30	-2.0	30.83	120.0	0.80	2.2	3.45	3.20	2.94	10.7	11.6	3.78	3.53	9.8	10.5	21,354	790.1
Assets $2.5 - $10.0 Billion:							**-10.1**		**209.1**		**2.8**				**11.3**	**12.8**			**11.0**	**12.4**		**790.3**
Associated Banc-Corp	WI	ASBC / OTC	2	$25.45	$41	$20	-18.3%	$13.30	191.4%	$1.16	4.6%	$2.60	$2.41 ↓	$2.34	9.8 x	10.6 x	$2.71	$2.52 ↓	9.4 x	10.1 x	69,230	$1,762.1
Charter One Financial 3/	OH	CF / NYSE	1	22.75	27	15	19.0	11.73	193.9	0.72	3.2	2.65	2.35 ↓	1.53	8.6	9.7	2.68	2.38 ↓	8.5	9.6	209,504	4,766.2
Commerce Bancshares 1/ 3/	MO	CBSH / OTC	1	34.75	40	26	2.6	17.67	196.7	0.62	1.8	3.15	2.85	2.59	11.0	12.2	3.27	2.97	10.6	11.7	61,610	2,141.0
Fifth Third Banc.	OH	FITB / OTC	3	68.00	75	44	-7.3	13.41	507.1	0.96	1.4	3.20	2.80	2.15	21.3	24.3	3.28	2.88	20.7	23.6	309,680	21,058.2
Firstar Corporation 3/	WI	FSR / NYSE	N	25.56	30	16	21.0	6.46	395.7	0.65	2.5	1.70	1.50	0.87	15.0	17.0	1.82	1.62	14.0	15.8	970,026	24,796.3
First Tennessee	TN	FTN / NYSE	2	20.50	42	16	-28.1	9.67	212.0	0.88	4.3	2.20	1.90	1.85	9.3	10.8	2.25	1.95	9.1	10.5	130,406	2,673.3
FirstMerit Corporation	OH	FMER / OTC	2	18.94	29	13	-17.7	9.51	199.1	0.88	4.6	2.10	1.90	1.37	9.0	10.0	2.22	2.02	8.5	9.4	88,401	1,674.1
Huntington Bancshares	OH	HBAN / OTC	3	19.38	34	17	-18.8	9.45	205.0	0.80	4.1	2.05	1.90	1.82	9.5	10.2	2.17	2.02	8.9	9.6	221,982	4,300.9
National City Corporation	OH	NCC / NYSE	2	20.00	35	16	-15.6	9.71	206.0	1.14	5.7	2.45	2.20 ↓	2.22	8.2	9.1	2.57	2.32 ↓	7.8	8.6	606,228	12,124.6
Old Kent Financial	MI	OK / NYSE	3	33.25	45	24	-6.0	10.81	307.6	0.88	2.6	2.80	2.40 ↓	2.11	11.9	13.9	2.92	2.52 ↓	11.4	13.2	121,578	4,042.5
TCF Financial 3/	MN	TCB / NYSE	2	26.19	31	18	5.3	9.67	270.8	0.85	3.2	2.55	2.20	2.00	10.3	11.9	2.65	2.30	9.9	11.4	80,728	2,114.1
Union Planters Corp. 2/ 3/	TN	UPC / NYSE	1	31.25	50	25	-20.8	19.77	158.1	2.00	6.4	3.40	3.10	2.85	9.2	10.1	3.75	3.45	8.3	9.1	135,487	4,234.0
Assets > $10.0 Billion:							**-7.8**		**237.8**		**3.7**				**10.4**	**11.6**			**9.9**	**11.0**		**5,921.7**
Total Index Average							**-8.2%**		**184.2%**		**2.8%**				**9.9 x**	**11.2 x**			**9.5 x**	**10.8 x**		**$1,388.6**

Notes: 1/ Stifel, Nicolaus & Co. makes a market in one or more issues of securities of this company.
2/ Stifel, Nicolaus & Co. has provided investment banking services for this company within the last three years.
3/ One or more of the analysts has a beneficial interest in a security of this company.
4/ Cash earnings are calculated by adding back to net income: Core deposit premiums and Goodwill amortization (Tax-effected when applicable).
Investment Rating: 1: Strong Buy, 2: Buy, 3: Accumulate, 4: Hold, 5: Sell, N: Not rated.
An arrow indicates direction of change in Investment Rating or EPS estimate in the last calendar month. A = Actual, E = Estimate. NA = Not available, NM = Not meaningful.
All earnings per share figures are fully diluted and exclude the benefit of net operating loss carryforwards and extraordinary items.
Historical results are as originally reported in each year's annual report and subsequently adjusted for any stock splits and stock dividends.
Average figures for the group are unweighted and exclude the high and low values along with any figures that appear not meaningful.
Market Capitalization is calculated using shares outstanding at 3/31/00.

Stifel, Nicolaus & Company, Incorporated

ranked by assets in customer accounts. They provide lower-priced trades than full-service firms because they do not have to pay a staff to research companies or to give investment advice. They also provide investors with the ability to make online purchases of stocks, bonds, and mutual funds. New expanded services offer real-time quotes and after-hours trading.

Deep-discount brokers are known to have the lowest trading fees. They offer free stock charts for performing technical analyses and other research tools for the do-it-yourself investor. As with regular discount brokers, they also engage in after-hours trading and offer real-time quotes. In comparing their commission costs with full-service brokers, you will see why their popularity is growing, especially with young and middle-age investors. Large pension and institutional investors also use their services to save money when trading large blocks of securities.

The Internet Rewrites the Rules

Tech-savvy investors have thrived in this brave new world. Trading costs have shrunk, while online investing has become a national mania. Web sites are offering a variety of reports, charts, and graphs so that the do-it-yourself investor has more and better tools to make decisions. Although institutional investors have more financial data at their disposal to make decisions, the playing field has leveled so that individual investors can now have the tools to make their own well-informed decisions.

Over the past 10 years, we have seen a proliferation of new services from large brokerage houses to counter this revolution. For example, when their clients started grumbling about $100 commissions and threatened to begin using their computers for trading, big broker-dealers came out with *wrap accounts*. These accounts combine unlimited trading with old-fashioned full service for a low set fee that is based on a percentage of assets under management. To appeal to the growing number of do-it-yourselfers, many full-service firms now offer cheap online fees that rival the current $30 trades at discounters such as Charles Schwab.

In the meantime, deep discounters have begun an offense of their own. In January 2000, for example, the E*Trade Group completed a $1.1 billion merger with Telebanc Financial, the leading online bank. Likewise, TD Waterhouse and Ameritrade have teamed with Schwab and three venture capital firms to form their own investment bank. As different classes of brokers invade each other's turf, we will see an increase of this type of activity in the future. For example, in a move to target wealthier customers, Schwab announced in January 2000 its intention to purchase blue-chip asset manager U.S. Trust.

With all of the different kinds of accounts that can be used, not to mention all their available products and services, American investors have become more confused than ever. This intense competition has also generated lower costs along with more choices. Now, investors can balance costs with service considerations and factor in their personality types to determine the right broker for them. I encourage you to take the Temperament Test in Figure 10-3 to see which service type best suits your temperament.

Professional Investment Advisors

Today, people's anxiety levels seem to rise with the amount of assets that they own. In other words, the more money that they have invested, the more likely they are to seek advice from a professional. Studies show that the average American will tend to move away from self-directed investing to an advice-driven relationship when he or she passes the $100,000 mark. When investors are dealing with real assets of a significant number, especially in a volatile market environment, there is a lot more to lose —and the consequences of not seeking advice are much more important than ever.

But, deciding how much advice is needed depends on a number of factors. These include the size of the portfolio and the tolerance for unknown risk. Investors generally fall into three main categories: those who want to do everything themselves and feel completely independent; those who prefer to delegate it all and shift the responsibility to a full-service professional; and those who fall somewhere in the middle. Since we are in business to provide full service to clients, let's look at the various choices people have in receiving professional advice in today's investment arena.

The proliferation of Investment Advisors has mushroomed over the past 20 years due to the growing affluence of our American society. As the

Figure 10-3 *Temperament test.*

a test of temperament

Do you shamelessly beg stock tips from strangers? Or are you the kind of lone wolf who'd rather chew off a paw than ask for advice? With guidance from Dr. Robert W. Siroka, director of the Center for the Psychosocial Study of Financial Behavior in New York City, we've constructed a quick quiz to point you toward the type of broker you should consider: full-service, discount, or online.

Answer the following questions and add up the points to get your final score.

1. **You're:**
   Generally pessimistic. I expect the worst and usually get it. (3)
   Somewhat optimistic. I don't know what to expect but hope for the best. (2)
   Generally optimistic. I expect the best, period. (1)

2. **How readily do you share control?**
   Very readily: in fact, every chance I get. (3)
   Not very readily: only if I'm backed into a corner. (2)
   Not at all: they'll have to pry the remote from my cold, dead fingers. (1)

3. **How emotional are you?**
   Overly: I cry at the end of *60 Minutes.* (3)
   Somewhat: I cry at the end of *Forrest Gump.* (2)
   Not at all: I laugh at the end of *Forrest Gump.* (1)

4. **Others describe you as:**
   Friendly as a puppy. (3)
   Cool as a clam. (2)
   Mean as a snake. (1)

5. **When you're lost in a new city, do you:**
   Immediately stop for directions? (3)
   Consult a map, then try to find your own way? (2)
   Drive around until you run out of gas? (1)

6. **How communicative are you?**
   I don't make decisions without consulting my partner. (3)
   I consult with my partner but make most decisions myself. (2)
   Forget consulting: I decide. (1)

7. **Do you consider yourself:**
   An arts person? (3)
   A renaissance person? (2)
   A math person? (1)

8. **Which leadership profile best describes you:**
   Lineman: Just tell me who to go out there and hit. (3)
   Quarterback: I want to have some control over the outcome of the game. (2)
   Coach: I want to call every play. (1)

9. **Which of these statements sounds most like you?**
   Tell me what to do. (3)
   I have an idea I'd like to discuss. (2)
   I know what I want—get out of my way. (1)

SCORE

(22–27) Highly Dependent—Get thee to a full-service broker.

(15–21) Not Overly Confident—Avail yourself of the services that a good discount broker can provide.

(9–14) Self-reliant—Station yourself in front of a computer and let the trading begin.

Source: *Individual Investor Magazine*

economy expands and incomes increase, people have more disposable income to invest. Unfortunately, recent studies show that many Americans are very poor savers, averaging only 5 percent of their disposable incomes. In a free society built on the consumption of goods and services, we are tempted to spend more money that we actually make. In America, buying items on credit is so easy, and many people end up abusing this privilege.

Investment advisors come in many shapes and sizes, and we need to distinguish between those who are competent and those who abuse the professionalism of this industry. Our ultimate mission is to offer a service to the public that will help them improve their financial lives. As our industry becomes more competitive, we will see a falling out of those who do not provide quality service at a reasonable price. Let's look at the different classes of investment advisors along with the pros and cons of their business practices.

- **Stock brokers**—Have been around for the longest time and are still very popular, especially with older Americans. People feel comfortable with traditional Wall Street brokers, and enjoy visiting their richly appointed offices to witness the excitement of a market trading atmosphere. All stock brokers must pass the Series 7 test to be legally registered to sell securities. To add value, they follow traditional investment strategies, such as trying to pick undervalued securities, stocks, and mutual funds for their clients. They often rely on in-depth reports from their firm's research department. This situation usually means higher costs to the investor in the form of commissions. But many are reducing these costs due to increased competition. They can also offer proprietary mutual funds, which are run by money managers employed by the investment firm. One important point to remember when considering employment with a large wirehouse or well known broker-dealer: If you leave the firm, they will claim that all of your clients still belong to their company. If a broker builds a book of clients and attempts to take it to a new firm, there could be legal complications as well. Once more, the broker-dealer will give these clients to other registered representatives in their firm to contact in an attempt to keep this business on the books. On the positive side, working for a large broker-dealer can have excellent benefits. For example, they offer retirement plans, health and life insurance, and sometimes an opportunity to partake in equity ownership. By working for a well-known company, there could also be management opportunities, such as becoming a branch manager for a local or division office, or for internal positions within other departments in the home office.
- **Investment consultants**—Normally work for Wall Street firms but specialize in advising clients about their investments. They usually charge an ongoing fee for their services, rather than commissions on individual transactions. This line of work will become even more popular as we witness the shifting from commission to fee-based services in the future. Investment consultants also focus on helping educate investors about activities in the capital markets. They perform this task by providing educational materials for clients and keep current by attending training conferences. They help clients by using the financial planning approach, which includes setting goals and drawing up recommendations to achieve them. Clients will generally know in advance what it will cost to do business when taking this approach.
- **Bank investment representatives**—Also have their license to sell securities, but work in the environment of a commercial bank. People still think of banks as giving the most trusted advice along with high quality service. Therefore, this atmosphere is an excellent place to build a new client base. A little background on this trend in in order here. When the stock market was rising during the '80s and '90s, banks were losing much business to traditional brokers and independent financial planners. Because they already had a solid base of customers, they only found it natural to hire and train new brokers to offer investment products. The idea was to keep the money

from leaving their financial institutions. One problem is that many older Americans are not use to having their bank offer investment products. The perception is that if they buy them at the bank, there is no risk of loss to their principal. However, unlike savings and CD accounts, various securities such as stocks, bonds, and mutual funds are not guaranteed by the *Federal Deposit Insurance Corporation* (FDIC). So, bank investment representatives must emphasize this fact through full disclosure, and make sure clients understand that the investments they sell can and do fluctuate in value.

- **Insurance company representatives**—Will go through similar training and licensing procedures as any other person who wants to sell securities. The difference here is that these advisors focus more on the selling of insurance products for their respective companies, and therefore tend to obtain a Series 6 license. We have found that insurance products are viable and can be right for many individuals in given situations. However, a professional in this industry must be careful not to only push these products, and reassure clients of an unbiased approach. Unfortunately, the general public already has a negative perception of salespeople who work for the insurance industry. While most insurance companies have excellent training programs and fringe benefits for representatives, it might be more difficult to establish a career in this area. Before committing to one of these firms as a representative, make sure that they offer excellent support in your chosen area of specialization.
- **Fee-only financial advisors**—Develop financial plans for individual clients and are paid a flat fee to do so. For this reason, they are perceived as having no conflict of interest because they do not sell investment products. This approach is becoming more popular with the general public, and these professionals have access to all mutual-fund vendors that do not charge sales commissions. They do not get paid for selling investment produts, but rather for creating a plan, and charging either a flat fee or by the hour. They usually work with more affluent clients, and will charge a percentage each year based on assets under management. They must obtain a *Registered Investment Advisor* (RIA) designation in order to conduct business in their state of origin. To maintain competency, they should belong to the *National Association of Personal Financial Advisors* (NAPFA), an organization of fee-only planners that holds regular meetings on topics related to this type of financial planning.
- **Chartered financial consultants (ChFCs)**—Financial planner designation awarded by the American College. Educational requirements include eight courses of sequence of financial planning topics plus three years of business experience. There are also ethics and continuing education requirements. There are currently 33,000 ChFCs in practice. Website: www.amercoll.edu.
- **Certified financial planners (CFPs)**—Are identified as individuals who have met the education, examination, experience, and ethical standards established by the *Certified Financial Planner* (CFP) Board of Standards, Inc. The CFP board owns the CFP certification mark and licenses qualified individuals to use it every two years.

The CFP mark identifies people who are dedicated to the highest level of professionalism in the financial-planning field. CFPs can be licensed representatives, independent financial planners, or fee-only planners. They must fulfill a biennial continuing-education requirement in order to stay up-to-date on planning strategies and financial trends affecting their clients. In addition, the CFP board monitors compliance with its *Code of Ethics and Professional Responsibility*. This monitoring includes investigating consumer complaints, removing licenses from CFPs who are found to be in violation of the code, and continually reviewing reports from other regulatory bodies and the press. A new organization, the *Financial Planning Association* (FPA), is dedicated to continuing education of CFPs and the promotion of their business to the American consumer.

Your Ultimate Career Decision

An entry-level financial professional will want to be competent in many different areas in order to help a variety of clients. The most widely known and respected designation in this career field is the CFP. The CFP Board of Standards is committed to promoting the CFP mark in a number of ways for its members. As illustrated in Figure 10-4, this promotion includes a campaign designed to increase public awareness of the CFP designation around the country.

As explained in its 1999 annual report, in addition to national newspaper and magazine coverage, the board conducted sponsorship of *National Public Radio* (NPR) programming that reached an estimated 13.1 million listeners in all major markets. The board also hosted open forums in three cities in order to discuss issues that were of interest to CFP licensees and introduced a new consumer brochure, "Why You Should Choose a CFP Practitioner," in 1999.

There has been an increased use in the CFP board's Web site, www.CFP-Board.org, and the Internet in general. The board redesigned its site, making it easier to use, and frequently sends e-mail notices to CFP licensees concerning various topics of interest. Visits to the Web site increased by 47 percent to 253,353 in 1999.

Figure 10-4 *CFP public-awareness campaign.*

PUBLIC AWARENESS FACTS AT A GLANCE

	1998	1999
Calls to Toll-Free Consumer Number	5,484	19,698
Web Site Visits	172,170	253,353
Radio Public Service Announcements (PSAs)	25,198	19,579*
Media Impressions	220 million	307 million

* *Includes television PSAs for a total of $1.3 million equivalent time value.*

Among its major responsibilities, the CFP board sets education, examination, experience, and ethical standards for initial certification. The board authorizes qualified individuals to use the CFP mark and monitors the continuing education requirements of current CFP licensees. By year-end 1999, the number of licensees in the United States had increased to 34,656. Certification can be obtained either by enrolling in courses given at more than 100 approved colleges and universities in the U.S. or by taking a self-study course at home. All applicants must pass a certification examination covering six areas of competancy before being issued their license to practice as a CFP.

Figure 10-5 gives other important data showing the increasing popularity of obtaining this designation, as of December 31, 1999. A licensee profile is broken down by gender, age, and education level. Also shown is the type of business that these professionals are in and the various licenses they hold. There is also a further breakdown of CFP licensees by state of residence. By examining these statistics closely, you can relate them to your own personal profile to make a better decision on whether to pursue obtaining a CFP license.

How to Choose a Broker-Dealer

As a professional in the investment field, you want to offer services that are best for both you and your clients. Some important things that you want to look for when choosing a broker-dealer include the following:

- **Top-notch compliance**—This feature might not seem important, but you want a broker-dealer who makes sure that you are always in compliance with securities laws. Keep in mind that this industry is strictly regulated by the U.S. government, and you want to be in business for a long time. The compliance officer of your broker-dealer has the right to inspect your office at any time to make sure you are following securities laws governed by the rules of the *Securities and Exchange Commission* (SEC). Also, being able to call upon a broker-dealer for help with specific regulatory issues will free you to spend more time with clients. As our industry gets bigger, regulators must contend with an increasing amount of fraud. But for the most part, ethical planners will understand the need for stricter guidelines, more careful reporting, and prudent visits from regional supervisors. Look for firms that have plans to automate these responsibilities and a compliance department that takes the edge off your shoulders as much as possible.
- **Sales and marketing expertise**—Depending on what you want to do or specialize in, find a good broker-dealer who has a proven reputation for outstanding sales and marketing programs. The idea here is to make building your practice challenging but fun at the same time. You should look for a turnkey system that helps you accomplish this goal. Experienced people from the home or regional office should also be available to help you set up operations if you are establishing an independent office. This includes offering secretarial assistance or advice on how to take the paperwork burden off

Figure 10-5 *Increasing popularity of obtaining the CFP designation.*

LICENSEE PROFILE
(As of December 31, 1999)

GENDER		AGE		LEVEL OF EDUCATION	
Male	75.2%	40-49	37.4%	Bachelors	88.0%
Female	24.8%	50-59	29.1%	Masters	29 7%
		30-39	19.6%	Associate	3.3%
		60-69	8.8%	Juris Doctorate	3.1%
		20-29	2.0%	Doctorate	1.8%
		70+	1.5%		

BUSINESS TYPE

Personal Financial Planning	43.5%	Banking	4.0%
Securities	15.7%	Education	1.3%
Accounting	7.5%	Law	0.8%
Insurance	7.5%	Real Estate	0.6%
Tax Preparation/Advice	4.2%	Human Resources	0.3%
Other	4.1%	Government/SRO	0.3%

LICENSES HELD

Securities	67.0%	Real Estate	5.5%
Insurance	66.3%	Attorney	2.8%
CPA	15.7%		

1999 CFP LICENSEES BY STATE

Alabama	251	Louisiana	315	Oklahoma	250
Alaska	43	Maine	124	Oregon	406
Arizona	584	Maryland	851	Pennsylvania	1,777
Arkansas	123	Massachusetts	1,244	Rhode Island	131
California	4,150	Michigan	1,136	South Carolina	239
Colorado	890	Minnesota	900	South Dakota	98
Connecticut	671	Mississippi	111	Tennessee	497
Delaware	114	Missouri	599	Texas	2,193
District of Columbia	79	Montana	112	Utah	191
Florida	2,215	Nebraska	189	Vermont	75
Georgia	734	Nevada	114	Virginia	938
Hawaii	171	New Hampshire	181	Washington	802
Idaho	94	New Jersey	1,628	West Virginia	76
Illinois	2,058	New Mexico	161	Wisconsin	751
Indiana	632	New York	2,512	Wyoming	34
Iowa	377	North Carolina	766	Foreign/Territorial	52
Kansas	363	North Dakota	69		
Kentucky	215	Ohio	1,344		

your shoulders so that you can concentrate on being with clients. Also, find out if they offer a system for solving problems that otherwise would take away from the work you really want to be doing—building assets under management through a long-term client relationship.

- **Guidance and technology**—Naturally, you will try to be all things to all people. But in reality, no one is expected to be an expert in everything. When clients come in with specific issues, it is nice to be able to call the office or regional office to tap their resources for answers to specific questions. They should also give advice on individual stock selections and updated research reports on mutual funds. Technology is critical in remaining competitive in this industry. We cannot stress enough that your broker-dealer should be on the forefront of the Internet and should have an attractive Web site for clients to inspect. Up-to-date software, downloadable forms, online order entry, and office automation are essential to help you run a smooth operation. Simply put, the more support in technology and automation from your broker-dealer, the easier your practice will be to run and the more profitable it will be in the future.

- **Products and services**—The broker-dealer you choose should be current with all products and services available in the industry so that you can remain competitive. This means having one person in the home office in charge of due-diligence on products and vendors. The initial screening process is essential for dealing with companies whose products you will use for client portfolios. For example, there should be highly reputable investment companies offering mutual funds and "A" rated insurance companies offering variable annuities that have excellent track records for performance and service. Your broker-dealer should also give you choices for setting up self-directed accounts with major clearing firms and the flexibility to offer several fee-based programs. Because the future of the investment business means the gathering of assets under management for a long-term relationship, you should be able to offer programs for both personal and tax-advantaged plans.
- **Networking with professionals**—Educational programs are a major benefit when working with a broker-dealer who is committed to the excellence of its associates. The broker-dealer should have several meetings per year that you can attend in order to keep current with changes taking place in the industry. Most importantly, the information should be relevant to your business so that you can become even more proficient in dealing with clients. One critical area is being able to network with other professionals one on one. This networking is especially important for advisors who work in small offices. It enables them to exchange ideas and to learn how to solve the common challenges that they all face. Ideally, a broker-dealer will offer several such meetings each year, and even have a workshop to train marketing and administrative assistants. Most importantly, this training is on the forefront of technology and gives us the tools necessary to run a highly efficient and profitable practice.

Building Competency as a Financial Professional

Ultimately, clients will make the choice based on faith and trust. A client must be encouraged to pick an investment advisor who will service his or her special individual needs. Likewise, the more personal and specific this process is defined, the easier the selection process will become. The more services that the investment professional can offer, although a client might not need them all in the beginning of a relationship, the more flexibility a client has to use them later.

For this reason, I would encourage any entry-level professional to go the extra mile and obtain his or her certification as a financial planner—to become a CFP. Passing a Series 6 or Series 7 examination just to sell securities or to oversee assets under management will not be good enough in the future. You must be perceived as having the credentials to provide a variety of personalized services for many years to come. In building a practice, you want to obtain accounts where you will have the best opportunity to increase assets under management.

A few years ago, the *International Association for Financial Planning* (IAFP) developed the following definition: "Financial planning is the process of providing advice and assistance to a client for the purpose of achieving the client's financial goals."

1. Financial planning has a logical six step process:

   a. **Data gathering**—Obtain as much information as possible about the personal and financial status of the client. This information is obtained from the income statement, balance sheet, and personal budget. The interview process should also include gathering data on insurance policies, income taxes, investments, various retirement plans, wills, and trusts. Simply put, the more information that you have about a client's financial situation, the better you can analyze and make recommendations to help that client achieve financial success in the future.

   b. **Goal setting**—Establish major objectives that are important to the client. This action includes determining short-term (one to three years), medium-term (four to eight years), and long-term (eight years or more) goals. Examples could be accumulating money for a down payment on a new home in three years, building funds for a child's college education in seven years, or accumulating a nest egg for a planned retirement in 15 years.

   c. **Identification of financial problems**—Conduct a thorough analysis of all of the information you collect in Step a. Also, each client will tell you what situation or special problem he or she is trying to solve. People go through traumatic experiences in life, which includes the death of family members, divorce and separation, and the birth of new children. Anything you can do to help solve financial problems related to these areas will build their trust and loyalty in your professional abilities.

   d. **Preparation of written alternatives/recommendations**—Deliver a thoroughly prepared written plan of your findings and recommendations to help solve their specific problems. There are several choices in this area. You can conduct a comprehensive analysis of their entire situation, which would mean the development of a large plan. Or, you can focus recommendations on one or two areas of most concern in their current situation. Either way, this step is critical for bringing everything to a head. This process helps clients know exactly where they stand financially, and what can be done to solve problems or improve their financial lives in the future.

e. **Implementation of the agreed-upon recommendations**—This step will help you complete the financial-planning process. After doing all the analysis and work in coming up with the correct recommendations for a client, it is only right that you should implement and follow through in order to fortify your long-term relationship. At this point, clients will also want your assistance in following up with your recommendations and more advice to continue building on a successful relationship.

f. **Review and revision of the plan**—On a periodic basis, make sure that the client is on the track toward achieving his or her established goals. As with following a road map to a particular destination, you want to monitor the plan closely in order to arrive at the desired objective. A periodic review will also determine whether any revisions need to be made based on changing family circumstances or other life-changing events.

2. A financial-planning client can be an individual, a family unit, or a legal entity. Each one requires special attention based on needs and circumstances. For example, individual clients might need an investment program to build future retirement capital. A family unit might want proper estate planning to minimize taxes so that more assets can be passed on to heirs. A small business might need a new retirement plan for employees or want to assure that future ownership will be passed to the right people.
3. Comprehensive financial planning will include the basic areas of financial planning, along with other areas of concern to the client. The basic areas of financial planning include financial statement analysis, insurance planning, investment planning, income tax planning, retirement planning, and estate planning. Other areas of concern can include cash management, education funding, charitable giving, and business-succession planning.
4. The financial-planning process can be applied to meet the client's needs in any of the following ways:

   a. A complete and comprehensive plan to cover all financial areas
   b. A subset or limited plan to meet the client's needs on a more limited basis
   c. A focus to meet a single client goal on a more specialized basis

While this list describes a general theme of what financial planning is all about, I would suggest using the following criteria for what financial planning will mean to consumers in the future:

- The six-step process previously described.
- The analysis and recommendations must always be presented to the client in writing for their examination and subsequent decision-making process.

- The review of financial circumstances must be comprehensive in nature, including an analysis of the client's personality for risk purposes. The financial planner must also determine the client's tolerance for staying with an investment program in order to reach long-term objectives.
- The flexibility to do single goal or specialized financial planning for a lower fee. Clients will often use other trusted professionals for insurance, banking, and estate planning. This means you don't have to draw up a comprehensive plan each and every time. For example, if you focus on investment and retirement planning services, you may not need to do a comprehensive plan that includes all the other areas (unless requested by the client).
- As a financial planner, you must acknowledge being in the role of a fiduciary—that is, acting *only* for the client's best interest at all times (with a clear explanation that there will be no conflicts of interest).
- Explaining up-front how the financial planner will be compensated for services rendered. The more flexible you can be in this area, the more trusted business relationships you will develop.
- How services are rendered is likely to affect the client's current and future financial situation. In other words, recommended strategies must be explained fully, including both pros and cons, so that a fair evaluation will lead to a rational decision by each client.

Selecting Investment Advisors: Using the Seven Cs

In addition, as an entry-level professional who seeks to become highly competent in the investment field, you should encourage clients and prospects to choose their investment advisor according to the **Seven Cs** that are used by accountants, bankers, and attorneys:

1. **Credentials**—What educational background does this person have? How does this individual keep current with changing economic and market conditions? Does he or she belong to one of the industry's trade associations, such as the *Financial Planning Association* (FPA) or NAPFA? How many years of active business experience does this person have? What types of people make up the client base? What licenses does the individual have to conduct business for his or her practice?
2. **Competence**—Did this person ask a lot of questions so that enough data is gathered to make sound recommendations? Will the plan be presented in written form and tailor-made to address critical financial problems? Will the recommendations be both generic and specific?
3. **Compensation**—Will this person be compensated by fee only, by commission only, or by a combination of both? If this person is a fee-only planner, how will he or she carry out the full financial-planning process (including implementation)? Is there a chance for a conflict of interest if this person is a commission-only planner?

4. **Confidentiality**—Has this person stated that all information will be held in strictest confidence? Has the planner offered to give referrals of existing clients whose situations and objectives are similar? How would a portfolio be constructed to address the concerns of special situations?
5. **Commitment**—Does this person wish to establish a life-long relationship or just want to make recommendations in order to sell investments? What type of follow-up service is being offered, and how often will reviews be conducted?
6. **Creative ability**—How will the plan or recommendations be tailored to my unique situation? Can I see a sample plan and envision how it might relate to my goals and objectives?
7. **Caring personality**—Does this person give me a feeling of warmth and friendship? Would I give this person responsibility over my money when it comes to a trusted relationship? Do we have compatible personalities and similar thoughts in dealing and thinking about money?

Conclusion

This chapter focused on the issues related to investment services. We will continue to see an ever-expanding array of opportunities to help individual clients become financially successful in the future. The ever-changing face of financial services along with more modern advancements and tax law changes will continue to challenge our existence as investment professionals. Faced with this reality, are you up to the task? Are you willing to take the bull by the horn and ride off into the sunset with a determination to face future challenges?

With more competition facing us every day, we need to make a solid commitment as to the type of services that we will provide to clients and stick with it. Most importantly, you must decide which areas in the investment field you like the best. If you could become an expert in just one area, what would it be, and how would you plan to make a future career practicing it? How do you plan to become known as an expert in your field? How will you market yourself as a financial professional? These are the questions that you must answer now as you prepare for the challenges that lie ahead in the 21st century.

Conclusion

This book has given you the opportunity to learn about the fundamentals of a dynamic stock market as it relates to the 21st century. Needless to say, we have an ongoing challenge to stay ahead of our competition as the financial services industry changes in the future. Our clients look to us to attain the highest level of competence and to apply our knowledge to help improve their financial lives. Are you up to this ongoing challenge for the future?

As a professional certified financial planner, I am prepared to fit the responsibilities of the **Client's Bill of Rights** (see Appendix). When someone comes into my office, he or she can ask questions that pertain to each amendment, and I am prepared to answer each one. Most importantly, my job is to prove that I can live up to his or her expectations.

As an entry-level or seasonal professional, you should also be asking serious questions about how you want to develop and keep clients in the future. This includes the type of firm in which you would like to affiliate with for a career. Large broker-dealers typically have extensive training programs, good retirement benefits, and extensive home-office support. The tradeoff is that should you ever decide to leave and take your book of clients elsewhere, you might lose a large number of accounts that will be claimed by the broker-dealer as being proprietary. Therefore, investigate your options thoroughly before affiliating with any investment company.

On the contrary, should you decide to become your own boss and open an independent business, there are tremendous rewards as well as some risks. As an entrepreneur, you run a business in order to make a profit. You will be in control of all income based on how hard you work. Likewise, you should manage expenses by being well organized. Independent broker-dealers are set up in order to help professional people run their businesses efficiently and minimize failures.

As the president of your own company, you should be completely free to pick and choose the investment products that you feel are best suited for each client. There should be no conflict of interest regarding which investments you have to sell or to whom they are sold. An independent broker-dealer can give extensive office support for your business while offering many quality investment products to solve client financial needs.

Should you decide to explore this avenue, I highly recommend you consider independent broker-dealers who are prepared for the challenges that lie ahead, especially with regard to future technology. Not only visit their Web sites, but talk to financial professionals whom you know and trust, and who can tell you about reputable firms. I have found that many of my clients want to work with someone who is independent so they never have to worry about conflicts of interest when I recommend investment products. In this way, I am completely free to fulfill their Bill of Rights at all times.

Should you have questions regarding any topic in this book, please feel free to e-mail me at busbwyss@admiral.umsl.edu. You can also visit my Web site at www.creativeassetmgmt.com or call me in St. Louis at (636) 256-2666. Good luck in your future endeavors, and I look forward to hearing about your highly successful career.

Appendix

A Client's Bill of Rights

Amendment 1. I have the right to deal with someone I can trust.

Amendment 2. I have the right to deal with someone who has a special area of expertise or unique capability not found in other people.

Amendment 3. I have the right to deal with someone who listens to me and takes an interest in my needs and concerns.

Amendment 4. I have the right to deal with someone who not only critically evaluates a variety of investment and insurance products, but also offers them with an eye towards appropriateness and suitability.

Amendment 5. I have the right to expect performance. This means not only from the investment and insurance products we select, but also from performance in enhancing my overall financial well-being.

Amendment 6. I have the right to deal with someone who instills in me the feeling that my money is being treated as though it were their own.

Amendment 7. I have the right to deal with someone who prioritizes my short- and-long-term goals, and develops a plan so I can achieve them in the most efficient manner.

Amendment 8. I have the right to deal with someone who delivers information to me at a level which I can understand.

Amendment 9. I have the right to deal with someone who is committed to working with me over a long period of time.

Amendment 10. I have the right to deal with someone who, by virtue of education, experience, technical competence, and adherence to ethical practices, is recognized as a top professional in their field.

Index

Note: **boldface** numbers indicate illustrations; italic *t* indicates a table.